W9-CLY-406

DATE DUE

DEMCO, INC. 38-2931

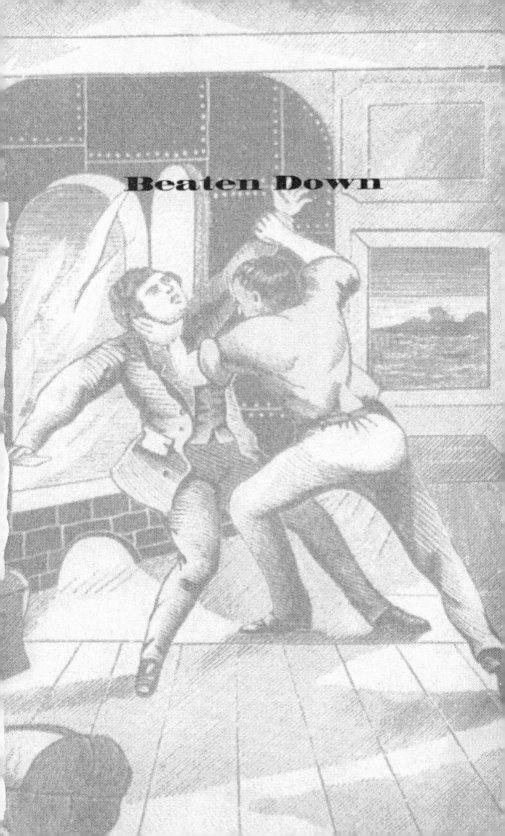

Beaten Down

BEATEN DOWN

A History of Interpersonal Violence in the West

DAVID PETERSON DEL MAR

UNIVERSITY OF WASHINGTON PRESS

Seattle and London

Copyright © 2002 by the University of Washington Press
Designed by Pamela Canell
Printed in the United States

Library of Congress Cataloging-in-Publication Data
Peterson del Mar, David, 1957–
Beaten down : a history of interpersonal violence in the West /
David Peterson del Mar.
p. cm.
Includes bibliographical references and index.
ISBN 0-295-98260-8 (alk. paper)
1. Violence—West (U.S.)—History.
2. Violence—British Columbia—History.
3. Interpersonal conflict—West (U.S.)—History.
4. Interpersonal conflict—British Columbia—History.
I. Title.
HM886 .P474 2002   303.6'0978—DC21   2002072684

The paper used in this publication meets the minimum requirements of American
National Standard for Information Sciences—Permanence of Paper for Printed
Library Materials, ANSI Z39.48–1984. ♾ ◉

Illustrations on pages i and 1: From *Specimens of Theatrical Cuts* (Philadelphia:
Ledger Job Printing Establishment, c. 1875). Illustration on pages ii–iii:
Engraving by Frederic Remington, from Theodore Roosevelt, *Ranch Life
and the Hunting Trail* (New York: The Century Company, 1888).

FOR PETER

CONTENTS

6

Big as God Almighty
and Undemanding as Dew:
Violence and People of African
and Japanese Descent 136

ACKNOWLEDGMENTS

IT IS A PLEASURE to thank the many people who helped prepare this book for publication. I was fortunate to enjoy the services of excellent research assistants: Riley Adams, Connie Barnes, Chris Beach, Melanie Buddle, Bonnie Cernak, Claudette Gouger, Kurt Nordstokke, and especially Mia Reimers. Mina Carson, Ken Coates, John Findlay, Robin Fisher, Michael Grossberg, Theresa Healy, and John Lutz read parts of the manuscript. Richard Maxwell Brown, Robert Johnstone, Mary-Ellen Kelm, Mia Reimers, and Jill Schlessinger read all of it, as did three anonymous referees for the University of Washington Press. Julidta Tarver of the press advised and encouraged me, and Jacqueline Ettinger provided both a very useful critique and a close editing of the text. Several undergraduates at the University of Northern British Columbia shared with me the fruits of their research: Darren Bradley, Eva Doerksen, Owen Haley, Judy Larson, Kurt Nordstokke, Shannon Pickering, and Anne Marie Sam. Several friends and family members shared their homes during my research trips: Karen Blair, Matt Fairbanks and Michele Besso, Muril Helen and Bob Demory, Georgie Hendrie, Shelly MacNaab, Armand and Dolores Smith, Nicole Smith, Mark, Eileen, and Bridget Summit, and Lisa Varga. Of the many archivists and librarians who assisted me I am especially grateful to Diana Thomson at the University of Northern British Columbia and to the kind staff of the Boys and Girls Aid Society in Portland, who always managed to accommodate me in the midst of their very hectic and important work. Mike Badnin provided clear, easily understood technical instruction and never said "jump" unless I needed to. To all of the above people I offer my heartfelt gratitude for their generosity.

I am also grateful to the Social Sciences and Humanities Research Council of Canada for providing a three-year grant to fund my research and to the University of Northern British Columbia for a seed grant.

My deepest debt is owed to my family. Wendy del Mar has offered me unstinting encouragement and support, even when my research took me away from home. She is a peerless critic and precious life partner. Peter del Mar arrived midway through this book's creation and has enriched its author with his gentle spirit and joy for life. He is already trying to create a world that is both peaceful and just, and I only hope that Wendy and I can keep up with him.

Since this book deals with many potentially embarrassing episodes, I have chosen (and at times been required) to obscure the identities of some historical actors, particularly for the twentieth century. I have purposefully kept some of the references vague, and indicated in the notes where information has been withheld, to ensure that the privacy of these people and their descendants will be respected.

Beaten Down

INTRODUCTION

EVERY OTHER FRIDAY, one by one, we filed forward, bent over, and took our medicine: one or more "hacks" from a wooden paddle. It was the late 1960s at Lewis and Clark Consolidated, and the students who had been bad were suffering for it. Our teachers, paying homage to a cultural revolution that had filtered down even to rural Clatsop County, Oregon, called these events "happenings."

Not many of us feared these women. Our physical education teacher was much more imposing. He administered his infrequent punishments with a bat, behind closed doors—though the sound of hard plastic on taut buttocks resonated across our small gymnasium. The highly public happenings were, by contrast, something of a spectacle, a peculiar blend of sixties trendiness and old-fashioned discipline, tinctured, I now think, by sadism. The pain inflicted was more apt to be emotional than physical. One of my most vivid images from elementary school is of my classmates snickering as Mrs. Gramson daintily returned my ubiquitous packet of tissues after paddling me, thereby implying that I had acted the coward and put them in my back pocket to cushion the blow.

Other writers from Clatsop County have occasionally described unremarkable acts of violence. In the 1960s and 1970s Sam Churchill recorded his memories of growing up in an early-twentieth-century logging camp. Churchill depicted a community that was generous but rough, one in which violence flared repeatedly but seldom with results that seemed consequential. A crude but big-hearted neighbor woman beat her obstreperous boys. The loggers routinely used their free time to fight each other. Churchill's mother, who hailed from New England, never accepted the community's ready use of physical force. Her son recorded an instance in which she separated two combative men and demanded to know why they were fighting.

"My God, Mrs. Churchill," blurted one of them after an awkward pause, "do we have to have a reason?"[1]

Other accounts of violence lay folded tightly in filing cabinets crammed in the basement of the county courthouse in Astoria. Charlotte Smith, the daughter of a prominent Clatsop Native woman and a white father, filed three divorce suits against successive spouses, and in each she described sundry acts of cruelty. Sylvester Ingalls, whom she had married in 1864, would not make a fire for her when she was sick with menstrual cramps, had farted in bed and then held the covers over her head, had not sufficiently provided for her, and "swears at me all the time." He had also committed adultery. Three years after this suit, in 1874, Charlotte married Charles Dodge. Just two weeks after the wedding he "got mad & cursed me & threatened to leave me." He had "treated me roughly all the time" and had hit and pushed her, at least once because she had tried to keep him from whipping her boy from the first marriage. They divorced in 1879. Charlotte wed Henry Brallier a year later and divorced him in 1892. This third suit's documentation is relatively sketchy, although Charlotte cited an instance in which Henry had hit her with his fist and a fire steel.[2]

Is this the stuff of history? Not according to most historians. Emma Gene Miller's history of Clatsop County devotes considerable space to schools and lumbering without treating violence. She thinks it noteworthy that Charlotte Smith once gave a little girl some material for a dress, but she has nothing to say about her four marriages. Nor have more scholarly accounts of North American history much troubled themselves with prosaic acts of interpersonal violence. Historians of violence have largely concerned themselves with collective deeds easily categorized as political, such as riots, strikes, and vigilante movements, although growing numbers are paying attention to homicides. When Kenneth McNaught criticizes historians for overlooking violence in Canada and calls for an approach that is more sensitive to local history, he is not referring to wife beating, rape, or child abuse. When Carlos Schwantes remarks that labor strife seldom turned violent in British Columbia, he cites the absence of riots and gun battles like the handful that erupted in Washington, not whether miners and loggers routinely brawled in saloons and bunkhouses. A child being turned over his parent's knee, a pair of inebriated men squaring off, a husband slapping his wife: these events are deemed historically inconsequential, a sort of white noise that has, like the poor, been with us always, humming quietly during and between explosive acts of violence.[3]

Yet the very pervasiveness of intimate violence makes it worthy of concerted historical examination. The fact that automobile accidents are apt to yield only one or two fatalities does not mean that safety experts concern themselves only with airline crashes, events nearly as rare as they are catastrophic. By the same token, the average North American has been and is much more likely to be injured or even killed by a parent, spouse, or friend than by a member of a vigilante or terrorist group. Events like the Oklahoma City bombing are so spectacular and episodic that they mask the steady drumbeat of blows that suffuse many people's lives. If historians are concerned with violence, should we not study its most common forms?

Many social scientists certainly do so. Criminologists, sociologists, and psychologists take prosaic acts of interpersonal violence much more seriously than historians do. The topic is addressed in innumerable books and by several journals, including *Violence and Victims* and *Victimology.* As these titles indicate, such scholars, like Sam Churchill's mother, approach violence as a problem. They associate it with deviance and are primarily concerned with measuring, predicting, and preventing it.

This sort of work is very important, but it can also be misleading. The characterization of violence as a uniquely harmful act, the automatic conflation of violence with pathology, can distort, obscure, and mislead. Much of the voluminous work produced by Murray Straus and Richard Gelles, probably our most influential students of domestic violence, is burdened by this assumption. At the heart of their analysis is a "conflict tactics scale" that classifies violent acts by type (slap versus kick, for example) with no consideration of the principals' size, strength, or status, let alone an assessment of the broader social context in which such blows are administered. Hence the scale would indicate that my stint as a day-care provider, when I regularly absorbed the cuffs and blows of enraged toddlers, was far more harrowing than a childhood during which I continually expected, but never received, a thrashing from my father.[4]

Anthropologists more often succeed at linking particular violent acts to larger social and cultural patterns. In *Hunting Humans: The Rise of the Modern Multiple Murderer,* for example, Elliott Leyton argues that his subjects represent "the logical extension of many of the central themes in their

culture—of worldly ambition, of success and failure, and of manly aveng-
ing violence."[5] Leyton is concerned not simply with the number and personal characteristics of serial and mass killers, but with what his subjects
are attempting to accomplish through their horrible acts and how these goals
relate to ones shared by the rest of us. Nigel Rapport's *Talking Violence: An
Anthropological Interpretation of Conversation in the City* considers less dramatic behavior. He argues that people's remarks about violence "testify to
the complex drama of their own lives" and serve to "reflect upon community, about those who share one's definition of proper behaviour and the rules
of its description, and those who do not."[6] A number of other social scientists have used the topic of violence as a point of departure for broader concerns. Emanuel Marx argues that beleaguered residents of an Israeli town use
violent assaults as "appeals" to demonstrate and elicit recognition of their
desperation, to "communicate things which ordinarily are not clearly stated,
and sharply bring home familiar truths which had been half ignored."[7] From
serial killers like Ted Bundy to young men arguing over whose hometown
has the toughest bars, violence is related to complex questions of identity,
status, and power.

Interpersonal violence can be like Clifford Geertz's Balinese cockfight: more
important for what it signifies than for what it constitutes. To be sure, the
three scenarios that open this book can simply be interpreted as abusive or
unnecessary acts of violence. Most of us can agree that schoolchildren and
wives ought not to be hit and that grown men should find nonviolent means
of amusement. But to assert this is to leave much unsaid and unexamined.
The pupils at my school and Charlotte Smith were struck for very particular
reasons: we disobeyed or challenged people who considered themselves our
superiors. The violence we suffered therefore emerged from a hierarchical
relationship, a relationship that usually maintained itself without recourse
to physical blows. Indeed, Smith accused her first husband of abuse that did
not include violence. Violence, furthermore, has often erupted from above
or below when a husband's or teacher's authority was least, not most, secure.
Its appearance, as Linda Gordon has pointed out, commonly denotes resistance as well as dominance.[8] The Clatsop County loggers' violence is still more
difficult to contain in conventional moral categories. The loggers were peers,
their violence consensual and, to Mrs. Churchill's bemusement, apparently

without purpose. But, as we shall see, such fights commonly served both to determine a pecking order within a male society of equals and to set the members of that society apart from their purported inferiors: children, people of color, and of course women.

Acts of interpersonal violence almost always constitute an attempt by one or both participants to exercise power. I define power as the ability to control one's own life and the lives of others. An infant has very little power and must depend upon the whims and judgements of others even to eat or move. A wealthy corporate head, on the other hand, lives more or less as he (or occasionally she) pleases and can throw thousands of other people out of work with the stroke of a pen. Power, then, has to do with both the extent to which others can impose their wills on us and the extent to which we can impose our will on them. A person's power can vary considerably from place to place and relationship to relationship. A man may enjoy little of it at work and a great deal of it at home.

How are power and violence associated? At first glance, that relationship seems clear enough: dominant people use violence to control subordinates. But, as we have already seen, social arrangements are never this simple. Even the most marginalized and oppressed people possess at least a modicum of power; as any reflective parent or administrator will attest to, no one can fully control another's actions. Violence, furthermore, is a relatively crude and sometimes costly means of exercising dominance. It often invites legal sanctions and disrespect. Violence is therefore frequently abjured by those with the most power and employed by those who lack other coercive tools, such as status or money. These people may use violence as an act of protest. Such protests can be direct, as when a student or worker hits an overbearing teacher or superior. But they are often indirect, as when a pair of unemployed and uneducated men square off in a bar to demonstrate their mettle.

Like many social scientists, reformers are often tone-deaf about how interpersonal violence relates to power and dominance. Expressions of concern over violence can serve to point out the abuses of powerful people, such as parents and husbands. But they can also obscure larger patterns of dominance. Indeed "moral panics" focused on violence commonly divert public attention from social inequalities and inequities to less discomforting explanations of social and cultural strain. Focusing on violence as a social problem enables powerful people to define social ills and assign blame for them, leaving unquestioned their own privileges and abuses.[9]

Dominance does not necessarily require the use of physical force. Michel Foucault shows how criminal justice shifted in the eighteenth and nineteenth centuries from the work of literally tearing apart and torturing the bodies of wrongdoers to a program that instead fastened onto their minds. The new system appeared much more humane. Criminals were now rehabilitated, not punished. The state aspired to change their thoughts, not abuse their flesh. But this new system was both more ambitious and more subtle. "Power," as Foucault put it, now acted "while concealing itself."[10] The state had become skilled at imposing its will on others and at disguising that coercive act.

This book suggests that a similar process transpired on the micropolitical level, within communities and families. Powerful mid-nineteenth-century men of the north Pacific slope (British Columbia, Washington, and Oregon) were not shy about using fists, whips, or switches to validate their social position. High status entailed the right or even obligation to hit others. Today, on the whole, it does not. Refusing to use violence has become a mark of masculine social distinction—a choice that typically disturbs the status quo not one whit. Like Foucault's prison administrators, powerful men's renunciation of violence more often obscures than undermines existing patterns of dominance and control.

Interpersonal violence should therefore not be studied as an end unto itself. It is inextricably bound up in larger cultural processes and moral problems, and its causes and significance cannot be understood aside from social relations of power. That is the thesis of this book.

The word "violence" has become highly elastic. Some lament the violence of poverty, others the violence of abortion. I have adopted a relatively narrow and literal definition: for the purposes of this study, violence is a deliberate physical act, typically a blow, that causes direct physical pain to another person.[11] This book focuses on interpersonal acts of physical force: violence within families and schools, between relatives, friends, and acquaintances. It will say little about warfare or sports or other types of collective, organized violence, such as riots, lynchings, vigilante movements, or struggles between labor and management. I am concerned with micropolitical acts of violence, particularly violence between people who knew each other well.

This is cultural as well as social history. I am interested in how people have practiced and talked about violence. Which acts have various groups of people condoned or condemned? What sort of violence has been identified by political leaders as a social problem, a crime warranting or requiring the intervention of the state? Answering these questions reveals that talking about violence has also constituted an act of power, an attempt to expand the influence of one's own group at the expense of others.

Since I am primarily interested in exploring the relationship between power and interpersonal violence, this book is not an orthodox history in its organization or its methodology. Its geographic boundaries are clear enough: the land that today constitutes the states of Washington and Oregon and the province of British Columbia. It also progresses chronologically, from pre-contact Native societies to the present. But this is not primarily a regional or comparative study, nor an attempt to render an exhaustive history. It uses various locales and successive periods not to offer a complete history of violence in parts of the United States and Canada but rather as a vehicle for exploring the manifold and complex relations between violence and power. Change over time and distinctions of nationality have, to be sure, affected both the nature of interpersonal violence and its relationship to power. But I am more interested in using time and place to explore the nuances of that relationship than in simply focusing on the history of violent acts. This book may therefore be more properly understood as historical anthropology or historical sociology, in which the past is used as an analytical tool, than as a traditional history concerned primarily with charting and explaining change.

The book's chapters reflect this goal. They address not simply change over time, but different aspects of interpersonal violence and its relationship to power. The first illustrates how the colonization of Native people transformed the political nature and significance of their violence. The next examines how violent acts among settlers constituted both dominance and resistance. Chapter three shows how these patterns of dominance and resistance persisted into the 1890s, even as social relations became less contested and interpersonal violence more rare. The following chapter examines how the region's urban newspapers vacillated over whether to treat marginalized people's violence as potent or impotent in the twentieth century's first decade. Chapter five treats the 1920s, a decade during which public celebrations of masculine physical contests waxed while men's actual practice of violence increasingly occurred not among or before peers, but in private, against children and wives.

The final chapter compares the very different ways in which two marginal ethnic groups, people of Japanese and African descent, encountered and practiced violence during the twentieth century's first half. The epilogue addresses the recent explosion of concern around many types of interpersonal violence.

The north Pacific slope is a good place to conduct a multifaceted history of violence. Its major geographic features—its coastline, mountain ranges, and most of the Columbia River—run north to south, across an international boundary. The Chinook peoples of the lower Columbia River shared more in common with the Haida of the Queen Charlotte Islands far to the north than they did with the Nez Perce or Cayuse of the Columbia Plateau, just as modern residents of Vancouver have arguably more closely resembled residents of Seattle than residents of Fort St. John, in British Columbia's northeastern quarter. This is not to say that nationality has never trumped geography on the north Pacific slope. But its victories were hard won, at least in the nineteenth century. British Columbia has in many respects more closely resembled the U.S. West than Washington and particularly Oregon have: it developed very rapidly, around mining, and attracted many footloose young male adventurers while Willamette Valley farmers were creating and maintaining highly stable communities. Society north of the border was therefore decidedly more masculine, mobile, and ethnically diverse than it was in Oregon or Washington. Physical and cultural geography inverted British and American ideals of order and individualism and made it difficult for authoritarian British Columbia officials to impose their vision of a peaceful and orderly society on their volatile charges. That despite these difficulties British Columbians soon became less violent than their more settled counterparts to the south suggests that cultural ideals could mitigate demography.[12]

The north Pacific slope has seemed like a relatively peaceful place. British Columbians soon indulged in the Canadian habit of contrasting their orderly, peace-loving society to that south of the line. Although Oregon and particularly Washington had some vigilante movements and lynchings, their histories have been much more tranquil than most parts of the West. Yet the province and two states offer abundant and divergent historical sources describing violence. Many fur traders and ethnographers described Native peoples. Oregon, Washington, and British Columbia have ample repositories of newspapers dating from at least the 1850s and some very useful oral history collections and autobiographies. Vancouver and Portland have extensive arrest records for much of their history. British Columbia has very strong criminal court records and many published reminiscences. Oregon and to a lesser extent Washington have detailed accounts from divorce suits.

Each type of source offers particular pitfalls and possibilities. Newspaper accounts are perhaps the most tempting; a few days' work in most any period will produce a stack of easily digested renditions of violent encounters. These accounts can easily mislead, however. They are a collection of violent acts deemed newsworthy by their editors, not a trustworthy sample of all violent acts actually committed. Hence when Roger McGrath asserts that, aside from prostitutes, women of two western U.S. mining towns "suffered little from crime or violence" and that "young toughs" committed "no violent crimes," what he has actually established is that newspapers and the court systems seldom noted such acts.[13] Arrest records, like newspapers, are more useful for assessing how community leaders perceived and punished violence than for tracing actual levels of violence, for the vast majority of assaults have always gone unrecorded. Inasmuch as a dead body usually generated legal notice and newspaper stories, homicide statistics are much more accurate.[14] I use them to indicate the level of extreme violence in particular places and times. More useful still have been qualitative accounts by participants in violent acts. Some of these accounts are from autobiographies, reminiscences, or oral histories. Reliable and detailed descriptions of criminal acts can be found in court documents, particularly the preliminary hearings for assaults and homicides that occurred within a few days of an altercation. To be sure, witnesses tailored their testimony to fit their desires. But their statements nonetheless convey a great deal about social and legal expectations of violent behavior, and the use of witnesses by complainants and defendants alike provides a check against bias. These legal materials, generated by a wide variety of people, offer detailed depictions of violent acts seldom recorded elsewhere.

As I have already argued, these accounts are important not simply because they describe acts of violence that historians have neglected, acts that have harmed and humiliated most North Americans. They also suggest and detail other neglected and pernicious aspects of our collective past: the shifting but stubborn lines of power and authority that have divided colonized from colonizer, person of color from person of privilege, working man from gentleman, wife from husband, child from adult, son and daughter from mother and father.

Interpersonal violence has been and is a pressing social problem. But it has occurred alongside still larger problems that it has often obscured: social inequalities and injustices that have both shaped and transcended the blows that have punctuated and diminished the lives of so many of us.

1

A White Fist on Their Noses

Colonization and Violence

AROUND 1900 AN ELDERLY KWAKIUTL told a local Indian agent that his people had been "living in a state of warfare" for countless generations. Then the white people arrived and brought peace.[1] Colonizers have of course been eager to hear and construct this sort of history. The belief that conquest constituted a civilizing process in which missionaries, government officials, and educators saved Indians from themselves has proved reassuring to whites confronted by Native anger and poverty. If a senseless series of brutal massacres had dominated precontact life, the newcomers could argue that colonization solved more problems than it caused and that the solution to Native problems lay not with Native tradition, but with a still larger dose of assimilation.[2]

Colonization did in fact end warfare among Native peoples of the north Pacific slope in the nineteenth century, in the United States and Canada alike. A Puget Sound village was much less apt to be awakened by the cries of club-wielding raiding parties from the north in 1900 than it had been in 1800.

But this sort of physical safety was a direct consequence of conquest, of losing control over one's affairs. Groups who had lost their political autonomy were no longer free to fight.

Nor were these conquered peoples free from violence. Large- and small-scale acts of physical force of course accompanied conquest, especially south of the border. And violence did not end once subjugation began. Indian agents, missionaries, and educators commonly beat the Native peoples they governed, particularly children. Violence was an integral part of the process and practice of domination. Violence also festered within conquered groups. It had seldom marred intravillage relations before contact and conquest. By the nine-

13

teenth century's close, however, acts of physical force between Native people who knew each other well had become more common.

Assessing the impact of colonization on Native people's experience of violence entails more than simply calculating shifts in the risk of being hit or murdered. It requires attention to the changing nature and sources of violence, to the changing contexts in which those acts occurred. The rest of this book will not treat collective violence or warfare. This chapter does, for otherwise the relationship between colonization and violence cannot be discerned.

Native societies on the north Pacific slope developed as four broad culture groups during the millennia preceding contact. The Northwest Coast peoples utilized rich ecosystems to create relatively populous and stratified societies. The Plateau peoples of the semiarid Columbia River drainage system constituted the major interior group and stretched from what is now south-central Oregon well into the British Columbia interior. They lacked the abundant salmon resources enjoyed by their coastal counterparts and were more dispersed and egalitarian. Populations were still more scattered in the northern interior of what would become British Columbia, home to sub-Arctic peoples, and in the arid southeastern quarter of what would become Oregon, where the Northern Paiutes of the Great Basin culture group resided. Political authority within all these culture groups was much more diffuse than in Meso-America or Europe during the same centuries.[3]

Political divisions often led to violence, but set battles were relatively rare and bloodless. Robert Stuart, who arrived at the Columbia River's mouth in 1811, remarked that a contest fought over several days and involving more than one thousand men might produce only a dozen killed and wounded. Northwest Coast groups, in particular, much preferred ambush to open warfare because the element of surprise dramatically lowered the risks for attackers. George Gibbs, who observed Natives of the Puget Sound in the mid-nineteenth century, concluded that "the real method of warfare among them was by murder, overpowering individuals by numbers, or killing them by stealth and unawares."[4] Likewise, a fur trader living among the Carrier early in the nineteenth century remarked that these sub-Arctic people regarded "a murder . . . committed on a person belonging to a tribe with whom they are at enmity" as "a brave and noble action."[5] Europeans living in huge, politically centralized nations with standing armies conducted warfare much differently. War was a discrete event with a clear beginning and end and thousands of casualties. Native warfare struck such people as both unethical and halfhearted. But these small-scale conflicts added up. Donald Mitchell, after examining over seven hundred historical and ethnological sources, concludes that "predatory warfare . . . for plunder and captives, was engaged in by virtually all Northwest Coast societies."[6] By the eighteenth century the more powerful northern peoples, such as the Haida, were especially aggressive, as were smaller groups to the south, such as the Lekwiltok of Vancouver Island and the Klallam of northern Puget Sound. The more widely dispersed Sekani, Beaver, and Carrier peoples in what is now the northern interior of British Columbia also commonly fought each other in the eighteenth century, as did many Plateau peoples to the south. Natives recalled a decade-long conflict between the Shuswap and Sekani that ended in a crushing defeat for the latter in about 1790, a series of attacks by the Snake and Paiute on the middle Columbia from the mid-eighteenth to the early nineteenth centuries, and repeated conflicts between the Shuswap and the Okanagan around 1700 and the Klamath River and Shasta peoples around 1800.[7]

Some groups tried to avoid warfare and raiding. Several peoples on or near Puget Sound, including the Upper Skagit, the Puyallup-Nisqually, and the Twana, seldom initiated large-scale armed conflicts. The Lillooet people whom James Teit interviewed around the turn of the century "acknowledge that they were not so warlike and rapacious as the other tribes of the interior," although they "often fought determinedly when attacked on their own ground."[8] The strongest case for nonviolence among Plateau peoples has been made by Verne Ray, who in the late 1920s began studying the Sanpoil and Nespelem of what is now northeastern Washington. Ray's "informants denied that any major conflict had occurred 'as long as could be remembered,'" and he concluded that even "heinous offenses by raiding parties were left unrevenged."[9] In a broader, more synthetic study, *Cultural Relations in the Plateau of Northwestern America,* Ray granted that southern Plateau groups such as the Nez Perce and Cayuse had engaged in armed conflicts long before white contact, but again emphasized that some northern groups, particularly the Sanpoil and the Southern Okanagan, articulated and practiced pacifism.[10]

Ray overstated his case. Wayne Suttles cites nineteenth-century descriptions of Sanpoil feuding and raiding, as well as archaeological evidence of earlier conflicts. Sanpoil leaders indeed emphasized peacefulness, since peace facilitated the efficient operation of their profitable fisheries. But this does not mean that peace always prevailed. Even Ray granted that not all Sanpoil "conformed alike to the ideals of peacefulness and equality."[11]

Likewise, the Twana of Puget Sound emphasized peace but were ready for war. Informants recalled that they rarely engaged in raiding and fighting during the early nineteenth century, in part because they lived on a relatively inaccessible part of Hood Canal. Yet one, Harry Allen, remarked that they "were always ready for raids from outside," and they related many instances of armed conflicts, including a major attack around 1845 in collaboration with other Puget Sound groups in retaliation for continual slave raids from the north.[12] William Elmendorf, who conducted these interviews, concluded that Twana pacifism inhibited "aggressive warfare" but did not preclude various forms of intergroup conflict, including defensive fighting, the use of magic, and joining counterstrikes organized by more aggressive peoples, like the Klallam.[13]

Armed conflict was too important a political tool to be discarded. Brian Ferguson follows Morris Swadesh in arguing that "material conditions" lay behind Northwest Coast warfare, particularly the lure of accumulated food stores, productive territory such as salmon streams, and control of trade.[14] On the Northwest Coast in particular, groups perceived as weak were vulnerable to attacks from distant parties seeking slaves and other forms of booty. Retaliatory strikes served notice that a village or set of villages could not be raided with impunity and that their food sources could not be exploited by interlopers.[15]

Warfare enhanced the status of individuals as well as groups. This was particularly so among Plateau groups who, like their counterparts on the Great Plains, used warfare as a proving ground of masculine courage and competence. Tum-a-tap-um, a Nez Perce leader, reportedly reacted to early fur traders' attempts to establish peaceful relations by remarking that his young men "delight in nothing but war" and asked if he should throw all of his war trophies away and "forget the glory of his forefathers."[16] Prowess in war brought status, such as the right to display prestigious emblems. Franz Boas reported that Kwakiutl warriors could "wear grizzly bear claws on a headdress" after killing several enemies, for example.[17] Among the Nootka, younger brothers of prominent leaders reportedly relied on "the fortunes of war" to win prerogatives that their elder siblings already possessed.[18]

But the skulls impaled on stakes in front of villages along the Northwest Coast did more than attest to the prowess of particular individuals. They also bore mute testimony to the risks of attacking that group. The ostentatious ferocity of Northwest Coast warfare spoke to the importance of reputation and intimidation in both winning and avoiding conflicts. "It was the desire of all tribes to win the most terrible name for bloodthirstiness," remarked one of Edward Curtis's informants.[19] The capacity to inflict violence on other groups was an essential political tool.

Kinship shaped the nature of intergroup violence. Native peoples perceived themselves not primarily as discrete individuals, but as parts of collectives, members of groups to whom they owed their identities and allegiances. Sometimes these allegiances escalated conflicts. Boas explained that among the Kwakiutl the loss of a relative "was felt as an insult to one's dignity, as a cause of shame and sorrow" and stimulated a desire "to make someone else . . . feel sorrow and shame at least equal to one's own."[20] A single death could initiate years of blood feuding, particularly among the politically decentralized peoples of the northern interior. One such conflict between the Carrier and Chilcotin reportedly began with the death of a leading Chilcotin and ended several years later with the massacre of nearly an entire village.[21] But ties to others could also deter violence. Ferguson argues that the ubiquitous food and wealth redistribution networks of the Northwest Coast served to defuse volatile situations: "Hoarding food when your neighbors are hungry is a very dangerous thing to do."[22] Sharing material resources was far less costly than chronic warfare. Potlatches, feasts, and marriages created familial bonds between people who might otherwise have distrusted each other.

Allegiance to kin and village certainly served to calm relations within the group. Native peoples placed an extraordinary emphasis on social harmony. Among the Coast Salish, intergroup relations were reportedly characterized by suspicion, but "the preservation of peace and unity" within the extended family "was a practical and moral necessity."[23] Likewise, the Skagit socialized their children "not to take offence readily," and "adults who received insults without retaliating were given the highest praise."[24]

This emphasis on agreeableness bore fruit, especially on the Northwest Coast. A fur trader among the Nootka in the mid-1780s "never saw any quarrel among them, or ever heard them abusing each other."[25] A botanist at Nootka Sound for several months in 1792 recorded that Spanish officers who visited several villages were unfailingly "impressed by the affection and gentleness they had observed in everyone."[26] Other observers and later scholars made the same point.[27]

Harmony characterized most marriages. To be sure, Charles Bishop, captain of a trading ship that wintered among the Chinooks at the Columbia River's mouth in 1795 to 1796, remarked that husbands "sometimes beat" their wives "unmercifully."[28] But traders farther north came to much different conclusions. Captain James Strange, among the Nootka in the mid-1780s, remarked that spouses "appeared exemplary in love & attachment to each other."[29] One of Strange's charges remarked that he "never during our whole stay saw one instance of a quarrel between Husband and Wife, or any squabbling between the Sexes."[30] Camille de Roquefeuil, who arrived three decades later, asserted that women "are treated with much mildness by their husbands" at Nootka Sound and elsewhere on the coast.[31] Oral traditions also indicated intolerance for wife beating. Coast Salish husbands who struck their wives were reportedly obligated to make a public distribution of property, and a Quinault account describes how a man dared not visit his wife's Makah kinsmen because he had "often quarreled with her and abused her."[32] Much farther south, among the Tolowa, an abused woman's kin would reportedly be "forever shamed" if they failed to protest her ill treatment.[33]

Abused Native wives did not simply wait for their families of origin to intervene. They acted on their own behalf. Divorce was not uncommon on the Northwest Coast, and wives often left physically abusive husbands. Wives married to such men in the interior generally enjoyed fewer options, but here, too, some groups allowed them to escape violent spouses.[34]

Wives were most apt to face violence if they committed adultery. Almost universally, in the interior and on the coast, those suspected of the practice could face severe physical punishments, including beatings, disfigurement, torture, or even death. The families of such women might retaliate, but not if they believed that the wife was guilty.[35]

Adulterous wives were much more likely to face violence than were adulterous husbands. Among the Klamath of the southern tip of the Plateau, a woman married to an unfaithful husband could beat his paramour, but apparently not him. Indeed, adulterous husbands did not fear so much their wives as the husbands of their lovers.[36]

Women could also face violence if they did not properly comport themselves upon their husbands' deaths. Among the Kalapuya of the Willamette Valley, a widow who refused to marry her deceased husband's younger brother might be killed. A fur trader who remarked that the Carrier were "remarkably fond of their wives" noted that widows had to serve their deceased husband's family for several years and "are frequently beaten with a club or an axe, or some such weapon." The grieving kin of dead men reportedly forced widows to stand as close as possible to their funeral pyres. Women who shrank before the heat were met with spears. For some time after this harrowing event, "every child in the village might command her and beat her unmercifully."[37]

This sort of violence certainly suggests that Native marriages did not constitute a feminist utopia. Wives were more susceptible to spousal violence than their husbands were, and that violence could be extreme.

Yet such violence spoke more to the needs of the group than to the jealousies and prerogatives of individual husbands. Violence against wives, certainly in its more extreme forms, was structured, even predictable. It occurred around a husband's death or, more commonly, around a wife's adultery. In either instance, his lineage had a deep interest in the woman's behavior. A widow who did not show proper respect to her dead husband, like a wife who had sexual intercourse with another man, threatened the bedrock of social relations. Rebecca Morley observes: "Unlike the 'privatized' West, wife beating in traditional societies may be inextricably linked to the political context of kinship."[38] For women to bear children whose paternity and lineage were not what they seemed, not what was required, was to endanger the entire group's very identity and survival—now and for generations to come. Hence wives accused of adultery were subject to a great deal of castigation. But other wives were not.

Child beating was more rare than wife beating. Early fur traders among the Nootka remarked on parents' deep affection for their children. Most ethnologies from the Northwest Coast date from the early twentieth century, several generations after contact. But even accounts from people who grew up in the mid to late nineteenth century do not generally describe extensive physical punishments. Ronald Olson stated that Quinault children under age five "were never punished," and that "only low class people whipped their children" at any age.[39] Several ethnographers described whipping or other forms of violence as toughening rather than as punishment. Parents often avoided these rites, for they did not wish to hurt their children.[40]

Nor did children in the sparsely settled sub-Arctic or Great Basin suffer much violence. Paiute parents seldom used corporal punishment. Carrier parents, according to an ethnographer who interviewed them in the 1920s, "occasionally" beat their children but more often corrected them indirectly, through storytelling. His informants remarked that "the shame and humiliation inflicted by this method were harder to endure, and more efficacious, than the severest thrashing."[41]

Violence toward children was more common on the Plateau, but here, as on the Northwest Coast, it had more to do with training than with punishment. Withstanding pain prepared one to risk one's life for the good of the group, as a warrior or in bearing children. Pain was often self-inflicted. Shuswap boys commonly cut themselves as they prayed for stoicism, and girls burned heaps of dry fir needles on their skin as they prayed for the courage to withstand the ordeals of childbirth. A Kittitas woman recalled in the late 1920s that "an old man . . . beat the short ones, so that the short ones would grow up to be strong and invincible."[42] Ethnologist James Teit's vivid and detailed account of the Thompson people's winter child-whipping ceremony illustrates that Plateau children were not simply passive victims of violence. Boys who bravely stepped forward and made a speech to the elderly whipper who visited each house would generally not be whipped. Children over age eight who refused to dance and sing and pretend to pick berries were subject to four blows, but children might choose the whipping "to show their courage." Indeed, some called for additional lashes. The bloodied boy who wore out the switch without flinching "had done a great feat"; his courage would exempt the other children from such ordeals for a long time to come. The next morning the whipper would invite the people of the house, particularly the children he had hit, to a feast. The whipping ritual, according to Teit's informants, "was to help the children overcome their bashfulness," to teach them courage, and to train boys for warfare.[43] This ritual could be harrowing, but like other types of violence Native children experienced, those with sufficient poise and determination could shape its outcome and meaning. The goal of such violence, furthermore, was more instructive than punitive: to prepare youth to act courageously and independently, not simply to defer to authority.

Precontact Native peoples, then, struggled to maintain both internal peace and at least the capacity for external violence. Parents and other relations treated children gently, but boys, in particular, needed to be trained to inflict and withstand violence, to put their lives at the disposal of the group's welfare. This was not schooling in recreational violence; an ethnographer remarked that the Lummi fought not "with fists but with short straight knives."[44] These men were to be ruthlessly aggressive in combat, patient and forbearing with their kin, their wives, and their children. Not all succeeded. Some warriors and many shamans were dreaded outside and inside of their villages. Group norms of harmony and cooperation did not always restrain them. Nor did the links of kinship always promote peace. Intermarriage and other exchanges knit villages and lineages together, but real or perceived slights could rend those linkages and create extensive and lengthy conflicts. A wife suspected of adultery or a husband thought to be abusive, for example, could both divide a family and stimulate animosity among the spouse's kin.[45]

Yet these societies' micropolitical organizations generally served to contain internal and to generate external conflicts. The survival of the group, after all, depended both on maintaining group harmony and on being able to negotiate, through nonviolent and violent means, with many similar groups. This need for cohesiveness shaped all types of violence. It discouraged the use of physical force among those who knew each other well, except when wives were suspected of betraying their husbands' kin through adultery or when children required training. Strangers were much more inclined to meet with violence, for they constituted a potential threat, and allegiance to the group presumed a willingness to risk one's life for its welfare.

The arrival of Europeans on the north Pacific slope would eventually invert this equation by eliminating warfare and exacerbating intragroup relations. But the changes were at first more subtle than profound.

Europeans influenced Native peoples long before direct contact. Disease is the most obvious example. Around 1780 smallpox traveled from the Plateau along the Columbia River to its mouth, then northwards, between Vancouver Island and the mainland and up the Fraser River. It is difficult to know the proportion of people who died in this epidemic, but estimates range from one- to two-thirds. Smallpox and other diseases repeatedly visited the heavily populated Northwest Coast throughout the fur-trade era. Rapid depopulation created social instability and mobility. It may have also created a sense of crisis. Elizabeth Vibert argues that Plateau peoples attributed spiritual causes to the first epidemic, that they interpreted the deaths as "a symptom of deep unease or imbalance in the spirit world."[46]

Microbes were not the only newcomers. Horses arrived on the Plateau in the early 1700s, about a century before the first white explorers or fur traders.

This revolution in transportation facilitated trading, raiding, and warring. Peoples from the western Great Plains used horses to cross the Rocky Mountains and attack the Nez Perce and their neighbors. The Cayuse used the new animals to subjugate the nearby Walla Walla and to conduct raids to the west and the south. The Okanagan, too, used the horse as a military tool of expansion, particularly at the expense of the Shuswap. Several groups rode their horses over the Rocky Mountains to hunt buffalo and fight the Blackfoot and other Plains peoples. Horses also altered internal political dynamics. They added prestige and status to men more commonly than to women, and to men of war more commonly than to men of peace. In the sub-Arctic, foreign Native peoples foreshadowed whites' arrival, as the Beaver and Sekani contended with Cree propelled westward by the fur trade. Indirect contact with whites tended to exacerbate Native political conflicts.[47]

The fur trade stimulated intergroup conflict, particularly at first. Early access to firearms allowed some to expand at the expense of others. The Nez Perce welcomed the Lewis and Clark Expedition in 1805 largely because they hoped to gain the reliable access to firearms that their enemies across the Rocky Mountains enjoyed. Coast Salish villages suffered at the hands of Kwakiutl armed with guns, and, to the north and the east, gun-wielding Beaver reportedly terrorized groups of Sekani. These sorts of mismatches became rare as the novelty of firearms wore off and their use spread. But access to trade remained a point of contention. Meares observed Nootkan villagers attacking members of another group who attempted to trade with the Europeans. Relations were particularly strained near and around Fort Simpson, a Hudson's Bay Company post on the north coast established in the early 1830s. The Tsimishian who clustered near the trading post often quarreled with both the Haida who came to trade from the Queen Charlotte Islands and with the Gitksan who had established themselves as middlemen between the coast and the interior. These forts generated conflict by drawing traditional enemies to the same ground and by stimulating profitable trade that Native groups vied with each other to control. Ferguson observes that Northwest Coast peoples had traditionally fought each other over "the control of subsistence resources." Now they killed each other in a struggle "over the control of trade goods."[48]

The fur trade also altered political relations and violence within groups. Ferguson observes that "a few local groups became so wealthy and powerful that they were immune to attack" and therefore had little reason to curb their aggression.[49] The same could be said for ambitious individuals. Gaps between rich and poor widened as wealth and possibilities for upward mobility increased. Some, like Concomly of the Chinooks, became powerful through trade. Increased raiding for slaves and goods enriched many others, and successful warriors enjoyed unprecedented status. June Collins observes that Patius, a Skagit leader in the mid-nineteenth century, "violated the traditional concepts of proper behavior" by "killing members of his own village over trifles." Yet his people felt compelled to tolerate this war leader, for "villages which did not have adequate leadership were either wiped out during this period or deserted."[50] The fur trade brought great wealth and power to some people fortunate enough to survive its epidemics, but marginalization and subordination to others.

This is not to say that white traders directly encouraged conflict among Natives. To be sure, Meares made an attempt "of binding the chiefs" at Nootka "unalterably to us, by furnishing them with some fire-arms and ammunition, which would give them a very decided advantage over their enemies."[51] But the Hudson's Bay Company, in particular, favored pacific relations between Natives. Indeed, Governor George Simpson complained of "the Constant Broils among the tribes" that interfered with trading, and the factor at Fort Langley lamented that "warfare keeps the Indians of this vicinity in such continual alarm that they can not turn their attention to anything but the care of their families."[52]

But the white traders' attempts to promote peace sometimes did more harm than good. Alexander Ross described how the Northwesters at the Columbia River's mouth tried to tap the supply of furs to the north by drawing How-How, a leading Cowlitz, to Fort George with guarantees of safety from the Chinooks, his people's enemies. But the party had hardly left the post on its way home before some Chinooks shot at them. When a stray shot hit the fort, its sentinel surmised that the departing Cowlitz had turned on their white hosts, and the post's men joined the Chinooks in firing on the beleaguered party, wounding two. Hudson's Bay Company leaders at Fort Simpson tried to avert such misunderstandings by stipulating that they were only able to offer security to visitors within the post's walls.[53] It was a humbling, if truthful, admission.

Natives soon noted that whites could be extremely violent—even among themselves. Daniel Harmon remarked that the North West Company's rank

and file in the northern interior celebrated New Year's Day in 1811 "as is cus-
tomary for them—Drinking & fighting."[54] The fur trade's gentlemen almost
always reserved their violence for the rank and file. The penalty meted out
to a pair of Sandwich Islanders who attempted to desert in 1847 simply consisted of "knocking the men down, kicking them until they got up, and
knocking them down again until they could not get up any more."[55] Some
factors became highly skilled at flogging. When Simpson in 1843 remarked
in a letter to John McLoughlin that "I have . . . always Believed Kindness to
Be the Best Disciplinarian," the bemused chief factor retorted that Simpson
was "writing for Effect on others" and found it peculiar that his superior,
who had inflicted some brutal beatings of his own, had "become all at once
very sensitive about striking the men."[56] Violence functioned largely as a
form of recreation or, if men of consequence involved themselves, a means
of discipline.

Natives were nonplussed by the newcomers' violence. Those at Stuart Lake
who observed the fur traders' drunken brawls on New Year's Day in 1811
"thought the White People had become mad," and "hid themselves under
beds & elsewhere."[57] Fistfighting seemed especially peculiar. "However
expert the Indians may be at the knife, or the spear, or the gun, they are invari-
ably taken aback by a white fist on their noses," boasted Simpson.[58] Skilled
at killing enemies, Natives were unaccustomed to using less lethal forms of
violence.

White leaders, for their part, were offended by Natives' willingness to kill.
William Tolmie recorded an extended discussion in which a chief trader
on Puget Sound asked several local Native men "to confess to him all their
evil actions beginning with the murders & next the thefts." One of them,
Babyar, "after coughing, blowing & humming frequently, declared himself
guiltless of any evil action but recollecting himself shortly after said that he
had killed 5 men & stolen their property, also stole two slaves." Chiatzaan,
another local Native, said "that he had never done any harm, but afterwards
acknowledged himself the murderer of five, (besides those killed by his medi-
cines)." Their inquisitor then "pointed out to the worthy assemblage" the
"enormity of the crime of murder," elicited promises from the men that they
would "never again . . . commit the action" except "in self defence," and
"made" them "mark with a pen a sheet of paper on which their names were
written." The tone of Tolmie's remarks suggests that he had his reservations

about the efficacy of this exercise. But a year later, at Fort McLoughlin, he had his own disagreement with a man who described a fellow Native, who had lately committed a murder, as "a brave fellow not afraid of a bull—a complete warrior." Tolmie retorted that "in my opinion he had acted in a treacherous & cowardly manner having taken his adversary by surprise," an argument that "of course" struck the man he was speaking to as "very absurd."[59]

From the time of early contact, many of the newcomers tried to impose their way of doing violence on Native people. Walker described a particularly intricate example from 1786. The British, irritated by the Nootka's thievery, decided to make an example of a man who had taken a kettle and two jackets. They first asked Kurrighum, a local leader, to restore the goods. Kurrighum retrieved the kettle, but "insisted" that he could not recover the jackets. The British insisted that the offender be produced. The Nootka soon presented both the purported thief and the clothing. "But," continued Walker, "the recovery of the Property was not judged sufficient, and it was determined to carry the Thief on board, and there to give him corporal punishment," an eventuality that "neither he nor his friends expected." The Nootka leaders protested, and the prisoner "made a violent attempt to escape" that provoked a number of blows that caused him to bleed. The shore party then hailed the men on board the ship for a boat, but those men mistook the agitation ashore for an attack and fired on the Natives. This of course alarmed the Natives still further; they now seemed to believe that the captive was about to be killed and eaten. Kurrighum therefore offered ten sea otter skins and then "all that he was worth" for the captive's release, but to no avail. The party insisted on taking their prisoner to the ship. But once there, they found him "half dead with fear, . . . his teeth fast clenched, and his Mouth foaming with blood." Fearing that the man "would die," they concluded "that he had been sufficiently punished by the fright he had received" and released him. He then walked away "without any assistance"—which suggests that his injuries had been feigned.[60] The European traders had badly garbled and bungled whatever lesson they had hoped to impart.

Most interracial conflicts, moreover, were not so one-sided. Avaricious and desperate captains at times resorted to kidnapping or plunder to extract sea otter pelts from experienced Native traders. But Natives responded in kind. The Haida attacked at least five trading ships. John Jewitt noted that his Nootka master, Maquinna, recounted instances in which captains had stolen forty sea otter skins, slain four chiefs, and killed at least twenty Natives in retaliation for the theft of a single chisel. Maquinna had long nurtured "an ardent desire of revenge," a desire he satisfied in 1803 by overcoming the ship on which Jewitt served.[61] Land-based fur traders from the United States also clashed with Native peoples. Employees of the Pacific Fur Company often disputed with Native peoples around Fort Astoria and farther up the Columbia River during their short tenure in the region. John Clarke in 1813 executed a Native man for stealing a silver goblet, and a few months later the Natives retaliated by killing several of Clarke's men. In 1829, Natives in what would become southern Oregon reacted to high-handed treatment by members of the Jedediah Smith expedition by killing most of them.[62] The fur trade harmed Natives in some respects. But it did not rob them of their political autonomy or their ability to inflict violence on the white newcomers.

To be sure, interracial relations became more pacific as trade increasingly fell into the hands of British land-based companies. But neither the North West Company nor the Hudson's Bay Company conquered the north Pacific slope's Native peoples. Neither organization succeeded in imposing its understanding of violence on them. Simpson boasted of the latter organization's "never allowing an insult or outrage [to] pass without retaliation & punishment" on the one hand and of its "judicious firm and conciliatory measures" on the other.[63] Indeed, the company on several occasions attempted to attack and kill Native people it deemed guilty of murder. But it lacked the resources to do so consistently and effectively. Necessity therefore made a virtue of forbearance. Peter Skene Ogden, one of the Hudson's Bay Company's leading men on the north Pacific slope, put the whites' viewpoint plainly: "Look at our numbers compared to theirs; look at the many opportunities they may have of committing murder; look at their treacherous character," and "the weakness of our establishments in the summer."[64] A white trader who administered a violent punishment to a Native might soon find the tables turned. Harmon, for example, succeeded in thrashing Kwah early in the nineteenth century, when he thought the Carrier leader was trying to intimidate him. But a few years later Kwah conspicuously spared the life of James Douglas, a prominent fur trader, vividly demonstrating that interracial power relations were much more equal than the newcomers liked to admit. The Hudson's

Bay Company reaped great profits from the fur trade on the north Pacific slope. But it could not subdue or subject its indigenous peoples.[65]

Hudson's Bay Company employees also had difficulty controlling their Native wives. The Fort Simpson post journal noted that one woman returned to her family after her French-Canadian husband beat her and that a local Native leader beat a Hudson's Bay Company employee for hitting the leader's daughter.[66] Native wives who moved away from kin did not enjoy such protection. Celiast, the daughter of a leading Clatsop man, married Basile Poirier, a baker at nearby Fort George in the early 1820s, and the couple soon relocated one hundred miles upriver to Fort Vancouver. According to one of Celiast's children from a second marriage, Poirier was an abusive alcoholic. Chief Factor John McLoughlin noted in his correspondence that another employee wanted to elope with Celiast, a plan that she probably helped to hatch and that he vetoed. But not many years later, in the mid-1830s, Celiast left Fort Vancouver with another man: Solomon Smith, a recent arrival from the eastern United States who had been teaching school at the fort but was not a regular employee. Other Native women who had married fur traders also exercised independence. Samuel Parker, a minister who arrived at Fort Vancouver shortly after Celiast and Solomon left, was told by company employees that "these Indian women do not understand the obligations of the marriage covenant, and . . . might through caprice leave them."[67] Even in the most intimate interracial relationships, then, whites could not simply impose their will on Natives.

The same could be said for the Natives whom whites employed. The British and U.S. fur companies routinely hired and abused Natives from Hawaii and the Great Lakes region. Locals proved more difficult to control. When David Douglas, a British naturalist on the Columbia River in 1826, prepared to give his guide "a little corporal chastisement," the Native man "lost no time in making his escape."[68] Joseph Thomas Heath, a farmer for the Hudson's Bay Company Puget Sound Agricultural Company, recorded in detail his ineffectual attempts to discipline his Native workforce in the 1840s. Early in 1845 he complained of his "house full of Indians." He wished to "lay my stick about them," but could not afford "to offend them as they are the only laborers I have to depend on." He lamented that he did not "know how to manage . . . my people." He once put a rope around the neck of a man he suspected of killing one of his lambs and dragged him "to a tree before releasing him." Nearly two years later, after catching two employees stealing food, he asserted that he had tried "everything in my power to make them comfortable and pay and feed them liberally and yet cannot prevent them from stealing, but please Goodness, will do it, or go without Indian labourers."[69] But Heath could not in fact go without such workers. Corporal punishment might drive them away and in any event failed to keep them from working at their own pace or from taking what they pleased.

The fur traders used violence much differently from their Native counterparts, and at times they tried manfully to impose their style of discipline and punishment. But they met with little success.

The balance of power began to tilt on the north Pacific slope in the mid-1840s, as thousands of overland immigrants arrived from the United States and when Great Britain ceded the Oregon County south of the forty-ninth parallel. Most of the newcomers went to Oregon's Willamette Valley, a fertile agricultural area stretching more than one hundred miles south from where the Willamette River empties into the Columbia River near Fort Vancouver. About three-quarters of the Kalapuya and other Native groups had died in a malaria epidemic in the early 1830s, and, by the mid-1840s, whites easily outnumbered the beleaguered Native peoples they hired as cheap labor or kept as slaves. Treaties negotiated in the 1850s removed the survivors to coastal reservations, away from the main concentrations of white settlement.[70]

Conquest was more extended and bloody in those parts of Oregon and Washington in which the newcomers did not simply overwhelm indigenous peoples. The Cayuse War in 1848 was the first large-scale conflict. A series of battles on Oregon's eastern and southern borders three decades later involving the Modocs, the Nez Perce, and the Bannock marked the end of organized hostilities. In between were battles in southwestern Oregon, on Puget Sound, and on the plateau of southeastern Washington. These clashes often lacked well-marked beginnings and conclusions. One historian denies that they "deserve to be called wars," that they instead resembled "exercises in reciprocal mayhem and murder."[71] Local volunteers rather than federal troops often began military campaigns, and killings began long before settlers organized themselves into regiments. The Rogue River War of 1856, for example, was preceded by many years of bloodshed between Native peoples and explorers, miners, and settlers. Nor was violence easily contained within the boundaries of organized battles. Both sides attacked nonparticipants, and volunteers and army officers alike executed Native prisoners summarily. Indeed, the notion of Native warriors enjoying the prerogatives of combatants struck some whites as absurd.[72]

A great deal of violence, moreover, occurred outside even the most elastic boundaries of "war." Many whites were prepared to beat any Native who displeased them. Such violence was a form of intimidation and punishment, pure and simple. Indeed, the colonizers often whipped Natives as if they were erring children. A lieutenant remarked in 1853 that the Native peoples of Puget Sound "are easily controlled," that "a good whipping makes one of them very obedient."[73]

Most of these punishments were dispensed without using the formal legal systems of Oregon and Washington. One of Seattle's founders noted that "when an Indian would steal anything" in the early 1850s "it was our custom to tie him up & lynch him."[74] A few years later, a group of men abducted a Tillamook Native who was being held for trial in the burning deaths of a minister's wife and child. According to a Portland newspaper, they "hung him from a convenient fir." "There is little or no interest manifested to find . . . out" the lynchers' identities, the writer noted.[75] Indeed, a Puget Sound newspaper remarked in 1858 that "it would perhaps be impossible in this country to obtain a jury that would find a bill against a white man for killing an Indian."[76] Race did not always determine the outcome of criminal trials. Washington courts sometimes acquitted Natives accused of killing whites. But many such Natives never got their day in court. Washington's official legal culture emphasized fairness, but its popular legal culture, in the words of Brad Asher, "stressed a race-differentiated justice system, in which due process was the preserve of whites and Indians were subject to exercises of private discipline."[77] A Willamette Valley man put it more bluntly when he set out to avenge himself on a Native woman who had just hit him with a board: "There is no law against killing Indians."[78] There was such a law, of course. But it did not count for much when so many denied or ignored it.

Natives did not meekly submit to whites' assertions of sovereignty and superiority. The Rogue River and Yakima Wars occurred in part because Natives resented and resisted whites' sexual assaults. A Nez Perce man accused in a Washington court of murdering a white man reportedly stated that the deceased had accused him of stealing a spyglass, and after some words were exchanged "the man tried to draw his Pistols." The accused wrested the weapon away "and offered to return the pistol if he would return the spy glass," but the deceased then "drew a knife," which so angered the Nez Perce that he killed and robbed the man.[79] Likewise, a Willamette Valley newspaper reported in 1861 that Natives in eastern Washington had killed two men because one of them "had chastised an Indian boy for stealing."[80]

But interracial violence became increasingly one-sided. When the relatives of an eleven-year-old Native girl on the south Oregon coast threatened to avenge her abduction, a group of whites reportedly went "to the Indian ranch . . . tore down their house, and beat" several of the Natives with ax handles, causing at least one death.[81] The Indian agent at Kitsap in western Washington reported in 1858 that Natives "compelled to resort to theft as a means of preventing starvation" were "tied up and mercilessly whipped" for "stealing a few potatoes or a little wheat."[82] Some three years later an Olympia newspaper reported that a Mr. Wood had shot and killed a Native man for "running off with a sack of flour."[83]

A deadly earnest political struggle lay behind these altercations. Natives' violence served to defend their sovereignty and autonomy. White violence served to deny it. A. J. Splawn recalled with rare candor how he and his fellow settlers in eastern Washington set about punishing and intimidating the Natives who outnumbered them in the early 1860s, that F. M. Thorp whipped a Native horse thief so brutally that the man died of his wounds and beat an aggressive Native leader until the man begged for mercy. Likewise, a western Washington settler kicked unconscious a Native man who tried to charge him for drinking out of the river. The intent of such acts was not simply to punish particular acts of insubordination. The blows were calculated to establish that Natives were, in fact, subordinates, inferiors who had better learn to act the part and to conform to their superiors' mores. Hence James Swan noted that a coastal settler gave a Native who had borrowed his boat two dozen lashes upon the craft's return, with "an injunction for the future to let the white men's property alone."[84] Such beatings were acts of political dominance.

Interracial politics were not so clear-cut north of the line, where settlement was less extensive and race relations more pacific. Large numbers of non-Natives did not arrive in British Columbia until the Fraser River and Cariboo gold rushes of the late 1850s and mid-1860s, and most did not tarry for long. British Columbia's leaders, moreover, prided themselves on possessing a justice system free from racial prejudice. Anglican bishop George Hills enjoyed explaining to Natives "that in British territory no one could take the law into his own hands," for "the law was equal against all & for all."[85] Even after a group of Chilcotin killed some thirteen whites in 1864, a British Columbia newspaper asked for "the same impartial justice . . . in dealing with the aborigines that we would desire to have meted out to ourselves" and urged a "most careful discrimination between the guilty and the innocent."[86] This difference was not simply rhetorical. With the exception of a clash involving U.S. miners discussed below, nothing in British Columbia resembled the Indian wars so common in Washington and Oregon. This difference was of course not confined to the north Pacific slope. Large-scale armed conflicts between Natives and whites were next to nonexistent across Canada, and Washington and particularly Oregon were more pacific than most of the United States. The British emphasis on law and order served to defuse conflicts that might have erupted into warfare south of the line.

British Columbia's leaders also tried to impose British law on small-scale conflicts. Victoria's charge or arrest books indicate that magistrates did not discriminate against Native defendants. All four Native men accused of assaulting white men over a six-month period in the late 1860s received fourteen-day sentences, the same penalty imposed on three of the four white men arrested for assaulting Native men.[87] British Columbia's officials were able to exercise greater judicial and political power than were their counterparts to the south, and the colony's Native people were therefore less vulnerable to settlers who took the law into their own hands.[88]

But this difference in means should not obscure the similarity of ends. For the British, judicial fairness was the handmaiden of colonization. To hunt down Natives who had committed acts considered criminal under British law, to clap them in irons, transport them to a British jail, and then require them to answer questions before a British court was to demonstrate, to prove, that these peoples had been conquered, that they no longer enjoyed sovereignty. Racially blind sentencing simply underscored that Natives were subject to the same law, the same authority, as their white counterparts. It constituted and legitimized British colonization. Hence Chief Justice Joseph Needham in 1866 told a grand jury examining three cases of intra-Native homicide that they "must not be swayed by the idea that Indians are not equally responsible with whites," for the defendants "were English subjects and amenable to English law."[89]

Even so, British justice was not always fair enough or strong enough to ensure equitable treatment of Natives. A Nanaimo newspaper complained that they suffered "punishments unknown to the law," including a brutal flogging for petty theft.[90] Government records reveal that thirty-three out of thirty-eight people sentenced to death over a six-year period were Native, three Chinese, one Hawaiian, and one of unrecorded ethnicity. British justice, moreover, was not as pervasive as its proponents wished it to be. The great majority of the thirty thousand miners who flocked to the Thompson and lower Fraser Rivers in 1858 were from outside the empire, most from the western United States. These men reacted to sporadic Native resistance by organizing into several military companies and carrying out a bloody campaign. The surviving Natives were, in the words of a miner from Washington, "so cowed that they would beg, but dare not steal."[91] James Douglas soon succeeded in extending British authority to the goldfields. But sporadic violence continued. Squiss Ovia explained to a court how he learned in the spring of 1859 that his brother, who had accompanied several white miners to the Fraser River, had been killed by an "american." Ovia "wept bitterly for four days" and then borrowed his uncle's gun. He met a man "having much resemblance to those that Indians had said to me to be the murderers of my brother," then shot and wounded him.[92]

Lofty pronouncements regarding the impartiality of British law did not keep whites from routinely attacking Native people even in the colony's core. Violence toward Natives was both common and well documented in Victoria, which acted as a magnet to thousands of whites and Natives alike. Whites assaulted Natives in the course of robbery and sexual assault and to punish those who had informed on liquor traders. As in the United States, a strong sense of racial superiority shaped many of these acts. Captain William Mouat, who reportedly remarked that Natives were "not worthy of any better fate than skinning," took the law into his own hands in 1865 by twice whipping a Native man who had broken a door on his property.[93] William Lidgate, barkeeper at a whiskey house just outside Victoria, testified in 1864 that one of his patrons, William Jackson, called a Native man who had asked for a glass of beer a "black son of a bitch" and then kicked him. When one of Jackson's companions remarked that "he had not given it to the Indian enough," Jackson "went out again" and clubbed his victim over the head.[94] Men like Mouat and Jackson believed in making an example of Native men who acted as if they were their equals. "The white men kick the Indians about like dogs," remarked a visitor to Vancouver Island, "and the more they kick them the better they are liked."[95]

Native people also used violence in interracial encounters, but their use of force became increasingly defensive as their power shrank. Settlement proceeded more slowly and fitfully in British Columbia than it did south of the line; in 1871 it had about three times the land mass and one-tenth as many residents of European descent as Oregon did. Whites still constituted less than a quarter of the new province's population by that date. Yet here, too, many aboriginals felt beleaguered. The *Colonist* complained in 1859 that Natives were continually harassing farmers outside of Victoria by shooting their cattle and threatening their persons. Robert Brown, a botanist, related the Natives' perspective a few years later, noting that an Irishman farming part of the Cowichan Indian Reserve had let his pigs run loose in their potato patches. When the farmer shot one of the Native dogs with a ball that came close to hitting two Native women, the Cowichan became "much excited and begged of the priest . . . to be allowed to kill him."[96] Retaliation for personal insults motivated many such attacks. Quawish admitted to killing a white man in a schooner off Vancouver Island, but asserted that the court "would not be angry with me" if it "knew what the white man did to me," for the deceased had "struck me & knocked me down & took my blanket from me & I was ashamed."[97]

Natives learned to confine their attacks to the most marginalized newcomers. Some reportedly believed themselves superior to people of African descent. But immigrants from China were the most common target of aboriginal violence. The *Colonist* frequently reported on affrays between Victoria's Native and Chinese residents, often noting that Natives started the altercations. Bishop Hills, who in 1860 toured the goldfields where thousands of Chinese labored, observed that Natives held them in "contempt" and was amused by "their patronizing manner when they spoke to 'John Chinaman.'"[98] To be sure, Natives often had concrete reasons for resisting Chinese settlers. In 1868 Satcha, a Fraser River Native, described an argument with Ah Tchong that began when Tchong complained of his horses "running over his Land." Satcha retorted that "it was not his Land, that formerly it was Indian Land, and that the Indians were accustomed to go along the Trail." The two then fought. Tchong, for his part, claimed that Satcha had been purposefully walking through his turnips and had asserted that "this is my ground and not yours" when asked to walk in a ditch.[99] Native violence toward white and Chinese newcomers alike was interwoven with the broader theme of dispossession, but it was much safer to attack Chinese than whites.

British Columbia Natives did not, on the whole, suffer from as much violence as did their counterparts to the south. They were far less likely to die violent deaths, far less susceptible to summary, extralegal justice. Even so, the relationship between colonization and violence was in many respects the same on both sides of the line: whites used violence to underscore their right to rule, Natives used it to protest that right, and those protests became more muted and indirect over time.

Increasing numbers of Native groups were losing their autonomy on the north Pacific slope. Scholars point out that loss of territory and associated resources was crucial to this process. Treaties negotiated largely in the 1850s, often after Natives had lost armed conflicts, concentrated most surviving Natives in Oregon and Washington onto reservations, often far from their homes. Faced with marginal and unfamiliar land and insufficient supplies, forced to live side by side with traditional enemies, and subjected to repeated bouts of disease, their numbers continued to shrink until early in the twentieth century. Those who did not conclude treaties often found themselves in even more dire circumstances, at least if they resided near whites. A western Washington Indian agent noted in 1857 that most of the Natives of his district lived "among the settlements, with no one locality which they can confidently call their own, no place for a village which they can have any security that they will not be compelled to abandon the very next season, and no grazing spot from which their horses may not be excluded the next week by the fence of the settler."[100]

British Columbia Natives were not defeated in wars, and only a handful of groups signed treaties. But they were subjected to the same broad historical forces. A Native leader on Vancouver Island told an early settler that his people feared "that more King-George men will soon be here, and will take our land, our firewood, our fishing-grounds." "We shall be placed on a little spot, and shall have to do every-thing according to the fancies of the King-George men," he concluded."[101] His prediction was not far wrong. Settlers, unlike the fur traders who had preceded them, saw Natives as "at best irrelevant, and at worst an obstacle," as Robin Fisher puts it.[102] Many of these newcomers chafed under the administration of James Douglas, in part because the old Hudson's Bay Company employee remained relatively sensitive to Native rights. But Douglas's tenure as governor ended in 1863, and subsequent leaders were much more responsive to popular white opinion. They quickly and consistently moved to reduce Native land rights and autonomy.[103] Natives in remote corners of the province continued to maintain at least an approximation of their traditional hunting, fishing, and gathering activities, largely because few white settlers were present to circumscribe or contest them. But the die was cast.

Colonization's progress could be gauged by measuring white officials' progress at imposing their understanding of violence on Native people. Elijah White, appointed in 1842 as Oregon's first sub-Indian agent, proposed a type of tribal governance that included a system of powerful chiefs and constables to administer laws punishing crimes ranging from trespass to murder. A number of Plateau leaders decided to adopt White's system, largely because it enhanced their personal power. But many resisted the new laws, particularly the provision for whipping. Plateau peoples were either unaccustomed to being whipped or perceived the process of lashing as some sort of reciprocal act, in which the recipient proved his mettle and won praise. Hence some leading men asked "a reward for being whipped," complaining that they "had been whipped a good many times" under White's system "and had got nothing for it." When White explained "that they need not expect pay for being flogged, when they deserved it," that the whippings were simply a punishment, the men "laughed heartily at the idea, and dispersed."[104] Why would a free man subject himself to a beating for no reward? Likewise, Sciats, a Wasco leader whom White had flogged, asked the missionaries at The Dalles to read the portions of the Bible that described the apostle Paul being whipped and then "turned away, muttering, with great complaisance, 'Ah, Paul was whipped! Paul was a good man. Sciats, he was whipped.'"[105] Elijah White could introduce new legal practices to unconquered peoples, but he had little control over how they implemented or interpreted them. Such Natives persisted in determining the moral and political lessons of the beatings that the aspiring colonizers inflicted on them.

This violence became much less amenable to interpretation once Natives were conquered and confined to reservations. Major C. H. Rumrill in 1864 reported to the Washington superintendent of Indian Affairs that he punished the Natives under his charge by imprisoning, whipping, and executing them. Other reservation personnel routinely used corporal punishment. Ben Simpson, who became the agent at the Siletz Agency on the Oregon coast in the early 1860s, reportedly made frequent use of the whipping post. Located far from their supervisors, among peoples they regarded as inferior, these men might literally get away with murder. William Barnhart wrote in 1862 from northeastern Oregon that he had shot and wounded a man who had pursued "a defenseless old Indian woman that he had just previously cruelly beaten" to the Umatilla Agency. Barnhart expected the man "to recover to be punished for the dastardly outrage."[106] T. W. Davenport, another agency employee, offered a less flattering depiction of Barnhart's judicial practices. A few months after the above incident he asked the post's half-Native interpreter, whom he identified only as "Antoine," why he had not protested when Barnhart stole some cattle from local whites: "Mr. Davenport, I am an Indian, and Mr. Barnhart shoots Indians." This man soon disappeared. Barnhart "conjectured" that he had become drunk and had fallen into the Umatilla River. But Davenport later learned from Antoine's sister that his body had been found many miles away, in the Columbia, with a bullet hole in his head. "He was a half-breed Indian," remarked Davenport, "and as a rule inquiry as to the cause of death in the whole- or half-breed Indian stops at the bullet hole."[107]

Missionaries joined government agents in mingling violence with colonization on the north Pacific slope. They began arriving in large numbers in the 1840s and met with a mixed response. Some Native leaders welcomed them as a tool to augment their power. Groups seemed particularly willing to integrate at least selected aspects of Christianity into their culture after periods of great turmoil, for missionaries offered both explanations for these disasters and institutions like temperance societies and authoritarian leadership to mend them. These new programs were apt to include corporal punishment. Early, Native-led religious movements influenced by Christianity emphasized harmony or incorporated whippings in ways that dovetailed with Native traditions. But the missionaries insisted that the purpose of beatings was to punish, to teach obedience. Elkanah Walker, a Protestant missionary among the Spokane of the Plateau, remarked in 1843 that the Natives exercised "control" of their children "mostly by threatening them without any intention of putting it in force, which is teaching them to lie."[108] The missionaries aspired to change this. They did not always succeed. A critic of missionary Henry Spalding noted in 1840 that he had "failed not unfrequently in getting individuals whipped when he has attempted." Indeed, when Spalding had a woman flogged for running away from her husband, a white employee of the mission who had reportedly abused her, the angry Nez Perce very nearly succeeded in whipping the husband.[109] Missionaries in British Columbia, where Native-white relations were generally less contentious, faced less resistance in implementing corporal punishment. William Duncan, the noted Anglican missionary to the Tsimshian, used it. The Oblates, a Catholic order, employed the Durieu system of strict discipline that included whipping, a punishment that Native men appointed by these priests often carried out.[110]

Whites' growing power also manifested itself in the most intimate interracial relationship, intermarriage. Native women who lived with fur traders were not, as we have seen, free from abuse. But they retained much of their traditional independence and could not simply be abandoned by husbands employed by the Hudson's Bay Company. Soldiers, miners, and settlers were free from such constraints. Military officers in southern Oregon reportedly forced even married Native women to cohabit with them and then left them. Others preferred more episodic forms of rape. A Native woman on the lower Fraser River stated in 1859 that William Henry Pollard had "asked me to sleep with him for two dollars and half," and then pushed her to the ground and kicked her when she refused.[111] More permanent liaisons did not disappear altogether. Even as late as 1880, one out of every ten households in western Washington's Clallam County was headed by a white man who lived with a Native or mixed-race woman, and intermarriage remained common in British Columbia. But the conditions that such women lived under had often deteriorated. In 1863 the *Colonist* remarked that "a young Indian woman, who has been for some time past cohabiting with a white man" had just given birth "in the public highway" of Victoria, intoxicated and "surrounded by a crowd of . . . rowdies . . . who were jeering her upon her painful condition."[112] Four years earlier an inquest on a deceased Native girl, age twelve or thirteen, established that she was a "Northern Indian" who had recently arrived on the lower Fraser River to live with William Peterson. A witness believed that the woman "had suddenly left" because "she was unhappy and pined at having left her friends." Her body turned up three months later, bearing the marks of starvation and exposure. The witness believed "that Peterson treated the squaw with kindness," but it is well documented that many white husbands of Native wives did not.[113] This is not to say that these women were helpless. Husbands were still apt to complain that their Native wives were independent sexually and otherwise—"habitual stubborn cruel & ill tempered so as to make it impossible . . . to live together," as a western Washington man's divorce complaint put it.[114] But such women had fewer options than before as Native people's autonomy and power shrank.

Colonization also increased levels of violence among Natives. This was partly a function of increased contacts between groups. Like the trading posts that preceded them, white towns and businesses drew Natives from hundreds of miles away. The Strait of Georgia and Puget Sound, in particular, were by the early 1850s heavily trafficked by Natives traveling to and from trading and employment opportunities in Victoria or western Washington. These journeys regularly put parties in contact with enemies or strangers. When returning home, northern Natives commonly "raided, robbed, enslaved or beheaded" those they passed, as John Lutz puts it.[115] Conflict might also break out once the travelers reached their destination. Several died when a Coast Salish group who lived near Nanaimo attacked a Kwakiutl group who had come to work at a sawmill. Large-scale confrontations declined markedly in the 1860s, as the British and Americans extended their authority along the Pacific coast's waterways.[116] But altercations between the diverse Natives drawn to white cities and towns were much more difficult to eradicate. Groups like the Tsimshian and Haida generally managed to avoid each other in their neighboring homelands, but not on the streets and the outskirts of Victoria, where several Tsimshian were murdered in late 1859 and early 1860. A Tsimshian complained to Bishop Hills of the Haida's aggressiveness: "'Fight, Fight' is the word. 'Fight all day, all night.'"[117] Not that the Haida were the only Native combatants in Victoria. In 1867 the *Colonist* reported on a "drunken free fight" between the Tsimshian and Bella Bella, and throughout the 1860s it regularly noted a number of armed and unarmed assaults involving a variety of Native peoples.[118] Oregon and Washington newspapers described the same phenomenon around their cities. The Portland *Oregonian,* for example, in 1863 complained that Natives who had been living on the edge of town for several months engaged in "midnight brawls" on an "almost nightly" basis, and a year later it recorded "another row . . . between *siwashes,*" when one Native stabbed another.[119] Relatively abundant amounts of money, trade goods, and alcohol drew diverse groups of Natives from many miles away to Victoria and Portland, often with violent results.

Colonization also increased Native people's violence toward each other in the countryside. This was particularly so on the early reservations of Oregon and Washington, where Native groups unfamiliar with or hostile toward each other were thrown together. A Native man taken captive as a young boy in the Rogue River War later recalled the difficulties he faced at the Siletz Reservation, where he repeatedly fought coastal Natives, once losing his front teeth when they pelted him with rocks: "That's rought times!"[120] Indeed, the agent at Siletz noted in 1863 that he was trying to separate the reservation's various bands to avoid the "broils and disputes, so common among Indians where different tribes are placed too closely together."[121] Native peoples north of the line were spared this sort of radical relocation, but there, too, intra-Native violence seemed to be increasing. Some thirty-two members of two Tsimshian groups along British Columbia's north coast reportedly died in internecine quarrels from 1861 to 1863, for example.[122]

Much intragroup violence involved shamans. Native peoples held shamans responsible for deaths they caused purposefully and for cures that failed. As the number of Native deaths rose, more and more shamans were killed. One historian counts twenty cases of shaman killings from 1837 to 1855 around The Dalles, on the Columbia River.[123] A woman whose family settled in the Willamette Valley in 1844 recounted that a shaman came to their house seeking protection: "He said his patients all died so the Indians were going to kill him for claiming he could cure them and not doing so."[124] Whites of course dismissed such beliefs as preposterous and sometimes prosecuted shaman killers. But Natives had increasing recourse to shamans as more explicit forms of aggression became problematic, thereby creating a spiral of suspicion and retaliation.[125]

Some forms of family violence also increased. Violence toward children remained uncommon, even under trying circumstances. Swan wrote that during his three years among the Natives of Shoalwater Bay on the south Washington coast he had "never known of an instance, during their wildest drunken freaks of fury or rage, where one of their own children was hurt or badly treated, although at such times they are very apt to treat their slaves with barbarity."[126] Violence toward wives, on the other hand, became more common. A woman who arrived in the Willamette Valley in the mid-1840s recalled that Native men "often beat their squaws."[127] Likewise, Bishop Bagshaw in 1860 recorded that two Native women at Cayoosh talked about "husbands beating & killing their wives."[128] Much of this violence centered, as before, on Native women's purported sexual conduct. Native women's growing reliance on prostitution along with white men's propensity for sexual assault made both extramarital sex and the punishments associated with it more common.

By the century's close, trends discernible a few decades before had become more pronounced. The relative numbers of Native people had plummeted. In 1881 they had constituted a majority of British Columbia's population. Two decades later they made up just 16 percent. They were only 2 and 1 percent, respectively, of Washington's and Oregon's population by 1900. Economic and social marginalization accompanied this demographic shift. Those who lived far from white settlements, such as the Makah of coastal Washington or Natives in most of northern British Columbia, were relatively insulated from these changes. Natives near the Fraser River's mouth in southwestern British Columbia reportedly earned 35 percent of their income from wages, those of the Babine–Upper Skeena region in the north 16 percent, and those on the north coast just under 3 percent. The three day schools in the Babine–Upper Skeena region enrolled only 81 students from a population of 524 school-age Natives, and the average daily attendance was only 38. Acculturation also varied within reservations and reserves. The 1891 report from the Siletz Agency, on the Oregon coast, said that its Natives were "in every degree of advancement, from the old salmon eater, who hasn't a care apparently except to fill his stomach, on up to the thrifty, intelligent farmer, mechanic, and schoolboy."[129] Chief Joseph, a leader of the Nez Perce's tragic struggle to escape to Canada in 1877, was the best-known traditionalist. Colville Reservation agent Albert Anderson complained in 1898 that Joseph's band had persisted "in following their ancient traditions and indulging in their primitive customs." They were "strictly 'blanket' Indians," who were making little or no progress at civilizing themselves.[130] But the choice facing aboriginal peoples on the north Pacific slope in the 1890s was not nearly as clear-cut as these agents claimed, was not simply a matter of choosing tradition and poverty or acculturation and prosperity. Even those Natives who strove to conform at least outwardly and to participate as equals in wider society were frustrated by inadequate access to land and other resources, an overdependence on unreliable wage labor, white officials' unwillingness to surrender control of religious and political institutions, and pervasive racist attitudes inside and outside reserves and reservations. Well-founded cynicism no doubt fueled much of the behavior that agents chalked up to stubborn traditionalism.[131]

Whites' violence toward Native peoples underscored the latter's decided subordinate status at the century's end. W. M. Halliday, who lived with the Kwakiutl, recalled that he and his brother beat a group of Native boys for playing in the haystack of a missionary couple. The boys' fathers resented the beatings and remarked that "they didn't want any whites there, would drive them out if they didn't behave." In the altercation that immediately followed, Halliday felled one of the Natives, who from that point on "became very friendly," often complimenting Halliday "on my great strength and skill in having knocked him down." Lack of power made a virtue of obsequiousness. A few years later, a young English immigrant killed four Native dogs that were bothering his cattle. The man who owned the dogs returned with two Native policemen, but the whites refused to cooperate and smashed the nose of one of the Natives. The aboriginal officer persisted, and took the Englishman to the white constable in Alert Bay, who arrested the Natives for detaining a man without a warrant! This lesson in interracial law enforcement had, Halliday remarked, "a very wholesome effect in keeping the Indians in Kingcome Inlet in check."[132] Other types of white violence were more prosaic. Native children, in particular, were subject to sanctioned and at times extreme violence from their white schoolteachers north and south of the line, in day and residential schools alike. British Columbia's civil leaders occasionally challenged the Oblates' right to set up separate legal systems for the province's Native peoples, but missionaries and their appointees continued to administer whippings to Natives guilty of moral infractions.[133]

Natives' violence toward whites became rare as whites' violence toward Natives became commonplace. This is not to say that Native people stopped resisting their oppression; indeed, some groups, such as the Nisga'a of northern British Columbia, mounted explicit and formal political protests to colonization. But anything remotely resembling concerted armed resistance was virtually unheard of by the 1890s. The British Columbia Coroner's Register recorded only one instance of a Native killing a white between 1893 and 1899, and less extreme acts of violence were also uncommon. Ethnologist A. F. Chamberlain, who worked among the Kootenay of southeastern British

Columbia, recalled that one of the Natives he was measuring "suddenly rose to his full height, drew his knife from his sheath, and made a motion to strike" him, a trick that greatly amused the other Natives present.[134] Resistance now hid its face in harmless pantomime.

The handful of Natives who attacked whites tended to be desperate. A Native said that he shot and killed a white storekeeper in the Cariboo whom he had worked for because "he would not give me any wood to make a fire, nor axe to cut any with." Indeed, the justice of the peace noted that Natives had been breaking into the homes of settlers to steal food and clothes, that some Indian families "are in great need of help."[135]

But whites and Natives alike commonly blamed the latter's violence not on hunger or resentment, but on alcohol. When Squamish Charlie asked to stay the night at James McRorie's cabin near Vancouver, McRorie replied, "I don't want any Siwash around here." Charlie finished a bottle of whisky, "got thinking," and killed the man who had insulted him. But in explaining the killing, he emphasized to the court his intoxication rather than McRorie's insult.[136] Likewise, Annie, an Okanagan Native, said that her husband, Frank, shot Gavin Hamilton only after Hamilton had put him out of the house and she had started "hollering" for help. But Frank simply said that he was drunk and did not remember what had happened.[137] This became a common refrain. A Native man accused of killing another told the court: "I did not know anything about it; . . . I was very drunk, did not know anything."[138] Whites eagerly concurred. Newspapers remarked that "a drunken Siwash is about as amenable to reason as a mad dog" and that alcohol "temporarily deprived" them "of reason."[139] An Okanagan judge asserted that those who sold whiskey to Natives risked the life "of every white man in the place," for alcohol served to "take away their brains, and make fiends of them."[140]

The simplest approach to interpreting these sorts of assertions is to agree with them. Indeed, many popular and scholarly observers of Native life, not a few of them Natives, have argued that Native people have been genetically predisposed to alcoholism. But researchers are not agreed on this issue and, in any event, people's behavior while intoxicated is not predetermined. It varies widely according to culture and social context. Alcohol was not indigenous to the north Pacific slope; Natives learned how to drink from observing drunken fur traders, sailors, miners, or settlers. An oral tradition from the Lillooet of British Columbia's southern interior describes how a young

Native stole a barrel of whisky from some white miners in the late 1850s and explained to his fellow villagers how whites used the drink to "fight, dance, stagger around, and have a great time!" "Now we can all try this medicine," he concluded. The participants sent the women, children, and older people away. "This will be just for men, and we can have a good time, like the white men," remarked one. After gulping several drinks they began singing and yelling and dancing. Then they "bumped into each other" and began fighting. "That's what the white people do!" said the young man who had stolen the whisky.[141]

Natives' dwindling power only made liquor more attractive. The attempts of white authorities to keep Native people away from it underscored its apparent potency and desirability. Intoxication also offered an opportunity to disinhibit, to cast off the role of complacent Indian without the risk that more overt rebellions would have entailed.[142] For whites, Natives' apparent inability to "hold their liquor" underscored their inherent weakness. It also implied that Natives who were in their "natural" colonized state were tractable and agreeable. Natives became surly and aggressive only when liquor rendered them insensible and fiendish, to paraphrase the British Columbia judge quoted above.[143]

The people most likely to be victimized by drunken carousing were not, however, white colonizers, but rather fellow Natives. This sort of violence bequeathed a power of sorts, but it was not a power that much altered the status quo.

For missionaries, government officials, and other colonizers, Natives' acts of drunken violence simply indicated that colonization had not yet reached fruition, not that the humiliating process of dispossession and domination had turned Native aggression inward, upon friends and family instead of enemies and strangers.

Native peoples during the precontact and fur trade eras usually directed their violence outward, toward members of other groups. Indeed, much intragroup violence—the whippings and other trials that young men suffered through—served to prepare them to risk their lives in conflicts with outsiders.

Colonization made these risks unnecessary by bringing warfare and raiding to an end. But it did not end violence. Violence against wives escalated along with Native women's forced and voluntary sexual liaisons with white soldiers, miners, and settlers. Other forms of intragroup violence involving adults also rose, as white settlements, towns, reservations, and reserves drew and forced various Native peoples together. White violence toward Native people also grew dramatically with settlement; miners, settlers, soldiers, and others whipped, beat, and killed members of a race they considered inferior. Much of this violence was illegal, and occasionally it was prosecuted. But much was also mandated, not just in warfare, but in schools and churches and on reservations, by the very people whom Natives were told to obey and trust. Native people often resisted, particularly south of the line, but this resistance became increasingly veiled, indirect, and even displaced as Natives became weaker and more dependent.

The unifying factor beneath these seemingly disparate changes was Natives' loss of sovereignty and power. When Oregon Indian agents tried to discipline Natives for killing some shamans, they reacted angrily: "We are not your slaves that you should punish us for executing our own laws. . . . Why do you meddle with our own business?"[144] The question ultimately was not so much whether or not shamans should or should not be executed for certain crimes, but rather who controlled such decisions, whether Native people had the right to formulate and enforce their own ethical and legal systems.

The north Pacific slope's Native peoples may well have been more safe from violent death at the outset of the twentieth century than they had been several generations before. Death from disease had become much more common, of course. But raids for slaves and heads were over, as were other types of large-scale, armed conflict. Yet intragroup violence had increased, and white missionaries, government agents, and teachers regularly subjected Natives, particularly children, to blows. These whippings, moreover, were calculated to induce obedience and subservience, not bravery and independence. Colonization may not have changed the overall level of Native violence. But it transformed its character, context, and purpose.

Native violence became still more internecine during the twentieth century. The breakup of residential schools at last ended the violence and sexual abuse that so many of British Columbia's Native peoples had faced at the hands of their white teachers. But spousal violence and violence among friends and neighbors has become widespread on many British Columbia reserves—though violence against children has remained relatively uncommon. British Columbia's Natives have been victimized by homicide at over ten times the rate of their non-Native counterparts, the great majority of them killed by fellow Natives, often family members.[145] A man bearing a tattoo reading "Born to hate cops" was gunned down on a northern British Columbia reserve in 1960 not by a police officer or truculent white man but by another Native.[146]

Washington State's Sherman Alexie, the distinguished writer, has plumbed the nature of this sort of violence. His fiction often describes Native men who are both alienated and violent. Thomas Builds-the-fire, the smallest man on the Spokane Indian Reservation, is regularly beaten up by cruel peers. Two uncles are "slugging each other with such force that they had to be in love."[147]

Racism lies beneath this violence. Alexie attributes a violent 1976 New Year's Eve party to a storm that gave to each Native "a specific, painful memory." One remembered his father being spit on in Spokane. Another recalled being sterilized immediately after giving birth. Two brothers remembered growing up in poverty, hiding crackers in their bedroom at night to stave off hunger. The memories deepened the pain, intensified the storm, until all the adults were "out on the lawn, dancing in the snow, fucking in the snow, fighting in the snow."[148] The line of causation between humiliation and violence is not always readily apparent. Alexie's aside that Victor Joseph's wardrobe of "silk shirts and polyester pants" made him "an angry man," seems nonsensical. But Joseph's clothes, purchased thirteen years before, during the disco era, symbolize his poverty, his inability to join in the American dream, for he "had never had any money since."[149] "My father got completely out of control once because he lost the car keys," writes Alexie in another story. "Explain that to a sociologist."[150]

The bitter fruits of conquest and colonization have outlived Indian wars and residential schools alike.

To Take Your Own Part

Violence among the Settlers

ON 13 FEBRUARY 1834 William Fraser Tolmie, a Hudson's Bay Company physician, attacked one Charbonneau, a "rascally Canadian noted for laziness & dishonesty" who had been engaging in lewd conduct behind the doctor's house. Tolmie "thought it right to make an example of him to the others & accordingly" planted "a hearty kick" on his bottom together with some other blows. Charbonneau soon fought back, grappling with his superior and scratching his face. Another of the post's leaders then arrived "& hurled the fellow to the earth & another kick on the posterior completed his punishment." Tolmie remarked that "Mr. Manson's interference probably saved my credit," for Charbonneau "is a brawny fellow of nearly 6 feet." But he hoped that "my pommelling him will show the others that I am not to be trifled with."[1]

Tolmie's attack on Charbonneau is representative of the way prominent Hudson's Bay Company men used violence against rank-and-file employees. Tolmie decided that one of these men deserved and required a beating, and he administered it, with the help of a peer, so that the recipient had little chance of successful resistance. The relationship between power and violence was simple and clear: Tolmie and people like him had the right and responsibility to use physical force to punish the insubordinate acts of their inferiors, to show who had power and who did not.

This traditional conception of violence by no means disappeared with the arrival of thousands of newcomers seeking land, gold, and other opportunities on the north Pacific slope a few decades later. We have already seen how these men treated Natives, how they paired their claims for land with an eager willingness to whip and humiliate aboriginals who resisted them. But Native people were only the most obvious target of the powerful newcomers' violence. People of high status asserted and often benefited from their right to use nonlethal violence against a wide range of others: men from China, wives, and children. They shared Tolmie's understanding of violence and power. Some subordinates accepted that understanding. But others used their fists and their bodies to contest, like Charbonneau before them, this hierarchical version of social relations.

Thousands of whites from the Midwest and upper South flooded into Oregon and then Washington in the 1840s, drawn largely by agricultural opportunities. They set up relatively stable communities, particularly in Oregon's fertile Willamette Valley. By 1860 Washington had over eleven thousand people, Oregon over fifty thousand, and four out of every ten Oregonians was female. Settlement proceeded much more slowly and fitfully north of the line. Vancouver Island had fewer than one thousand whites in 1854. It and the mainland colony boomed a few years later when the gold rush drew thousands to Victoria and to the Fraser and Thompson Rivers. But mining had declined by 1871, the year British Columbia joined Canada. The young province then had fewer than nine thousand white residents, another fifteen hundred or so from Asia. Females made up less than 30 percent of its non-Natives.[2]

British Columbia had all the makings of a lawless frontier: wide expanses dotted with settlements of unattached and mobile males. Yet leading British Columbians styled themselves as tradition-minded colonials. Hudson's Bay Company employees held key governmental positions long after the fur trade's decline, and even the mining boom did not bring a democratic revolution. Indeed, Bulwer Lytton, Secretary of State for the Colonies, proclaimed in 1858 that "the grand principle of free institutions" should not be entrusted to "settlers so wild, so miscellaneous, perhaps so transitory, and in a form of society so crude."[3] The two colonies (Vancouver Island and British Columbia did not merge until 1866) required a well-regulated, orderly society.

Those south of the line, on the other hand, associated settlement with individualism. Hence a young man traveling the Oregon Trail in 1852 later recalled that the journey took his party "beyond the realm of social constraint, conventional usage, and the reign of law," and that many "seemed to exult in their so-called freedom."[4] Law preceded settlers in British Columbia. It followed them in Oregon and Washington.[5]

British Columbia's elite cherished and exaggerated the differences between their society and the less inhibited one to the south. Edmund Hope Verney, a naval commander, remarked in an 1862 letter to his father that he preferred the mainland's New Westminster to the busy port of Victoria, since the former settlement had "more English feeling, more English sabbath-observance, and less American democracy and equality: among that very small society reigns good-feeling, gentlemanly-kindness, and courtesy."[6] The distinguished actor Charles Kean expressed pleasure upon reaching Victoria in 1864 to be "away from those dreadful snuffling, spitting Yankees' *[sic]*, with their boastful impudence."[7] Such observers often asserted that Americans' predilection for anarchy and disorder expressed itself through their tolerance and practice of violence. George F. G. Stanley, a British army officer, visited The Dalles in 1860 and marvelled that its residents bragged "that no one has ever been hung there for murder."[8] British Columbia leaders prided themselves on enforcing the law firmly and consistently. The *Cariboo Sentinel* of Barkerville did not always approve of Chief Justice Matthew Baillie Begbie's civil decisions, but applauded in 1866 "his unswerving application of the law" in criminal cases.[9] The next year, after two murderers had just been sentenced to die, the newspaper found it "reassuring . . . that in a British colony, and even in such an isolated portion of it as this, such wretches will not be permitted the exercise of such horrible instincts with impunity."[10] At stake were political and social principles, not just abstract notions of justice. Begbie reportedly lectured a group of U.S. miners in the Cariboo that they were mistaken to "look upon liberty as a condition of life which gives them the right to defy the laws of their country, and to govern it according to their wishes by the might of the bowie knife and Colt's revolver." "Liberty," Begbie explained, "is the power of doing what is allowed by law."[11]

Settlers south of the line did in fact articulate and practice a different sort of criminal justice. Men expected each other to look after themselves. One who came to the western United States in 1852 and spent much of his life in eastern Oregon recalled that a man who went "to law for protection" made "himself a pusillanimous object for every vagabond to spit upon and kick."[12] The *Portland Oregonian* responded to reports of late-night vandalism around the city's businesses in 1853 by suggesting that "every order-loving citizen" should "shoot at the first midnight drunken brawler" who approached "his store, office, shop or house."[13] Much of this sort of hectoring was of course rhetorical. Yet juries and judges in Oregon and Washington were much more lenient with those who took the law into their own hands than were their counterparts in British Columbia. Murderers were less frequently given the death penalty south of the border than north of it. Oregon apparently averaged less than one execution per year from 1850 to 1865. British Columbia, despite a much smaller population, sentenced at least thirty-eight to die in just a six-year period. Richard Maxwell Brown's aptly titled *No Duty to Retreat* describes how western Americans, in particular, altered traditional English law so that men could stand their ground and use violence rather than withdrawing when confronted with an adversary likely to do them great bodily harm. Hence a San Francisco newspaper thought it novel that Begbie did not believe that "the circumstances of one party attacking, or firing first, is generally considered as sufficient excuse for the other party following up and killing his antagonist, even when his own life appears to be no longer in danger."[14] Washington and particularly Oregon were tamer than California and other parts of the American West, but their legal systems interpreted self-defense more broadly than British Columbia's did. Hence noted gunman and Confederate sympathizer Ferd Patterson won an acquittal on the grounds of self-defense after he had shot and killed a man in Portland who was trying to get him to drink a toast to President Lincoln. Indeed, it was not uncommon for angry men in British Columbia to threaten to kill their enemies "if I ever catch you on the American side."[15]

Community leaders might interject themselves where the law would not. Extralegal groups were organized in southern Oregon and on Puget Sound. The largest vigilante movement before 1865 arose in and around Walla Walla in eastern Washington during the Civil War, where citizens hanged several reputed livestock thieves. As in other parts of the West, Walla Walla's vigilantes and their sympathizers presented themselves as respectable and concerned citizens who were simply doing what legally constituted authority could not or would not. Myron Eells, a Protestant missionary, recalled in 1892 that the Walla Walla vigilantes were "good, brave, determined men" who had "waited for the law to do what it ought to until long after patience ceased to be a virtue, and then they went to work."[16] Another man acquainted with the vigilantes' handiwork later asserted that they established "the foundation . . .

for the well-regulated and prosperous Walla Walla city of today."[17] Most non-governmental executions were carried out not by highly organized vigilantes, but by spontaneous lynching parties. Several such killings occurred across Oregon and Washington before 1865, in both mining and agricultural settlements. The victims of these groups were typically marginal men deemed to have committed outrageous crimes, particularly cold-blooded murders. Groups of citizens sometimes whipped purported offenders instead of killing them, and in 1861 a Coos Bay group tarred and feathered two men before running them out of town. British Columbians rarely even considered such measures, and there were apparently no vigilante movements or lynchings there.[18]

British Columbia administered criminal law much differently from Oregon and Washington. British justice was more certain and centralized. Criminals south of the line, even murderers, were more apt both to escape the state's criminal justice system and to die at the hands of groups of private citizens frustrated with that system's leniency. A man who bludgeoned another to death after an apparently trivial quarrel near Walla Walla reportedly did not fear punishment by "the civil authorities, but he did fear the Vigilantes."[19] Political and judicial authority was much more broadly distributed south of the line than north of it—including the right to inflict deadly force.

These divergent reactions to violent acts can obscure the extent of that violence. Respectable British Columbians associated American murder and mayhem with excessive democracy and therefore dwelled fondly on any examples they happened across. D. W. Higgins, who arrived in Victoria in 1858 and eventually owned its leading newspaper, recalled that "the crack of the revolver, and the whizz of the rifle ball, were sounds familiar" to the residents of Port Townsend, Washington, around that time.[20] Stanley, the British army officer, made the patently absurd assertion that an average of one man per day was "ruthlessly shot down" in Walla Walla's streets in 1862.[21] John Wunder has pointed out that Washington settlers, self-consciously aware of the American West's reputation for violence, also exaggerated its salience in their communities. Judge William Strong, Washington Territory's first supreme court justice, confided to his diary that he and some of his fellows had amused themselves by describing the country as "very dangerous" to a nervous, newly arrived schoolteacher, "although it was perfectly peaceable."[22]

Yet homicide statistics suggest that the settlers of Washington and Oregon were no more violent than their peers north of the line. An examination of British Columbia newspapers and coroner's records from 1859 through 1871 yields a total of forty-three homicides not involving Native people, or about 16.6 per hundred thousand people per year. Two sources indicate a virtually identical rate in the Pacific Northwest. Newspapers from 1850 to 1865 suggest a rate of 16.9 per hundred thousand people per year for Oregon, the 1860 census a rate of 14.0 per hundred thousand for Oregon and Washington combined.[23]

Even so, early British Columbia's homicide rate was surprisingly low. It was, to be sure, much higher than it is today—and much higher than the rate for eastern U.S. cities in the mid to late nineteenth century. But its rate of 16.6 compares very favorably to places south of the border that shared its demographic features. The rates for three mining areas in California and Nevada during the mid-nineteenth century ranged from 48.6 per hundred thousand to 95.5, three to six times higher than in the British colony.[24] Oregon's homicide rate was low for a western state. But its population was much less volatile than British Columbia's, more oriented to farm and family. The quintessential British Columbian, on the other hand, was the miner, an unattached, mobile, and often pugnacious young man, precisely the sort of fellow who was apt to get into a shooting or knifing scrape. These people came from a wide variety of places and cultures. People from the United States dominated, particularly Californians, and were joined by Germans, French, Chinese, Italians, Spaniards, Poles, and nearby Native peoples. A German mathematics professor who visited Yale, the hub of the Fraser River goldfields in 1858, remarked: "It would have been difficult to find in one place a greater mixture of different nationalities." He counted six women in the population of three thousand. Most dwellings were tents.[25] The primary goal of such men was not to build a lasting and harmonious community, but rather to make money and leave as quickly as possible. Gold attracted not simply miners who expected to get rich quick, but people who hoped to get rich off the miners: merchants, prostitutes, gamblers, and thieves—"human vultures that feed and fatten upon the frailties and follies of their fellow-men," as one observer put it.[26] The tumult and acquisitiveness of mining towns spilled over into the regional transportation centers through which miners and the goods they required passed, towns like Walla Walla, The Dalles, Victoria, and the small communities strung along the Fraser River. These were violent places. "There was more life in The Dalles in a day than there was in Portland in a month," remarked a man who moved to the former town in 1864.[27] A. J. Splawn traveled widely in Oregon, Washington, and British Columbia during the Civil War, and his recollections make it clear that the violence and disorder that accompanied mining spilled across the border. A roadhouse between the Cariboo mines and Yale, for example, "was full of lawless men, drinking, gambling, swearing, and fighting."[28] Washington and Oregon had a few places like this, too, but mining culture was much more influential north of the line than south of it.

Why, then, were miners much more inclined to kill and be killed in California or Nevada than in British Columbia? Roger Lane, a meticulous historian of murder in the United States, concludes that the use of handguns rose dramatically in the 1850s and that "there is no question" that this "affected the murder rate."[29] Begbie and other law enforcers would have agreed; they tried to limit the number of guns in British Columbia. Yet an assistant to Begbie in 1859 observed that the Fraser River's miners "all carry revolvers."[30] Indeed, an examination of settlement-era homicides involving non-Natives indicates that about 56 percent died from gunshot wounds in British Columbia. This was not much lower than Oregon's rate of 64 percent, and it was higher than rates for the United States as a whole, which stood at just 33 percent for 1846 to 1860 and 48 percent for 1860 to 1900.[31] Killers in British Columbia were about as apt to use firearms as their counterparts south of the line were. Hence attempts to discourage firearms apparently did not much depress its homicide rate.

Culture is a more plausible explanation for why British Columbia had a lower homicide rate than California's mining towns. Judge Begbie in the spring of 1859 expressed surprise that there appeared to be "on all sides a submission to authority" on the Fraser River, a willingness to obey English law, "which, looking to the mixed nature of the population, and the very large predominance of the Californian element, I confess I had not expected to meet."[32] Legal and popular culture south of the line were more sensitive to individual liberty and freedom, the right of a man to take the law into his own hands without fear of suffering much judicial punishment for it, even if that claim to freedom meant killing another man.[33] British Columbia's relatively low homicide rate indicates that legal culture could affect behavior, could influence how readily men (very few murders involved women or children) resorted to acts of violence that might prove lethal.

The great majority of violent acts between grown men consisted not of murders but of ordinary fights carried on without firearms or knives. Officers of the law, writers for newspapers, and other observers seldom paid much attention to such altercations, which makes it difficult to trace even their relative frequency. But they clearly occurred often, and on both sides of the border. Victoria newspapers regularly noted fights during flush periods in the mining economy.[34] In June 1865 the *Cariboo Sentinel* proudly pointed out that not a single criminal case had come before the area's magistrate for the past twelve months, "notwithstanding the large population, composed of persons of nearly every nationality, gathered into the district of Cariboo."[35] Less than a month later, however, a Barkerville resident complained of frequent fights at night, and that same year the newspaper quoted a justice of the peace as remarking that "he regretted to say that rows were of frequent occurrence in Barkerville."[36]

Such fights typically began over trifles. Male peers often fought each other over personal slights—actual or imagined. A Victoria newspaper reported in 1861 that one man called another "a pup" in an argument over some slops outside of one of their homes. The insulted man lashed his adversary the next day, proclaiming, "Sir, you called me a 'pup,' and I promised to cowhide you."[37] A few years later the same newspaper described how one Herbert Gaston knocked the hat off another man's head after he had "made some assertion which Gaston thought was a reflection on his veracity." The man whom Gaston had assaulted pressed charges. But Gaston, an American, remained unrepentant. He told the police magistrate that "he had acted in a moment of irritation and he regretted it," and he was willing to apologize to the court for his actions. He would not, however, make any amends to the man he had assaulted, for "if the same thing occurred again he should feel in duty bound to take the same course."[38]

To let an insult go unpunished was to admit that one was not much of a man. W. Everman claimed that he murdered a Willamette Valley man to cover up a theft: "I would rather the news would get home that I had killed a man for trying to injure my character, than for news to go home that I [had] stolen a watch."[39] A man in southern Oregon's mining fields in the early 1850s recalled that the miners "acted on the great law of honor, and to the fact that to call a man a liar or to impeach the honor or his origin, or to use towards him any epithet imputing dishonor, was to invite the contents of a pistol into the accusers physical economy."[40] Indeed, a man about to be hanged in Jacksonville for shooting an antagonist who called him "a liar and a thief" predicted that those who passed by his grave would remark "there lies a man who would not be insulted."[41] Violent quarrels across Oregon, Washington, and British Columbia often started when one man ridiculed another.[42]

Fighting repaired the social equilibrium that such ridicule had disturbed. It restored harmony among male peers. Combatants showed each other respect by putting their hard feelings aside after hitting each other. James Swan wrote that the settlers on Shoalwater Bay in the 1850s would, if they "got vexed with each other, . . . step out and settle the difficulty with a fist-fight, and then the trouble was over."[43] Likewise, an intermediary trying to calm one of the principals who had just been in a fight in eastern Washington "told him it was all over now" and "not to resent it."[44] The ideal fight resembled a boxing match in which two men who respected each other determined who was, on that day, the "better man." Hence two Victoria-area men who had engaged in "a bruising match" of twenty-two rounds in 1865 reportedly "left the field on the best of terms," although one had been knocked down twenty-one times.[45]

Fighting, like drinking, expressed male sociability. Kinahan Cornwallis noted at some length the drinking habits of several Yankees on their way to the British Columbia mining district in 1858. "Let's liquor" were "momentous words" that caused the party to repair immediately to a saloon. The drinkers gave each other "a nod of the head" and then "swallowed our respective 'drinks.'" They then "proceeded, one by one, to return the compliment and stand drinks all round likewise, the treater saying 'My respects,' as he nodded his head."[46] Fights could easily break out in this highly charged, highly public environment in which inebriated men regularly asserted and defended their status. Indeed, a Washington paper attributed a free fight to "what is commonly called 'fighting whisky.'"[47] Likewise, a Victoria man charged with an 1869 assault had been heard to say that "he was drunk" and "that he meant to remain drunk until he had whipped" his victim.[48] But men also drank to heal ruptured friendships, to signal that their differences had been settled. A witness to an 1860 altercation in Victoria testified that one of the parties struck a blow, "said, 'now come up and I'll treat,'" and handed his adversary a bottle.[49] Another Victoria man, caught by the father of the nine-year-old girl he had just sexually assaulted, tried to exculpate his act by remarking "oh lets settle it, come in and take something to drink—though the father refused."[50] Drinking, like fighting, expressed social intimacy, and one often accompanied the other.

These contests resembled duels, the classic expression of respectable men's violence in England, Canada, and the eastern and particularly southern United States. Duels consisted of a highly ritualized series of events that began with the perception of an insult to one's honor and ended in an armed showdown. Each step bore witness to the high status of the principals. The person aggrieved by a perceived threat demanded "satisfaction" in the form of a public apology. If the two parties could not reach a mutually satisfactory resolution, they faced each other with pistols. This act of risk, which occasionally ended in death, served to illustrate the combatants' courage and status. "Each man allowed his adversary to shoot at him," notes Kenneth Greenburg, "and therefore paid him the compliment of acknowledging his social equality." To fight a duel, then, was both to settle an argument with an enemy and to exchange the gift of mutual recognition of each other's superiority to lesser men. Hence one was under no obligation to accept a challenge proffered by a social inferior.[51]

Dueling had become much less accepted and common by the mid-nineteenth century, but the assertions of masculinity and status that lay behind it continued to inform unarmed confrontations. A newspaperman who described an argument between the editor of another paper and a British lieutenant was appalled when the "officer and gentleman struck another English gentleman on the heart with his foot." The man thereby injured had retorted: "Sir, I am not your servant."[52] Socially prominent men were not supposed to use violence to degrade each other. They certainly were not prepared to suffer confrontations initiated by their inferiors. Verney, the naval officer, complained in an 1862 letter to his father, a powerful English landholder, of obnoxious behavior by "a half intoxicated miner" at the Victoria post office. The ruffian first stared in Verney's face and then, when "I took no notice of him," he "very rudely elbowed himself in front of me." Verney continued to ignore the man, who "began speaking to the bystanders: "I say, what a swell we are in our regimentals, ain't we?" and then thrust some tobacco in Verney's face, remarking, "I say governor, have a chaw?" This act at least succeeded in eliciting a glimmer of recognition from Verney, who retorted, "No thank you," and, "I think it is like your impertinence speaking to me at all." The miner's final gambit was to insist on paying the cost of Verney's letter. Verney told the clerk that "this gentleman will pay my letter," and then snubbed his tormenter by walking away.[53] The persistent miner at first employed crude, physical confrontation and then attempts at gift-giving in asserting his equality to a distinguished-looking Englishman; a fight and a present were each cut of the same egalitarian cloth. Verney would have none of it; he turned up his nose at both offerings and was gratified to learn that the miner had not made good on his offer to pay Verney's postage.

Working men were much more apt to pick fights with each other than with their social superiors. Conflicts described as "free fights" were particularly violent; they entailed either disorganized affrays involving at least several people or conflicts in which the principals cast all inhibitions aside by biting, eye-gouging, or using dangerous weapons. Observers recorded such fights between soldiers, sailors, miners, and other men of marginal means on both sides of the border on the north Pacific slope. In 1858 about a dozen men reportedly emptied from a Steilacoom saloon in western Washington and "commenced an indiscriminate or 'free fight,' . . . and amused themselves for some time knocking each other down."[54] University-educated William Hilleary wrote in 1865 that his fellow soldiers were "fiddling, writing letters, selling apples, mending, reading, dancing, running, scuffling &c. according to the mood each soldier was in."[55]

For respectable onlookers, such behavior simply illustrated the participants' brutality and inferiority. The staunchly Republican *Oregonian* was delighted to comment on a "disgraceful" fight between the editors of two local Democratic newspapers in 1857, remarking that "these leaders of the *unwashed*" should "know that public sentiment regards with execration such proceedings."[56] The writer who described the above free fight in Steilacoom termed it "disgraceful" and asserted that the brawlers "were and are strangers here; none of our townspeople caring to distinguish themselves in this manner."[57] Fighters of Irish descent were particularly apt to be condemned and lampooned. An 1861 western Washington newspaper described how one Irishman "dared another to step on his coat tail," a challenge that touched off "an exciting Tipperary fight . . . in which about a score of fun-loving Hibernians participated, each knocking down the man nearest to him, regardless of his being friend or foe." This "amusing scene . . . was decidedly the most entertaining event of the day."[58] In the same year, a Victoria newspaper regaled its readers with the story of how one McAllister defended himself in court against a charge of kicking in a door and assaulting two Native women. The sailor began by "hitching up his trousers at the waist, and spitting on the floor" as he described how the two women had laughed at his intoxicated condition. He had then rushed toward the "'eathens" and "couped one of 'em, yer honor, with my right and I wumbled another on 'em with my left." When a third party appeared, "I wumbled him too—blast his heyes," a pronouncement that provoked "uproarious laughter, in which the whole Court joined."[59] The newspaper's rendition of McAllister's antics, complete with attempts to render his dialect, laid before Victoria's literate citizenry a familiar and amusing stereotype: a drunken and pugnacious Irishman. A judge in the Cariboo went so far as to remark in court that "a black eye might not hurt an Irishman, but it might hurt an Englishman."[60]

Yet respectable men were by no means prepared to leave fighting to their unrespectable counterparts. Physical force, the ability to subdue another man with one's bare hands, was still a key component of masculinity in recently settled parts of North America in the mid-nineteenth century. Hence a Puget Sound newspaper was pleased to report in 1861 that when an Irishman, "spoiling for a fight, challenged a quiet, peaceable Englishman," the latter, once "his courage was called in question . . . pretty thoroughly demolished his antagonist."[61]

Yet most man-to-man violence occurred among peers. It served to unite, not to divide. Men's fights with each other illustrated their honor and courage, their manliness. Even the loser had, as Elliott Gorn puts it, "demonstrated his mettle and maintained his honor." The use of violence was particularly important to marginalized white men. It allowed them, in Gorn's words, "to shout their equality at each other."[62] If others were on hand to observe, so much the better. These men's ability to risk and absorb considerable physical punishment expressed both a moral courage that their social superiors could not exceed and their superiority over African Americans and women, people deemed unable and unworthy to participate in such brawls. Michael Kaplan, writing of mid-nineteenth-century New York City, observes that working men "fought each other . . . to demonstrate the democracy of their manliness to each other."[63] Saloon brawls were not simply a vehicle for letting off steam. South of the line, especially, they reflected key tenets of Jacksonian Democracy: the political autonomy, equality, and solidarity of white men.

Such men practiced a much different sort of violence toward people they considered their inferiors. Chinese immigrants constituted, on many parts of the north Pacific slope, the largest group of nonwhites. Crop failures, warfare, and banditry in China coupled with opportunities to make relatively large sums of money in the mining regions of Oregon, Washington, and British Columbia drew many thousands of Chinese men in the 1850s and 1860s. They became particularly numerous in British Columbia. Some three thousand resided at Barkerville, the heart of the Cariboo gold country, in the mid-1860s. By that time the Chinese of the north Pacific slope had diversified and could be found working at road building, domestic service, cooking, farming, and gardening. They generally continued to keep to themselves, in part because they faced so much legal and informal discrimination, discrimination that tended to grow worse over time. They labored under very difficult and overcrowded conditions. Many spent their earnings, meager by white standards, on gambling, opium, or prostitutes. Violence apparently flourished under these conditions, although official indifference and Chinese wariness of outsiders make it difficult to trace its extent and causes. Money lay at the center of some disputes. In 1869 a Chinese man living in the British Columbia interior admitted to shooting and killing Ah Chou, whom he suspected of stealing his gold. "I saved this money long ago," he remarked, and the theft "made me so angry that I shot him."[64] Two years later Ah Soun and Ah Sam cut each other in Victoria in a disagreement over the repayment of a debt. Gambling also provoked violent altercations. In 1871 two Chinese men climaxed a quarrel in a Victoria gambling house by drawing knives and stabbing each other. Other violent altercations occurred in Victoria's Chinese houses of prostitution.[65]

Whites were not much concerned over Chinese men's violence. They repeatedly asserted that Asians were weak, their violence ineffectual. Well-to-do British Columbians made a virtue of this purported submissiveness, for they preferred subordinate men to act the part. Johnson praised them as "hard-working, sober, and law-abiding—three scarce qualities among people in their station," particularly the truculent Irish.[66] Verney, the British gunboat commander, referred to them as "a wonderful race, . . . patient and enduring. I never saw a Chinaman looking otherwise than contented, and I never saw one the worse for drink."[67] If only poor, uneducated whites would be so tractable and sober—and weak. The Victoria *Colonist*'s 1860 report on a fight between a Caucasian and a Chinese man noted that "as usual, poor John got worsted."[68] Indeed, Chinese men were much more likely to be victims than aggressors in interethnic altercations. Homicides in Oregon and British Columbia apparently included two instances in which a white man killed a Chinese man, but none in which the tables were turned. Assaults were of course much more common, and they served to express the aggressors' contempt for Asians. John Thompson, for example, removed Ah Took's hat and then hit him for objecting to it. R. B. Johnson, who arrived in British Columbia in 1862, observed that the Chinese of British Columbia were "treated like a dog, bullied, scoffed at, kicked, and cuffed about on all occasions."[69] Relations were the same south of the line. A Civil War army officer in southern Oregon remarked upon "the ubiquitous Chinaman, moving from mining locality to mining locality, fleeing from the kicks of one to the cuffs of the other."[70]

By the mid-1860s, however, concerned whites were noting that Chinese violence was becoming more effectual. The Victoria police court magistrate informed two combative Chinese men in 1865 "that they used to be very peaceful citizens but had lately been very fond of taking the law into their own hands."[71] Two years later the *Colonist* remarked that "the Chinese are fast becoming civilized"; a Seattle "Celestial" had recently shot a man who had attacked him "instead of meekly submitting to the chastisement."[72] To become "civilized" was to aspire to equality, to assert that one ought to enjoy just as many rights as a white man did.

A similar dynamic occurred around violence between spouses. Indeed, the *Colonist* in 1861 asserted that "the habit of beating Chinamen is about on a par with woman-whipping—not quite so mean, but full as cowardly and despicable."[73] Women, like Chinese men, were deemed too weak to constitute a proper fighting foe. The Victoria *Colonist* condemned the practice a number of times, describing wife beating as the "cowardly" practice of brutes.[74] Oregonians, too, commonly associated wife beating with unmanliness. The *Portland Oregonian*, a staunchly Republican newspaper, remarked that a leading Confederate was "a jail-bird and wifebeater."[75] But such condemnations depended upon women's submissive inferiority. Jason Lee, an

Oregon Methodist missionary, confided to his diary in 1838 that he "felt especially indignant at that man who could tyrannize over an innocent, lovely
and defenceless female." In the same sentence he excoriated "that woman
who was ever grasping after the authority of the husband, and then always
seeking to exhibit her prowess, in browbeating him on all occasions." Not
all women, it seems, were "innocent" and "defenceless." Still, "I have generally been disposed to fix the heaviest censure upon the man, . . . believing
it to be in his power to introduce and maintain a system that will in most
cases secure harmony, order and peace in the family circle."[76] Lee expected
more of men because he considered them women's superiors. Male dominance and paternalism dovetailed. South of the line, groups of men occasionally lynched or flogged men for "insulting . . . respectable females," as
one newspaper put it.[77] One William Smith reportedly assaulted a man for
making "a remark derogatory to American ladies" in or near Victoria in 1863.[78]
Like the husbands who killed their wives' lovers, these acts of violence
occurred over the heads of women, creatures who, it seems, were incapable
of defending themselves.[79]

Ann Austey was precisely the sort of abused wife that respectable men liked
to help. She had married Francis Austey in Detroit in the mid-1850s and had
come to Victoria with their young son in 1862. The couple's neighbors soon
noticed that all was not well. Major John Biggs observed the couple closely
and concluded, as he later put it, that Francis "was a drunkard, and a self
degraded, abandoned character, who had reduced himself and family thereby
to destitution." Francis "was unnaturally brutal" toward Ann, "so much so
that upon some occasions she sought the protection" of Biggs and John
Waddell. Biggs and Waddell decided that the best solution to this difficulty
was to put the Austeys in charge of a rented house, where they could keep
boarders. Francis might make good with such an opportunity, and Ann's sympathizers could keep a close eye on him. But Francis spurned these men's
attempts at "effecting a reformation" in his "habits and conduct," persisted
in his "outrageous" behavior, and left his family within two months—whether
by his own volition or at the insistence of the couple's frustrated patrons is
not clear. Several contributors then provided the abandoned wife and child
"with lodgings in a respectable private family." Ann began making a living
for herself, applied to a Victoria court so that she could control her own earnings, and then left for Washington where she "has maintained herself and

child . . . by her own industry," as one of her Victoria friends put it. She applied for a divorce there in 1865. Francis was by then living in a Puget Sound shingle camp with a Native woman, a condition that, for his critics, underscored his moral depravity and his wife's virtuous suffering.[80]

Respectable people had much less sympathy for abused wives who failed to behave so passively. The companionate model of marriage had made some headway in the United States and Canada by the mid-nineteenth century, but not primarily on the north Pacific slope. Most men on both sides of the border still expected wives to obey their husbands, and many believed that those who did not deserved or required at least moderate physical punishment. Margaret Hunt, writing of eighteenth-century England, points out that "a society suffused with personal relationships of dominance and submission . . . saw violence as a necessary, if not always optimal, way of maintaining order in any hierarchical relationship."[81] U.S. law went further in its critique of wife beating than did English or Canadian law, but many jurists still defended a husband's right to hit his wife. Hence an eastern Oregon magistrate remarked in 1865 that a divorce suit presented him with evidence showing both that the wife had "suffered violence" from her husband and that she had given "good cause for the use of means on his part which might elsewhere be improper."[82]

Mid-nineteenth-century Oregon husbands were in fact most apt to strike their wives when these women acted assertively. Alice Holister recalled that her husband hit her and told her that "he would learn me better than to be saucy to him" when she objected to him coming home three hours late.[83] Peter Brusan reportedly told his thirteen-year-old bride that if "she did not mind him and do everything he told her, he would whip her until she could not stand up."[84] Husbands often became violent when women thought, spoke, or acted independently. Their blows constituted an attempt to restore the marriage to a state of patriarchal equilibrium. Unlike violence toward a peer, moreover, these fights were supposed to be one-sided and unfair. Husbands did not square off with their wives and give them a fighting chance; they beat them any way they could, fair or foul. White men hit their wives for the same reason that they hit Chinese men: to punish insubordination.[85]

But women did not always follow these scripts. Many were isolated from each other and their kin, marginalized socially and politically, and engaged in hard farm labor. But these very conditions often encouraged independence and strength. Men commonly asserted that women were the weaker vessel, but experience told women otherwise, and many were willing and able to take their own part against a domineering husband. Harriet Wunch filed for a divorce from George in western Washington in 1852. They had married in Oregon just six years before, when she was eighteen. Her complaint asserted that her German-born husband would "become ferociously mad" and threaten to shoot her. George's answer countered that Harriet showed her hatred for him by placing "sticks of wood under his back in the bed," trying to destroy her fetus, attempting "to cut their bed in two," and by endeavoring to stab him when he interfered. Harriet evidently did not wish to be a mother or to have sexual intercourse with her husband, and she took her own part. George concluded that "he had ample cause for all the anger he ever manifested toward his said wife."[86] Husbands' and wives' violence, then, typically occurred around particular instances of the latter's resistance to the former's authority. It indicated both men's determination to dominate and wives' determination to refuse that domination.

Settler women employed violence outside as well as inside of marriage. In 1862 a man was "accidentally shot in the leg" in a Portland "row with Madam Reeve, a strong-minded woman, whose lecture . . . he criticized some weeks before, and for which he was threatened with a cowhiding at the time."[87] Women, like their male counterparts, also quarrelled over the Civil War. Several female Confederate sympathizers reportedly tried to cut down a flagpole flying the U.S. colors in the Willamette Valley. The leader flourished a butcher knife and asserted that she "would stab the first man who threatened to interfere."[88] British Columbia women also used violence, but apparently not as freely as their counterparts to the less hierarchical south, where patriarchal marital arrangements were somewhat less secure.[89]

Indeed, contributors to British Columbia newspapers could hardly broach the subject of women's violence without snickering. The *Colonist* referred to a woman accused of beating her husband as "an old woman of a strong gipsy cast."[90] It repeatedly poked fun at women who used their fists by referring to them as "Amazons."[91] An 1865 story entitled "Amazonian" described how "a fair complexioned damsel, of tartar-like propensities, and a combative native had a 'set-to' on Yates street last night, amidst the hooting and yelling of delighted multitude."[92] Men shook their heads over such spectacles when they were not chuckling about them. A Cariboo *Sentinel* writer "could scarcely suppress the exclamation, alas for humanity!" when he espied "two finely dressed and good-looking women" opposing each other at court. One of them seemed "graceful," but soon betrayed "a passion so uncontrollable" that even the court could not restrain her "torrent of uncomplimentary language." The author dropped several hints regarding this woman's occupation: she had an alias, "considerable personal attractions," and engaged in "unseasonable promenades."[93]

Such stories had a clear message: normal, respectable women did not use violence. It was a lesson preached south of the border, too. Men fought in wars, men engaged in fair fights, and boxing was a "manly art." Hence a southern Oregon miner critical of the peace settlement brokered by General Lane in 1853 went around Jacksonville collecting money to buy Lane a petticoat. The *Colonist* in 1868 lampooned a man by suggesting that he was only able "to scratch, gouge and pull hair, like any other old woman."[94] White men expressed their superiority over women both by refusing to fight them fairly and by asserting that women were not capable of fighting—though white women, like Chinese men, sometimes gave the lie to that assertion.

Parents asserted and enjoyed more freedom to punish their children than husbands did their wives. George Miller, brother to the noted poet Joaquin, said that his father had been raised by Quakers and that "he never struck one of his children, as he did not believe in physical force as a method of settling disputes."[95] At the other extreme was A. R. Dillon, an eastern Oregon physician who reportedly asserted that his three-year-old daughter "was his own & he would whip her when he please[d]" and "kill her if she did not mind."[96] Most parents of course fell somewhere between these two views. They commonly described physical punishment as a form of moral instruction, an act of discipline administered in response to particular acts of disobedience and misbehavior. Children who grew up in mid-nineteenth-century Oregon recalled their parents hitting them for slipping away during a prayer meeting, laughing in church, and taking a bite out of a cheese. A man who grew up with sixteen siblings simply recalled: "Father usually spoke once, and then struck."[97] Parents commonly hit children with particular objects, such as switches or straps, indicating that such beatings were deliberate, considered decisions, not sudden acts of passion. Community members intervened in the parent-child relationship only in reaction to extreme cases of abuse. In 1864, for example, the *Portland Oregonian* reported that a child living with a local family had been imprisoned in a privy for several days without adequate food or bedding and had apparently been beaten and scalded. Authorities rescued the child and put the father in jail. Parents who stopped short of torturing or maiming their children seldom faced such consequences.[98]

Yet the widespread acceptance of corporal punishment does not mean that it was used extensively. Indeed, few people who grew up during the settlement period recalled frequent beatings from their biological parents.

Why was this so? Why did the settlers not hit their children more often? Because parents generally did not hit obedient children, and mid-nineteenth-century children typically accepted their parents' authority. The man whose father "spoke once, and then struck" proudly recalled that "he sure trained us to habits of industry and brought us up the way we should go."[99] Parents usually struck their children for particular acts of insubordination, for a specific, instrumental purpose. Since children, unlike many wives, accepted their subordinance, fathers and mothers rarely felt the need to use physical force to keep them in their place.

Children were much less likely to accept the authority of a stepparent or foster parent, and these adults often responded with violence. In the Willamette Valley in 1865, John Baker married a woman with several children. Two years later he sought a divorce. "The trouble mostly originated with the oldest children when I tried to correct them," he recalled. When they called him names, "I started to whip them," and his wife "took their part."[100] J. W. Cullen came to Portland with his mother in 1847, and shortly after their arrival she married Frank De Witt. De Witt "was a firm believer in the efficiency of the rope's end," and some nights Cullen's back was "so bruised and sore I could hardly sleep." He ran away from home at age thirteen, after a particularly brutal beating. His mother talked him into returning, and De Witt promised that he would stop whipping him. A few weeks later De Witt became enraged at Cullen and, to keep the letter if not the spirit of his word, repeatedly "picked me up and threw me on the floor as hard as he could" instead of whipping him. Cullen "watched my chance" and slipped away again, this time apparently for good.[101] Many others had similar childhoods. A woman orphaned at age seven in the early 1850s lived with many different families in the Willamette Valley and by the age of fourteen "had been whipped so often and so hard that I was used to it."[102] Several men who grew up in Oregon recalled severe beatings from their stepfathers. One who arrived in 1852 at age five had "scars all over my body" over seventy years later from his step-mother's beatings.[103]

The blood tie uniting children to their birth parents spared most children such horrors—until they went to school. Settlement-era children were more apt to be hit by their teachers than by their parents. To be sure, corporal punishment was coming under increasing criticism in Canada and the United States during the nineteenth century, and these attitudes occasionally made their way to the north Pacific slope. British Columbia's 1872 Public School Act stipulated that teachers would eschew corporal punishment "except when it shall appear . . . to be imperatively necessary."[104] But most adults up to that time had not much troubled themselves about violence toward children. In 1860, the Victoria *Colonist* had objected to the punishment meted out to a five-year-old pupil. But this child's injuries were exceptional: he had a two-inch cut, a swollen knee, and his back and legs were "completely covered with black, blue, and yellow stripes, evidently inflicted with a heavy rod."[105] A subsequent article asserted that the boy had received a "clubbing" rather than a "birching."[106] At issue was not whether a young student had been whipped; rather, community leaders were concerned over whether or not the child had suffered, as the judge in a similar case put it, "undue violence."[107] Moderate acts of corporal punishment seldom excited concern. A parent remonstrated with southern Oregon teacher Oliver Applegate— who styled himself "knight of the Birches"—for hitting his boy, but apparently only because Applegate had struck the child in the face.[108] The reminiscences of early Oregonians indicated that teachers who "ruled by smiles and love rather than by the rod" were the exception.[109]

Like stepparents, teachers commonly became violent when students contested their authority. Children recalled being hit for failing to master their lessons, but also for whispering, for making fun of the teacher, for playing too loudly, or to intimidate other students who were likely to misbehave. Teaching was not a highly regarded or regulated profession in recently settled areas. School directors consisted largely if not wholly of local parents with little education who usually hired inexperienced young men willing to teach for a few years or months until a more lucrative opportunity presented itself. For such men and their women counterparts to maintain order in school rooms that included boys in their late teens was very difficult. Indeed, many employers cared more about a teacher's physical constitution than about his or her intellect. The directors of a Willamette Valley school reportedly told a prospective teacher in 1865 that "the prime requirements" for the job were "to be able to lick the big boys." He succeeded, for "if the rod didn't do the work I used my fists or a club."[110] Another Willamette Valley settler recalled "a regular free-for-all fight . . . a knockdown and dragout fight" between her teacher and "some of the big boys" who had become "tired of having Professor Hull whip them so much."[111] The stakes in such battles were high. A teacher whose students could beat him physically was not fit to teach. Boys might literally demonstrate their mastery by throwing their instructor out of the school. A man who grew up in southern Oregon, for example, recalled that "the big boys put" one of his good teachers "out of the schoolhouse through the window and ran him off."[112]

School, then, was a place where boys learned not only to read and write, but also the relationship between violence and power. Schoolteachers assumed a dominant attitude toward their charges. The ubiquitous assortment of rods or switches that stood near their desks represented their right to punish, that they stood in relation to their students as a parent to a child. But a teacher's authority was much more contingent than a birth parent's. It resided in an ability to control students, ultimately in the ability to beat them. Young men could rid themselves of male teachers, at least, by showing that the pupil was in fact the better man, by physically overwhelming them. In the classroom, as outside it, power ultimately depended on force, and as boys neared adulthood they were more reluctant to receive violence, more able and eager to inflict it.

Boys were schooled in violence outside the classroom, too. A man who came to the Willamette Valley in 1853 at age five recalled: "Every boy was taught to hunt the deer, the bear and the elk."[113] Another Oregon boy born in 1855 remembered a childhood of hunting, horse breaking, and physical games such as shinny, which incorporated a wooden ball and long wooden clubs and "was a terrible game on a boy's shins." Winter brought organized snowball fights that, "when bad blood was stirred," included soaking the missiles in water "until they were as hard as rocks, and then some one was almost sure to get hurt."[114] Boys with snowballs were at times a public nuisance in Victoria, where a lad apparently lost an eye to one in 1865.[115]

Boys commonly fought each other, and for reasons that were not much different from those motivating their fathers. Peers commonly staged fair fights. A group of Victoria students, ages ten to sixteen, gathered in 1861 to witness a fight between boys from opposing schools and reportedly drove away a man who tried to stop the affray. A man who spent much of his boyhood in the Willamette Valley recalled that he fought one of his classmates "almost every day," for no apparent reason except that "I thought the day would come when I could wear him out and lick him."[116] For young males, as with older ones, violence was the handmaiden of camaraderie. A farm boy who visited Corvallis and got in a dangerous fight with a local lad who called him "a country jake" recalled that his adversary "was friendly" at their next meeting "and we never had any more trouble."[117] Likewise, Frank Langlois became "good friends" with another teenage boy after the two fought.[118]

Parents encouraged boys' violence. Samuel Thurston, Oregon's first territorial delegate in Congress, wrote to his wife from the nation's capital in 1850 to instruct her to tell their three-year-old son that "he must not fight, but must be good, and kind." But he also asserted that "I would *not* have [you] weaken" the boy's "combativeness by any means. . . . for it is a giant in this world of war." He should "always be ready to make peace—*never to ask it.*"[119] Gentleness was well and good, but a boy needed to learn to take care of himself in a dangerous, strife-laden world. William Barnet Simpson came across the Oregon Trail in the mid-1840s and later recalled that during the journey an older boy regularly licked him once he discovered that Simpson, mindful of his parents' admonitions "to turn the other cheek" and not "settle . . . differences with . . . fists," would not fight back. Simpson's mother got wind of the situation and told him that "the time has come for you to take your own part," to "whip this bully within an inch of his life or I will give you a worse licking than ever he gave you."[120] Even peace-loving parents believed that a boy who did not learn how to take his own part would never truly become a man.

Parents had very different expectations for their daughters. Girls, as we have seen, occasionally suffered beatings at home and school, though seldom as often as their brothers did. They also received far less encouragement to use violence. This gendered distinction of course pointed to the different roles that females and males were expected to fulfill. Indeed, Karin Calvert's examination of over six hundred portraits of young children painted in the United States between 1830 and 1870 reveals that artists most commonly depicted girls with dolls and boys with pony whips, an object that "succinctly summed up the approved masculine characteristics of physical courage, control, and dominance."[121] Little boys, after all, would eventually become men.

The relationship between violence and dominance was often complex during the north Pacific slope's settlement period. Boys grew to be men, and people expected men to be adept at violence. But men were not all of one piece. The forty-ninth parallel was one key divider. The government north of the border asserted a monopoly on law enforcement and killing. Officials south of the line were less active and granted citizens more freedom to defend their person and honor without fear of legal repercussions. Class and status markers also divided men. North of the line, particularly, a commoner had no right to challenge a gentleman. Respectable men depicted working men and Irishmen as being prone to violence, arguing that this truculence marked them as crude and vulgar. But they also liked to believe that if it came down to it they could beat these rowdies. Marginal men interpreted their own violence differently. They associated it with courage and manliness, traits that their well-to-do counterparts could not monopolize.

Social relations of dominance and insubordination also shaped the nature of violence in homes and schools. Husbands, parents, and teachers commonly used physical force to punish insubordinate wives, children, and pupils. Hence violence was apt to erupt where relations of power were clouded and contested, such as with older boys and their stepfathers or teachers, or between strong-willed, independent wives and their tradition-minded husbands. Such violence, moreover, was not always one-sided. Some subordinates successfully used physical force to refute their subjectivity, like the students who literally threw their teachers out of school.

Pacific intimate relations, then, often indicated not equality, but the acceptance of inequality, the willingness of children and wives to respect the authority of their parents and husbands. By the same token, violence commonly indicated not just the presence of a domineering father, mother, or husband, but of children or wives who found that dominance unfair or unbearable.

Violence was not, as powerful people hoped, simply an act imposed on an insubordinate and hapless inferior. It was an act arising from and interwoven among countless other acts of dominance and resistance, assertion and counter-assertion.

3

I Was Not There to Fight

The Decline and Persistence of Violence
in the Late Nineteenth Century

JOHN PERSON WAS NOT, he assured the court, a fighting man. The railroad laborer claimed that John Daly had committed an unprovoked and unwarranted assault upon him in the Kootenays of British Columbia in 1895. His version of the altercation began when Daly remarked that "if that big Swede s. o. b. wants something, he can have it," removed his coat, and advanced toward Person. Person took off his own coat "for my self-defence," but Daly "did not wait till I was ready" and immediately struck him. Person endeavored to run away, but Daly caught him and bit his ear and two of his fingers. Person "of course . . . was stronger"; he eventually subdued his persistent antagonist. Indeed, he emerged from this description as the better man in every way: he did not like to fight, he fought fair, and he beat a belligerent opponent who did not.

Under cross-examination, however, the colors of this self-portrait began to smudge and then to run. Person admitted to having remarked that "Daly thinks he is a better man than I am" and that he had called this claim "foolishness" and asserted that "I am not afraid of him." He also admitted to hitting a man at a nearby mill, though "he struck me first." Yes, he had boasted that "I can prove that I am the strongest man on this Division." But "I meant to lift, not to fight."[1]

Three years later another British Columbian, Okanagan farmer James Simpson, described an unprovoked and cowardly attack that left him unable to use one of his arms or to sleep. But Simpson's self-portrait, like Person's, grew increasingly implausible under cross-examination. He at first asserted, "I only have had one [other] row," which was with a man who "clinched me first." But he soon recalled "a row with a man at Pitt Meadows." Upon being asked if he had encountered any difficulties with a man named Wilson, he at first denied knowing any such person, then recalled a "Siwash Wilson" whom he "never had any trouble with . . . here," although "I had trouble with him at Okanagan Lake." "I do not know the nature of that trouble," he explained, but allowed that the two "had a racket . . . might have been a fight." Neither of them had "suffered greievous [sic] bodily harm," and "Wilson did not accuse me of biting his hand," at least not "when he was sober."[2] The more Simpson talked, the more obvious it became that his history was far from peaceable.

These instances aptly illustrate two salient trends regarding interpersonal violence on the north Pacific slope in the 1890s. Men, parents, and spouses were less likely to describe themselves as ready to employ physical force than they had been a few decades before. British Columbia, Washington, and Oregon had become much more settled and less isolated by the century's turn, and an ethos of self-restraint had eroded the combatant masculinity of previous generations. The law was more powerful, and more people expressed a willingness to submit to its dictates. But probes beneath the surface of nonviolent protestations by people like Person and Simpson revealed much more continuity in people's actual behavior than met the eye. Violence between men and toward children and wives had declined on the north Pacific slope by 1900, but not as dramatically as public and popular pronouncements suggested. The causes of that violence, moreover, the relationship between violence and power, remained largely the same.

The north Pacific slope had changed dramatically by 1890. The number of non-Natives in British Columbia had increased seven times over in just two decades to around 70,000, nearly three-quarters of the province's total population. Oregon and Washington were much larger. The former had over 300,000 residents by 1890, a more than three-fold increase in just two decades, and Washington had surged from just 24,000 in 1870 to 350,000 in 1890. Transportation revolutions prompted these remarkable population gains, as railways brought thousands of immigrants to Washington, Oregon, and British Columbia and carried the products of their farms, forests, mines, and industries to the rest of the continent. The region's demographic and economic boom slowed during the depression of the mid-1890s, but resumed by the century's turn.

The late-nineteenth-century boom only superficially resembled earlier periods of growth. To be sure, many newcomers settled in lightly populated areas. Much of eastern Oregon, eastern Washington, and British Columbia's Kootenays quickly filled up with ranchers, wheat farmers, and miners, respectively. Many arrivals were, like their earlier, mid-nineteenth-century counterparts, young, single males. Yet the context in which these men worked had changed dramatically. Agriculture and the extraction of mineral and timber resources still lay at the heart of the region's economy, but these activities were now linked to national or global systems of production carried out by large companies. Miners and loggers were wage workers employed by huge concerns that they could hardly hope to own. Farmers and ranchers were producing, as efficiently as possible, for distant markets. Women's domestic work also shifted, as railroads and an increased standard of living made the home production of many foodstuffs and clothing unnecessary. Men's work, then, was increasingly centered around disciplined and regulated production for the market, women's around the raising and nurturing of children.[3]

These developments are of more than passing interest to those studying the history of violence. Roger Lane argues that homicide became less common in the western world as work fostered more "regular, predictable, cooperative behavior."[4] Communities also became more feminized as women's direct contributions to the economy waned and their participation in social and cultural institutions waxed, for women, like employers, were apt to emphasize the importance of self-regulation. The shift to a production-oriented society transformed Europe and North America in ways both subtle and profound, molding and shaping societies that were more disciplined, more self-controlled, and less violent.

An increasingly powerful state facilitated this shift by more consistently intervening against acts deemed criminal. British Columbia retained its reputation for law and order—among criminal and respectable residents alike. A man imprisoned on suspicion of a pair of 1894 murders reportedly remarked that making "a man talk when he don't want to" was the "one thing this bloody English Law can't do."[5] But the man he had confided in was an informant; English law had prevailed again.

Oregon and Washington continued to lag behind British Columbia in prosecuting those accused of violent crime, but the gap was closing. An editorial in an eastern Washington newspaper complained not that those accused of homicide went free, as had often been the case a few decades before, but rather that killers were being "let off . . . with a term in the penitentiary" rather than being executed.[6] Washington apparently saw only one full-blown vigilante movement in the 1890s: a Stockmen's Protective Association organized against rustlers along the state's eastern border early in the decade. Spontaneous lynchings were more common but were largely confined to lightly populated areas of the states, and newspapers were more critical of these practices than they had been a few decades before. Community members occasionally organized to dispense less extreme forms of extralegal justice. Some fifty masked residents of North Yakima, in eastern Washington, gave a Chinese man accused of exposing himself a "good stripping with switches" and warned him not to return.[7] Residents of a western Washington town reportedly "organized a mob" to drag through a river a hard-drinking man who had driven his wife and children from his home. They relented only when "he begged for mercy" and signed a pledge to abstain from alcohol.[8] But the likelihood that such men would receive extralegal punishment decreased from what it had been at midcentury.

British Columbia courts continued to define self-defense narrowly, and Washington's courts had become more like British Columbia's. The defendant in an assault case in the British Columbia mining town of Golden established that his adversary had struck the first blow, but the magistrate nevertheless rebuked him for "meddling with the complainant" before the fight started, an admonition that prompted the accused to ask, "Can't a man defend himself in this country?" and to wonder if when "a person hits me again I must run to the Courthouse."[9] Washington courts allowed combatants more room in which to maneuver, though not as much as they had several decades before. The state's supreme court defined self-defense in a unanimous 1895 decision: "neither in defense of person nor property can one go further than is reasonably necessary for that purpose."[10] That court, as well as a lesser one, also emphasized the importance of the defendant's apprehension of great bodily harm. "If in good faith he has a reasonable belief from the facts, *as they appear to him at the time,* that he is in imminent danger," remarked a judge, "if he honestly believes such to be the case then he had a right to act in self-defense."[11] Hence one could kill another if one feared great bodily injury or worse from an assailant who could not be stopped by a lesser act of force. But did one have an obligation to retreat from such an assailant? The Washington State Supreme Court in 1896 overturned an eastern Washington court's murder conviction in part because the judge had implied "that it was the duty of the appellant, notwithstanding that he was upon his own premises, where he had the lawful right to be, to retreat from any assault then being made or threatened by the deceased."[12] Other jurists repeated the lower court's error. The right to stand one's ground and fight had become more cloudy and contested in Washington by the 1890s, as an increasingly powerful state viewed violence more critically while reserving for itself the right to administer justice.[13]

Yet British Columbians continued to compare themselves favorably to the United States in matters of law, order, and violence to an extent that caricatured conditions on both sides of the border. A Victoria newspaper in 1896 observed that once within the province's boundaries "miners and mining camp followers seem to have dropped their lawless habits and predilections almost without an effort." Hence "no one, even in a saloon, attempts to settle a dispute with a revolver." Even "miners from the neighboring states seem gladly to have adopted the quiet and peaceable ways of British Columbians."[14] When revolvers and knives did appear, the province's leaders tended to blame non-Englishmen. Hence the judge in Dominick Teragnolo's murder trial pointed out to the jury that "we have now men of foreign blood coming in among us" who were accustomed to wielding knives.[15] Shortly afterward, in a similar trial, the same jurist remarked on "the influx of foreigners who are accustomed to using the knife in settlement of their quarrels, instead of their fists, as in the Old English fashion."[16] Foreigners from south of the line often came in for particular condemnation. *Black Rock,* a popular novel written in the 1890s, describes how "Idaho," a professional gambler, learns "that a 'gun' was decreed by British law to be an unnecessary adornment of a card table" and expresses his "amazed disgust at the state of society that would permit such an outrage upon personal liberty."[17] The same point appeared in nonfictional sources. A Rossland paper in 1897 noted that Peter Costello, "the Spokane [Washington] tough," viciously kicked an unsuspecting man in the head and told another that he wished "that he had him in the States where he could smash him."[18] Indeed, Lady Aberdeen, one of Canada's leading reformers, praised Rossland's constable, John Kirkup, for keeping the young mining town orderly despite the presence of "wild and lawless" men from the other side of the border who "are accustomed to cut a gash and shoot at one another without any let or hindrance."[19] Frances Macnab, a British traveler in British Columbia in 1897, followed up his charge that people of the United States believed in "the utmost freedom to the individual" with the remarkable—and, as we shall see, wildly inaccurate—assertion that the United States had a homicide rate fifty times as high as Canada's.[20]

Popular fiction set in British Columbia did not champion violence. Presbyterian minister Charles William Gordon, who wrote under the pseudonym of Ralph Connor, was one of Canada's most widely read novelists around the century's turn. He drew from his experience at Banff, on the Alberta–British Columbia border, to write *Black Rock,* an account of the area's miners and lumbermen that appeared in the late 1890s. The novel does not much object to certain types of violence: good, clean fights calculated to right a wrong. But the principal burden of *Black Rock* is moral; it is suffused with the themes of duty, sobriety, and self-restraint. M. Allerdale Grainger's *Woodsmen of the West* makes the same point, though more obliquely. Grainger describes a number of violent altercations, some involving "a hideous, great hulk of a hobo from the States," but he claims that loggers "are a most peaceable class of men." The narrator himself manages to avoid fisticuffs, and he praises a friend who was "good tempered . . . where many another man would have given way, weakly, to silly violence."[21]

But the most popular Pacific Northwest novel of the 1890s went much further in condemning violence than did Gordon or Grainger. Frederic Homer Balch grew up in Washington and Oregon, and, like Gordon, he became a minister. *Bridge of the Gods: A Romance of Indian Oregon* appeared in 1890, one year before Balch died at age twenty-nine. The novel features a New England minister, Cecil, who made his way to the Columbia River around 1700. Cecil's general self-restraint, and in particular his abhorrence of any sort of violence, sets him apart from the Natives he has come to convert, people whom Balch describes as cuffing their wives around as if they were dogs and delighting in warfare.[22]

By 1900, then, the legal and popular cultures of Oregon, Washington, and British Columbia were more critical of men's interpersonal violence than they had been a half-century or so before. But culture and society are not one and the same. To what extent did violence actually decline on the north Pacific slope in the late nineteenth century?

The homicide rates in British Columbia and Oregon in the 1890s were less than one-half of what they had been in the 1850s and 1860s. British Columbia kept a coroner's register from 1893 forward. Its annual average was only 5.9 killings per hundred thousand people, and the rate declined during the decade's last years. *The Oregonian's* list of homicides for 1895 computes to almost the same rate, 6.3. These rates were higher than those recorded in eastern U.S. cities (Boston and Philadelphia had a rate of about 2.5 per hundred thousand in the 1890s), but much lower than those for more recently settled parts of the western United States (the rate in Las Animas County, Colorado, fluctuated between 10 and 26.6; the rate in Gila County, Arizona, from 69 to 70 for whites, higher for Apaches). Comparisons across time and space therefore show the same pattern: social stability fostered lower homicide rates. Men in their twenties constituted 16 percent of Oregon's white population in 1850, just 9 percent in 1900. The people most liable to commit homicides were becoming more civilized, and they were losing demographic ground to women, children, and older men.[23]

Demography also shaped less extreme acts of violence. Fights remained common in places dominated by young, unattached working men. British Columbians, as we have seen, asserted that their mining towns were orderly and law-abiding. A newspaper in Nanaimo, one of British Columbia's leading mining areas, in June 1890 remarked that the town "may well boast of being the most moral city on the Pacific Coast," as its police docket had been empty for the past ten days.[24] But a series of violent crimes soon had Nanaimo's leaders on the defensive. Later in 1890 one of its ministers noted that a man in Vancouver had recently referred to Nanaimo as having nothing "but diphtheria, gambling and murder."[25] Nearby Wellington was particularly violent. A Victoria police officer who visited in February 1891 reported "that fully two hundred men were drunk, and disorderly between Saturday, and Monday," all of them employed in the Dunsmuir mines. "I have been told," he continued, "that these drunken rows take place every pay day, and last from two to three days." He had confiscated two revolvers and a razor and feared that "a serious shooting, or cutting affray" was inevitable.[26] Recently settled ranching areas tended to be the most violent places south of the line. By 1897 Umatilla County, in northeastern Oregon, had only 4 percent of the state's population and 11 percent of its penitentiary inmates. A young man who left "the purity and innocence of Hood River's chaste way of life" to drive some wagons deep into eastern Oregon's interior found many of the local men visiting Prineville "in a state of somewhat pugnacious exuberance."[27] Parts of eastern Washington were particularly violent. In 1891 a resident of Alki in eastern Washington wrote that the community "is noted for being under cowboy control" and related instances in which young men had shot out the lights at a schoolhouse during community meetings. A year later a newspaper reported that a fatal knifing and an armed altercation between a "posse" from Garfield and a nearby gang of "young toughs" had begun when the latter "undertook to 'paint the town' because of the report that Garfield was not legally incorporated, and consequently had no legal officers."[28] Witnesses at the ensuing preliminary hearing testified that the ruffians had yelled, "There is no law in Garfield," that they would "do up the whole ——— town" and "show 'em who runs this town!"[29] Seven years later another set of disputes erupted between "the church people and the saloon element," as a Colfax newspaper put it, including an incident in which a bartender jerked a cigar from a minister's mouth and then beat him when he attempted to retrieve it.[30]

But places like Alki and Garfield were becoming exceptional by the turn of the century. The law, as we have seen, was more established by 1900 than it had been in 1860.

Indeed, complainants in the assault cases of the 1890s were more likely to stress that they were not prone to fight than was the case a few decades before. Two enemies in Alert Bay who wrote to British Columbia's attorney general in 1891 claimed to have acted nonviolently in the face of substantial provocation. Stephen Allen Spencer, an entrepreneur, said that Constable Phillip Woollacot had "called me a long legged Yankee son of a bitch and threatened to lick me and challenged me then and there to fight." Spencer claimed that he had refused this invitation, although he feared "that at any moment I may be forced in self defence to commit a breach of the peace."[31] Woollacot denied using abusive language and said that Spencer's brother-in-law had assaulted Woollacot's children several times. Woollacot "was naturally enough anxious to catch him at that kind of thing, but only to put him on his defense in a court of justice," not to take the law into his own hands.[32]

Respectable men's growing attraction to nonviolence was not just rhetorical. William Thomas, while sailing from Port Angeles, Washington, to his home in Victoria in 1898, was remarking to a companion on the peculiar course of the ship when the vessel's captain, William Owen, took exception, telling Thomas "that I was shooting off my mouth about something that I did not know a damned thing about." He called Thomas "a fool and a sardine." Thomas retorted that "if you are displaying now the quality of your intellect by the manner you are sailing the boat, it is not very bright," and wondered aloud where Owen would end up if he set out to traverse the Atlantic Ocean. Owen then called Thomas some more names and invited him to "come down to [the] main deck and I will fight you." Thomas "replied that I was not there to fight." Owen then attempted to drag Thomas down the stairs and desisted only after an ineffectual minute or two of "pulling and hauling." Thomas informed the captain that he owed him something for the torn overcoat and put his hands in his pockets and started to resume his conversation with his companion. Owen then hit him on the face, opening a "deep gash over the cheek bone." Thomas recovered and held his adversary, who was still endeavoring to strike him, "in a firm grip" until several passengers parted them. A number of witnesses substantiated Thomas's account, and none disputed it. Thomas had apparently refused to fight Owen, even after Owen had twice assaulted him and despite his apparent ability to hold his own with the captain.[33]

Men like Thomas preferred to go to law to settle disputes. George Frye of eastern Washington tried to buy the silence of George Kreitz after threatening him with a gun in a disagreement over some wire and fence posts. Kreitz agreed, but then went to Colfax to swear out a warrant for Kreitz's arrest after learning that Frye, in the words of a local newspaper, "had boasted to a neighbor of drawing a gun on" him.[34] This incident neatly illustrates two competing systems of resolving disputes: by personal aggressiveness and intimidation or by the law. Those who were physically weaker were, of course, more likely to rely on the latter than on the former. A western Washington man responded to an invitation "to square matters" from an antagonist who outweighed him by thirty pounds by telling his adversary that "he would settle with him over town." He then attempted to lure his stronger opponent into the arms of the police before the fight could begin.[35] Growing numbers of men even south of the line were willing to go to legal authorities to restrain bumptious adversaries by the century's close.

Most men nevertheless still seemed to believe that a man should fight when challenged to. Several western Washington men noted in 1898 that Frank Grimes was "very much disinclined to engage in quarreling and fighting" to such an extent that men "tormented" him "purposely to draw him into difficulty and quarrelling" and "considered they could run on him taunt and 'guy' him with impunity." Hence Grimes had "to endure the epithets of being afraid."[36] Grimes's nonviolence made him peculiar. J. E. Ballaine, an eastern Washington editor, was more typical. When Shorty Brown, an angry reader, encountered Ballaine, he "straightway peeled off his overcoat, at the same time applying a profusion of pot house epithets." The editor "kept his overcoat on," but when Brown made "a pass, . . . a fight had to come."[37] To punch a tormenter in the nose might be illegal, but most did not find it immoral. A British Columbia newspaper account of a man being fined for assault and battery noted that "when very foul language leads up to such pugilistic exercise, we do not wonder at the public sentiment when it decidedly leans with the [physical] aggressor."[38]

To be sure, well-to-do people often associated criminal violence with men they deemed unrespectable or cowardly. A Nanaimo newspaper reporting on an unprovoked assault linked it to "the congregation of Indians, Negroes, and so called white men" along a road "and their high handed, unlawful and disgraceful proceedings."[39]

This did not mean that respectable white men expected each other to submit to such treatment. One H. Finger, who ran an ice plant, accused a rival of acting like "a Chinaman" for spreading rumors about Finger behind his back. He also asserted that "any man" who "would take" that insult must be a Chinaman. "I wouldn't take it," Finger remarked.[40] A white man was no better than a Chinaman if he let someone get away with calling him a Chinaman. Respectable men were still supposed to use violence to defend their honor. A Nanaimo newspaper in 1890 recounted how "a big Irishman" was "insulting most every person passing" and knocked off the hat of "a lithe young man." When the young man objected, the Irishman rushed toward him, "remarking 'O'l smash the life ov yez.'" The young man then proceeded to pepper his opponent's face with blows before "he coolly walked away, remarking 'don't seek to interfere with a respectable man again in a hurry.'"[41] This story had a double-edged moral: it illustrated both coarse men's alleged propensity toward violence and the ability of honorable men to beat these brutal men at their own game.

The goal of most men's fights remained the same as it had a few decades before: to resolve arguments and hard feelings. A Washington newspaper reported that a man who "had been aggrieved by some words or action of" another man "proposed to square matters with him" by fighting.[42] Another reported that "a war" between two men that left one with a "broken ear" had successfully "settled the affair."[43] Likewise, a young eastern Washington man reportedly asserted at a dance that "he would get satisfaction before long" from his rival.[44] This desire for "satisfaction" arose from a wide variety of causes: contests over women, disagreements over money, arguments great and small. A quarrel in a British Columbia railway station started when one man told another that he could not ride a bucking bronco.[45] Resorting to physical force, to a fight, ended arguments that could not otherwise be settled.

To "settle" with another through fighting was to touch another man in ways that were brutally corporeal. The owner of an eastern Washington shooting gallery, frustrated that a customer ignored his demands for payment, "took his pay out of Mitchell's hide."[46] A western Washington man told his antagonist that "he would knock the shit out of" him.[47] Others challenged adversaries by inviting them to try to "take it out of me."[48]

Fighting men sometimes expressed violent intimacy in sexual terms, as if intercourse were the ultimate representation of male power. Indeed, a frustrated would-be rapist in the interior of southern British Columbia told his intended female victim that he would "fuck you to death."[49] Sexual epithets also accompanied men's violence toward each other. John Barr, a lumber foreman in the Kootenays, reportedly said, "Damn you I'll fuck you" as he struck the first blow in a fight with another man.[50] Those involved in another British Columbia conflict reportedly told their adversary to "come on you son of a bitch, you cock-sucker, come outside."[51] Sexual epithets played a crucial role in provoking a fight between two friends, Charles Williams and John Sullivan, as they were at work hauling logs in the Cariboo. An observer recalled that Sullivan was remarking on the "very nice girls in Prince Edwards Island," in eastern Canada. Williams's retort that "if he had his p___ in one of them I wonder how she would like it" irritated Sullivan, and he turned the tables by remarking that his companion "can't open your mouth without using that kind of language; your mouth is full of p___ks," which suggested that Williams, not the "very nice girls in Prince Edwards Island," was sexually subordinate. Williams then asserted that Sullivan "should not call a man those names." His friend retorted, "What are you going to do about it, you cock sucker." The intolerable insult stayed on the table, and the two began fighting.[52]

For one man to assert that another was sexually subordinate, effeminate, was to declare that he was less than a man. But white men's fights with each other more often expressed a sort of rough social equality between the participants. A man might refuse to fight a man he did not consider his peer for the same reason that he would refuse to fight with a woman: not simply because he feared losing, but because to fight with a social inferior was to admit that the person was not, in fact, inferior. The sheriff of Atlin (a remote town in northern British Columbia), who was said to possess "all the superior airs of the English upper class," refused to engage a small drunken man who was challenging all comers to a fight; "he evidently thought that he would lose caste by brawling with a commoner."[53] Possessing the willingness and courage to fight made one a member of a community of peers, and one's success at fighting determined one's ranking within that community. Barr, a Kootenay foreman, remarked in court that "a man would be foolish to go into a fight if he did not think himself the better man."[54] But one might not be "the better man" for long. The results of one contest could be quickly overturned by a subsequent battle. Hence when the winner of a western Washington fight remarked to the loser that "you got a good licking," his antagonist replied, "You cant do it again."[55] The winner of a fight in the Kootenays reportedly asserted that "I had the best of the man and made him shake hands," to which the loser retorted, "it was not the last of it."[56]

As in the settlement period, one showed respect to one's peers by fighting fairly. These physical contests followed an elaborate set of rules. A British Columbia railway laborer defended his behavior in a fight by claiming that he had not kicked his opponent, "did not strike him hard except when he was standing," and stopped fighting and shook hands when his adversary said "enough." He faulted his opponent for hitting him before he took off his coat.[57] Combatants were also supposed to be of roughly the same age and physical condition and were not to receive assistance from bystanders. Nor were teeth, knives, or firearms to be resorted to. Hence a participant in a British Columbia fight reportedly said to his opponent: "You s.o.b. you bite me, you don't fight square."⁵⁸ Likewise, when Fred Owen and fellow workman George Smith of the lower Fraser River confronted each other with knives, Owen put his away, remarking, "If you want to fight I will fight you fairly, I don't want to use a knife."⁵⁹

This is not to say that combatants never tried to get an advantage any way they could. But shootings and stabbings tended to occur when the rules of fair fighting broke down, such as when one man was not sure if another had a gun or not, or when a more powerful man insisted on taking on a weaker one. Young Don Wolf used a knife on an older and heavier adversary, asserting, "You have no business in picking on . . . me."⁶⁰ When a western Washington man told a neighbor with whom he had been arguing over property that "he would wollop the earth with me," the smaller man replied, "Mack you are a big man and can whip a half dozen of me, . . . I will warn you to keep your hands off of me, or I will fix you so you cant." He then shot and killed the larger man as he advanced toward him.⁶¹ Knives and pistols served as equalizers for smaller, less powerful men. John Barr of the Kootenays testified that when he and Harold Redgrave went outside "to settle" a dispute, Redgrave remarked that he had "made a mistake," for Barr was "a bigger man than me, and I dont know that I can fight you." But Barr insisted on a clear-cut, public victory; he told Redgrave to go back to the crowded house they had left and admit that "you are afraid to fight me." Redgrave worried aloud that Barr was "taking me back to make a fool of me," pulled a gun, and shot him.⁶²

The nature of violence between white men on the north Pacific slope, then, had not changed dramatically by the end of the century. Though less celebrated than during the settlement period, its causes remained substantially unchanged, and men's use of nonhomicidal violence did not decline precipitously.

Nor had the nature of violence toward children much altered. Canadians and Americans of the late nineteenth century viewed children in a much more positive and sentimental light than had their grandparents, a change in attitude that prompted some educators and other opinion makers to criticize corporal punishment. But most residents of the north Pacific slope continued to accept violence toward children, even if most parents did not frequently avail themselves of this perceived right.⁶³

Disaffected wives and husbands who complained that their spouses had abused their children usually cited only very violent acts. A letter from William Brimsmead of eastern Washington accused his wife of whipping his daughter from a previous relationship "black & blue" and locking her in a closet.[64] Another man said that his wife had struck her children with her fist and on at least one occasion bloodied her daughter's nose. At issue here was not a spouse's right to hit a child, but rather the extent of the blows. Hence a western Washington woman remarked that her husband would whip their children "harder tha[n] he ought sometimes."[65] An eastern Oregon woman explained that she had told her husband that "if he wanted to whip them that he could whip them in the right way" rather than hitting them over the head with sticks and kicking them.[66] A witness in another case remarked that a mother did not have "a right to abuse the child, but she should have a right to correct it and whip if necessary."[67] Likewise, Mary Miller of eastern Washington asserted that her husband had punished their children "too severely" by punching their little girl in the face with the child's own fists and slapping their baby on the head. These blows sometimes left the children bruised, and she cited one instance in which he held their son's head between his legs and "beat him severely on the bottom until he evacuated his bowels." Joseph said that he had punished their son "very reasonably," that he "had spanked him with my hand," and that "I never saw any marks on him." A neighbor testified that he had never seen Joseph "whip children extremely," but that Mary had struck one of the children with a horse whip. Mary reacted to these charges much as her husband had. She denied ever using a whip or leaving marks on her children, though she "very often switched" one of them "when he merited it."[68] This contested evidence makes it difficult to grasp how the Millers actually disciplined their children. But it clearly indicates how they wished to be perceived before the law: as parents who spanked and switched but did not bruise; who hit but did not abuse.

The law was very clear that parents had a right "to administer such moderate physical punishment as may be reasonably necessary to enforce" their "authority in the home," as one eastern Washington judge put it.[69] Indeed, parents were responsible for controlling their children, and those who could not occasionally appealed to the courts to send their children to someone who could. Hence a father turned his twelve-year-old son over to the Boys and Girls Aid Society of Oregon "in order that he may be disciplined, having gotten beyond his control."[70] British Columbians seemed even more desirous that children remain under the regulation of adults. A man who grew up in and around Hope on the lower Fraser River said that the emphasis on respecting elders was so strong that "even the neighbour would spank the other ones' children sometimes . . . so they would be brought up properly."[71]

Yet, as during the settlement period, most parents on the north Pacific slope apparently hit their children infrequently. Lillian Scott, born in western Washington in 1891, said that her Welsh father "was strict and . . . would jaw at me." Yet she could not recall her father "ever laying a hand on me." Nor did her Norwegian-born mother hit her, although she did spank her two little sisters for playing on a dead tree that they had been told to stay away from.[72] Indeed, many children apparently feared being struck only for what they saw as especially egregious sins. Some of the most heartrending court testimony from this period describes young children who expected to be punished by their parents after someone else had sexually assaulted them. The mother of an eleven-year-old girl raped in Nelson described how her daughter came to her "crying and . . . asked me not to whip her."[73] Likewise, a four-year-old girl, also from British Columbia, recalled pleading "Mamma don't whip me" after such an attack. Her mother, not comprehending what had just happened, tried to reassure her by explaining that she would beat her only if she had been playing on the street.[74]

Stepparents and foster parents were not so sure that they enjoyed a right to hit their children. The Boys and Girls Aid Society placed the children of deceased, impoverished, unfit, or beleaguered parents in private, generally rural homes. Frustrated foster parents were often at a loss over how to control these troubled and often recalcitrant boys and girls. An eastern Oregon woman wrote to the agency's head that the boy placed with them had become "perfectly impudent." She attributed this to their unwillingness to hit him: "If we had whipped him & made him mind in the start, we could of got along better," she remarked, "but he said we dident *dare* to & I dident know & you dident say."[75] Another adult complained that "I kant do nothing with" the boy sent by the agency, for "I dont liek to whip him without outhority and he gnos that."[76] Not all foster parents were so reticent about using violence, but most seemed hesitant to hit a child who did not really belong to them.

Educators felt much the same way. Settlement-era teachers faced with contentious children had commonly employed violence with little fear of being criticized for it. But this had changed by the 1890s in Oregon and Washington. A Willamette Valley teacher was fined five dollars for slapping a boy in 1896. An eastern Washington teacher charged with pulling out a young girl's hair and inflicting dangerous wounds upon her head was bound over for trial for a sum of fifty dollars after his preliminary hearing. The girl's father dropped the suit only after the teacher agreed to resign. The educator claimed that the incident was an accident, that he only "cuffed her ears" and inadvertently tangled his hands in her hair. But he "acknowledged a violation of the law in striking the child on the head," as a Colfax newspaper put it.[77] To be sure, those who grew up in remote parts of Washington and Oregon in the late nineteenth century recalled very severe and uncriticized acts of corporal punishment, and few parents or community members questioned a teacher's right to at least occasionally employ physical force as a form of discipline.[78] But students in the 1890s faced much less violence than their grandparents had, and teachers who used it were more likely to be challenged by the community.

Relations between teacher and pupil changed more slowly in British Columbia. The average number of reported corporal punishments fell from about 115 per hundred pupils in the early 1880s to around 30 per hundred for the 1890s. Yet some teachers continued to hit their students readily, and those who protested seldom got much satisfaction. In 1898 the mother of ten-year-old William Cates complained that the principal of Nelson's public schools, J. H. Soady, had whipped her child excessively with a rubber strap. The beating, she said, left William so sore that he could not eat his dinner that night. Four days later the marks from the punishment were still easily discerned. William's mother did not dispute Soady's right to hit her child. Indeed, she had asked him to, for he often refused to go to school and "was getting too big for her to handle." But she felt that he had gone too far in this instance. The school board disagreed, one member noting that "nothing but severe punishment" could keep some of the boys "in check." The justice in charge of the mining town's police court concurred with the school board and, according to a Nelson newspaper, "availed himself of the opportunity of reading" young William "a severe lecture."[79]

In only some instances, then, had violence toward children become less common and more frequently criticized by the century's close. Teachers and foster parents in Washington and Oregon used violence more gingerly than had their settlement-era counterparts, and they were more apt to face criticism when they did hit. Violence against schoolchildren declined on both sides of the line, although British Columbians seldom censured teachers who continued to employ corporal punishment. Biological parents in British Columbia and the Pacific Northwest alike apparently did not use violence often, probably because their children still respected their authority. Hitting children remained noncontroversial where tradition was strongest: in British Columbia and particularly in conventionally constituted families on both sides of the boundary.

Wives' status expanded more fully than their children's in the late nineteenth century, especially south of the line. Most historians of gender relations mark the nineteenth century as a time in which husbands' dominance became more conditional. By the century's close this trend had become well established even in many rural parts of the north Pacific coast. This was partly a matter of demographics. In 1891 the average age gap between British Columbia spouses still exceeded ten years, and in 1901 females made up just 29 percent of the province's non-Native population. But females constituted 42 percent of Washington's inhabitants at the century's turn, 45 percent of Oregon's. Women's organizations waxed along with their numbers. Well over one hundred Woman's Christian Temperance Union chapters and other clubs devoted to improving self and society flourished in Washington and Oregon by 1900. British Columbian women gained ground more slowly. The WCTU had only two chapters outside of Victoria and greater Vancouver by 1900, in Vernon and Nelson. Nor did the woman's suffrage movement engage many women outside of the province's two major cities until after the century's turn.[80]

It grew easier for wives in Oregon and Washington to get a divorce. Washington's divorce rate increased from 88 per hundred thousand in 1870 to 184 per hundred thousand in 1900, the highest U.S. rate.[81] In 1893 a member of the Washington State Supreme Court claimed that only women who came "into court with clean hands" were entitled to a divorce, but his four fellow jurists overrode him, arguing that a husband's ill-treatment was bound to affect a woman "and may have provoked her to acts and sayings which otherwise would not have been excusable."[82] British Columbia's divorce rate was much higher than the rest of Canada's but remained minuscule compared to Washington's and Oregon's: just 3.2 per hundred thousand for 1901 to 1905. Only four couples divorced in the entire province in 1900. These different rates reflected different views of wedlock. For Canadians, the institution remained, in the words of James Snell, "the bulwark of the social order."[83] People in the United States, on the other hand, increasingly saw marriage in terms of personal fulfillment and freedom, values that overrode traditional understandings. Indeed, when the father of a divorce-seeking Washington woman described his son-in-law as a "self-willed, stiff-necked, little fellow" who "wants everything his own way," the judge remarked: "He is an Englishman, isn't he?"[84] Old-fashioned patriarchy struck such men as un-American.

Popular opinion had tolerated moderate forms of violence toward wives in the settlement period, but by the 1890s any blows directed toward a wife were suspect among many Washington and Oregon residents. Men accused in divorce suits of hitting their wives seldom defended even relatively slight blows delivered under highly provocative circumstances. Joseph Miller of Walla Walla claimed that Mary had hit him in the mouth with a cream pitcher, loosening his teeth and drawing blood. Yet he testified that he "did not strike her, other than to ward her off." His wife had "dared me to strike her," had flourished a butcher knife at him, and spit in his face. Yet he "always went away and left her as quick as I could."[85] Joseph McCarty's answer to Maude's divorce petition recounted an instance in which she had beat him with her fist and a broomstick. He, "to protect himself, retaliated by slapping the plaintiff with his open hand twice." He then tried "to escape," but was slowed by rheumatism and unable to elude his angry wife, who "beat and bruised him over the head and shoulders with the broomstick until she broke the same over his head and across his shoulders."[86] Nicholas Dupuis's answer to his wife's divorce petition admitted to slapping her in February of 1893, but claimed that he did so in the "heat of passion" because she was continuing to keep company with a man with whom she had conceived a child some fifteen years ago, long after she and the defendant had married.[87] Women commonly contested these stories, which may have been fictional or exaggerated. But settlement-era husbands seldom felt compelled to apologize for using violence against wives they described as disobedient and willful. Divorce-seeking wives, furthermore, now often described very abusive husbands who used violence not at all or only after years of name-calling and threatening.[88]

The virtual absence of divorce in British Columbia deprives its historians of detailed documentation on violent marriages, but occasional newspaper accounts criticized violent husbands. The *Nanaimo Free Press* remarked in 1890 that "it is an open secret that there is more than one person—we will not call him a man—who is in the habit of beating his wife." It then published the stern remarks of a local magistrate as he sentenced a husband who had been convicted of assaulting his spouse, a warning that the jurist hoped would deter both the offender "and other habitual wife beaters."[89] The newspaper and the court seemed less sympathetic to the wife of Alexander Matheson, who "allowed that sometimes she prevented" her husband from beating her by "using the poker."[90] As during the settlement period, violent British Columbia husbands were most apt to be censured when their wives appeared helpless.

Linda Gordon points out that "condemnation of female violence went along with the romanticization of female passivity," a belief that "contributed to women's participation in their own victimization."[91] Wives on the north Pacific slope, like their husbands, did in fact seem to be using less violence, and using it less readily, than had their peers earlier in the century.[92] Women were affected by the same ethos of self-restraint that men were. Wives were less likely to be hit than before, but it was also less permissible for women to hit back or to use violence or threats of violence as a strategy to deter abusive husbands.

Yet wives who used violence toward their husbands typically did so for the same reason that their grandmothers had: to assert their autonomy. Maggie Otto, on her fourth marriage by age thirty-two, reportedly gave her husband a black eye when he objected to another man visiting her. Thomas, the husband of Elizabeth Allred, claimed that when he "remonstrated with" his wife not to keep company with disreputable men, "she told me to go to hell and called me a bastard, and hoar master son of a bitch." On other occasions, he said, she hit him. Nor was Elizabeth about to exchange one ruler for another. A witness who described her as "one of the lowest hoars in Centralia" had observed her walking with another man when a fellow she commonly kept company with "told her he wanted her to come and go with him." But she retorted, "You go to Hell you d—d son of a bitch, I will finish this fellow up and will then come and give you all you want."[93] This woman's blatant transgression of community mores, her extreme sexual independence, and her ready use of violence were all of a piece and marked her as an outsider. To be sure, more respectable wives might also use violence. Martha Rudd of

Galiano Island, near Victoria, insisted on keeping a letter away from her husband even when he pulled at her dress pocket, threatened her with a shotgun, and threw her down and twisted her neck and wrists "till I screamed with pain." Their children tried to pry his hands off, and Martha, "unconscious of what I was doing thro' pain," struck him on the head with a saucer.[94] George Croll of western Washington described a wife with "a powerful temper for a woman" who used violence less reluctantly. She reportedly struck him and called him a liar when he accused her of being out late and then hit him on the head with a stick when he slapped her face. At issue here was whether Emma Croll had the same rights as George did. When his wife's attorney asked sarcastically if George "had charge or control of her," if he were "her guardian," he retorted, "No, but I was in my own house." George viewed Emma as an erring child. Hence he "picked up a stick" and told his wife to "behave herself" when he judged that she was verbally abusing her mother. "She is a good natured girl when she is in a good humor," he told the court, "the best kind of a girl."[95] But Emma Croll, by her own admission, did not behave like a submissive "girl."

As during the settlement period, husbands were especially inclined to be violent when wives were not submissive. Mary Logan of eastern Washington said that her husband "threw me to the floor, and said 'God damn you I have a right to do what I please with my own'" when she hid his horse bridle to keep him from going to sell their house so that he could buy more liquor.[96] Eastern Washington's Lizzie Wood recounted a harrowing altercation with her spouse, J. D., which began when their daughter Myrtle did not take some medicine that Mary had told her to. J. D. remarked that "if I was not capable of making my children mind, he would do it for me." When Lizzie told him to "hush, and don't let us have trouble," he hit her with a fire poker and declared that "he would beat my brains out." J. D. had "been a cruel master to live with" and was tolerable only "as long as every thing went just to suit him."[97]

As with other types of interpersonal violence, traditional patterns persisted beneath growing denunciations of wife beating. Many husbands continued to hit wives who contested their authority. As marriage became more emotionally intense, however, couples found themselves quarreling over a broader range of issues.

Spouses increasingly clashed over sex. Husbands had become more prone to jealousy, even of relationships with other family members. One reportedly remarked that his wife's little brother "was a dammed fast kid" after the boy had kissed her. He told her not even to speak to male acquaintances, "for he said I was [a] dammed good looking woman and he did not want them to fall in love with me."[98] Women's refusal to submit to their husbands' sexual advances might also be met with violence. Nellie Murray recalled that William commonly came home late and intoxicated and forced intercourse on her by pinching her and holding her down. When she resorted to a separate, locked bedroom, he pried open the door and took her to their bed. Insisting that one's wife submit to sexual intercourse was, for many men, the ultimate emblem of masculine authority. California Joy ran a Centralia, Washington, boardinghouse and hotel, and her husband Joseph was reportedly a poor provider. One summer day in 1891 he was "ugly to me all that day" and in front of some of the staff accused her of being intimate with one of the guests. At bedtime he "came to my room . . . and said he was going to room with me that night, was going to sleep with me." When she demurred he asserted that "I am not going to be run out of my own bed." When she said that she would leave the bed to him and sleep with their daughter, he blocked her way, "raised his hand and said damn you I have a notion to kill you now."[99] George Stephens, also of western Washington, reportedly began a long quarrel by complaining that his wife would not go hop-picking and culminated it by slamming her "against the wall" when she refused his sexual demands.[100]

Such men asserted a broadly understood right to sexual intercourse. A man was not to marry simply "to gratify his lust," but neither were wives to deny a spouse "the privileges of a husband."[101] Hence an attorney asked Asa Evans of eastern Washington if his wife had permitted him "to have sexual intercourse when you required it?"[102] Women who refused husbands this requirement usually defended that refusal by citing exceptional circumstances. Some claimed that their spouses engaged in intercourse for several hours at a time and could not ejaculate, a description that neatly paired two grounds for divorce: physical brutality and impotence. Ida Rose, for example, testified that Joseph "would attempt to have sexual intercourse with me nearly every night, and . . . would continue three or four hours at a time." A physician stated that Ida was in poor health and that Joseph's "efforts in having sexual intercourse would probably shatter her nervous system."[103] Indeed, divorce-seeking women who complained of sexually aggressive husbands commonly cited very poor health. They also argued for a right to refuse sex during and around menstruation, pregnancy, childbirth, or miscarriage. But some of these wives went further and suggested, even to the court, that husbands' rights to their bodies were contingent on husbands' good behavior, a claim that their grandmothers had seldom ventured. Felanise Eddy cooked, washed, and kept house for Israel, but "was not able to love him like a woman ought to." He had "been abusing me too much," she explained.[104] Clara Donaldson, also of coastal Oregon, remarked that her husband "was too rough with me" from the first day of their marriage fifteen years before, and that she sometimes "put him off."[105] In sum, growing numbers of wives were struggling to place conditions on conjugal rights that their husbands considered absolute. The invention of the term "marital rape" lay decades in the future, but women were establishing the groundwork by the 1890s, even in the teeth of their husbands' determined and often violent resistance.

Violence against wives had become less common by century's end, yet its range of causes had become broader. Husbands were now liable to become violent not just when their wives disobeyed or criticized them, but also over actions relating to jealousy and sexuality. This suggests both that wives were exercising greater social and sexual independence than the women of earlier generations had and that husbands were becoming increasingly sensitive to matters having to do with marital intimacy, behaviors that were more difficult both to define and to control than the relatively clear-cut ones that their grandfathers had taken exception to.

Most types of interpersonal violence, inside and outside the home, had declined on the north Pacific coast by 1900. The homicide rate had dropped significantly from the 1850s and 1860s. Men were more likely than before to resort to the law to settle their disputes. Some people used corporal punishment on children less readily. This decline in violence was not, for the most part, dramatic. The homicide rate's decline lay in changing demographics, not just changing attitudes. Spanking disobedient children was still a widely accepted disciplinary tool. Men still expected each other to be handy with their fists. But peers, parents, teachers, and husbands had, on the whole, less frequent recourse to physical force than was the case a few decades before.

Ideals shifted more profoundly than actions. Popular fiction represented violent men as more barbaric than heroic, growing numbers of people depicted themselves as reluctant to engage in fisticuffs, and legal sanctions against violence stiffened on both sides of the line. Men were much less apt to defend hitting a woman than they had been during the settlement era, and violent teachers and foster parents were under much more scrutiny than before.

Tradition hampered the implementation of these nonviolent ideals. Many residents of the north Pacific slope still lived in societies dominated by young, single males in the 1890s, places that had only recently become settled. Nor were traditional understandings of masculine pugnaciousness or parental authority easily altered in more developed regions. It was one thing for novelists and educational reformers to describe violence as silly or harmful, quite another for men or parents to "take" insults or insubordination without physical retaliation or correction. New ideals and practices regarding violence coexisted with old ones. They shaped people's beliefs and actions. They did not transform them.

4

Plucky Women and Crazed Italians

Representing Violence and Marginality
in Seattle, Portland, and Vancouver

EARLY IN 1905 a Seattle newspaper reported the victory of "sunny Italy . . .
over darkest Africa." The contest occurred not on the field of battle, but on
a train bound from Portland to Seattle. It began not with a volley of rifle fire,
but when a "big colored porter" asked Mr. and Mrs. Kranberg for their tick-
ets. Mr. Kranberg immediately objected: "Ah no talk to ze colored pusson—
to ze—ah—to ze—what you call 'em—ze coon." "Don't you go to callin' me
no names," retorted the porter, "shaking his ebony finger" at the diminutive
man. "Dere ain't no dago as kin talk to dis chil' lak dat. See?" "The excited
little Italian, dancing around like a hen that has been but recently separated
from its head," repeated the racial slur. The Black man prepared to hit his
tormentor. But then "little Mrs. Madame Kranberg" intervened. She "leaped
nimbly over two grips and . . . planted a dainty little bundle of fives right
between the thick, protruding lips of darkest Africa." Her husband scurried
off to safety.[1]

This account from the *Seattle Daily Times* is not reliable social history. It
purports to present the intimate details of a complex interchange, as if several stenographers or reporters had recorded every word and gesture. The
newspaper had instead relied on the recollections of a single bystander, a person who almost certainly could not have recalled exactly what he had seen,
let alone heard. Indeed, the article's tone suggests that it was less concerned
with rendering a precise account of an argument than with telling a hack-

neyed, bigoted story of a burly, slow-witted Black porter comically defend-ing his honor, a diminutive and pugnacious Italian man farcically asserting his stature, and a woman proving to be more brave and capable than either of the self-important men. White, English-speaking readers were invited to chuckle at the spectacle of a Black and an Italian squabbling over their supposed dignity.

But the light tone of the piece did not render it innocuous. Writing of how western intellectuals have treated the Near or Middle East, Edward Said argues that "the Oriental is *contained*" as well as "*represented* by dominating frame-works."[2] Relations of power shaped these discourses. The above account was not just a funny story; it was a story that conveyed purported truths about two maligned ethnic groups, a story told over and over again, until its mes-sage became conventional wisdom, self-evident truth. Stories from leading newspapers had a political purpose; they reflected the sensibilities of the com-munity leaders who owned and read them. Accounts of violent altercations, letters to the editor, and editorials therefore tell us a great deal about how powerful people interpreted violence—what sort of violence they found news-worthy, what sort of violence they found objectionable, and what causes they attributed that violence to. Widely read newspapers sowed their interpreta-tions of violence regularly and broadly, bequeathing them a legitimacy that counter and alternative explanations could not match. This book's previous chapters are largely social histories, accounts of how people acted in violent altercations. Newspaper stories are occasionally useful in such histories, but they are much more helpful for examining powerful people's representations of violence and the people who used it.

Newspapers certainly took pains to clarify the social identities of violent men and women. These actors were not simply individuals. The *Seattle Times* story, for example, was not about two passengers and a porter. It was about "Italians" and "Negroes." Unprecedented numbers of nonwhites, immigrants, laborers, and working women arrived in Seattle, Portland, and Vancouver in the first decade of the twentieth century, and race, ethnicity, class, and gen-der profoundly shaped how newspapers represented violence.

What sort of stories did urban newspapers tell about the violence of people of color, despised immigrants, women, and laboring men? In many instances, such as the story of the Kranbergs, the press lampooned them. Comical renditions of marginal people's attempts to assert or defend themselves simply underscored their ineffable inferiority. But some outsiders elicited fear as well as loathing. Their violence was much more difficult to pass off, and stories about such acts betrayed trepidation along with prejudice.

Growth was the most obvious fact of life in Vancouver, Seattle, and Portland during the early twentieth century. Vancouver's population increased nearly four-fold from 1901 to 1911, when it stood at just over 100,000. Seattle tripled, expanding from 80,671 in 1900 to 237,000 in 1910. Even staid Portland doubled to 207,000 by 1910.

This population was divided. Race or ethnicity constituted the most remarked upon difference, with people of Asian ancestry constituting the most visible minority. At the century's turn they accounted for over 10 percent of Vancouver's population and about 5 percent of Seattle's and Portland's, although these proportions would fall significantly over the next ten years. Other racial minorities were far fewer in number. Vancouver had nearly one thousand Native people in 1901, but their numbers declined as the city grew. Only a few hundred lived in or near Seattle, many fewer in Portland. People of African descent were more numerous south of the line. There were about one thousand in Portland by 1910, more than twice that many in Seattle, and less than two hundred in Vancouver. Whites born in North America or northern Europe dominated all three of these cities. Some 85 percent of Vancouver's population had been born in Canada, Britain, or the United States. Over one-half of Seattle's immigrants and nearly one-half of Portland's came from Canada, Sweden, Germany, or England, and many of the cities' foreign born had lived elsewhere in the United States before moving to the Pacific Northwest. Immigrants from southern or eastern Europe were more rare. Those from Italy made up about 2 percent of Vancouver's population by 1911, a little less than that in Seattle and Portland. Russian immigrants were a bit more numerous than their Italian counterparts in Portland, a bit less in Seattle, and were scarce in Vancouver.

White Protestants dominated all three cities and tended to divide along class rather than ethnic lines, even though the cities lacked a large manufacturing base. Transient laborers occupied the lowest rungs of the occupational ladder. Skilled men enjoyed relatively high wages and could hope to make a good living, have a family, and own a house. Urban opportunities drew single women as well as single men, but not nearly as many. Males made up about 60 percent of Vancouver's population, nearly 58 percent in Seattle and Portland. Women residents were more likely to be employed than were their rural counterparts, but less likely to work outside the home than urban women in most other North American cities. In 1911, for example, they constituted less than 13 percent of Vancouver's paid workforce, more than 25 percent of Toronto's.

These cities were small and homogeneous compared to New York, Montreal, or Chicago, but they were much more exotic and diverse than most of the north Pacific slope. Seattle had a well-deserved reputation as a wide-open town that tolerated vice. Reformers worried about urban conditions in general, and about women working outside the home, the habits of wandering laborers, and the impact of Asian immigration in particular.[3] A rural schoolteacher who arrived in Portland in 1903 complained of "the stench of stale beer and whiskey" and remarked on the "swarms of nautical men, . . . mingling with the lumberjacks and sawmill hands."[4]

If newspapers are any guide, prominent residents of Vancouver and Portland were not much concerned with violent crime as the population of their cities exploded in the twentieth century's first decade. In 1904 the *Oregon Daily Journal* observed: "On the whole there is no more generally peaceful community anywhere than Portland."[5] The Vancouver *Daily Province* was still more content. A lengthy editorial that appeared in the summer of 1905, in the middle of an increase in arrests, remarked on the growth of violence and crime not in Vancouver, but in "the once quiet and respectable province of Ontario."[6] A few days later the newspaper noted that the city "has no distinctively hardened criminal population" and that nineteen out of twenty of those arrested and sent to police court were "common, ordinary drunks."[7] Indeed, the likelihood of being arrested for simple assault fell dramatically in Vancouver during this decade. In 1901, Vancouver police made some 82 arrests, or one for every 329 residents. Nine years later, when the city had more than tripled in size, it had only 137 such arrests, one for every 679 residents.[8]

Even Seattle newspapers remained largely mute on the question of violent crime. The most spirited denunciations often appeared in the *Seattle Republican,* a weekly owned and edited by Horace Cayton, the region's most prominent African American and an ardent critic of the city's corrupt leaders. Late in 1900, for example, it attributed a spate of recent murders, holdups, and robberies to Seattle's "wide open policy" of tolerating vice.[9] Another weekly, the iconoclastic *Patriarch,* used violent crime to grind one of its favorite axes; it attributed such acts to the "cuckold mill," liberal divorce laws that made it easy for wives to leave their husbands and thereby played a major role in the undermining of western civilization.[10] But Seattle's powerful dailies, the *Post-Intelligencer* and the *Times,* often opposed urban reform and seldom addressed the prevalence or causes of violent crime.[11]

Newspapers' solutions to violent crime underscored their belief that such crimes were exceptional. The *Province* followed British tradition in locating lawful behavior in certainty of punishment and respect for authority. Control ultimately rested on a willingness to use force—the rod for children and execution for adults. The United States denied this fact, with results that were, to Canadians, plain enough. The *Province* noted early in 1908 that Oregon had not executed a single killer during the previous year, this despite some fifty-six murders in the state. "Human Life Held to Be Cheap by Courts of Oregon State," the headline remarked.[12] The conservative *Oregonian* concurred on the salutary benefits of corporal punishment. An editorial commenting on a Vancouver, British Columbia, judge's sentencing of a man to be imprisoned and whipped concluded that "sturdy fathers of a past generation" had inflicted physical punishment on "unruly boys, that thereby they might become orderly men, with a wholesome respect for the governing power immediately over them—first parental authority, after that the law."[13] Other editorials celebrated the paddle as "a means of grace" that had "redeemed" many a boy and linked "the modern repugnance to whipping bad boys and impertinent little girls" to "the prevalent materialism of the age." "The fashionable dislike of anything that makes the flesh tingle is, to put it baldly, nothing better than a form of atheism," the editorialist concluded.[14] The *Oregonian*'s lamentations over the decline of corporal punishment served more as a launching pad for diatribes against mushy-headed reformers than as an explanation for violent crime, a problem that the paper seldom addressed. The Democratic and reform-minded *Oregon Daily Journal* approached violent crime much differently. Articles, editorials, and letter writers identified handguns as the culprit. The *Journal* published at least ten editorials against them in 1907 alone. "Without the revolver" even whiskey would not cause a killing, for a dispute would result in "nothing more than a fisticuff."[15] Criminal violence, then, was the creature of momentary and uncharacteristic impulses, and revolvers were so objectionable because they made killers out of men who were normally law-abiding and peaceful. The *Journal* confronted violent crime much more consistently than the other urban dailies on the north Pacific slope, but it laid this problem at the doorstep of technological, not social, changes.

Whether the north slope's leading newspapers ought to have been more concerned about violent crime is of course a subjective question. It is extremely difficult, even with extensive police court records, to get much of a sense of whether commonplace assaults were rising or falling during the twentieth century's first decade. Homicide records offer a much more reliable calculus. Portland's homicide rate was 6.4 per hundred thousand per year from 1900 to 1910, Vancouver's just 3.9, a substantially lower rate than the rest of the province had. These rates rose during the decade, however. Portland's increased from 5.3 per hundred thousand for 1900 to 1903 to 7.2 for 1907 to 1910. Vancouver's more than doubled, rising from 2.2 per hundred thousand per year to 5.4 per year for the same dates.[16] In the 1990s, as we shall see, concerns about urban violence would increase even as the homicide rate stabilized or declined. The reverse was true at the century's advent.

These cities' rapid growth and polyglot composition seldom provoked widespread fears of violent crime in the early twentieth century. Yet newspapers represented some marginal groups as more benign than others.

Women of course constituted the largest and most familiar marginal group in these cities, and newspapers nearly always depicted their violence as exceptional. It was "not the usual thing to see three women fighting with a man on Vancouver's streets," as the *Province* put it.[17] Newspapers occasionally reported such violence without recourse to humor or sarcasm, such as when women used violence to defend their honor or person. Portland newspapers, for example, commonly referred to women who resisted mashers or robbers as "plucky."[18] If "plucky" denoted a certain inherent frailty, it also suggested courage and resourcefulness. But turn-of-the-century urban newspapers more commonly depicted violent women as laughable. A 1907 article on a fight between Mrs. Ella Reimhoff and Mrs. Frank Bradbury in Portland featured a drawing of one of the women with her fist cocked and quoted a deputy city attorney's advice to one of the principals: "Madam, you are hiding your light under a bushel. You should enter the field of pugilism." Reimhoff, the target of this jibe, "acknowledged the delicate compliment with an ominous optical jab that penetrated the prosecutor through and through."[19] Women who used their fists were peculiar. Indeed, a Seattle daily's story of a violent woman described her as "the irrepressible Nell, who delights to wear male attire and travel under the name of Harry Livingston."[20]

Husband beaters were particularly newsworthy. "HE RELISHED NOT WIFE'S LOVE TAPS," read the *Oregon Daily Journal*'s headline for a story that went on to treat a husband's charge that his spouse had hit him with a telephone, slapped him with a slipper, and struck him on the arm with a wine bottle.[21] Two days later a piece entitled "WIFE USED POKER ON HUBBY'S RIBS" noted that a husband who had suffered two broken ribs and a scalding "has found married life . . . too strenuous."[22] Albert Crosby's divorce suit alleging that his wife had hit him with a flat iron provoked the *Journal* to observe: "The original hen-pecked husband of the jokesmiths, and a woman who can throw straight have been discovered."[23] Such marriages, then, were classical cases of gender inversion in which women's use of violence on their weak and pathetic husbands turned the marital relation upside down and usurped masculine authority. Newspapers occasionally represented women's violence as potent, if it involved a gun, or heroic, if it occurred in fighting off a lecher or a robber. But most accounts were crafted to elicit a chuckle, not fear or admiration.

Nor did boys' violence provoke much concern. To be sure, some concern over their disruptive behavior occasionally found its way into the cities' newspapers. One article in the *Province* complained that Vancouver's "bad boys . . . make rackets, . . . use profane and obscene language, and . . . indulge in vile actions."[24] Another asserted that "young hooligans" had blocked streets, shattered windows, disrupted church services, and used vile language.[25] But neither article complained of violent acts. Indeed, newspapers seldom represented boys' violence as potent. A *Province* article entitled "NURSERY DAY IN THE POLICE COURT" described in detail how a young boy charged with assault repeatedly burst into tears as his mother and a neighbor woman carried on a spirited quarrel before the magistrate.[26] Likewise, an *Oregonian* story on a fistfight between two messenger boys ended by noting that their mothers "took home the young hopefuls" from the police station.[27] Seattle's *Patriarch*, a weekly whose title bluntly conveyed its anachronistic editorial position, repeatedly criticized juvenile courts, claiming that they protected "youthful criminals" and had been foisted on the city by "degenerates" from Colorado, an "anarchy-stricken . . . effeminate, degenerate state."[28] But even the *Patriarch,* a paper loudly and proudly out of step with modern times, did not seem primarily concerned with a youthful crime wave. Rather, it complained that the juvenile court "undermined the parental authority."[29]

Nor did the cities' newspapers represent their dwindling numbers of Native people as dangerous. Vancouver's papers occasionally referred to brutal killings among those elsewhere in the province, but aborigines constituted a largely ignored proportion of the city's population. "Once the lords of the soil," Vancouver's "native sons" were "now only Siwashes to be pushed into the corner of a reservation and denied even the white man's recreation, booze-fighting," observed one piece.[30] Seattle newspapers also portrayed Natives as innocuous. A piece in the *Mail and Herald* in late 1902 marked "the season when the gentle, mild-eyed and sluggish Siwash appears in Seattle" and remarked that the "constitutionally tired" Natives of the region "bears about the same relationship to the Indians of the plains, as a cayuse does to a through-bred."[31] According to newspapers, these phlegmatic peoples might occasionally harm each other but posed little or no danger to whites.

Newspapers also depicted violence by people of Chinese descent as innocuous. To be sure, writers seemed eager to exaggerate Chinese men's propensity to attack and kill each other. Portland newspapers reported the outbreak of "tong wars" in 1906 and 1908, linking the murders of prominent Chinese American businessmen to violent factional struggles. The *Oregon Daily Journal* announced in the latter year that the killing of Lee Dai Hoi marked the declaration of "a bitter tong war" and that "some of the most prominent Chinese in the city have been marked for slaughter." Portland's Chinese community disappointed this expectation; the city's coroner recorded no Chinese homicide victims over the next six months.[32]

Other accounts used instances of internecine violence to depict the Chinese as exotic and sadistic. One described how "Lee Moon, the bold young Celestial who dared to cast covetous eyes on the slave-girl of Chee Fow," lay wounded and closely guarded by his fellows at a Portland hospital, where only "those who bore a strangely marked slip of green paper" could enter his room.[33] Meanwhile, "the cause of the trouble, the almond-eyed vermilion-painted girl with the smoothly brushed hair, sits dreaming in her little room that is heavy with the odor of punk, and smiles slowly on her sisters, who call her thrice blessed because the blood of a man has been shed for her."[34] Other pieces referred to "the dark secrets of Chinatown," a place of "thick and sticky and dimly lit" rooms concealing "knives . . . whetted to razor keenness.[35] The *Vancouver Daily Province* evinced a deep interest in "highbinders," a criminal organization that, according to one expert, fully three-quarters of North America's Chinese belonged to. He explained that the order expected its members to take 108 different oaths, vows "opposed to decency and civilization." They must drink their own blood, "walk along a heated metal board . . . stand between scorching flame," and be "pricked with daggers" before crawling "abjectly between the feet of the master." These barbaric rituals had transpired "dozens" of times "right in Vancouver."[36] But the newspapers pointed out that these victims were fellow Chinese Canadians—not whites.

As in the mid-nineteenth century, the Chinese were much more likely to be depicted as victims than as perpetrators in violent interracial confrontations. The *Oregonian* asserted that Chinese American gamblers almost always ran away or "took their arrest philosophically" rather than fighting back.[37] Likewise, the *Seattle Daily Times* described how steamship officers using just "clubs and fists" had "waded into" and put to flight a "band of blood-crazed," knife-wielding "coolies."[38] An *Oregon Daily Journal* story seemed still more unlikely. It recounted how two Portland policemen surprised "35 celestials" engaged in gambling. One of the officers went for help, while the other, drawing his gun, managed to hold the rest "at bay." Then, "after 15 minutes of commotion, weeping and wailing, the officers tied the 35 prisoners by the hands and led them away to headquarters."[39] The account described the men's physical impotence manifesting itself in a feminine display of frustration.

This purported physical cowardice did not render the Chinese innocuous to newspaper writers; their supposed capacity to degrade white people bequeathed to them a potency of sorts. A correspondent to the *Province* complained in 1907 that "it was absolutely impossible to pass through Chinatown after dark without being accosted every few steps" by "wily curbstoners" trying to draw one into illegal "gambling joints."[40] Indeed, a Vancouver police officer remarked in 1908 that "we have more trouble with Chinamen than with any other class in the community."[41] A Portland newspaper article entitled "EVIL CHINESE CURBED" quoted a police official who warned parents that "certain of the Chinese" were "teaching Oriental vices to young boys and girls," namely smoking opium. "Numerous instances have been heard of recently in which girls were sent on the downward path by the Chinese" through the "body and soul-destroying drug."[42] Likewise, a *Province* story on three Chinese Canadians accused of sexually assaulting a five-year-old girl noted that it was "another warning against the danger of allowing female children to become familiar with Chinese servants," for this was "by no means the first case of the kind."[43] Such descriptions suggested that the cowardly, unimposing Chinese were surreptitiously eating away at the underbelly of respectable society. But explicit acts of violence played a very small role in that purported threat.

The newspapers found the Japanese more dangerous than the Chinese. One writer argued that "a Chinese coolie is satisfied to remain one. . . . He is content to be a gardener, a cook, a scavenger or whatever nature designed him for, and to remain one." But the Japanese Canadian "sets up for himself" as soon as possible, for "it is not only the coarser forms of labor the Jap aspires to." "Let the Jap have full fling in this country," the writer warned, "and in a few years he will soon change the complexion of the Province from white to brown."[44] Later in 1907 the same publication, the *British Columbia Saturday Sunset,* cited Japanese Canadians' "aggressiveness, pugnacity and . . . utter disregard for the rights of others" as traits that might enable them "to overrun the country."[45] "Let Japan have all the credit due her as a rising and powerful nation," remarked the *Sunset,* "but let her might and power be exercised where it belongs, in the Orient." British Columbia's Japanese immigrants, like the Chinese and the Hindus, had to be tolerated "until we can do without them, and the man . . . who can show this Province how to dispense with Oriental labor and keep Orientals out of the Province will be its greatest benefactor in every sense in which the word can be written."[46]

People of Japanese descent constituted a much smaller proportion of the populations of Seattle and Portland, and those cities' newspapers did not expend as much ink on them as Vancouver's did. Yet they occasionally echoed some of the same attitudes. The *Seattle Mail and Herald,* a weekly, referred to "the coolie Jap" as "a peaceable-looking little beast" who was in fact "a treacherous animal, quick to anger, vicious and revengeful."[47] Portland's *Journal* warned in a 1908 editorial that the Japanese love of native land made them uniquely dangerous: "It is not as individuals in a detached sense that they are egotistical, persistent, valorous, inquisitive, pugnacious, polite and unscrupulous, but as citizens of Nippon." "If a Japanese lived here 100 years he would still be thoroughly Japanese," and "in no sense or degree American."[48] A letter writer to the *Journal* paired Japan's military successes with the attempts of Japanese Americans to gain equal educational opportunities for their children, suggesting that the latter was a sort of unarmed invasion, an aggressive act by a people who were intrinsically inferior, but whose innate aggressiveness made them capable of defeating white opponents.[49]

Newspapers described Japanese men as being much more physically dangerous than their Chinese counterparts. To be sure, occasional stories referred to them in such terms as "little brown culprit."[50] But newspapers also fashioned headlines like "SAVAGE JAPS TRY TO KILL WHITE FOREMAN" and "MURDEROUS JAP WIELDED RAZOR."[51] A *Province* story on a Japanese Canadian who attacked some Chinese Canadian residents of Vancouver bore the headline: "WANTED BLOOD. Warlike Jap Thirsting For Gore and Pig-Tails."[52] The newspapers asserted that violent Japanese men threatened whites, as well. The *Province's* account of two Vancouver police officers' attempts to subdue "a demented Jap" armed with a long knife dwelled on the culprit's skill. The pair were able to disarm T. Fumu, but only with great effort and risk, for he was "an expert swordsman and fencer."[53] Fears of a Japanese attack were most palpable during the Vancouver Riot of 1907, when a mob of whites smashed the stores of first Chinese Canadians and then Japanese Canadians. The *Journal's* headlines emphasized the dangers that the Japanese posed, not the white men who had instigated the conflict. "JAPANESE MOB ATTACKS WHITES WITH SANDBAGS," read one; "VANCOUVER JAPS ARE ORGANIZED AND ARMED," warned another. A few days later it asserted that the contagion had spread to Portland: "LOCAL JAPS ARE ARMED."[54]

Japanese immigrants, then, were feared as well as scorned. A *Seattle Post-Intelligencer* story entitled "TESTED JIU-JITSU UPON WHITE WIFE" expressed whites' deepest fears. It described in great detail the purported cruelty of a Japanese man who had gained the upper hand over his "American wife." He had battered her "until her wrists were almost broken" and nearly twisted "her shoulder blades . . . from their sockets." To make matters worse, Mary Tanaka had no idea when her inscrutable husband would inflict such punishments. So terrified had she become of these unpredictable tortures "that whenever the wife thought she had aggrieved her husband she walked over to him and handed him her wrist, preferring immediate punishment to waiting around for it in apprehension."[55] The story's moral was clear: this was the sort of predicament that white men and women alike could expect to find themselves in if Japanese immigrants overran their city.

The violence of unfamiliar European immigrant groups also elicited concern. Newspapers especially associated Italians with violence. A *Province* piece on an Italian Canadian man found seriously wounded bore the headline "STABBED IN USUAL WEEK-END BRAWL." It explained that these "foreigners" habitually drank on Saturdays and Sundays and then usually engaged in "a free fight of a more or less serious nature."[56] The *Province* liked to identify the ethnicity of violent immigrants in its headlines: "ITALIANS FOUGHT WITH STILETTOES," "ITALIANS IN A STABBING AFFRAY," and "ROUGH HOUSE AT AN ITALIAN WEDDING."[57] "ITALIAN ATTACKS WOMEN" preceded a story on a "crazed foreigner."[58] Seattle newspapers were not as apt as Vancouver's to identify violent people's ethnicity in their headlines, but they often did so in the text. A story on Basqualla Mariella's shooting of Earl Young, for example, repeatedly referred to him as "the Italian."[59]

These articles often described Italians' violence as unpredictable and irrational. The *Seattle Post-Intelligencer* explained that a "desperate fight" in "an Italian lodging house," which left one of the principals with a dangerous knife wound, began because two men "came home late at night, waking up the two babies of Raphael Columbo . . . and persisted in smoking in the parlor."[60] "FIVE-CENT POOL GAME CHARGE ANGERS ITALIAN," read the *Oregonian* headline for a story on an "unknown Italian" who punctured Michael Ram's lung with a stiletto in an argument in a Portland saloon.[61] Disappointment in love was the most common motive offered for Italians' murderous assaults. A *Journal* piece on Frank Guglielmo, killer of Freda Garacia, claimed that Guglielmo attributed the crime to "the passion of his race" which had "swept over him."[62] A *Province* article entitled "CRAZED ITALIAN SHOT WOMAN AND HIMSELF" identified "insane infatuation" as the cause of a murder-suicide in Seattle. One Pastor Valentine, "a son of sunny Italy," had fallen "wildly in love with one of Italy's daughters." "He pleaded as only an Italian can," and when the widow remained steadfast in her refusal, he shot and killed her before turning the gun on himself.[63] A *Province* headline on a murder-suicide in Vancouver bore the headline: "LOVE-CRAZED ITALIAN KILLS SWEETHEART."[64] According to newspapers, Italians' violence was both embedded in their makeup and almost always aimed at other Italians.

As with the Chinese, newspapers often seemed more concerned over Italian criminality than with violence per se. The *Province* published a lengthy story on the Sicilian mafia in 1909 that remarked that the institution, "devoted practically to combatting justice," could "have but one result, that of encouraging criminality."[65] Other stories described knifings associated with the "Black Hand" or mafia, an Italian organization involved in extortion and other types of organized crime.[66]

Newspapers argued that Italians' criminality and aggressiveness made them un-Canadian or un-American. Vancouver's pro-labor *Western Call* claimed that this "alien race" committed "a very large percentage of violent crimes" and would "take a lot of assimilation before they become good citizens."[67] A piece in the Vancouver *Sunset* asserted that "a couple of dago contractors" were jeopardizing "lives and property." It went on to describe how the contractors' use of dynamite near R. D. Rorison's home had shattered its windows and threw stones and mud into its rooms, nearly killing the owner's wife and child. The men engaged in the blasting were reportedly unconcerned, an attitude that infuriated the *Sunset*. "If you don't move out of your own home at the dictation of a greasy dago," the editorialist remarked, "he says he will blawa you up and if you getta da kill datta alle same your own fault." "The lives and property of citizens" were being endangered by these aggressive foreigners.[68] A *Province* article entitled "BLASTING ITALIANS WRECK RESIDENCE" commented on the same incident and asserted that "the laborers from the land of macaroni and malistas were exceedingly haughty, even impudent" in speaking to the police about the matter.[69] Such men were in Canada, not of it.

Vancouver, Portland, and Seattle newspapers characterized several other ethnic groups as aggressive and exotic outsiders. Headlines identified violent Greeks, Spaniards, Russians, Jews, Irishmen, Belgians, a "TERRIBLE DANE," and an "INSANE GERMAN."[70] Different meant peculiar. Court reports from the *Province*, for example, made reference to a drunken Swede "with an unspellable name" and a German complainant "who owns a name that took up two lines on the information he swore to."[71]

Unfamiliarity commonly bred contempt, particularly of Russian immigrants. A *Journal* headline identified a group of them in Portland as "FOREIGN THUGS," and the article described them as "part of a gang that infests Lower Albina."[72] An *Oregonian* article on Henry Shafer, one of three Portland wife beaters to be whipped under Oregon's whipping-post law, identified him as "a gigantic Russian, who weighs at least 250 pounds," before describing how he "ferociously attacked" his spouse.[73] The *Province*, two weeks before publishing its extensive story on the Sicilian mafia, presented a long piece on political affairs in Russia in which it quoted "an old Russian exile" on the barbaric conditions there: "It is impossible for the Englishman, sitting at home in his comfortable armchair, to realize that in the twentieth century, and in Europe, too, there lives a nation steeped in the miseries and oppression that one reads of in Mediaeval history."[74] It hardly needed to be pointed out that peoples from this nation were making their way to the north Pacific slope, and newspapers depicted their exoticism, sadism, and destructiveness as being of a single piece.

Violence by the Irish, a much more familiar ethnic group by the turn of the century, struck newspaper writers as more humorous than dangerous. They particularly liked to quote their accounts of fights. A *Province* article recorded Sydney Kenwater's rendition of a "scrap" in a Chinese restaurant: "The two Chinamen 'it me with a chair, Yer Honner. . . . I bowled one of them hover with me fist. I dashed for the door, and in some way they struck against hit an 'it hit. Four or five of them pursued me, sir, through the door, sir, and me a-runnin' hup the halley as 'ard as hever I could."[75] A brief piece in the *Vancouver Daily News Advertiser* recounted an "amusing ten minutes" in the city's police court when "Mrs. Cormier, a lady with an Irish temper," defended herself from assault charges.[76] Likewise, the *Seattle Mail and Herald* recounted a quarrel between "Mike" and his red-haired wife in which the latter belted an overly curious male onlooker and informed her intoxicated husband that it was "luck to ye, Moike Casey it wasn't yersilf that got it."[77] A *Province* story described how Jimmie Ryan, "a big Irishman, with a bad court record," pointed a gun at two Italians who had been sitting in a restaurant "joking together over a combination of spagetti Italienne, coffee Anglaise, and a petite opera bouffe porkio et maka de rone de beano on the side." Ryan explained to the police magistrate that he meant no harm and was merely having some fun: "Begorra, whin yiz pints a goon at a man, yez don't allus mane nurthin', becus it mayn't be lothened."[78] Many descriptions from the mid-nineteenth century had depicted truculent Irishmen as dangerous. But their descendants seemed harmless.

People of African descent had resided on the north Pacific slope for as long as the Irish, but turn-of-the-century newspapers described their violence much differently. They typically identified the race of Black perpetrators in their headlines and often went on to describe particularly vicious attacks. A Seattle story entitled "SHOT AFTER APOLOGIZING" described how an African American cook first demanded an apology from one Harry Lewis at gunpoint and then wounded him after receiving it.[79] An *Oregon Daily Journal* article recounted how a "murderous negro wielded his knife with maniacal frenzy" in subjecting a white longshoreman to "a savage onslaught."[80] For the *Mail and Herald,* one of Seattle's opinionated weeklies, such acts underscored the alien nature of African Americans. "Two 'Coons' met in a dark alley of this city the other night and proceeded to do each other up in a truly artistic 'Coon' style, with razors," the writer remarked. "How they live I do not know."[81] Ignorance, it seems, was a virtue when it came to understanding Blacks. But lack of knowledge did not preclude making some sweeping generalizations about the relationship between race and violence. "As a class," another piece asserted, "the negro has not the moral force to control his baser passions."[82]

Vancouver newspapers were less shrill in their descriptions of Blacks. The *Saturday Sunset* remarked that "the negro is about one-tenth as undesirable as the Jap or Chinaman."[83] Stories of Black people's criminality were as apt to provoke laughter as fear. The *Province* related how one John Lewis exhibited his ignorance by telling the police court that he "came here from Canada," having most recently lived in Kansas. He explained the "ugly-looking butcher knife" that police found on his person by stating that he used it "for cutting shoestrings."[84] Likewise, the *Province* quoted Charles Thompson's reaction to being charged with carrying a concealed revolver: "I had me coat off and de handle of de revolver, it stuck up, and was in plain sight. . . . it wuzn't co'sealed noways whatever, Jedge, Yer Honah."[85] Newspapers' accounts of Blacks' dialect and attempts to exonerate themselves made their violence seem silly and childish, not dangerous. But even Vancouver's opinion makers took Black men's violence toward white women seriously. A *Province* article described how a white woman appeared in police court "with large welts on her neck . . . where her negro mate had clinched his long, bony fingers." It noted that the judge had asked a question that many readers no doubt shared: "How did you ever happen to marry a black man?"[86]

Class did not figure as prominently as ethnicity in newspaper accounts of violence, but it was far from insignificant. Working-class violence was of course most prominently featured during strikes. But stories describing more isolated acts of violence commonly emphasized that the principals were men who worked with their hands. Headlines identified violent men as fishermen, loggers, railway workers, sailors, longshoremen, blacksmiths, teamsters, firemen, and a "Discharged Laborer."[87] "GARBAGE COLLECTOR AND DRAY-MAN FIGHT," read a *Province* headline.[88] Newspapers occasionally drew inferences between crime and occupation more explicitly. The *Province* asserted in 1905 that "the return of the fishermen is reflected in the increased activity in police circles."[89] The *Seattle Mail and Herald's* piece on "The Seattle Hoodlum" equated criminality with class; such people used "cheap tobacco" and wore "dirty clothes" or "bargain sale finery."[90] Crudeness of dress dovetailed with crudeness of morals in these accounts.

If newspapers depicted violence erupting naturally and easily from immigrant and working-class men, violent criminal acts by the well-to-do required an explanation. Some newspaper stories on wealthy men's criminality were simply descriptive or recounted their attempts to escape punishment by trading on their high social and economic position. But treatments of murders by prominent men strained to explain how a respectable person could commit such an act. Roscoe James, son of the Oregon State Penitentiary's superintendent, in 1907 killed the young woman he loved and then himself. The *Oregonian* at first asserted that the woman's "fickleness" had "goaded" James "to desperation" and that his previous "escapades" had been "merely boyish pranks."[91] The following day it decided that James was the fickle one, a "typical wayward boy" who had caused his prominent parents "much trouble."[92] The *Journal* focused on James's mental state, remarking that he was "crazed by his love" for the young woman he killed and "insanely jealous" of her.[93] Another 1907 murder-suicide occurred when Harry Liebe, a jeweler, killed his estranged wife and then himself. The *Oregonian* described Liebe as "maddened" by his spouse's refusal to live with him. But it suggested that the ultimate cause lay in his family's peculiar psychology. A cousin had killed an uncle and committed suicide in 1893, and two other family members had killed themselves. The prominent Liebe family contained "a suicidal mania."[94] Seattle newspapers included similar stories. When John Hiestand Tripple, son of a mining company president, killed his wife Lydia, the *Post-Intelligencer* quoted two people on the murderer's damaged mental state.[95] Violent passions, according to the newspapers, were more or less endemic to marginalized urban residents, such as the Italians or Japanese. Among the well-to-do, such acts were anomalies created by rare genetic flaws or powerful but temporary impulses.

Police court records are also useful for gauging how community leaders assessed the potency of various groups. Both Portland's and Vancouver's have survived. The thick ledgers listing those accused, the charges against them, and complainants offer seemingly exhaustive accounts of violent crime. The historian who devotes day after tedious day to wading through these interminable volumes would certainly like to believe so. But most assaults generated no arrests, and those that did were not random samples. Arrests depended on the proximity and willingness of a peace officer to intervene and often on the readiness of complainants to lay a charge.[96] Police courts, the urban equivalent of justice courts, were consequently populated largely by men of little status, people who carried out their quarrels in public or semi-public areas: saloons, streets, and boardinghouses. Hence a Vancouver resident who described himself as "an obviously respectable man" complained to the city's police commissioners that people like himself should not, in the unlikely "case of a dispute with a constable," be "made to consort with the dregs of humanity until he is either bailed out or his case dismissed the following morning."[97] Likewise, the *Oregonian* referred to the novelty of a physician appearing among the usual collection of "vagrants, drunkards and beggars" in Portland's police court.[98] Indeed, "laborer" was the occupation listed for 82 of 299 people charged with assault in Portland during a ten-month period in 1910. Men with prestigious occupations were much more scarce: two real estate agents, one physician, one insurance agent, one editor, and one attorney.[99]

In sum, arrests for simple assault, like the newspaper stories discussed above, tell us little about people's actual violent behavior. But such records are useful for telling us how law-enforcement officials defined and punished violent crime.

Ethnicity and gender clearly influenced sentencing. This was particularly so in Portland. If one discards the murky "discharged" category, most defendants received a fine. African American men received by far the highest average ones, $62.88. Immigrant, non-Asian males were next, at $30.05, not much above the average of $25.75 for white, native-born men. Asian men were fined an average of just $12.50, women of all ethnicities just $11.47.[100] Vancouver magistrates were much more consistent in their treatment of men and women. They sentenced non-Asian males to an average of 17.8 days for assaults, women to 13.3 days.[101] But they took violence by people of Chinese or Japanese ancestry much more seriously than did their Portland counterparts, sentencing such men to an average of 32.2 days in jail.[102]

Nor were arrests spread evenly over the population. Women constituted less than 7 percent of the Vancouver arrestees, less than 6 percent of Portland's. Asians were arrested at a rate that approximated their proportion of the cities' population. But African Americans constituted about 0.5 percent of Portland's population and African American men alone were 3.9 percent of those arrested. Foreign-born, non-Asian immigrants constituted about 21 percent of Portland's population and 29 percent of its arrestees.[103]

In general, these variations in arrests and sentencing mirrored the attitudes reflected in Portland and Vancouver newspapers. Most obviously, both the number of arrests made and the sentences handed out suggested that violence by women was relatively harmless and violence toward women relatively noxious. Violence by people of Chinese or Japanese descent elicited a much more mixed response; Vancouver magistrates imposed relatively stiff sentences for such violence. Asians constituted a much smaller proportion of Portland's population, and that city's magistrates imposed relatively light fines on them. Non-Asian immigrants cannot be easily identified in Vancouver's arrest records. Portland magistrates fined such men a bit more heavily than their American-born counterparts. But the highest arrest rates and average fines by far were inflicted on Portland's tiny complement of African Americans, a group that its newspapers commonly associated with violent criminality.[104]

This association of violence with blackness was no coincidence. Whites commonly categorized African Americans as the quintessential outsiders, the unassimilable aliens who could never become respectable.

Indeed, the north Pacific slope's newspapers commonly attributed criminal violence to strangers. British Columbians were most prone to make this claim. A *Province* editorial recounted Judge Begbie's heroic work in crime suppression "when the valley of the Fraser and the creeks of Cariboo swarmed with desperadoes . . . from every part of the world." Now, a half century later, British Columbia's rapid settlement made it inevitable that the province would "acquire an undesirable element," particularly "criminals from across the boundary."[105] Five years before, in 1904, a *Province* article remarking on an increase in crime over the past six months asserted that the police court docket revealed "beyond possibility of dispute that a large proportion of the offenders are recent arrivals from the other side of the line."[106] The Vancouver Moral Reform Association worried in 1906 that the San Francisco fire had driven large numbers "of the low, the vicious, and the immoral" northward.[107] Respectable

Vancouverites were particularly worried over their close proximity to Puget Sound, for a criminal who "was even run out of Seattle" was a tough charac-ter, indeed.[108] By the same token, Seattle and Portland police pointed out that many of their criminals came from elsewhere, particularly California. Moral depravity, like the temperature, apparently rose as one traveled southward. Cities could also be infected by their rural hinterlands. Loggers were perhaps the most notorious examples, as they commonly punctuated their isolated labors with trips to cities for bouts of drinking, whoring, and general hell raising. The *Vancouver Daily World* quoted a man charged in the city's police court with drunkenness as explaining that he had just returned from the north, where "things are run differently."[109] Likewise, an *Oregonian* article on a murder in a Portland rooming house remarked that the killer and his companion "present types seen in the remote rural districts who resort to gunplay over trivialities."[110] Tramps were automatically suspect. The *Oregonian* in 1900 noted that holdups had become rare "as the police department has been active and vigilant in round-ing up the hobos and thugs and ordering them to leave town."[111]

Newspapers also underscored the marginality of violent criminals by asso-ciating them with the most marginal areas of their cities. Seattle's pointed out that violent altercations occurred in its "tenderloin district," and head-lines identified "THE VICE DISTRICT," a "DIVE SALOON," and a "notori-ous resort."[112] Portland headlines commonly noted that crimes had occurred in the city's dilapidated north end, and Vancouver's pointed out violent acts from its east end, which housed "shacks . . . well known to the police."[113] The *Province* cited an even more noxious, though smaller, area in a story on the mysterious death of a Native woman. "Tar flats" had "been occupied as a rancherie and camping-place by the lowest class of Siwashes and half breeds ever since Vancouver has existed," and had seen numerous "orgies and fights."[114] Areas thickly populated by new arrivals were also depicted as dangerous. On the other hand, an attack on a prominent wealthy woman in Portland's exclusive Irvington section reportedly threw its "conservative atmosphere" into uncharacteristic "excitement and consternation."[115] Violence and respectability were supposed to be mutually exclusive.

Major newspapers in Seattle, Portland, and Vancouver consistently depicted violent criminals as outsiders. Marginality predicted criminality.

This is not to say that all marginal groups were deemed physically potent.

The violence of women and children was of little consequence, was simply laughable. The Chinese were much less familiar, and the newspapers identified their moral habits as a threat to their readers. But their purported cowardice undercut that threat and illustrated their inferiority. They were described as cunning, not manly. The violence of Japanese Canadians, African Americans, and new European immigrants, on the other hand, was depicted as potent and corrosive—alarming, not amusing. Dominant discourses around marginalized people's violence denied or exaggerated their power, illustrating their inherent impotence or organic brutality.

Horace Cayton's *Seattle Republican* expressed a radically different view of marginalized people's violence. Cayton expected no privileges for his fellow African Americans. But he demanded fairness. "Let the law take its course . . . whether the criminal be white or black," was his motto.[116] He, or someone writing for him, also suggested a reason for marginalized people's violence that other newspapers assiduously ignored. The *Republican* related how "a well-known colored man" of Seattle had wreaked a great deal of havoc in the city's eating and drinking establishments by breaking up dishes and glasses, knocking one man unconscious, and drawing a gun on another. To other newspapers, such acts simply illustrated the innate and irrational barbarity of even the most prominent African American. But the *Republican* had a different interpretation. It pointed out that this ordinarily "peaceful" man became aggressive only when "some one draws the color line on him."[117] A Black man's violence could not be understood aside from the social context in which he lived, including racism and discrimination.

The *Seattle Republican* is an exceptional historical source. Since history belongs to the winners, to the powerful, most extant descriptions of oppressed people's violence comes to us from those who neither fathomed nor wanted to fathom the daunting difficulties confronting a Japanese Canadian in Vancouver, an African American in Seattle. Outsiders therefore remained strange and exotic, people to be laughed at or feared—not understood.

To Do Just as He Pleased

Violence in the 1920s

YOUNG RUTH JONES had never seen anything like it. As she lay watching in the shadows of an eastern Oregon orchard, Sam Delaney, a cowboy, confronted the charming LeVeq. LeVeq threatened Delaney; Delaney called his bluff. The two turned to each other, "stripped of their birthrights of centuries and eons—as in an earlier and more primeval gloom hairy shapes had faced each other, teeth bared." The woman from the East found the scene "appalling." "Never before in her sheltered life had she seen two men face each other in just that way."

Ruth Jones had a lot to learn about the West. Here good triumphed over evil not when honorable men went to the law or turned the other cheek, but when they screwed up their courage and literally beat bad men down. By the close of Robert Ormond Case's *Riders of the Grande Ronde,* the unassuming Delaney had rescued Ruth Jones from the villainous LeVeq after battering and squeezing him into submission. He had also won her heart.[1]

Other male novelists across the north Pacific slope were telling the same sort of story by the 1920s. The ideal man was skilled with fist or gun; his moral courage manifested itself in a willingness to hurt and be hurt, to kill and be killed. Men hit and shot each other frequently—and with good reason. Women at first objected, then capitulated. Victorian platitudes about self-restraint melted away in the face of this new, violent man.

Yet accounts of people's actual lives on the north Pacific slope indicate very different trends. Violence between male peers in fact continued to decline in the 1920s and became more, not less, regulated. Protagonists were more likely to face each other across the line of scrimmage of a football field than across the dusty streets of a cow town. Acts of unregulated violence increasingly occurred in a highly private venue, within the family, where men hit not each other, but their sons, daughters, and wives. Male violence had a life outside the covers of male adventure novels. But it was women and children, not powerful peers, who increasingly bore its brunt.

British Columbia and the Pacific Northwest lost much of their distinctiveness in the early twentieth century. Virtually every corner of the north Pacific slope had joined modern society by the 1920s. The combined population of the province and two states exceeded three million by the decade's close, nearly triple what it had been thirty years before. These people tended to live close to each other. More than four out of every ten British Columbians resided in greater Vancouver by 1930, when about one-half of Washington's population lived in places with more than ten thousand people. Technological changes accelerated the spread of an urban ethos. Telephones, automobiles, and airplanes shrank distances as movies and radios homogenized culture. These mediums helped spread an ethos of self-realization and the pursuit of pleasure across the map. Government also increasingly made its way into people's lives, particularly in British Columbia, where the welfare state began expanding well before the Depression's onset. In Washington and Oregon, too, the government routinely affected people's lives through swelling school enrollments, Prohibition, and closer regulation of child rearing. By the 1920s the outlines of what some would later term "mass society" were very discernible on the north Pacific slope. Men and women were more apt to pursue self-fulfillment than ever before, in spite or because of living in an increasingly regulated society.[2]

These changes profoundly affected the ways in which people approached violence. Men, in particular, hoped that violence would compensate for the growing regulation and domestication of their lives. Leading North Americans alarmed by modernity's emasculating tendencies had prescribed violent sports, among other cures, around the century's turn, and activities like boxing, lacrosse, and football had become popular and respectable middle-class pastimes on the north Pacific slope by the 1920s.[3]

Yet these sports bore the imprint of the very strictures that so many men were chafing against. Indeed, middle-class men did not want to kick over the traces of civilized society altogether. They assured each other that the structured, controlled nature of their violence set them apart from mere brawlers. Arthur Mayse, the son of a Baptist minister in Nanaimo, recalled that at the end of his first day of school a crowd of boys that included the "tough son of a Welsh coal miner" initiated him into fistfighting. His father countered by teaching Arthur and some of his friends how to box, a style of combat more appropriate for a minister's son—although some of the boys' mothers thought not.[4] Likewise, a teacher in the Peace River country of British Columbia who had a "YMCA background in boxing" let two of his students who had started to fight each other at recess "go to it, but stood by to referee fair play and prevent any real damage."[5] These boys were allowed and even encouraged to hit each other—but only within the constraints of rules established and enforced by adults.

The first football game played in Goldendale, Washington, aptly illustrates the transition from unregulated to regulated violence. As the game commenced, onlookers reportedly poured onto the field "to such an extent that it was impossible for the referee to distinguish players from spectators." The audience learned that they had to stay off the gridiron, but some became so "imbued with [the] spirit of the game" that "they raced back and forth on the side lines to keep in close contact with the plays." Late in the game one of them, exercised that the visitors from The Dalles were "using unfair tactics in making such a vigorous effort to keep" the home team from crossing the goal line, picked a fight with an opposing player. Goldendale at last scored during the fracas, and "a rough and tumble free for all fight" nearly ensued.[6]

A quarter century later, in the 1920s, violent but highly structured games were a common part of boys' educations. Physical education, particularly boxing and team athletics such as cricket, rugby, and soccer, were key components to building character in British Columbia's private schools in the early twentieth century. Over three thousand students received regular military training in the province's public educational institutions by 1923. Educational institutions across North America used sports to build a sense of social solidarity, not to mention bureaucratic regimentation. Highly regulated, team-oriented activities prepared young males for lives of service in hierarchical governments and corporations. But sports also offered release to middle-class boys chafing at the constraints of a prolonged adolescence spent toiling away within the tedious confines of stultifying schools. A man who grew up in western Oregon recalled that football taught him "fellowship," "teamwork," and "discipline," but, more important still, stood out among all his high school activities in offering "the chance to put myself wholeheartedly into something, to do it with all my might, to give of my very best effort."[7]

Popular fiction of the 1920s also indicated respectable men's growing interest in violence, even in British Columbia. Alex Philip's novel *The Painted Cliff* exemplifies the association of physical and moral power. Peter, convalescing from World War I at the book's opening, eventually beats the evil, bull-like Morlock to a pulp during a bloody contest in which each peeled away the "thin veneer of civilization, battling with the elemental hate and fury of his cave-dwelling forebears." The fiction of Bertrand W. Sinclair and Robert Watson is more complex; their heroes have flaws, their villains are not without virtue. Nor do the protagonists win all of their fights, even those at or near the close of the novel. But they are, to a man, muscular and imposing. Physical strength alone does not ensure their success, but a man is not a man without the courage and capacity to test his fists and body against powerful adversaries.[8]

The growing literary affection for violence was still more apparent south of the border. If physical self-restraint had symbolized masculine self-control in Balch's *Bridge of the Gods* during the 1890s, the capacity to use violence marked the self-realization of heroic men three decades later. This theme was most consistently represented in westerns, a genre inaugurated by Owen Wister's *Virginian* at the century's turn. Ernest Haycox was the Pacific Northwest's leading writer in this genre and published his first western, *Free Grass*, in the late 1920s. Set on the expansive Great Plains rather than the forested hills of the author's home, this novel follows the violent coming of age of Tom Gillette after he returns to the West from the feminized and emasculating East. Other Oregon adventure writers told essentially the same tale. In *The Splendid Summits*, Charles Alexander's young protagonist, Esper, finds in the Oregon Cascade mountains a massive, cruel adversary on which to forge his manhood. Esper wins the final confrontation with a "man's blow" that contained "all hurt and all pride, all things done to him when he groped, a wavering boy."[9] Likewise, Edison Marshall's *The Isle of Retribution* traces the history of a morally and physically flaccid young Portland man who becomes hardened by physical labor on a remote North Pacific island. Ned Cornet gains his masculine birthright and his freedom at book's close when he overpowers Doomsdorf, the animal-like Russian trapper who had held him captive.

Other novels, like Haycox's *Chaffee of Roaring Horse* and Case's *Riders of the Grande Ronde*, feature heroes who had become larger than life well before the novel's first page. Unlike their British Columbian counterparts, these men are simply incapable of losing a fight, for their physical and moral superiority are completely bound up with each other.[10]

These authors were not simply appeasing popular tastes. They believed what they wrote. Alexander, a newspaperman in the Willamette Valley, prided himself on being a fellow who knew his way in the woods, warning a friend to "think well before pilgrimaging with me," for "I'm rough in most every way you can imagine." He urged this companion to wear a pistol on a hike: "You never know what you'll meet."[11] James Stevens, a much more sophisticated writer than Alexander, knew only too well that pistols were no longer needed in western Oregon by the 1920s. In *Brawny-Man* and a collection of short stories called *Homer in the Sagebrush*, Stevens celebrated the raw, premodern Pacific Northwest of the nineteenth century. His heroes are decidedly less wholesome than Alexander's or Haycox's, but they are just as violent. For Stevens, physical strength and the courage to use one's fists are part of a normal, healthy young male's makeup. These men are threatened not by anything so clear-cut as a dastardly villain; right and wrong, good and bad are slippery and often inverted in his work. The only evil force is modern life itself. Indeed, in a letter to H. L. Mencken in 1923 he recalled with patent fondness his childhood among people "as remote from civilization as the Neanderthals, and praise god, . . . as remote as they from the safety expert and the cock-eyed democrat." It had been "a hard violent life." But the Pacific Northwest of 1923 was "regimented," plagued by newspapers and movies, peopled by laborers who had become "slaves, serfs, unworried, full-bellied."[12] Most writers of masculine fiction south and north of the border alike seemed much less concerned about the incursions of modernity. Indeed, a number of them featured heroes who were adept both with their fists and at making money, men who were abetting the very forces that Stevens abhorred. But Stevens and his less sophisticated counterparts agreed on this: a man who was not a good fighter was not much of a man.

Stevens's association of progress with pacification was accurate, for men of the 1920s were still most apt to fight other men in places where women, children, and other modern amenities were scarce. Sam Churchill lived in a

remote coastal Oregon logging camp from his birth in 1911 until 1922. He
recalled Saturday night dances and Sunday baseball games regularly punctuated by fights. "It was just logger exuberance," his aunt Blanche explained.[13]
A sociologist studying Shevlin-Hixon, an eastern Oregon logging community of some eight hundred people, recorded "not infrequent" feuds. "These
people often take offense at the least provocation," he explained, "and even
the mention that one does not like the taste of another's beer may lead to
serious developments."[14] The same pattern prevailed in British Columbia. A
policeman at a 1921 rodeo in Williams Lake, a new town in the Cariboo, could
do little more than keep the large numbers of brawling men away from its
business area and from "breaking windows."[15] A woman who came to Fort
St. John in northeastern British Columbia in 1929, when the town consisted
of "about a dozen wooden shanties, vaguely sprung up on each side of a
straight mud road," remarked that a local dance had been "pretty typical of
the bad sort of Fort St. John revels. Most of the men got drunk and before
the end were brawling and fighting, and the one police officer of the district
was far too drunk himself to interfere."[16] But logging camps and cow towns,
though common enough in male adventure novels, were becoming more
scarce by the 1920s.

Acts of extreme violence between adults in fact became more infrequent
as the region's population became more settled. Oregon's homicide rate had
been 6.3 per hundred thousand in 1895. In the 1920s it declined to 4.5.
Washington's rate was only slightly higher, at 5.1. British Columbia's rate
plunged from 5.9 per hundred thousand in the 1890s to just 2.7 three decades
later. Roger Lane explains that the homicide rate in the United States continued its downward trend during the first decades of the twentieth century
because "the ongoing urban industrial revolution was still demanding . . .
rational regimented behavior."[17] This decline was more pronounced on the
north Pacific slope and in British Columbia in particular than elsewhere
because the modern economy and the culture which it bred had only recently
taken root. The rate therefore had more distance to fall.[18]

Novelists of the 1920s celebrated spontaneous, masculine violence much
more readily than had their counterparts from the 1890s. Yet such violence
remained common only on the margins of modern society, and the rate of
extreme violence continued to decline. Respectable men were more apt to

engage in violent sports and to read books celebrating violent heroes than their fathers or grandfathers had been. But they were less likely to fight or kill each other.

Other forms of public interpersonal violence were also falling. Violence toward schoolchildren was increasingly regulated and more rare. Like Foucault's penal reformers of a century before, educators were becoming professionalized, more devoted to inculcating obedience through subtler means than beatings and terror. A western Washington school board in 1918 adopted a code stating that teachers who "are most successful in controlling their pupils and maintaining good order without the use of corporal punishment" would, other factors being equal, receive preference in hiring and promotion.[19] Even a principal in remote Prince George, a town of under three thousand in northern British Columbia, argued against hitting juvenile delinquents. The editor of a small western Washington town was probably more typical of mainstream public opinion when he allowed that "moral suasion" was often "the best and most effectual means of making a good boy or girl," but that "a good application of the rod, if used with judgment, and not in anger," was at times "a surer method of bringing certain juveniles to a realization of their misdeeds."[20] Indeed, Washington law stipulated that "a parent or his authorized agent, a guardian, master, or teacher," could lawfully use force "to restrain or correct his child, ward, apprentice or scholar" if done "in a reasonable and moderate manner."[21] Canadian statute law, too, still gave "every parent, . . . schoolmaster or master" the right "to use force by way of correction towards any child, pupil or apprentice under his care, provided that such force is reasonable under the circumstances."[22] Local authorities sometimes disciplined teachers whose punishments exceeded "reasonable and moderate" bounds, although more than a few teachers continued to use violence extensively. But even former pupils who recalled frequent blows seldom mentioned severe beatings that left cuts or bruises. Teachers, for their part, described themselves as using corporal punishment rarely and reluctantly. A young instructor in northern British Columbia confided to her diary in the early 1920s: "A minute or so ago I did it. That which I was afraid would come: [I] strapped Constantine. . . . I believe I was as shaky as he but it had to be done."[23] Grace Brandt Martin complained to her diary that the eighth graders in her northeastern Oregon classroom were incorrigible: "Even the drastic methods of corporal punishment do not do the trick. I've tried it. What haven't I tried!"[24]

Most educators, like Martin, used physical punishment rarely, as a last resort. British Columbia Department of Education Annual Reports showed about thirty uses of corporal punishment per hundred students per year in the 1890s. By the early 1930s the figure had declined to less than ten per hundred for Vancouver schools. In one western Washington school only twelve out of thirty-one students had been struck during the 1922–1923 school year, a rate considered high.[25] These official counts no doubt missed some violent acts. Yet violence against schoolchildren was becoming both less common and less acceptable.

But if children were less likely than their parents and grandparents to face violence in public institutions, they were apparently as likely as ever to face it in the privacy of the home. Indeed, a man who grew up in a Washington coal-mining town recalled that "if you got a licking in school, you got two or three at home."[26] Tom McCall, who brought Oregon national attention as its unorthodox governor in the late 1960s and early 1970s, received frequent whippings with a shot-filled riding quirt wielded by his mother during his boyhood near Prineville. Richard Hugo, the poet, grew up just south of Seattle with grandparents who "subjected" him "to gratuitous beatings."[27] Beverly Cleary, the author of popular children's stories, spent her early years in the Willamette Valley town of McMinnville and recalled an early spanking for pulling a playmate from his chair. Less prominent men and women raised in the 1920s described more extreme punishments. Merritt Des Voigne's memoir of his eastern Washington childhood—artlessly entitled *Being Small Wasn't Bad At All*—remembered being slapped, beaten with a razor strop, and lashed in bed with a buggy whip. Phil Gaglardi, who became the mayor of Kamloops, British Columbia, recalled that his father had an "explosive temper" that he indulged by tying his children in chairs or lifting them by their ears, a practice that several times left the lobes of one of Phil's brothers "split and bleeding."[28]

Homicide statistics also indicated that violence toward children was becoming more extreme. According to newspaper reports, parents virtually never killed their children in the nineteenth century, aside from infanticides. From 1900 to 1910 Multnomah County coroners recorded the homicide of only one person between the ages of one and thirteen, just under 1 percent of the cases that included the victim's age. From 1908 to 1910 children aged one to nine accounted for 2.6 percent of the homicide victims in Washington.

In the 1920s the proportion had risen to just over 3 percent for Washington and Oregon combined.[29]

Extreme forms of violence toward children rose because of both children's and parents' behavior. Children were testing parental authority more than ever before. Popular culture had become more youth oriented, and teenagers increasingly socialized with their peers rather than with their families. Childhood, the years that sons and daughters spent under the authority of their mothers and fathers, had lengthened, and most adults still expected children to do as they were told. An eastern Oregon man illustrated a neighbor boy's good behavior by remarking: "I never saw him disobey his daddy in any way. He has always jumped every time he spoke to him."[30] More and more boys and girls were failing to meet these expectations and faced violence as a consequence. McCall's biographer asserts that Oregon's future governor "taunted" his mother knowing that it would bring a beating, "and often suffered the punishment with a satisfied smile."[31] But growing numbers of parents appeared to be hitting sons and daughters who were not challenging their authority, who were simply acting like children. A man wrote from the Willamette Valley to his mother-in-law in 1927 to complain that his wife beat their little boy, age five at the time of her divorce petition, "on the back with her hand as hard as she could hit him time and again just to satisfy her anger." When the child was "just learning to walk," for example, she "knocked him flat down on the floor for the only reason that he had come into the kitchen."[32] Infants were especially vulnerable to unreasonable violence, particularly, it seems, from their fathers. Divorce-seeking wives complained that their husbands beat, shook, or pinched their babies for crying. An eastern Oregon woman said that her son-in-law had beaten her granddaughter for refusing to nurse. A Willamette Valley woman recalled that her husband had declared that "he wasn't going to have that brat squalling any more" when their baby was but five days old and then "shook it hard several times." When she objected, he threw water into the infant's mouth every time the child began to cry. He also whipped this daughter with a ruler until she bled.[33] Another man, angry because his three-month-old would not sit still, reportedly crippled the baby's arm by twisting it.[34]

The great majority of punishments meted out by biological parents of the nineteenth century had been dispassionate and measured—a considered if arguably cruel response to specific acts of misbehavior. By the 1920s, increasing numbers of parents were attacking their children for no apparent reason, and with little restraint.

Indeed, some fathers' physical abuse shaded into sexual abuse. A fourteen-year-old British Columbia boy testified that his stepfather took him upstairs, "gave me a licking," a commonplace enough punishment, and then "made me sit on his cock."[35] Another British Columbia father admitted to having intercourse with his daughter over a period of four years, but claimed that he beat her not because she resisted his sexual overtures but "because I did not want her to go out." "I was very particular about my daughter," he explained.[36] Sexual intercourse constituted, for such men, the logical end of parental control. A British Columbia girl whose father had been having sex with her ever since she could remember noted that he had told her that "he wanted me to stay with him all my life and . . . to do just whatever he wanted." When she objected he asserted "that he had me and I was his own—soul and body." He then penetrated her.[37] Another British Columbia girl said that her stepfather "tried to make me get down on my knees and beg his pardon" when she slapped and pushed him for trying to rape her. When her mother "asked Daddy why he had licked me," he replied that his daughter "was a naughty girl."[38] Incest was so difficult for children to resist not simply because of differences in size and strength, but because fathers pursued it on the basis of their authority as the head of the family. Hence a girl told a British Columbia court that she had not reported her father's sexual abuse of her because "In the way of a father I obeyed him."[39]

The sexual abuse of children was not as exceptional as it seemed. To be sure, society did not openly countenance these acts. We know about these cases because the men who sexually assaulted these children were prosecuted. Yet many cases of incest went unreported. Some of the children in the above cases described relations that had gone undetected for many years. Nor was the sexualization of children confined to men who committed incest. A ten-year-old girl in British Columbia recalled a pimp telling her "that I was small and young and could make lots of money."[40] A Boy Scout leader on Vancouver Island combined the sexual abuse of two boys with fantasies of being hit in his own childhood. He asked the youngest to take off his pajamas, lay on his side, and pretend that he had done something wrong at boarding school before hitting him and forcing his penis between the boy's legs.[41] Incest and other forms of sexual abuse often emerged easily from unremarkable and seldom criticized types of interaction between men and children, particularly parents' widely respected right to control the lives of and inflict pain on their sons and daughters.

Dominance also shaped violent sexual relationships among adults. Rapists used violent imagery like "thrown it up her" or "gone off" to describe their orgasms, as if their ejaculations constituted a potent attack on women's bodies.[42] Sexual assault, like incest, could easily arise from unremarkable situations. A young British Columbia man who hit and raped a young teacher when she rebuffed him, for example, had been told by a fellow woodcutter that "he couldn't make love to the schoolteacher and make a date with her."[43] How quickly a seemingly innocent attempt to impress the local schoolteacher and perhaps steal a kiss had turned into something else. Likewise, the young men and women who testified at the trial of three Prince Rupert men charged with indecently assaulting a young domestic servant described much of what they saw as innocent horseplay. The complainant admitted that she had been to the park a number of times "smoking cigarettes and having a good time," and one of the witnesses said that he had seen her spooning with a number of young men there. Another noted that she and the defendants had been bumping each other playfully as they told her "how good looking she was." One of the young men then removed an unspecified article of her clothing. None of this seemed to strike any of the onlookers as untoward, and they walked away. A number of these witnesses soon heard her scream for help, but they had often heard her yell and did not think much of it. One nearby girl remarked, "I have already rescued one and I can't rescue another." The jury found the three defendants guilty in this instance.[44] But one wonders how many other young women hesitated to prosecute men for behavior that their peers felt was unremarkable.

Prostitutes were particularly vulnerable to men's violence. A British Columbia police officer arresting a young man for bruising and sexually assaulting a young woman reportedly told him that he should visit the town's red-light district "if he wanted to treat a girl like that."[45] A prostitute, by definition, could not be raped or otherwise abused.

Sexual violence threatened growing numbers of women outside the sex trade by the 1920s. Some divorce-seeking wives noted that their husbands had torn their clothes from them or spanked them. Late-nineteenth-century wives had described husbands who threatened or used violence to compel sexual intercourse. But violence itself had now become sexualized. A Willamette Valley woman, for example, complained not only that her husband insisted on gazing upon her naked body, but that he also, in the words of her divorce petition, "would handle the breasts of defendant in a rough and cruel manner" and bite them so that they remained painful for weeks on end.[46]

This sort of sexualized violence was part of a larger trend: like parents, increasing numbers of husbands were inflicting physical violence for reasons that were not, strictly speaking, instrumental, were not calculated simply to force a wife's obedience.[47]

Violence toward wives increased as its causes became more diffuse. In contrast to the 1890s, husbands now readily admitted to judges and to others that they hit their wives. Divorce-seeking wives less commonly described their husbands as using physical force reluctantly and more often as hitting frequently. This trend should not be exaggerated. It was one thing, many men seemed to be saying, to give a wife a slap in self-defense or to spank her when she had done something very objectionable, quite another to hit her repeatedly or with a closed fist. A man's answer to his wife's divorce complaint in an eastern Oregon court, for example, admitted that he had "struck plaintiff a light blow with his open hand," but only because he was fending off her blows and "persuading and compelling" her to leave a gathering "where her conduct and condition were of a scandelous character."[48] But during the 1890s men had not infrequently criticized even that sort of violence.

Judges seemed less inclined to change their views of hitting wives than husbands were. One in eastern Oregon remarked: "No man has a right to strike a woman, no matter what the provocation was."[49] The Oregon Supreme Court noted in its ruling on a 1921 divorce case that "no man has a legal or moral right to bruise or beat his wife, or compel obedience by physical strength or domineering force."[50] Public officials seldom troubled themselves over violence within the home. But, when they did, they displayed a greater willingness to condemn it.

The rub was that judges still expected wives of abusive husbands to be meek and submissive. This was particularly true in British Columbia, where divorce remained relatively rare. In 1928, for example, a woman in southwestern British Columbia complained of five years of continuous cruelty and cited several specific assaults, including instances in which her husband had tried to strike her with an ax, pointed a loaded gun at her chest, beat her, and pushed her down some stairs. But when asked if she had "a little temper" of her own, she replied, "I guess everybody has." The judge concluded that the plaintiff had not been frightened of her spouse, that the defendant "might just as well have had a lead pencil" as a gun. "To establish cruelty," one had "to prove real injury to her health." Hence he thought "she better make another try to live with her husband."[51]

Courts south of the line were much less exacting, but they, too, wanted divorce-seeking women to present themselves as victims. The Oregon Supreme Court noted in a 1921 decision that "cruelty which lays the legal foundation for a divorce must be unmerited and unprovoked, unless such cruel treatment is unjustified by the provocation and out of proportion to the offense."[52] The Washington Supreme Court asserted a similar standard, remarking in 1920 that "a person seeking a divorce must be innocent of any substantial wrongdoing towards the other party of the same nature as that of which complaint is made."[53] What this meant in practice was of course open to interpretation. Class was one variable. "What would be cruel to a delicate, sensitive woman might not be so to a brawling fishwife," the Oregon Supreme Court noted.[54] Indeed, a Willamette Valley man's legal answer to his spouse's charge of cruelty asserted that they had treated "each other . . . in accordance with the custom in the lumbering and logging camps" in which he had worked. Hence "each frequently has called the other a dam fool or liar over trifling matters, without any malicious meaning or ill-will . . . being implied thereby."[55] In sum, a woman who seemed to descend to the same level as an abusive husband was not likely to win much sympathy in court. An attorney in an eastern Oregon divorce asked a wife who complained of her husband's "beastly temper": "Did you fight back, or did you treat him as you should?"[56]

More wives were in fact fighting back. To be sure, some divorce-seeking women assured judges that they had treated their husbands just as the court wished. One, asked what kind of wife she had been, replied: "As good as I know how to be. . . . I tried to do everything he told me to."[57] Another eastern Oregon woman, when asked the same question, claimed: "I gave in to him and tried my best to make harmony in the home."[58] Third parties sometimes painted the same picture by describing wives who were "very submissive and dutiful," "did everything to keep from having trouble," and who "tried every way to pacify him."[59]

But wives, like children, were becoming more assertive. One recalled how she reacted when her husband persisted in referring to her, her mother, and her grandmother as prostitutes: "Well, I didn't take that, and I said, 'Well, you're a pimp.'" Her husband then became angry and slapped her, but to little effect. "It isn't my disposition to give in," she noted.[60] Another eastern Oregon woman, asked how she and her husband got along, replied that they did well "if I gave in to him in everything he wanted me to do, but that gets kind of old."[61] A district attorney repeatedly asked a woman who admitted to swearing at her husband to what extent she was to blame for the marriage's failure. She retorted that her husband was more culpable "because I would like to be with my children," and at another point remarked: "Well, I don't care for him, is one reason." When informed that wanting a divorce was not the same thing as deserving one, she admitted that she was partly to blame and had an "awful temper, and that has made it hard for us to get along," although "most anybody else would have . . . under the conditions." When the judge reminded her that neither spouse was entitled to a divorce when they were equally culpable, she assured him that she did not start their quarrels, but added that once her husband started one "of course I didn't just sit and say nothing." "You wouldn't yourself, I think," she remarked to the judge.[62]

Wives did more than "talk back" to domineering husbands. Increasing numbers seemed ready to use physical force in taking their own part. Some husbands claimed in divorce suits that their wives had struck them. A witness in a northern British Columbia case stated that a wife found in bed with another man rushed at her husband and slapped him in the face while remarking, "You son of a bitch You have caught me now."[63] A coastal Oregon man claimed that his wife had "chased me from the house, . . . kicked me in the testicles," and cut his lip.[64] Wives sometimes admitted to using violence.[65]

Most wives of the 1920s apparently did not use violence against abusive husbands, but neither did they simply defer to their wishes. As in the settlement period, violence often erupted because women disagreed with their husbands. Not a few wives contested their husbands' management of their finances. An eastern Oregon woman's spouse "pushed me right clear across the room" when she "remonstrated with him regarding some business deal, something that I didn't think was best."[66] Other men asserted a right to control their wives' earnings, a right that their wives often denied. One hit his wife when she refused to put the money she had earned into his bank account. A coastal Oregon man tied his wife up, threw her to the floor, and left their home when she refused to give him three dollars of her earnings. A marriage in which a wife's economic power exceeded her husband's was, to most men, inherently unstable. Hence a judge on the British Columbia Supreme Court explained a man's violent outburst in the restaurant owned by his wife by remarking that the defendant had "found himself in a menial position" and "was smarting under his subordinate position in the household."[67]

A number of violent husbands were in fact extremely sensitive to any challenges to patriarchal family relations. When an eastern Oregon woman told her eighteen-year-old son not to blow his nose at the breakfast table, her husband retorted, "If I had the relations that you have, I would not find fault." She countered "that I thought he had spent his sixpence at the celebration, and if I was him I would keep still." He then knocked her out of her chair and called her "a God damned Son of a Bitch."[68] A man in British Columbia's Okanagan region reacted still more radically when he perceived that his wife was laughing at him and egging on their sassy daughter. He picked up a poker and killed her.[69] Wives were struck when they protested against blows directed at their children. A Washington woman recalled that her father "was always beating us kids," and that when her mother "would try to interfere, . . . He'd beat her too and she'd cry."[70] Others described women who were hit for objecting to their husbands beating an infant or slapping and shaking a baby. Indeed, some husbands insisted that their wives had no right to discipline their children. Household authority was at stake in these disagreements. One man who reportedly shook and beat his babies until they were too exhausted to cry held his wife by the wrists to keep her from going to them, telling her that they were his children to raise as he wished. Likewise, a British Columbia woman who told her husband that "he should be ashamed of himself" when she caught him on top of her son, "using him as he would a woman," said that he then hit and kicked her to "let me see who I was," namely a person who had no right to question the way he ran the family.[71]

These aspiring patriarchs insisted that their spouses respect traditional male prerogatives. They were particularly keen on their wives preparing and serving meals whenever they required, even if they came home late and drunk. Such wives often tried to attach strings to their domestic service; they believed that cooking for and waiting on a man should be contingent on him behaving responsibly and respectfully. Abusive husbands denied these contingencies. To arrive home after bedtime and drunk and then to demand a warm meal cheerfully prepared was to assert that wives had no rights to speak of.[72]

Independent-minded wives were anathema to such husbands. Wives complained that their husbands hit them for visiting family, going to parties, or seeing friends. A Prince Rupert husband reportedly warned his wife to stay away from a woman he disapproved of or "she would be sorry for it" shortly before he killed her.[73] Violent husbands openly asserted a right to control the actions of wives who were behaving in ways they disapproved of. A husband's answer to his wife's divorce petition said that a violent altercation began when he "demanded that she leave" a party, and she refused.[74]

But growing numbers of women were insisting that husbands had no right to control how they socialized. An eastern Oregon woman recalled asking her husband, "What is wrong with you, are you losing your mind?" when he accused her of dancing too close to another man. She then sat out the dance and her husband started to argue with her and eventually slapped her. She filed for a divorce the next day.[75]

Wives' ultimate claim to personal freedom was to seek a divorce, a claim that many abusive husbands reacted explosively to. One wife recalled that when her husband "kept abusing me and saying mean things of what he would do . . . I told him that there was no use living together and fighting that way." He then "picked up an axe and swung it at me" and "told me if I wouldn't live with him he'd kill me."[76] Another divorce-seeking woman recalled a similar story. Barely three months after their marriage her husband had accused her of driving too much and took the keys from her. When she attempted to get them back, he knocked her down "and told me that I was lower than the lowest cur and that I would never amount to anything in all my life." She then packed her clothes and informed him that she was leaving. He locked her in the bathroom all night and "said if I ever left him he would kill me, that he wouldn't let me be happy with anybody else."[77] It was one thing for a husband to inform his wife that she would never amount to anything, that she was lower than a dog, quite another for her to conclude that their marriage ought to end. A third eastern Oregon woman recounted that on two days in succession her husband came to her house and beat her when she refused to return to him. He threatened to kill her if she sought a divorce and "has had me down with a razor right over my neck," saying "'Now move, just try to move.'"[78] This was the ultimate fantasy: to control a woman so completely that she could not even flinch without her husband's permission. A western Washington woman recalled meeting her estranged husband one morning and informing him, upon his query, that she had filed for divorce. He then threw her to the ground, beat her, and bit off the end of her nose.[79] Yet even these extreme acts of intimidation and abuse failed; both wives sought divorces.

Abusive husbands were sensitive not just to major acts of autonomy, such as divorce, but to trivial ones as well. An eastern Oregon woman recounted that her husband slapped and kicked her for taking a lamp into the bedroom and on another occasion struck her for not having "a meal ready just when he thought he ought to have it." Indeed, he became violent when "I was trying to do a little bit as I wanted to."[80] Other wives received beatings for "playfully" taking a cigarette from her husband's lips, for not washing the dishes immediately after dinner, for letting their dog out of the house when her spouse was preparing to beat it, for asking her husband to go to bed so as to be ready to work the next day, and for persisting in reading after being told to stop.[81]

Such husbands believed that even seemingly innocuous actions might represent an independent spirit. A witness in an eastern Oregon divorce suit testified that the husband, a jeweler, forcibly pushed his wife into a chair when she came home late. The woman remained seated, but not submissive: "She picked up a newspaper and started to read it and he jerked it away so she picked up a magazine and started to read it again and didn't say anything to him, just didn't pay any attention to him and he did the same thing."[82] A British Columbia wife recalled that her spouse "carried me into the sitting room," and "threw me to the ground and knelt over me, holding me down" after "I asked him if he had mended the governor on the tractor."[83]

In sum, husbands of the 1920s commonly used violence to show "who is the Boss round here," as one of them put it.[84] But such men were apt to confront wives who had agendas of their own—or at least who made their obedience and service contingent on their husbands' behavior. Violence against wives increased in part because these women were growing more independent.

It also increased because relations between the sexes had become more intense. Indeed, the lines that had separated women from men, wives from husbands, had blurred considerably by the 1920s, particularly south of the border. Growing, if still small, numbers of women worked outside the home, often alongside men. Young women and young men also spent more time together outside of work, often in intimate, sexually charged settings. Gender roles were changing even in remote corners of North America. Ray Nelson, who arrived in eastern Oregon's Malheur County in 1922, recalled: "There was a radical change taking place with the younger generation at that time." Men were dressing more stylishly, and women were discarding their corsets and "long dresses" in favor of clothing that allowed "a lot more bodily freedom." It was no longer rare to see one with a drink or a cigarette.[85]

Couples expected more of each other than before. British Columbia's divorce rate remained much lower than Washington's or Oregon's, but skyrocketed from 3.8 per hundred thousand in the first half of the 1910s to 32.6 per hundred thousand in the last half of the 1920s, over four times Canada's overall rate.[86] Many young brides wanted respect and freedom along with intimacy. A northern British Columbia woman, asked in court to elaborate on her charge that her husband had "abused me terribly," replied that "he would not let me go anywhere, and kept me home and would not help with the children" before she recounted his failure to provide her with "clothes and money."[87] A woman's letter to her husband in eastern Washington complained of sexual incompatibility. He would "use me to satisfy" his "own passions," and "sleep beside me all night as limp as a worn out mop rag," even when she "would beg" him "to love me."[88] Indeed, increasing numbers of men and women alike devoted themselves to searching for love—sexual and romantic. A wife wrote her husband to "not waste your life with me if you do not love me." He concurred: "Marriage is a compact which concerns two individuals alone. They alone know the infinite angle of a relationship that is either beautiful or unbearable." Since they had "*never*" enjoyed the "*companionship* and *love* which signify true mating," they should "both act in accordance with our conscience" and separate.[89] Separation was of course more appealing if there were another woman or man to go to, and married people assured their lovers that they owed it to each other to leave their spouses. "We only live once," wrote a British Columbia locomotive engineer to the other woman in his life, "so we might as well make the best of it[,] eh."[90]

This growing sense of freedom could be unsettling. Women's longstanding financial and social reliance on husbands was slipping. But those who still depended for their security on the goodwill of a dependable spouse had reason to feel less secure as growing numbers of men chafed at the nineteenth-century ethos of masculine self-restraint and responsibility. Men, for their part, seemed ill at ease with women's growing power. Oregon ministers who addressed the question glorified traditional mothers who, like Christ, set aside their own needs to serve happily their children and husbands. A well-to-do eastern Oregon sheep rancher reportedly put it more bluntly by proclaiming that "we would be better off if the women and lawyers and judges and bankers were all hung, we would have a better world." "Damn women," he would exclaim. "They break you and spend your money," they were "easy to get and hard to get rid of."[91] Women, like other powerful economic forces, seemed to be out to rob men of their independence.

A complex concoction of cultural and social developments had created a hothouse marital environment by the 1920s. Wives and husbands wanted more from each other than they had before—more intimacy, more consideration, more sexual pleasure, and more material comforts. Yet individualism increasingly characterized both women and men. Women could pursue a greater, if still constricted, range of opportunities outside the home, and there was a growing readiness among women and men to leave marriages in which they felt dissatisfied, in pursuit of greater autonomy, a more perfect love relation, or both. That people participated in these changes to varying degrees of course exacerbated matters. A woman whose understanding of marriage was firmly rooted in the nineteenth century might find herself paired with a man of more modern sensibilities, and vice versa. The rules of marriage were shifting beneath people's feet, and the changes were both exciting and disorienting. Violence was often the handmaiden of change.

Spousal violence also flourished in the shrinking parts of the north Pacific slope that were least modern, in highly isolated pockets that resembled settlement conditions of several decades before, places where embattled wives and children had no one to turn to.

Fred Frye and his wife Edith moved to a ranch south of McBride in the early 1910s. Fred made railway ties, an activity he forced some of their seven children to work at, and moonshine whiskey. He had always been a hard man to live with. The family's rough cabin had but two rooms, and he sometimes drove the children out of the house for the night. On 16 November 1922, he loaded a shotgun and stated that he would kill them all, that, as one of his sons later testified, "he was God and there was no power greater than he." Edith sent her children from the house. When they returned, she had shot and killed their father. Edith, asked why she had not gone to the police if her husband "had been continually abusing you," replied: "He wouldn't let me away from the house."[92]

Bill Smith, another patriarchal husband-father, also died at the hands of a family member in a remote part of British Columbia. They had recently moved to the province from the United States. Area residents testified that he had remarked: "God damn my family, I've given them a good education and they don't help me a bit. The only thing I see to do is kill the whole God damn bunch." He told the son who would kill him a day later: "If I thought you had any brains I'd crack your head open to see what they looked like." Another man recalled Smith remarking that he "was going home to 'clean-up,'" a statement that seemed insignificant at the time.

Bill arrived home from hauling logs that afternoon in a foul mood. A daughter recalled that "Mother wanted to read a clipping but Father drowned her voice by humming." The couple also had some sort of disagreement about money, with Bill apparently asserting that he did not intend to support his wife. But matters did not come to a head until the two went to bed. According to Mary, Bill said: "You God damned Son of a bitch lying there cold and saying nothing" and "pulled the covers off me." Mary then dressed herself. Bill called her a "Dirty fence corner Whore" and, when she objected to such talk, ordered her and then the children out of the house. She went out, coatless, and he followed and hit her. She then came back in the house, and he again ordered her to leave. She and one of her daughters then waited on the road for the other daughter. But Bill "came out, ordered me back and said something about Murder & Bloodshed saying it had to be settled right here, then grabbed me by the hair of the head and forced me down." Their daughter then pulled him off, and Mary ran toward the distant town. But "I knew I could not get away, so I turned back north," hoping to run to a neighbor. The daughter called out, "My God, help her he will kill her." Bill's eldest son then shot him. He told one of the sisters that he intended only to "stop" his father, but Bill Smith died a few minutes later.[93]

A third harrowing case of family violence in rural northern British Columbia did not end in death. The family consisted of Martha Shannon, her husband John, her teenaged daughter Jennifer (from a previous relationship), and an infant son. According to Martha and Jennifer, John had assaulted his wife a number of times. A few days before his arrest he had blacked her eye and struck Jennifer when she tried to assist her mother. The next day he uttered a threat that greatly alarmed Martha: "He came in from feeding cattle and told me he intended to do just as he pleased with Jennifer," that "as soon as you learn to understand I am going to put my hands any place I please on Jennifer the better we'll get along." He did not "want to fuck the girl," just to show her "a father's love." Martha retorted that he dare not. "Do you see my one black eye?" she asked. "Well I will take another; I will give the last drop of blood in my body, but you shall not do that to Jennifer." But John did not back down and remarked: "I would just like to kill you, you dirty old son of a bitch." Martha then told Jennifer to "appear to agree with him" to buy time, that John was likely to be away part of the next day, so they could get a letter to the police through a neighbor. Jennifer fought her way through deep snow to execute this plan the following day, and tried to sweep out her tracks as she returned.

John detected and misconstrued the tracks in the snow. He concluded that a man had come to the house in his absence and, as Martha put it, had been "using my body." John then remarked that "he would use my daughter and let me see how it goes." She "tried to pass" this remark "off lightly" and, that evening, "tried to be pleasant" as she mended his gloves. But John asked Jennifer, Mary's daughter, to read to him sitting on his lap. Mary "feared to protest against this, so said nothing." As Martha cared for the baby, John "told Jennifer she should come into his bed and warm his back." Mary "felt sure of what he was up to," but "Jennifer finally had to go to his bed before I could possibly get ready myself," although "she looked at me pleadingly." "I told her it was best to go, not to antagonize him as long as it was no worse than that," that they had to bide their time until the police responded to their letter. But John insisted on touching Jennifer's breasts, and she and her mother objected and resisted. There followed several hours of struggle between John and the two women. Neither was able to get at John's knife or to otherwise subdue him, despite repeated attempts. The best they could do was to strike a series of bargains that kept Jennifer's virginity at least technically intact and Martha from being killed. But the sight of John touching Jennifer's genitals or masturbating over her would compel Martha to again throw herself at John, despite his repeated threats to kill her and her daughter. John hit both women in these fights, cut Jennifer's finger with the knife, stepped on her face, twisted one of her breasts, and lifted her by her pubic hair. He repeatedly spat on Martha's face. Finally, some six hours after the three had gone to bed, John allowed Jennifer to leave after ejaculating between her legs. Four hours later he "wanted Jennifer to come into bed again," but Martha "protested and persuaded him to satisfy himself on my body." An hour later he again masturbated on Jennifer.

Martha then succeeded in checking her husband's sexual assault of her daughter by appearing to consent to it. "After all, John," she remarked, "it is not so bad if you only go that far." John then "asked me to lay on his arm and he said we could all be happy there if he could love Jennifer and me too." She then got him to promise that he would not have sex with Jennifer "until Wednesday, expecting, of course, the police to come Tuesday." John "said it would be all right then[,] only Jennifer must shape up to him when he was doing it" and that "if there was any offspring no one need know but what it belonged to me." According to Jennifer, John "planned with us to use mamma one night and me the next night." But Martha's plan trumped John's; the police arrived the next morning and arrested him.[94]

Community members were quick to condemn John Shannon once his actions came to light. The officer who arrested him noted that the neighbors were "so incensed over the harsh treatment" that he had inflicted on Martha "that they were ready to act on their own initiative . . . and to take the law in their own hands."[95] A northern newspaper said that Martha's deposition "was a record of fiendishness paralleling in brutality and depravity the most horrible versions of Armenian persecution and torture," and it described John as "a madman of the most devilish type."[96] But Martha and Jennifer, like Edith Frye, had been compelled to rely on their own wits and courage to escape a patriarchal man's abuse.

Northern British Columbia was of course an anomaly. Only a tiny proportion of the north Pacific slope's residents lived under such remote conditions. Yet these three families were not as exceptional as they seemed. A rising proportion of the north Pacific slope's population resided in cities or towns by the 1920s. But isolation accompanied urbanization. Fewer couples lived in boardinghouses, and the size of households shrank as children became less numerous and as lodgers, servants, and kin found accommodations elsewhere. Changes in attitude accompanied changes in household composition;

friends and neighbors were becoming more hesitant to presume to enter each other's private spaces and private lives, the emotionally charged places where family members nurtured and damaged each other.[97] The privacy that abusive husbands and parents like John Shannon enjoyed was therefore becoming more common even as the remote conditions that he and his family lived under were becoming more rare. The isolation that had long characterized so much of the north Pacific slope was increasing just as it seemed ready to expire. Growing numbers of wives and children—in city and countryside alike—would have to contend with men like John Shannon.

Such men were all but invisible in the north Pacific slope's popular culture. Its writers celebrated the bravery of good men who subdued bad men, not husbands who bit off their wives' noses. Its public spectacles featured violent, highly structured masculine displays of courage, such as football games, not fathers who raped their children.

But popular representations of violence and the actual practice of violence had diverged by the 1920s. The showdowns in streets and saloons so celebrated in fiction had become rarities. Men fought or killed each other less frequently. The state had become less tolerant of unregulated, public acts of violence.

Violence within the family, on the other hand, appeared to be rising after its late-nineteenth-century decline. Husbands more readily hit their wives in the 1920s than in the 1890s, and fathers and mothers seemed more apt to hit their children, or at least to use more extreme forms of physical punishment than their parents and grandparents had.

A culture emphasizing self-expression facilitated these shifts in several respects. First, it eroded husbands' and parents' capacity for self-restraint. Popular culture increasingly embraced violence even as governments more closely regulated its public manifestations. But—outside of assessing fault in divorce suits—public officials seldom concerned themselves with family violence. In the home, behind closed doors, the emphasis on self-realization fueled rising expectations, making marital life more intense, more capable of generating hate and love alike. This growing ethos encouraged subordinates—wives and children—to act more independently, in their own self interests. Parents and especially husbands resented this, and violence often ensued.

These trends are of course still very much with us. Newspaper articles, reports from battered women's shelters, and even the attenuated court transcripts from the twentieth century's last decades describe violence toward wives that was more extensive and extreme than that described in court documents from earlier in the century. Children were probably less commonly spanked late in the twentieth century than they had been before, but the violence they encountered was becoming less predictable. Gordon notes that late-twentieth-century parents have commonly hit their boys and girls not just for acts of disobedience, but simply for crying. Children, furthermore, have been more likely to be the victims of homicide near the twentieth century's end than at its beginning. In the 1920s children age one through nine constituted 3 percent of all homicide victims in Washington and Oregon. The figure rose to 4 percent for 1950 to 1964, to 5 percent for 1965 to 1969—this although children constituted a declining proportion of the population.[98]

The 1920s seemed, for a time, to be anomalous. It was followed by North America's worst economic depression and then by five years of war and two decades of relative conservatism. By the early 1970s, however, it was clear that the 1920s had constituted a foretaste of modern life—and, in many respects, of modern violence.

6

Big as God Almighty
and Undemanding as Dew

Violence and People of African and Japanese Descent

IT LOOKED AS IF Sandy Moses would have to move from his Seattle house in the late 1930s. The Ku Klux Klan had been driving out other African Americans in his neighborhood by burning crosses in front of their homes. A woman stopped by to ask if he was ready to sell. Moses brought out his rifle. Then he said, "Me and my friend is going to stay here." She evidently spread the word. Thereafter Moses "never had a bit of trouble."[1]

Monica Sone recalled a very different reaction to housing discrimination from about the same time. She and her mother asked about a summer rental in western Washington only to have the owner tell them that "we don't want Japs around here." Sone's mother said nothing. She took her daughter's hand and walked quickly away. "Ka-chan, there are people like that in this world," she later explained. "We have to bear it, just like all the other unpleasant facts of life. . . . when you are older, it won't hurt quite as much."[2]

People of African and Japanese descent who lived on the north Pacific slope differed from each other in many ways. One of those ways was their experience of violence. Of the two groups, African Americans were more apt to suffer from and to employ violence in the first decades of the twentieth century.

World War II changed these two groups' experiences profoundly. The war offered unparalleled opportunities for those of African descent, unparalleled hardships for those of Japanese ancestry. What did not change were their divergent approaches to conflict and violence. African Americans remained more likely to use and suffer from violence than did Japanese Canadians and Japanese Americans. The war accentuated patterns already well established by culture and circumstance.

People of African descent have experienced more violence than any other non-indigenous group in North America. Physical punishments were an integral part of slavery in the southern United States. Masters and overseers routinely whipped slaves for a wide variety of offenses, actual or imagined, or simply because they wanted to. Violence did not end with emancipation. The Ku Klux Klan and less formally organized groups of whites lynched African Americans suspected of crimes, or those who seemed too independent. White southerners executed nearly three thousand Blacks from 1882 to 1930, usually without using official legal mechanisms. Lynchings decreased in the mid-twentieth century, when southern African Americans found more economic opportunities, often by migrating to cities in the North or the South. But physical force remained an integral component of white dominance, particularly in the South. In the 1930s John Dollard found that the whites of a southern town were patently proud of their violence toward African Americans and defended it as a necessary part of race relations.[3]

Much more so than most ethnic groups, African Americans had to forge a sense of corporate pride and identity against the white heat of threatened and actual violence. Not surprisingly, violence became one of a number of problematic tools of resistance. To be sure, slaves rarely organized large-scale uprisings in the United States, and violence toward whites remained extremely risky long after emancipation. Dollard reported that southern African Americans acted very carefully and gingerly around whites. But he also noted that poorer Blacks in particular tended to idealize violence and to admire those among them who dared to use it. Indeed, Lawrence Levine points out that the heroic protagonists of African American folklore were commonly hard, ruthless men and women who acted with "total anarchy and lawlessness," people who "were pure force, pure vengeance; explosions of fury and futility."[4] For many African Americans, the willingness to employ violence in the face of overwhelming odds was the stuff of legendary bravery.

African American violence in the late nineteenth and early twentieth centuries was not simply the stuff of folklore, was not simply rhetorical. The white homicide rate in the United States was about 5.3 per hundred thousand from

1918 to 1927, the African American rate about 36.9, over six times as high. To be sure, many African Americans died at the hands of whites, particularly in the South. But, at least outside the South, African Americans were much more likely than whites both to be murdered and to murder. Roger Lane's study of homicide in Philadelphia indicates that African American men and particularly women were more apt to kill than were their white counterparts and that this difference widened in the late nineteenth century as the white homicide rate declined. Lane attributes this substantial and growing gap largely to African Americans' economic and social marginalization. The spread of industrialization imposed on most North Americans an ethos of self-restraint and, for those with decent jobs, a sense of investment in the established order. But Blacks remained largely outside that process. Philadelphia's African Americans also tended to be well armed, both because most were compelled to live in areas of high criminal activity and because racist harassment and attacks fostered in many of them a sense of "eternal battle-readiness," as Lane puts it.[5] To leave the South was, many African Americans felt, to gain the freedom to defend oneself.

These attitudes toward violence traveled west as well as north. A witness at the trial of a Black man accused of an 1863 killing in Victoria claimed that the defendant "has told me over and over again that he would think no more of taking any man's life, who had wronged him, than he would of taking the head off a chicken."[6] This point of view was extreme, but most African Americans shared a determination to resist insult and discrimination. Newspaper reports of race relations during the 1890s in Roslyn, a Washington coal-mining town, noted both whites' threats to lynch African Americans accused of crimes and African Americans' resolve that these threats would not be carried out. "The most bitter hatred exists between the whites and blacks," read one such account, "and the least act is liable to bring about a bloody scene."[7]

Bloody outbreaks between Blacks and whites were relatively rare on the north Pacific slope because so few African Americans lived there prior to World War II. Several hundred came to Victoria in the late 1850s, many from San Francisco. But their numbers soon declined, and few people of African descent lived in British Columbia by 1940. Oregon and particularly Washington drew a number of African American land seekers in the mid-nineteenth century. Washington was less discriminatory than Oregon, and African Americans generally preferred to settle in the former state rather than the latter. The 1900 census counted 1,105 Blacks in Oregon, 2,514 in Washington. By 1940 these numbers had grown to 2,565 and 7,424, respectively, although African Americans' percentage of the overall population was still under one-half of one percent. Relatively few of the migrants came directly from the deep South. A 1935 Seattle survey indicated that nearly three-quarters of its African Americans had been born outside Washington, most hailing from border states or the northeastern or midwestern United States. Seattle was by far the most popular destination of Blacks moving to the Pacific Northwest. In 1940 its African American population numbered nearly four thousand, Portland's around two thousand. These urban communities were family oriented: females constituted 43 percent of Seattle's African Americans, 46 percent of Portland's.[8] African American communities in smaller cities or towns were much more volatile. Vernonia, a remote northwestern Oregon town, in 1930 had seventy-one African American residents recruited directly from the South to work in a lumber mill. But the mill had closed by 1932, when only eight Blacks remained.[9]

Like their counterparts in other regions of North America, the Pacific Northwest's Blacks lived in a racist, hostile environment. Oregon and Washington were overwhelmingly Caucasian in the 1920s and 1930s, and most of their residents wanted to keep it that way. A sociologist studying Shevlin-Hixon, a small timber town in eastern Oregon, reported that all of its approximately eight hundred residents were white and that "their dislike for an oriental or a negro is so strong that when one comes into the community, conditions are made so unpleasant that he soon leaves."[10] Indeed, the mother of a divorce-seeking eastern Oregon woman criticized her son-in-law by recalling that he had expected her daughter to live in an apartment building that had "negroes living on one side of them, and a drunken bunch on the other."[11] Whites often associated African Americans with crime. A student at the University of Washington in the 1930s reported in a sociology paper that Seattle police viewed African Americans as "a degenerate, sluggish group."[12] Henry Broderick, who sat on the Washington parole board for several years, in 1934 described one prisoner as "a big, black buck, hard of face, sinister of eye" who "could have been convicted in any court on his looks alone." Blackness itself purportedly produced these traits, for Broderick identified the prisoner as "a real anthracite" or coal-black "African."[13] These attitudes confronted all

African Americans, wealthy and poor, law-abiding and criminal. Kathryn Hall Bogle remarked in 1937 that the African American high school student in Portland might well escape racist violence, but not "subtle omissions, exceptions, and other differences . . . that wound the spirit." "Outside his home," she concluded, such a student "is bombarded by assaults and propaganda against his race."[14]

Racist attitudes and stereotypes expressed themselves in highly concrete and structured patterns that ensured African Americans' marginalization. Employment discrimination constituted the most fundamental. Bogle remarked that the words "'we have no place for you.' . . . echoed and reechoed in my own ears" when she searched for work in Portland. She sought employment at "large and small stores of all descriptions," the telephone company, light and power utilities, and as an elevator operator and a clerical worker. Wherever she found a vacancy "I was told there was nothing about me in my disfavor—except the color of my skin," although a number of the people who refused to employ her at a business "offered me employment in their homes." "Were it not for this little quirk in a white man's discrimination," she concluded, "many thousands of Negroes could not earn the bare necessities for life."[15] Employment figures supported Bogle's generalization. Portland's African American women most commonly worked as maids. Some were elevator operators, a handful were stenographers. Portland's African American men worked largely at the bottom rungs of the service industry for railroads, hotels, and restaurants, or as janitors in office buildings. A few Blacks owned small businesses, such as shoe-shine stands or beauty parlors. A 1932 study identified the following professionals in Portland's African American community: one doctor, one dentist, three attorneys, five ministers, and twenty business people.[16] Seattle had offered numerous if modest employment opportunities for African Americans during its boom years early in the twentieth century, but here, too, the great majority of African Americans worked at jobs with little pay or status. In 1930 some 51 and 83 percent of employed African American men and women, respectively, toiled in some form of domestic service compared to just 5 percent and 25 percent for white men and women. In that year Seattle had two African American doctors, two lawyers, seventeen retailers, six restaurant owners, and forty-three barbers or beauticians out of a total Black workforce of nearly nineteen hundred.[17]

Washington and Oregon's African Americans faced substantial segregation. White landlords, realtors, and home owners did not establish impoverished, racially homogeneous ghettoes in Seattle and Portland, but by the 1930s they had excluded African Americans from most residential areas, thereby inflating the cost of the substandard housing that most of them purchased or rented. Hence a Black man who came to Seattle shortly after World War I found that his realtor would not take him to a house in the city's north end during daylight, and a Black woman who moved to Seattle in the late 1930s who objected to being shown a filthy rental was told that it was "good enough for niggers."[18] Seattle and Portland schools became nonsegregated between the two world wars, but some white-owned businesses in Seattle and especially Portland still refused to serve African American customers or, in the case of theaters, insisted on seating them in separate and inferior spaces.

African Americans objected to these racist acts. They created social spaces of their own. Churches were the most fundamental of these institutions, followed by fraternal groups like the Masons and the Eastern Star and a variety of women's and men's clubs. Some of these groups had explicitly political goals. Seattle had a branch of the National Association for the Advancement of Colored People in 1913, Portland a year later. Seattle added a branch of the National Urban League in 1930 and had two active, if short-lived, chapters of Marcus Garvey's Universal Negro Improvement Association. Black leaders worked within such organizations to end discriminatory legislation, criminal justice procedures, and social practices, and to improve employment opportunities. But few Seattle and Portland African American leaders were militant. Edwin C. Berry came to Portland to head its National Urban League early in World War II and described its African American community as "law-abiding, self-sustaining, and unobtrusive." African Americans "were not integrated into the free flow of the life in Portland," and had generally "accommodated themselves to the position . . . to which they had been assigned."[19] Quintard Taylor, author of a meticulous history of Seattle's African Americans, likewise notes that the city's relatively positive race relations "generated a marked complacency among many Seattle African Americans."[20]

But not all African Americans of the north Pacific slope were oriented toward integration. Seattle and Portland essentially housed two distinct African American communities. The self-styled leaders were the men and women who held stable and relatively remunerative jobs and who constituted the backbone of African American churches and other organizations. More noticeable to most law-enforcement officials and other whites was a much less stable population commonly involved in various criminal activities. People of African descent who found it difficult if not impossible to secure a decent living at respectable occupations—this on top of suffering the many other indignities that all African Americans labored under—often turned to illegitimate ways of making money. Horace Cayton, born in 1903 to Seattle's most prominent African American, recalled that his parents looked down on lower-class Blacks as a "great discredit to the race" and urged their children to avoid them. But, upon being expelled from high school, Cayton signed up with a crew of African American strikebreakers on a ship heading to Alaska. These sailors were "rough, tough, uneducated men." Most had been born and raised in the South but now floated from city to city as part of "the northern urban Negro proletariat." Unlike the educated African Americans with whom Cayton's parents socialized, they had little hope of race relations much improving, and they had no knowledge of or interest in Black leaders like Booker T. Washington. Cayton, who eventually became a distinguished sociologist, termed them "rebels against society." One of them aspired to own a whorehouse, another a gambling joint. One advised Cayton to "get along" with white people "until we have a chance to fight back and kill them." Until that day, which he did not expect to live to see, he intended to stay out of trouble unless a white man was to "corner me and abuse me."[21]

Many African Americans on the north Pacific slope were in fact cornered and abused by whites. Elva Nicholas described how as a little girl in Franklin, a Washington coal-mining town, "we had to *fight* our way to get to school," for "the whites was determined that no Negroes" would attend. On one occasion Nicholas dodged a schoolmate who intended to push her down a steep embankment, and the white girl's own momentum sent her down into berry bushes, leaving her badly bruised and cut. The injured girl's mother remarked that "she wanted that 'Nigger' sent to reform school, because . . . I had no business moving" when her daughter tried to shove her. Nor were Nicholas's teachers respectful. One beat African Americans with a rubber hose and refused to give them passing grades.[22] Years later, in the 1930s, Nicholas's eight-year-old boy faced the same sort of difficulties. A group of Seattle children told him that "they didn't want him at that school and to get out," held him down, and urinated on his face.[23] Not all African American children who grew up in western Washington early in the twentieth century recalled such prejudice.[24] But Black children were apt to face racially motivated violence, violence that was often extreme.

African Americans who ran afoul of the law were particularly vulnerable. Cayton began stealing at age sixteen and was soon arrested for assisting two older African Americans in a holdup. The Seattle sergeant knew his prominent father and sent him to juvenile court. He treated two older suspects, whom he referred to as "trashy southern niggers," less gently. "Rough 'em up a bit if you want," he advised his subordinates. Cayton avoided a police record by going to the state school for recalcitrant boys. But he did not avoid violence. Mr. Holding, one of his keepers, backhanded Cayton on the head one day after the boy's arrival and later beat him with an ax handle. Fights among the inmates were common. Indeed, Holding enjoyed forcing his charges to box each other—sometimes with bare knuckles.[25]

Fear of violence was one of many strands that bound Blacks together. So was a willingness to use it themselves. One of Cayton's earliest memories was of hiding with his family in the basement because his father had dared to hit a white man who had insulted him. His father expected his son to act the same way. Cayton recalled "constantly being chased home by the rougher Italian boys" in sixth grade until his father insisted that he "stand up and fight" them. Confronted on one side by his young tormentors and on the other by his belt-wielding father, he "turned on my pursuers with a violence that surprised them, and . . . won their respect."[26]

Other African American children learned the same lesson. A Vernonia resident who taught a first-grade class that included a few African American children in 1927 remembered that one of them justified shoving a child by explaining: "My Mama told me not to let any old white trash push me around, and he pushed me!"[27] Black parents, then, told their children to meet force with force. Nicholas recalled that her mother backed her up when the mother of a white child complained that Nicholas had pulled out some of her daughter's hair: "You tell your daughter to stop pulling my daughter's hair." African American parents seldom objected to corporal punishment per se. But they were very wary of whites inflicting it on Black children, and they raised their children to resist unjust punishments. Nicholas said that her father threatened to kill a notoriously violent teacher if he "put [his] hands" on her.[28] Marguerite Johnson likewise recalled that her mother backed her up when she hit a teacher who was pulling her hair and calling her a "little nigger."[29]

Relations between the north Pacific slope's African American and white children were often forged in a crucible of violence. Violence divided. But it could also integrate. Nicholas recalled that some white children in the small Washington town that her family had moved to at first threw rocks at her and her siblings. But "we'd throw back, and . . . The next thing you know, they was all piled up at the door playing."[30] Likewise, Juanita Proctor recalled that white children called her and her brothers names when they moved to a Seattle neighborhood. But "we'd whip 'em and get 'em straightened. . . . after that we didn't have any trouble with 'em."[31] Another Seattle woman said that she scratched a white classmate who "called me a 'nigger.'" Years later, as a young adult, the former schoolmate saw her on a streetcar, showed her the scar, and remarked that she "should have known better," and that she had not used the word "nigger" since.[32] As we saw in chapter two, white children's violence toward each other was often a prelude to intimacy. Interracial violence involving Black children was generally more extreme, but it, too, could lead to friendship or at least tolerance.

This sort of personal resistance to prejudice followed many of Washington's African Americans into adulthood. There was much prejudice to resist. The Ku Klux Klan was extremely popular in Washington's and particularly Oregon's cities and towns in the 1920s. Although the Pacific Northwest's chapters largely devoted themselves to denouncing Catholics and Jews, many if not most of the persons they confronted and abused were of African descent. Some police officers also used force on African Americans deemed to have stepped out of line. Letcher Yarbrough recalled that "a black man and a white woman, could not safely walk down Jackson Street" in Seattle "without the police questioning him and possibly beating him up."[33] Many African Americans refused to tolerate prejudice. Joseph Staton of Seattle had a contest with four of his Black friends to see who could cut out the most black faces on the spare tire covers that the Coon Chicken Shack restaurant gave to customers. Later, during the 1930s, he made a habit of tearing "We do not cater to colored" signs out of Seattle store windows and would "dare the fellow to put 'em back in." He and his friends also fought discriminatory theater seating: "If a person was militant enough . . . he would just sit in the middle, and the usher couldn't do anything about it."[34] Young whites sometimes assisted their African American friends in such work. Sons of some prominent Spokane families reportedly helped a Black high school classmate integrate one of the city's theatres. Like their children, adult African Americans sometimes found that whites who had been initially hostile would become friendly after being confronted. Genevieve Roberts recalled that a mob of armed white people tried to run them out of the house they bought in the eastern Washington town of Wenatchee. But her father and uncle stood their ground, and they eventually became "the best liked family in the neighborhood."[35] This sort of explicit resistance was risky. But it could be highly effective.

The Pacific Northwest's relatively small and often scattered African American communities did not create a tradition of concerted organized protest prior to World War II. But they nevertheless resisted racism. Resistance usually transpired on the family level, in acts that seldom made the minutes of local NAACP meetings or the columns of Black newspapers. African American children and adults used violence to create a modicum of tolerance, acceptance, and even friendship. Their willingness to employ violence might win the right to live in the houses they owned or rented, to attend nearby schools, and to walk home from those schools without being beaten up.

Washington and Oregon's African Americans remained on the economic and political margins of their communities on the eve of World War II. But they were less oppressed by daily humiliations and strict segregation than most of their counterparts living elsewhere. These relatively favorable conditions arose not simply from demographics and circumstance, but because so many of them had insisted that their white neighbors treat them with respect.

People from Japan arrived much later on the north Pacific slope than Black people had, and with somewhat different expectations. They began emigrating in the late nineteenth century, pushed by the dislocations of modern industrialization and pulled by unique employment opportunities. The great majority of the early arrivals were young men, most of whom did not intend to stay and who did not, at least at first, learn much English. In 1910, about 62 percent of Washington's Japanese were males between the ages of twenty and thirty-five, and they outnumbered women of that age by nearly a ten-to-one margin. Many toiled for Asian labor contractors, building railroads or working for lumber companies or canneries.[36]

This pattern shifted as the arrival of Japanese women encouraged family formation and a determination to stay in North America. By 1940 females made up 43 percent of the people of Japanese descent in Washington, 44 percent of those in British Columbia. The Issei, born in Japan, had by this time made themselves at home. Many who had started out doing contract farming for a set wage had moved on to tenant farming, leasing, and eventually to owning a few acres or more. By 1920 Japanese Americans possessed some seven hundred Washington farms, most near Seattle and Tacoma, and most specializing in vegetables and small fruits. The majority of the north Pacific slope's Japanese lived in Vancouver, Seattle, or Portland by 1940, where many owned and operated small stores. Nearly one-half of Seattle's Japanese American income earners owned a business in 1935, and another one-fourth worked in white-collar occupations. Many in the vicinity of Vancouver or elsewhere along British Columbia's coast made a living fishing.[37]

Immigration restrictions hindered the population growth of Japanese Canadians and Japanese Americans. Their numbers peaked south of the line in 1930. Washington and Oregon then had nearly eighteen thousand and five thousand people of Japanese descent, respectively. British Columbia had twenty-two thousand by that time. By the eve of World War II, the second generation, or Nisei, outnumbered their parents.[38]

Japanese Canadians and Japanese Americans created communities that were diverse, but highly cohesive. Place of birth—Issei or Nisei—was one obvious difference, one that became increasingly significant as the second generation matured. Religion also divided communities. Roughly one thousand Japanese Americans attended a Christian church in Seattle in the early 1920s, about half that number a Buddhist one. Yet people of Japanese ancestry formed tight communities on the north Pacific slope. All sprang from a distinctive culture that emphasized family and corporate obligations rather than individualism, and most Issei worked hard to perpetuate these values, regardless of whether they intended to return to Japan. As Linda Tamura puts it: "Issei lives reflected clearly prescribed roles, subordination of their own needs and well-being to those of the group, reverence for authority, and a conformity to rules for proper behavior."[39] Compared to people of African descent, who had lived in North America for many generations, they were little affected by Anglo-American culture. They had a strong sense of themselves as a separate people. For the Issei, North America was a place to succeed, not to integrate.

The Japanese on the north Pacific, like their white counterparts, became less violent as their communities became more settled. A man who in 1898 arrived at Steveston, near Vancouver, British Columbia, recalled that there were only three Japanese women there and that the Japanese Canadian community was "full of hotheads."[40] Another, speaking of the same time and place, said that its residents fought often, "as there were no women." "Later, when the brides started coming from Japan, their lives improved," he noted.[41] Many early-twentieth-century fights arose over frictions at canneries or mills where many young Issei labored. A foreman at a British Columbia lumber mill noted that a pair of employees "blamed each other" when he told them to work faster. When one claimed that the other was "too lazy to work" and accused him of sleeping, the accused first threatened to hit him, then picked up a picaroon and delivered a mortal blow.[42] Violence also occurred around criminal activities, such as gambling. But men's violence toward each other declined as Issei communities matured and their members married and left wage work for more stable and less exploitative forms of employment. Japanese Canadians and Japanese Americans had very low crime rates by the 1930s. "They are the only exception" to the generalization "that crime and poverty go hand in hand," remarked a 1942 editorial in a Seattle Black newspaper.[43]

Men of Japanese descent commonly dominated but did not beat their wives. Most Issei and Nisei grew up, like Vancouver's David Suzuki, with "the cultural assumptions of male dominance."[44] By the century's close, Japan's rural majority had undergone a process of "samuraization," meaning that the values of its urban warrior class had spread across society. These values included increased status for husbands and fathers, who expected respectful obedience from their families. North America reversed some aspects of this trend. Few Issei wives had to compete with powerful mothers-in-law for their husbands' loyalty, for those women almost always lived in far-away Japan. North American norms of equality and chivalry also influenced Japanese Canadian and Japanese American marriages. But most Issei women had a hard life. The majority came as picture brides and married men many years older who expected their young wives to do as they were told. Early in the century, especially, many lived under isolated and trying conditions and worked very hard for their families. A Vancouver Nisei woman observed that her father "didn't get a bride, he got a work horse."[45] These men seldom hit their wives. One recalled that her husband was at first very jealous and eventually became violent, prompting her to seek refuge at the Victoria Oriental Home. But few women of Japanese descent defied their husbands so openly. Midge Ayukawa concludes that "most picture brides . . . fulfilled their roles as subservient 'good wives and wise mothers.'"[46] Husbands, as we have seen in previous chapters, have been less apt to hit subservient wives. Hence two reported threats or attempts to kill women of Japanese descent came from spurned suitors, not respected husbands.[47]

Violence against children was also relatively rare among Japanese Americans and Japanese Canadians, and for similar reasons. The great majority of Issei and even Nisei parents expected their children to be submissive and hard-working, a credit to their family. S. Frank Miyamoto, who studied the Seattle Japanese American community in the mid-1930s, reported that fathers and mothers seldom neglected an opportunity "to remind the young of the virtues of obedience," that "no propaganda gets a more effective reiteration."[48] Monica Sone of Seattle said that the teacher at her Japanese school seemed to expect his students to possess "deep *rigor mortis* . . . no noise, no trouble, no back talk."[49] But parents and teachers usually employed shaming and other forms of verbal discipline rather than physical punishment to promote these ideals. A young woman who grew up in Hood River, Oregon, said that her parents struck her on only one occasion, when she tossed her head and said that she wanted to abort a hair-styling session that her mother was giving her. Suzuki's more volatile father would sometimes kick him, but then apologize for it. Such violent outbursts were exceptional, in part because Nisei children tended to conform to their parents' wishes.[50] Relatively patriarchal family structures, then, did not necessarily lead to high levels of family violence. Japanese American and Japanese Canadian families stressed and usually realized self-control by those with authority and obedience by their subordinates. Anglo norms corroded this tradition only a little. People of Japanese descent had lived in North America for only a few decades by World War II, and they remained a highly distinct people.

This distinctive people suffered a great deal of prejudice. Parents and children, husbands and wives all faced repeated acts of discrimination and racism on the north Pacific slope. Even modest financial successes could exacerbate these hostilities. Alfred Moltke, who grew up near Seattle, recalled that an "entire Japanese family, from six years old to seventy, male and female, could be seen working in the fields from sunup to sundown" and "never complained." They soon owned some of the best fields, for they would pay top dollar for good land and could make much higher profits than anyone else could. "Young white men who wished to pursue farming as a livelihood" therefore "had to leave the country and look elsewhere."[51] A Japanese Canadian recalled a conversation that began when a white man asked him why he painted his house every two years. When "I said I did because I liked it neat and clean," the man retorted: "You goddamned rotten Jap."[52] Caucasians commonly imputed to the Japanese a predilection for craftiness and underhandedness. Hilda Glynn Ward's 1921 novel, *The Writing on the Wall*, describes an intricate plot by Asian Canadians and their white lackeys to take over British Columbia. Racism expressed itself in both formal law and popular custom. Many restaurants and places of entertainment would either refuse to serve people of Japanese descent or would seat them in segregated and inferior sections. The Nisei, despite high levels of education, had difficulty finding good jobs outside their own communities. Ken Adachi recalls that in British Columbia, university graduates commonly toiled as clerical workers, gardeners, or mill hands. Only one Nisei garnered a teaching appointment in British Columbia. Unlike African Americans, who owned fewer businesses, many Nisei were able to work for their parents, but generally in subordinate positions. Given the community's emphasis "on 'getting ahead,'" Adachi notes, "there was a great deal of bitterness over having to accept inferior social and economic status as symbolized by menial positions and labouring jobs."[53] Whites on both sides of the forty-ninth parallel routinely inflicted other indignities on the Issei and their children, including threats and racial epithets.[54]

Racism sometimes expressed itself through violence. The most publicized incidents involved group acts: clashes between fishermen around the Fraser River's mouth in the early twentieth century, the Vancouver Riot of 1907, and attempts to drive Japanese Americans out of Toledo, Oregon, and Ellensburg, Washington, between the world wars. More commonplace acts seldom made the newspapers. A Seattle Issei in the early 1920s noted that young boys had thrown stones at him and that on one occasion an older man had knocked off his hat. Another recalled that "little rascals threw pebbles at me and sprinkled me with a hose" as he went to church on Sundays. A police officer remarked: "It's just kids' mischief," and "took no action at all."[55]

The typical Issei would not even have contacted the police officer. Gordon Hirabayashi, who grew up in a western Washington farming community, observed that "for most Japanese Americans the ultimate objective was survival, not confrontation." Since "the nail that sticks out is the one that gets hit. . . . to avoid trouble one should become inconspicuous, and, above all, avoid confrontation."[56] Those in British Columbia followed the same principle. Even before the 1907 riot, the Vancouver Nisei "were always very cautious in our actions so as not to agitate the situation any more than necessary," recalled Katsuyoshi Morita.[57] The second generation did, indeed, learn this lesson. A Vancouver Nisei, confronted by discrimination in the late 1930s, recalled that he and his friends reasoned that "we could enjoy ourselves in lots of ways, just like every other Canadian kid living in Vancouver, and if a couple of guys who ran restaurants, a few who ran theatres didn't like us, well, why worry."[58]

This is not to say that the Issei and their children never protested injustice, never fought back. Kibun Miyazaki wrote from eastern Washington in 1917 to describe how he intimidated a burly white co-worker who had sworn at him by remarking, "I don't like American-style fist-fighting or tackling. . . . my way to fight is with a gun."[59] Some recalled hitting schoolmates who taunted them. But the ideal response to such indignities was to win over one's enemy without the use of violence or intimidation. Yoshito Kawachi recalled striking, when "my patience broke," two white girls who persisted in plaguing him at a Hood River school—but this was only after he had impressed his other white schoolmates by giving candy to those who treated him well.[60] Fuyo Nishiyori was even more determined in gaining the friendship of the bigoted white women she worked with at Seattle's Pike Place Market. She one day offered part of her ice cream cone to one of these vendors, only to have the woman spit on it and knock it from her hands. But she was undeterred. Later that day, when the rude woman became ill, Nishiyori helped her by calling her son and putting away her merchandise. "After that," she concluded, the woman "changed her attitude toward me."[61] Such people protested racial discrimination discreetly if at all. Yaeshige Mochizuki's letter to a Washington theater that had insisted on seating him on the second floor assured the manager that "this letter is not a plea or a protest, but only for future reference" before asking to "please explain why you discriminate against Japanese?"[62] A Japanese Canadian recalled taking a more circuitous route in objecting to having to vacate a Vancouver swimming pool by 9:30, when the white people began arriving: "Just before we'd get out some of us, and sometimes all of us, would pee in the pool. . . . If you're going to swim in a city-owned pool and not let some of us swim in it because of the colour of our skin, then you're going to have to swim in some of our pee."[63] Nonconfrontation was not the same thing as passivity.

The pressures facing the north Pacific slope's Issei and Nisei increased dramatically during World War II. Umeo Uyeda, a Vancouver first grader at the time of Pearl Harbor, recalled attacks from older boys and "the terror I used to feel at the prowl cars" surveying Japanese neighborhoods at night.[64] As before the war, most anti-Asian prejudice took nonviolent though virulent forms. Kathy Hogan, who wrote a column for a coastal Washington newspaper, in 1943 lampooned the idea that "Japs" could become loyal citizens: "It has taken the rest of us thousands of years to get to be Americans, but the Japs—who were a tribe of diapered aboriginal fishermen when Commodore Matthew Perry let them out of their economic Pandora's box back in 1854— have beaten evolution to the draw and got to be Americans in less than a hundred years . . . by putting on little frock coats and glasses and learning to rattle off the preamble to the Constitution."[65] Racism also flourished north of the border, even though Canadians were not much engaged in the war's Pacific theater. A Vancouver woman recalled that "the Japanese were more our enemy than the Germans."[66] The war against Japan was, for many West Coast residents, a war against people of Japanese descent.[67]

The war came home to Vancouver early in 1942. A veteran and three other young Caucasians attempted to rob a small Japanese Canadian confectionary store. When Yoshiyuki Uno resisted, one of the thieves shot him dead. Early newspaper reports manifested more empathy for the victims of this crime than for its perpetrators. One termed the deceased's mother as "plucky" for chasing the four men out of the store.[68] The jury found the four guilty of murder on 18 April. The judge had no recourse but to sentence them to death, although the jury had recommended mercy. One of the convicted, Robert Hughes, took advantage of his opportunity to address the court and excoriated it for wanting "to string up four boys for some lousy Jap."[69]

This verdict and sentence provoked much public sympathy for the defendants. The Vancouver *Daily Province* had already referred to Hughes as a "tall good-looking Canadian soldier" whose father "had collapsed from the strain" of the trial, although it termed the trial "a justification and a vindication of our Canadian system of justice" in which "it made no difference . . . that the murdered man was the member of an enemy race or that the accused were of our own people."[70] Likewise, the *Sun* concluded that for the court to take race into account would be to "reduce the justice of Canada to the level of the justice of Japan."[71] Most readers apparently disagreed. Some simply objected to capital punishment or asserted that four men should not be executed for murdering one. But many injected race into their arguments. "M. B." lamented the taking of "four white lives" for killing one "Japanese."[72] Dorothy Lake argued that Hughes's willingness "to die for his country" constituted "loyalty to his race."[73] "Seething," who claimed to "know some really very nice Japanese people," asserted that he or she would "get four Japs for these four boys" if the Japanese invaded. R. W. Wilson argued that the nation was preparing "to kill Japs when they come" and that "we would have to also kill the ones that were here." Hence the four convicted killers should have the opportunity to "kill many more Japs."[74] Rarely did letter writers express sympathy for Uno or his family. A year later, when the jury in a retrial found the defendants guilty of manslaughter rather than murder, "an audible sigh of relief" arose from the courtroom.[75] The lessons of this case were not lost on British Columbia's Japanese Canadians: most whites evidently assumed that they would fight for Japan, that they were not loyal Canadians.[76]

These assumptions lay behind the forced relocation of coastal Japanese Canadians and Japanese Americans in the weeks and months following Uno's murder. The U.S. camps were located far inland; neither Washington nor Oregon had any, although near the war's end some former internees settled east of the Cascades. The majority of Japanese Canadians lived near or on the coast and were sent to centers located in the British Columbia interior, some in all-male work camps, others in larger camps dominated by families. Those who attempted to live outside of these camps faced substantial prejudice and pressures from the region's white residents. Over twelve thousand Japanese Canadians lived in cramped British Columbia relocation communities by the spring of 1943, though many would soon leave for work on the prairies or in Ontario.[77]

Forced relocation was a tremendous blow to the thousands of Issei and Nisei who had struggled so long and hard to make a home and a life for themselves in places like Steveston, Vancouver, Seattle, Portland, and Hood River. All had to go, foreign born and native born alike, those loyal to Japan and those loyal to Canada or the United States. The move itself was a shock. They received but a few days' notice and had to sell possessions for a small fraction of their worth, particularly in British Columbia. Many British Columbia men were separated from their families. One child remembered the night her father left them, "seeing all these men, most of whom had been big bosses in their own homes, . . . being sent . . . to a distant work camp."[78]

At this point, it seemed, Japanese Canadians and Japanese Americans did not have much left to lose. Their determination to endure oppression and prejudice largely without complaint, let alone violence, had not shielded them from a catastrophic relocation and a future pregnant with uncertainty. Perhaps these unprecedented pressures would prompt violent militantism.

They did not. Few Issei or Nisei actively resisted relocation and the indignities that accompanied it. One of the most cited instances occurred at the Vancouver impoundment center in May 1942, when a police officer struck several people in a crowd of internees who, reacting to a frightening rumor, had rushed out of the building. Eiko Henmi, a Nisei woman, confronted the man angrily: "What do you think you are doing! Do you think these women are so much cows that you can beat them back into place!"[79] Several hundred British Columbia Nisei husbands, some of whom sympathized with Japan, elected to defy orders separating them from their families, but they did not resist the arrests that quickly followed. Indeed, most Nisei counseled cooperation. The *New Canadian*, voice of Vancouver's educated second generation, urged its readers early in 1942 to "endure . . . endure . . . and still endure," to "forge a record of dignity and endurance to leave as a proud heritage for our sons and daughters to come."[80] The Issei were more inclined to be loyal to Japan—and to comply with Canadian authorities. "We could do nothing but grit our teeth, swallow our tears, and obey orders," recalled one.[81] Adachi concludes that "most Japanese did not resist evacuation but cooperated with a docility that was almost wholly in line with their background and their particular development as a minority group."[82]

This cooperation generally persisted in British Columbia's internment camps. A man reportedly remarked, "Shikata-ga-nai" (it can't be helped), to a woman who was weeping at her first sight of Sandon, the "little poky place" in which she and four of her children would have to live.[83] Men working in the road camps were more likely to protest, but they rarely employed violence against Caucasians.[84]

Relations within the Japanese Canadian community were not as pacific. Leaders who had cooperated with the evacuation process were often discredited and occasionally beaten. Those loyal to Japan resented Nisei or Issei who were not. Suzuki ran "a daily gauntlet" of bullying schoolmates at the Slocan camp because of his vocal Canadian patriotism.[85] Those who supported Japan were also angry and at times violent toward camp residents who elected to leave to become self-supporting or who opposed the repatriation program to Japan that the Canadian government offered near the war's close. Violence also erupted simply from the camps' crowded conditions and the strains of internment. These instant communities threw together Japanese Canadians of diverse places, religions, political beliefs, ages, and economic classes, all of them under tremendous financial and personal difficulties.[86]

Still, violence continued to play a relatively minor role in the lives of the north Pacific slope's Japanese Americans and Japanese Canadians, this despite the terrible toll that the war inflicted upon them. North America's Issei and Nisei had emphasized and practiced stoic endurance for decades. Wartime catastrophes did not change this.

Just the opposite could be said of the region's African Americans. World War II was a great boon for the Pacific Northwest's Blacks, and violence continued to loom large in their communities.

The war drew tens of thousands of migrants to the shipyards and defense industries of Oregon and particularly Washington. Seattle's African American community grew from less than four thousand in 1940 to at least ten thousand in 1945, when it constituted about 3 per cent of the city's population. An estimated twenty-three thousand African Americans made their way to the Portland area during the war. Many did not stay for long. But many others did—or resided across the Columbia River, in Vancouver, Washington, or in Vanport, a brand new city that was about one-third Black by 1945. Indeed, it was the racial mix of several small cities that changed most dramatically. The number of African Americans living in the Puget Sound community of Bremerton shot up from seventy-seven to over forty-five hundred in just five years. The Black community of Pasco, in eastern Washington, went from next to nothing to over three thousand. Many early workers came from the northeastern United States, but most came from the South in 1943 and 1944, when African American migration peaked. The migrants sometimes came as families, but often as single women and particularly men. Large numbers of Black servicemen were also stationed in parts of the Pacific Northwest.[87]

The newcomers received a chilly welcome. Mayor Earl Riley proclaimed that "Portland can absorb only a minimum of Negroes without upsetting the city's regular life."[88] A Reed College student interviewed Portland whites who contrasted African Americans from the South, who "know their place and work hard," with those from New York City, who were more prone to agitate.[89] Seattle police chief Herbert Kimsey remarked in early 1943: "We have had little trouble with the local Negro population." But he added that "those who have come here from out of the city" were apt to commit crimes.[90]

Some well-established African American residents agreed. One who had lived in Seattle for twenty years remarked in early 1943 that many Blacks were coming to the city "for the sole purpose of robbery, begging and using vulgar language on the streets, buses, etc."[91] Other longtime Seattle residents later recalled a variety of fearful reactions to the new arrivals. One said that "although we had our share of segregation we felt that we were better off if we were less visible," that the newcomers might make "a lot of noise" and then "we would all suffer."[92] Another woman remembered fearing that the shabbily dressed arrivals would "come up here in our wonderful country and spoil things."[93]

Longtime African American residents of Seattle and Portland feared that the unprecedented numbers of newcomers would upset race relations that had been generations in the making. How could they successfully absorb tens of thousands of largely uneducated young men and women?

The Pacific Northwest's African American communities were bound to experience a great deal of strain during World War II, regardless of how the new arrivals acted. The influx of war workers strained housing across the region, but continued segregation made Black neighborhoods especially crowded. Many restaurant and theater operators, alarmed by the rising numbers of African Americans, became more rather than less discriminatory, and the war did not end employment discrimination. Companies and unions generally succeeded in restricting African Americans to the most menial jobs in defense plants, and Blacks made very little progress in gaining access to professional or government positions during most of the war.[94]

Prewar African Americans in Washington and Oregon were not, as we have seen, passive in the face of discrimination. The newcomers were still more assertive. Seattle's NAACP and National Urban League chapters became more militant in resisting discrimination. So did individuals. One longtime Black resident observed that many of the recent arrivals were "awfully aggressive," a trait she linked to their changed circumstances. "Down there," in the South, "a lot of them had to step off the sidewalk and let the other fella pass by," she remarked. When "they got up here . . . they would push the other fellow off."[95] Escaping the South meant, to many newcomers, not having to tolerate racism. A combination of rising African American expectations, continued discrimination, rising numbers of highly racist white southerners, and the dynamics inherent to rapidly expanding and unstable populations made for volatile race relations.

The Pacific Northwest did not, like the rest of the country, see any race riots, but Blacks and whites often clashed in small-scale altercations—particularly at work. In 1944 six African American women in a Vancouver, Washington, shipyard were fired after complaining that their white supervisor regularly called them "niggers" and kicked them.[96] Joseph Staton, the Seattle man who had destroyed "whites-only" signs during the Depression, was the only Black in his work group. One day a white man from Arkansas showed up and "almost fainted right there" upon learning that Staton was his supervisor. He then told "nigger jokes *all* . . . day long." Staton reached his limit at mid-afternoon and grabbed the man's throat. He also recalled a fight between white and Black war workers that began when a Black woman slapped a white one for objecting to working next to her.[97] Likewise, Albert Smith recalled that an African American worker knocked down a white who "hollered" about having to sit next to a Black man in a Seattle-area cafeteria.[98] Race relations were particularly strained on the crowded buses and trolleys that carried war workers to and from their jobs. Elva Nicholas recalled that many white southerners "tried to bring the South up with 'em," and cited an instance in which she informed a woman who tried to eject her from her bus seat that "you're up here now, you'll have to get used to it or else."[99] Julia Hayes reported that passengers crowded her into a white man who called her names and threatened to hit her. She warned him that "he wouldn't look the same" if he tried it, but, at the urging of two friends, he kicked at her face. Once at the shipyards he again assaulted her, and she cut him on the arm with a penknife.[100] A year before, in 1943, two white men from the South reportedly chased a Black worker from a bus and beat him unconscious. Most transit fights were not this serious, but pushing and yelling between Blacks and whites was not uncommon.[101] Blacks and whites also clashed off the job, at the dining and entertainment centers of housing projects and at public restaurants.[102]

In the above incidents, African Americans seldom backed down from a fight and whites usually precipitated these conflicts, either by trying to eject African Americans from an integrated setting or through the use of racial epithets. They also indicate that wartime interracial violence seldom settled anything. Before the war, as we have seen, the violence employed by African American children and adults often served to both resist and overcome prejudice. It could serve as an ultimately constructive, if harrowing, step in winning acceptance and even friendship from white classmates and neighbors. But violent altercations between shipyard workers seemed only to express racial tensions, not to resolve them. Perhaps these wartime communities were simply too volatile and divided to foster much grassroots interracial understanding. Or perhaps, as established African American residents had feared, the region's whites were simply unprepared to deal with so many Black people.

Indeed, the war stimulated white fears of Black crime and violence. Portland's police chief, according to the *Oregonian,* "charged Negroes with a bulk of the major gun scrapes and knifings committed . . . during the war boom."[103] The *Native Sons of Washington,* a monthly publication, complained in 1944 of criminal activity by the region's African Americans, citing white slavery, liquor and marijuana sales, sexual assaults, and murder. "If this crime wave does not stop," it warned, "preventive measures will have to be taken."[104]

African American soldiers were responsible for the most blatant act of Black-on-white violence that occurred in the Pacific Northwest during World War II. In the summer of 1944 more than fifty African Americans stationed at Fort Lawton attacked some Italian prisoners of war. Several hours later the body of one of the Italians was found hanging from a tree. A white American soldier explained that his Black counterparts "were particularly sore because the Negro troops were doing all the dirty work" while the Italians "were compelled to do so little."[105] African Americans were incensed that white enemies were being treated better than Black patriots.

But African Americans were much more apt to kill each other than to kill whites. Whites were the victims of only four out of sixteen killings by Seattle Blacks reported between November 1941 and November 1945 in the city's primary African American newspaper. In none of these four shootings did race appear to be the primary motive for the homicide.[106]

The motives of African American intra-racial assaults and homicides are difficult to discern, partly because newspapers did not report them in much detail, but also because stabbings and shootings often began over seemingly trivial altercations. A Seattle African American said that he fractured another's skull in a fight that began when the dead man or one of his companions objected to him singing on the street late at night. A few months later, in the summer of 1942, two Seattle Blacks reportedly shot at each other "in an argument over a small sum of money."[107] A Black shipyard worker reportedly stabbed a Black soldier in a Seattle tavern in late 1944 after yelling, "I'll show you what a civilian can do to soldiers and sailors."[108] These fights were not unlike those that had been common on the north Pacific slope between and within many ethnic groups during the mid-nineteenth century, when disproportionate numbers of well-armed young men from diverse places and backgrounds easily took offense at each other's behavior and readily defended their honor.[109] But African American women as well as men more frequently used violence than did their white counterparts. Four of the sixteen killings reported in the *Northwest Enterprise* were by wives who said that they shot their husbands to protect themselves from abuse. All of these factors contributed to a very high rate of homicides by Seattle's African Americans during the war, well over fifty per hundred thousand per year.[110]

Faced with repeated and exaggerated accounts of violent African American crime, Black editors balanced condemning such acts with contesting white interpretations of them. A writer in the *Northwest Enterprise* asserted in early 1943 that a Black man's recent assault on a white woman "shocks the sensibilities of every Negro in Seattle, both saint and sinner," and that the accused deserved to die. But he hastened to add: "No race may claim a monopoly of vice or virtue."[111] Indeed, the *Northwest Enterprise* pointedly noted the absence of African Americans in particular criminal acts. In the summer of 1943 a headline declared that a riot had occurred in Vancouver, Washington, "SANS NEGROES."[112] A year later the paper published the photograph of a white shipyard worker accused of sexually assaulting and killing a fourteen-year-old Seattle girl. "DO NOT MISTAKE THIS BEAST FOR A NEGRO," the paper remarked. "WE ADMIT WE HAVE SPAWNED SOME BRUTES, BUT NOTHING AKIN TO THIS."[113]

Black leaders defended some African Americans accused of crimes. A number of Oregonians protested the execution of Robert E. Lee Folkes, who was convicted of killing a white woman on a train near Albany, Oregon, in 1944. Portland's and Seattle's NAACP criticized instances of police brutality several times during the war, as did other African American organizations. A *Northwest Enterprise* editorial likened the behavior of two Seattle police officers who reportedly beat a Black woman to "Gestapo" tactics, noting that a Black soldier viewing the episode remarked: "That is what I am wearing this uniform for?"[114]

Like Horace Cayton before them, Seattle's Black leaders viewed Black violence through a race-sensitive lens. The *Northwest Enterprise* asserted that no reason was "sufficient to justify" lynching the Italian prisoner of war.[115] But it also pointed out the many provocations that African American soldiers had suffered and that the evidence linking those soldiers to the Italian's death was less than overwhelming. One commentator concluded his observations on the trial of the African American servicemen by asserting that "there is no country that can compare with America if it lives up to . . . the Constitution of the United States" and that "the Negro" was "America's most loyal citizen." He looked forward to a day when "we shall all be free," would "all live the American way."[116]

Seattle's Black leaders expressed ambivalence over the death of Eugene Moszee. Moszee, who had come from Texas five years before, was shot in a 1945 gunfight with two Seattle police officers, one of whom he killed. An *Enterprise* columnist reported that the community's general opinion seemed to be that Moszee "had come in contact with so much discrimination that he had made of himself a one man committee to fight it in all its various and ugly forms." The writer, although sympathetic with Moszee's distrust of the police, could not support "his approach to the solution of the whole problem" of racism.[117] A second *Enterprise* columnist was easier on the police and harder on Moszee. "Discrimination is as odious to us as to any living Negro," he wrote, "but we will make no attempt to correct the evil by force." Discrimination would be ended "by reason." Moszee "brought his race more harm than good," and his "methods do not point the way."[118]

Such commentators were frustrated that they could do so little to control the acts of people like Moszee, African Americans who did not seem to share the Black leadership's hope for integration into the American dream. At about the time of Moszee's death, a writer took "time out . . . from exposes and complaints of injustices" toward Blacks "to take an introspective view of our race." He or she cited numerous homicides by Black Seattle residents over the previous year and vulgar "street groups" who exhibited "lack of respect

for themselves or the decent pedestrians who pass their way." "WHAT ARE
WE GOING TO DO ABOUT IT?" the column asked. Apparently not much.
"Our public men, our YWCA, our YMCA, our ministers, our interracial societies cannot become the keeper of the conscience of these derelicts," the author
asserted, "because their minds seldom meet."[119]

Indeed, the preachments of the *Northwest Enterprise* would likely have
struck the rowdies who lined Seattle's Jackson and East Madison Streets as
irrelevant and naive, just as a quarter century earlier Horace Cayton's ship-
mates violated the sensibilities he had been raised to respect and to practice.
For them, white privilege and hostility were intractable givens, facts of life
that Black people coped with as best they could, breaking conventional laws
and moral principles when it suited their purposes. In 1945, more so than
before, the Pacific Northwest's African Americans essentially constituted two
communities, those who believed that mainstream white society was capable of treating them justly and those who did not. Those who found American
society inherently and irreversibly racist had little incentive—outside of fear
of punishment—to observe its laws.

This pessimistic view of racism found vivid expression in the so-called Black
protest novels of the 1940s. Richard Wright's *Native Son* inaugurated the genre
in 1940. Wright's radical departure consisted of creating a protagonist, Bigger
Thomas, who is both the victim of suffocating racism and very difficult to
empathize with. Thomas is not the sort of man that the leading African
Americans of Seattle and Portland approved of. He is more attracted to thiev-
ing than to working, he votes only because he can thereby make a few dollars, he is unable to form affectionate relationships with others, and religion
strikes him as silly and pointless. He finds meaning and transcendence in violence. To be sure, his killing of the young white woman whose family he works
for is accidental. But Thomas quickly realizes that "all of his life had been
leading to something like this."[120] After killing Bessie, his girlfriend, "there
remained to him a queer sense of power," for "these two murders were the
most meaningful things that had ever happened to him." "For a little while
I was free. I was doing something," he remarks.[121] Wright's purpose was not
to confirm a racist belief in the inherent criminality of African American men.
Bigger Thomas and the actual men that Wright drew from in creating him
were not "essentially and organically bad." "Environment" had "produced
these men."[122] Chester Himes's *If He Hollers Let Him Go,* set in wartime

California and published in 1947, makes the same point. It is Bob Jones's sensitivity to racism, his acute awareness of white people's continual and offensive reaction to his color, that enrages him and makes him want to kill and rape, to make the white man who had hit and insulted him "feel as scared and powerless and unprotected as I felt every goddamned morning I woke up."[123] This decision to murder leaves Jones feeling "relaxed, confident, strong . . . just like I thought a white boy oughta feel."[124] It is a measure of Jones's impotence, his inability to "be a hero," that he does not kill.[125] In a highly racist society, murder became, as Thomas's lawyer asserted, "an act of *creation!*"[126] Intractable racism, Wright and Himes argued, turned conventional American morality on its head. It sapped the law of its legitimacy and transformed even heinous crimes into creative, life-affirming acts.

But these creative fictional acts were often inflicted on other African Americans. Thomas sadistically beats up one of his friends. He accidentally kills his white employer but purposefully murders his Black lover. William Attaway's *Blood on the Forge* follows the life of Big Mat, a powerful African American who kills an abusive white riding boss on a Kentucky farm and then flees to the steel mills of Pennsylvania. But Big Mat's violence is indiscriminate; it is also employed against the women of color with whom he lives and against striking workers. Indeed, he finds all violent acts intoxicating; they make him feel "big as God Almighty," like the brutal riding boss he had feared.[127] Likewise, it is not simply out of self-defense that Ann Petry's protagonist in *The Street* finally kills the African American man who is trying to rape her. She continues to bludgeon the prostrate Boots Smith long after he has lost consciousness, for "this impulse to violence had been in her for a long time, growing, feeding." Betrayals by African American men contribute to her rage, but as the blows become heavy and fast "she was striking at the white world which thrust black people into a walled enclosure from which there was no escape." The desperately poor and circumscribed Harlem street on which Lutie Johnson and her young son live and cannot escape symbolizes the hopelessness of their lives and the roots of her violence.[128] Humiliation, these writers argue, breeds hatred and violence, not long-suffering patience.

The north Pacific slope was a long way from Ann Petry's Harlem and from the emerging school of realist African American fiction. But the themes explored by these novelists help to illuminate the violence engaged in by poor African Americans across the continent. Wright, Attaway, Petry, and even

Himes were not attempting to glorify African American violence. Rather, they were explaining its prevalence in the African American community. Petry, in the words of Arthur Davis, set out "to show why the Negro has a high crime rate, a high death rate, and little or no chance of keeping his family unit intact in large northern cities."[129] These intellectuals crossed the boundary dividing relatively prosperous African Americans from their poorer and less educated counterparts to describe how intractable racism combined with a deeply felt rage against that racism could create individuals who were very violent outside and particularly inside the African American community.

In mid-August 1945, a few days after the United States had dropped a second atomic bomb on Japan, several African American soldiers and an African American police officer fought in a north Portland cafe. According to the *Oregonian,* some soldiers had been arguing over their bill and attacked Harry Payton, an officer in training, when he arrived to settle the quarrel. He fired several shots, some of which wounded one of the soldiers. The men beat him.

The *Observer,* Portland's Black newspaper, offered a fuller and more troubling account of the fight. It pointed out that the white officers whom Payton had called for assistance instead disarmed him, allowed the soldiers to assault him, then delayed taking him to the hospital. "This is the first time an incident has ever been brought to our attention where officers of the law outright refused to give protection and coverage to a brother officer," the editorial remarked. This writer both criticized and empathized with the violent soldiers who had attacked Payton: "The abuses to which most Negro soldiers are subjected in battle areas and in the United States is resented more than death is feared," and each "is determined that his return to a civilian existence will not be dotted with the same persecution as when he entered the service." Yet very often their "misdirected" resistance found "another Negro for the target."[130]

This story neatly illustrates some of the dynamics and ironies of African Americans and violence on the north Pacific slope in the mid-twentieth century. Violence, as the *Observer* pointed out, was a protest against racism, a signal that Blacks were unwilling to be pushed around. Yet, more often than not, it was other African Americans who absorbed those protests. Indeed, the white police officers who wanted Payton bloodied and humiliated did not have to skin their knuckles. They had only to disarm him and to step aside.

This example is unusual in its interracial nature. Blacks commonly attacked each other without the benefit of direct white intervention. But the episode was representative inasmuch as the soldiers' blows both protested racism and harmed a fellow African American. Such acts "simultaneously challenge *and* reinforce existing power relations," as Robin D. G. Kelley, writing of the early-twentieth-century South, puts it.[131]

Japanese Americans and Japanese Canadians suffered from and employed violence less frequently than their African American counterparts did. Recalling the forced move from Vancouver to the interior in 1942, Joy Kogawa writes in her acclaimed 1981 novel *Obasan* that she and her fellow Japanese Canadians "disappear into the future undemanding as dew."[132] This was not, as we have seen, universally true. Some Issei and Nisei protested relocation before and after the fact. Nearly a half century later Japanese Americans and Japanese Canadians would demand and receive official apologies from their governments. But aggressive resistance was the exception rather than the rule through the 1940s, particularly among those born in Japan. In a subsequent novel, *Itsuka*, Kogawa writes that the Issei possessed a "code of honour requiring them to gaman, to endure without flinching"; that their lives in Japan began with watching "the poverty of fellow villagers who suffered in silence, for the love of parents, for the honour of ancestors, for the sake of the whole."[133] People of Japanese descent directly challenged racism only rarely. One's inner attitude could transcend outward circumstances that could not be changed, could not be helped. Yet endurance was not the same thing as resignation. Persistent hope of a better life drew these men and women across the Pacific Ocean, helped them to create close-knit and economically viable communities under very difficult circumstances, and enabled them to endure the manifold humiliations of World War II.

As a marginalized, highly coherent ethnic group, the north Pacific slope's African Americans had much in common with Japanese Americans and Japanese Canadians. Their reaction to prejudice constituted one of the chief differences. Washington and Oregon's African Americans were more hopeful, less stoic. They commonly took prejudice on directly, particularly as individuals and as families, and they often used violence, the same coercive tool that had so often been inflicted on them, to defend themselves or to assert their rights. But that violent style was not simply a tactic used in interracial confrontations. It also flourished within the Black community—particularly during the heady but tumultuous days of World War II. African Americans were the quintessential Americans in that they had learned that equality meant not having to defer even outwardly, and that violence was American democracy's compatriot.

The divergent histories of peoples of African and Japanese descent in North America illustrate that racism could flourish with or without violence. The way that a given group experienced violence—as an external threat, a reaction to that threat, or an internal dynamic—denoted not just a certain type of oppression. It also signified a particular tradition of resistance.

Epilogue

Discovering Violence

ONE LATE SUMMER'S NIGHT in 1993 two young African Americans brutally beat a white man outside the Lloyd Center mall as his horrified fiancée looked on. The event was highly unusual. Blacks typically reserved their violence for each other, and they were much more likely to be victims than perpetrators of hate crimes. But the episode immediately became, as one observer put it, "Portland's version of the urban nightmare." Indeed, most of the over two hundred people who shared their reaction to the beating with the *Oregonian* expressed deep fear of violent African Americans. "The blacks seem to be the ones with the bad attitudes," said one. "I can't help it if I'm white and they're black and I feel like a target." Another vowed to never again go to the mall where the beating occurred. "Just from my experience watching TV and reading the news, there is a certain type of black man I find frightening," she remarked, "usually between the ages of 15 and 25."[1] As at the century's outset, many white Portlanders were afraid of the city's relatively small complement of African Americans.

Residents of the north Pacific slope had become more fearful of violence in general. A 1976 poll of British Columbians revealed that 49 percent felt less safe and just 2 percent more safe walking the streets than they had five years before. A 1993 poll of Washington voters found that about 80 percent believed that crime was on the rise, and they listed it ahead of health care as the number one issue confronting the nation. "We are being overrun by scary people who wait in the open for the opportunity to take what belongs to us and damage us in the process," complained a resident of downtown Seattle in 1991.[2] Being the victim of a violent crime had become the quintessential violation of one's humanity. A Prince George resident asked in 1995 whether fear of being attacked inside or outside one's home did not constitute "a total loss of basic freedom?"[3]

Violence has become such a powerful emblem of injustice that political adversaries often try to top each other's accounts of being victimized by it. The Oregon Citizens' Alliance campaign against homosexuality provoked numerous charges and countercharges of violent attacks in the early 1990s. A Portland man wondered how OCA organizers could be "so fascinated by what I might do in the privacy of my bedroom as to be willing to cause all this pain, all this fear and all this violence in our state."[4] A television ad explicitly linked the OCA's efforts to growing numbers of reported bias or hate crimes against gays and lesbians, including a Salem firebombing that had taken two lives.[5] Lon Mabon, the OCA's head, countered that his organization had condemned such acts and that OCA supporters had themselves been harassed. Indeed, in late 1993 someone shot at his home. He granted that "not every homosexual is a violent criminal," but he and his supporters argued that gay men were prone to pedophilia and sadomasochism.[6] Debates over issues like homosexuality now commonly turned on which side could most convincingly depict itself as the targets of violence, its opponent as the perpetrators.

The same dynamic has shaped recent debates over gun control. In 1997 attempts to charge an eighty-five-year-old Kamloops, British Columbia, man with aggravated assault for stabbing a much younger and heavier man who was attempting to break into his home provoked calls from indignant residents complaining that "criminals are getting the upper hand here."[7] Citizens needed weapons to protect themselves, to avoid being victimized. "Gun control looks much more like victim disarmament than criminal control," declared a Washington resident in 1993.[8] Gun registration would simply, as a Prince George editorial put it two years later, "hurt those who have never hurt anybody."[9]

Gun control proponents have pointed out that the world could not be neatly divided up between law abiders and law breakers. Many domestic homicides, for example, were committed by people who were model citizens outside the home.[10]

But many gun control advocates simply associate guns and their owners with aggression and violence. Portland's *Willamette Week* probed the silence and confusion that struck well-to-do leftists when one of their own, Marcia Moskowitz, gunned down her estranged husband in 1993. "This kind of thing just doesn't happen to our friends," remarked one. Another explained Moskowitz's act as a reversion to her modest roots: "Here's a working-class kid from the streets, with a working-class response to what she felt was injustice." A longtime friend of the couple explained such reactions as "a class thing." "These people of privilege can't even imagine anyone they know using a gun."[11] Good people, they believe, simply have nothing to do with firearms and violence.

A growing revulsion toward violence has also intensified and altered debates about the corporal punishment of children. Concern over and reporting of child abuse exploded in the 1960s, on the north Pacific slope as elsewhere on the continent. This early movement met little explicit resistance, in part because it focused on extreme examples. When a Vancouver writer asserted in 1976 that "child battering is without any doubt the most horrifying and prevalent crime tolerated in this community," few felt moved to disagree.[12] Indeed, highly publicized killings of children—particularly if they were young and white—commonly provoked a great deal of mourning and outrage, as if these innocent victims symbolized the vulnerability to violent strangers that so many adults seemed to feel.[13]

But child welfare advocates were soon testing this consensus by asserting that any use of physical force was cruel and unnecessary. British Columbia and then Oregon outlawed corporal punishment in schools in the 1970s. British Columbia Education Minister Eileen Dailly announced the change early in 1973, explaining, "If we want to reduce acts of violence in the community we must eliminate it in our schools. If we want to develop future generations into more humane people we must practise more humanity ourselves."[14] Many others echoed these arguments over the next quarter century. A Washington schoolteacher remarked in 1995 that spanking taught "that force is the way to solve problems."[15] The Oregon Committee for the Prevention of Child Abuse listed ten damaging lessons that spanking taught, including that children could not control themselves and "that it is OK to hit someone you love, which can perpetuate domestic violence."[16] But many simply asserted what seemed to them self-evident: "Let's not hit kids."[17] "I have never understood how one could hit or strike someone on the street and be charged with assault while a parent hits a child and it is accepted as discipline," remarked a British Columbian.[18] Oregon's movement against hitting children received considerable impetus in late 1997 when Governor John Kitzhaber, a Democrat and the father of a newborn, inaugurated the "Hands Are Not for Hurting" program by pledging that "I will not use my hands for hurting myself or hurting others."[19]

Traditionalists reacted defensively and angrily to these developments. "Please don't confuse beating a child with disciplining them with a spanking in love," asked a Puget Sound resident in 1997. "There's a big difference between a swat and a beating," added another.[20] Conservatives wish to retain the right to use at least a modicum of violence.

Yet the term "violence" has become so pejorative that even those who have defended its use have disavowed the word. Hence a proponent of corporal punishment in British Columbia schools remarked in 1973 that this sort of discipline was "not an act of violence" but "an act of love."[21] Likewise, a Seattle-area resident asserted in 1985 that "the corporal punishment I (and millions of others) believe in and practice regularly is not 'violent.'"[22] "Violence" has become, by definition, abusive.

To be sure, much of modern North American culture has celebrated violence. The ability to fight plays an integral part in the novels of Oregon's Pulitzer prize–winning Ken Kesey early in the 1960s. *One Flew over the Cuckoo's Nest* features a set of timid male sanitarium residents, McMurphy, the consummate individualist who eventually liberates them, and his foe, the domineering Nurse Ratchet, who, like the institution itself, represents modern therapeutic culture. McMurphy's eventual assault of Ratchet exposes her physical weakness, breaking her spell over the other men. *Sometimes a Great Notion* is much less misogynistic, but here, too, violence plays a crucial role. Hank Stamper returns from the Korean War "to find the Dodgers in a slump, frozen apple pie just like Mom useta make in all the supermarkets, and a sour stench in the sweet land of liberty he'd risked his life defending." His old friends on the Oregon coast "acted tired, scared, asleep."[23] Yet he manages to remain his own man, running the family's logging business contrary to the wishes of his union-minded neighbors and literally outfighting them whenever they challenge him. These men admire Hank's rugged independence, and they are disheartened when a modern union organizer, using social pressure rather than old-fashioned intimidation, brings Hank to his knees and shuts his operation down. Hank is also humbled by his seemingly ineffectual younger half-brother, Leland, who arrives from the East at the novel's outset with a chronic case of ennui. Leland is not as impotent as he seems, for he cunningly seduces

Hank's sensitive wife, Vivian. But Leland has an epiphany of his own at his moment of victory; when presenting himself to Viv as the helpless victim of a beating at Hank's hands he forgets himself and fights back for the first time in his life. Using his fists transforms and energizes him, and his unexpected masculinization snaps Hank out of his funk. The two brothers, freed from their preoccupation with Vivian, call off the truce with the union and float their log boom down the river. This association of violence with male self-realization in a sanitized mass society was commonplace in the United States by the 1980s. Violent criminals had become the ultimate chic nonconformists, a trend facilitated by popular Hollywood films such as *Silence of the Lambs* and *Natural Born Killers*.[24]

But the tide was changing by the 1990s. Washington's David Guterson became the most widely read writer of the Pacific Northwest, and he features male protagonists who struggle to understand others, not to beat or subdue them. Violence represents immaturity, not coming of age.[25]

This growing sensitivity to violence has affected our behavior. The general homicide rate rose precipitously in the 1960s and early 1970s and more or less stayed at that high level for the next two decades. British Columbia's went from an average of less than two per hundred thousand in the 1950s to a peak of over four in 1974. Oregon stayed between four and five per hundred thousand for the first half of the 1990s, Washington at more than five. But then the rates declined. British Columbia's sank to less than three in 1997 and stayed there. Oregon's fell to 2.7 in 1999, Washington's to three. It is too early to discern to what extent this recent decline in homicides, which has occurred in most of the rest of North America, is due to evanescent shifts in demography and drug use. But it probably also has to do with changing values.[26]

Less extreme forms of violence have also declined—even when the homicide rate was increasing. During the nineteenth century, virtually all boys were expected to know how to fight, to "take care of themselves." Many still are. But many of the boys I grew up with on the Oregon coast in the 1960s and 1970s, particularly those who planned to go to college, chose not to. Formal military training is no longer a routine part of education for young males, and most educated men have followed President Clinton in deciding that they need not prove themselves on the field of battle.[27]

Marginal men have been less ready to put down their fists and guns. Elliott

Leyton, a leading anthropologist of murder, asserts that U.S. homicides are "overwhelmingly committed by men of low socio-economic status."[28] As we saw at the close of chapter one, British Columbia's Native people are about ten times more likely to kill or be killed than are their white counterparts. Domestic violence has been more evenly distributed, but here, too, poor or unemployed husbands and parents have been at least somewhat more apt to use it than have those who enjoy greater economic security.[29]

That growing numbers of educated men are apparently abjuring violence is certainly cause for a certain amount of celebration. Powerful people are not as inclined to employ violence as they used to be, and violence is a particularly pernicious form of domination.

But, in contrast to the fur-trade era, modern forms of dominance seldom require violence. Indeed, well-educated men's attempts to stigmatize violence—including firearms and hunting—may strike those less privileged as just another insult. Marginal people's violence constitutes an act of political protest inasmuch as it often expresses—albeit indirectly—resentments over poverty, racism, and other forms of injustice. Robert Heilman writes eloquently of the difficulties and humiliations that working-class people face in his southern Oregon community, of worrying that your kids will not have enough to eat, of watching friends move away, get divorced, commit suicide, of being ordered around by college-educated supervisors with more income and job security than you but less experience and knowlege. Physical force— or intimations of it—serves to remind purported superiors that there are other ways to measure a man's prowess: "a foreman who is uncomfortable with the underlying violence of his crew becomes their target."[30] Violence serves as an accomplishment and a coercive tool that marginalized men can fall back upon. That so many high-status men now profess to be finished with violence only rubs salt in the wound. Pierre Bourdieu writes that this attempt to rework traditional norms of virility seems to threaten "one of the last refuges of the autonomy of the dominated classes, of their capacity to produce their own representation of the accomplished man and the social world." "The new therapeutic morality" of nonviolent masculinity is politically charged in that it asks working-class men to surrender the only form of distinction for which they can compete on even ground.[31] This goes a long way toward explaining why opposition to gun control has often been so dogmatic and seemingly irrational—and why a Washington man in 1997 would name "the world's richest man, [Bill] Gates" and "other Seattle elitists" as the evil forces behind the movement to limit access to guns.[32] Microsoft's head represents a brave new world in which knowledge, cunning, and wealth count for everything, physical prowess and courage for nothing.[33]

The changing relationship between violence and power has also shaped recent discussions of spousal violence. North Americans discovered wife abuse in the 1970s. The bruised faces of young, beautiful women staring out from magazine covers and television screens prompted women and men alike to conclude that these victims needed and deserved our help. Women's shelters and treatment programs proliferated, and the police began arresting men for behavior that the law-enforcement community had ignored a generation or two before.[34]

This focus on the most brutal and explicit acts of male dominance generated considerable sympathy for wives who had been physically abused. But the emphasis on bruised, often passive women suggested that violence and dominance were one and the same: all violence was abusive, and abuse entailed violence. Like their counterparts of the nineteenth century, abused wives elicited the most sympathy when they were the helpless victims of a violent husband. But by the 1990s growing numbers of studies indicated that wives were about as likely to hit their husbands as vice versa, and growing numbers of men and women—including some scholars—were arguing that we ought to therefore become much more concerned about husband beating. "Is there something special about women that makes violence against them more heinous than violence against men?" asked a northern British Columbia resident.[35] A British Columbian whose female partner had physically assaulted him complained in 1998 that attacks should not be broken up into categories such as "elderly abuse, child abuse, abuse of the female." "Abuse is abuse," he asserted, "it's not a gender issue."[36]

I disagree. But before explaining why, I wish to point out that this assertion represents an important historical departure. Men, as evidence presented here has shown, have traditionally denied that women were capable of hurting them physically. Women's supposed physical and general inferiority reinforced each other. Paternalism has had a misogynistic underside—and paternalism is quickly eroding.

That growing numbers of husbands are admitting or claiming to fear their wives' physical strength suggests that male dominance is abating and that women no longer require men's protection as much as they once did. But it also indicates that dominance is becoming unhinged from violence. That men are willing to say that they fear women does not mean that male privilege is dead. Rather, it shows that male privilege can coexist with male appeals to victimhood and vulnerability, that physical strength is no longer the litmus test for dominance.

We have been slow to acknowledge this. The last four decades of the twentieth century began with a growing sensitivity to violence against vulnerable adults and children: the Civil Rights movement and subsequent movements concerned with people of color, the discovery of child and then wife abuse. But widespread sympathy for African Americans, children, and wives has been contingent on their status as pacific victims of violence. We have offered far more empathy to civil-rights marchers cringing under fire hoses than to militant Black Panthers, have been more quickly moved to pity by the plight of bruised babies than by sexually abused and truculent street kids. With dominance less reliant on the use of physical force than before, racism and sexism and the broader exercise of power and privilege have become more veiled, more difficult to pin down, to name. We often fancy that modern social movements have set us all free, that the right to vote, for example, bequeaths universal equality, that people are not being dominated if people are not being hit.

Yet traditional forms of privilege and dominance are alive and well, outside and inside of marriage. Social scientists who have simply asked modern couples which of them has the final say in decision making have concluded too readily that the vast majority of heterosexual relations are egalitarian. Aafke Komter's classic 1989 study "Hidden Power in Marriage" found that considerable, if generally unspoken, dissatisfaction lay beneath wives' apparent consent to the structuring of child care, leisure activities, sexual relations, and financial decisions.[37] Indeed, more recent studies describe the persistence of male privilege in several key areas, from who gets to pursue a new job in a different city to who controls the family's choice of television programs. Men's determination to monopolize the remote control is consequential as well as humorous.[38]

Indeed, many women have been most deeply offended not by male violence, but by male privilege. In the early 1960s, for example, a British Columbia woman stabbed her intoxicated husband in the back when he told her that he was going to leave her. He admitted in court that he had been drinking heavily for the two months before the stabbing, that he had been unemployed more often than not for the past two years, that their electricity had been cut off because of his failure to pay the bill, and that their landlord was about to evict them for being behind in the rent. He added that he had just told his wife and daughters that he intended to send for the children after he left her. He could also turn violent. His wife told the police that he had assaulted her with a hammer a week before. But it was his freedom to come and go as he pleased while she cared for their impoverished children, his bringing over drunken friends, his failure to provide anything for his family that figured most prominently in her statement. She did not claim to be afraid when she knifed him. His repeated assertion of traditional male prerogatives, not the threat of violence, prompted her to attempt murder.[39]

Should the courts excuse the acts of wives maddened by male privilege? Of course not. But neither can male dominance, a factor so pervasive that it affects all heterosexual relationships, be simply factored out of an analysis of spousal violence. Gender inevitably affects the moral textures, the causes, content, and outcome of violent interchanges, as do race, class, age, and less obvious variables.

Sibylle Artz's work on violent girls in and near Victoria illustrates the importance of considering the gendered context of violent behavior. Rising rates of violence by girls is often pointed to as evidence that girls have become as violent as boys. But females' violence does not necessarily indicate the abatement of male privilege. Indeed, it is often learned within very patriarchal family structures. Artz's violent schoolgirls are much more apt than both boys and nonviolent girls to have been victimized by physical or sexual abuse and to come from families characterized by pronounced male dominance. These families taught them that violence was an appropriate way to punish perceived subordinates, and the girls follow this script by beating younger, assertive girls, particularly those who flirt with the violent girls' boyfriends. The schoolgirls' violence both arises from and reinforces hierarchical social relations. They understand that at school, as at home, some people have a right to hit others.[40]

Larger stories and patterns of dominance and abuse are easily overlooked when violence becomes the solitary or primary lens through which social problems are assessed.

Consider, for example, the series of altercations involving two couples in

Greater Vancouver in the early 1960s. The evening began uneventfully enough. Mary and Dan were visiting a married couple, Denise and Jim, and having some drinks. At one point, during a conversation about another man whom Mary had been seeing, Dan grabbed Mary and pushed her down. Jim then restrained Dan. After a half hour or so the two couples went to different parts of the home. Jim threw up, and Denise got a bucket of water to clean the floor. She "told Jim to get up and he wouldn't, so I hit him on the back of the head and of course, when I hit him, he turned around and hit me with his open hand." They continued to quarrel, and Jim smashed some glasses. This drew Dan from the bedroom, and, in Denise's words, he "told Jim he mustn't do that, and to leave me alone, he shouldn't hit me at all, he had no business to do that." Jim then fell asleep. "That's pretty good," remarked Denise, "I don't run around nor go out anywhere and yet I get beat up." Dan agreed: "You are a good kid, he had no right to do that." Mary, on the other hand, deserved a beating, for she "ran around on him all the time" when he was away. Denise demurred, for Dan "was not married to Mary" and did not support her. Dan insisted that Mary "was no good," though "he loved her." Mary, for her part, announced that she was going to call a cab and go home after Dan called her "a couple of names that weren't very pleasant." Dan accused her of wanting to call her other man and followed her into the bedroom, insisting that she show him the telephone number. Jim was by now regaining consciousness, and Denise washed his hands and face and sat down with him to watch a movie, leaving the other couple to work out their differences. Dan soon emerged from the bedroom covered with blood, and Denise went in to find Mary unconscious and "badly beaten." Mary was dying. Jim later recalled hearing slaps in the bedroom, but "I never thought anything of it at the time." "It wasn't like he was killing her or anything," he remarked when asked to recount the events surrounding her murder.[41]

This incident brings to mind Clifford Geertz's observation that "the same people who arrange chrysanthemums cast swords."[42] Jim and Dan both hit their own partners and told each other not to. The events also point out this book's central argument: that the context and meaning of a violent act cannot be understood without exploring relations of power. Many of the apparent inconsistencies and peculiarities in the above set of altercations disappear if they are analyzed through the lens of male privilege. Dan and Jim acted consistently. Each asserted a right to control his partner's behavior, to hit her when she violated his rules, and to stop each other from hitting a woman in his presence. Dominant men claimed a right both to punish and to protect. In either instance, they constituted themselves as woman's superior.

This is not to say that powerful people have always succeeded in dictating who gets to hit. At one point in the evening, Denise struck Jim. No one seemed to take the blow very seriously, and Jim quickly trumped it with one of his own. But subordinates' violence has not always been so ineffectual. One of the reasons that powerful people have typically preferred to dominate without recourse to physical force is that the outcome of a violent conflict is difficult to predict and to control. Working-class men, in particular, have often taken great pride in their fighting ability, and, at least until recently, their social betters have found it difficult to dismiss altogether this sort of manly prowess. Powerful, early-twentieth-century residents of Seattle, Portland, and Vancouver liked to depict other people's violence as ridiculous. But, in many instances, their fears outran their confidence, and the spectacle of marginal men's violence alarmed rather than amused them.

It is particularly important to consider questions of power when assessing the violence of people of little status. Marginal people have been most apt to fight each other. Prior to colonization Native peoples fought strangers, not fellow villagers. After colonization, after becoming marginalized, they turned their violence largely upon friends and family. This example suggests that the roots of violence among subordinated people reside in the dynamics of dominance and resistance rather than springing from Native or African American culture per se. Such violence has been and continues to be extremely costly to the social fabric of communities that have more than enough problems without it. But such violence has also offered a status of sorts to people with few other opportunities to distinguish themselves, as well as expressing discontent with oppressive social and economic arrangements.

By emphasizing the relationship between power and interpersonal violence, I do not mean to ignore variations over time and between places. Like other historians, I argue that people's propensity to employ physical force has generally followed a U-shaped curve, falling during the nineteenth century and rising during the last half of the twentieth century, in concert with the creation and erosion of industrialization and the production-oriented culture that accompanied it. These broad shifts disguise a number of countertrends, however. Spontaneous acts of violence among middle- and upper-class men apparently declined throughout the nineteenth and twentieth centuries on the north Pacific slope. During the late twentieth century, the Pacific Northwest and British Columbia, the United States and Canada, may have become more violent in the aggregate, but not within each of its social parts. The general public's acceptance and use of violence toward children has followed a particularly complex pattern. Very few non-Natives objected to corporal punishment during the settlement period, and very many do today. But the actual prevalence of child beating—at least extreme forms—has risen during the twentieth century as children have grown more autonomous and as the punishments meted out by parents have become less predictable. The recent campaign against spanking and abuse has not necessarily changed this. Violence has also varied by place. It has been more common in recently settled areas than in established ones, and British Columbians have been less disposed toward homicidal violence than have their counterparts in Washington and Oregon—particularly if one takes into account nineteenth-century demographic differences that inflated British Columbia's rate.

Detecting differences in violence over time and between places is difficult and important. But we must be careful not to assume that violence constitutes a reliable calculus of a society's general health. Many people of modest means have practiced violence as a social leveler. Hence British Columbia's relatively low levels of violence have indicated not simply that it was a safer place in which to live, but also that its populace was less apt to challenge authority—inside and outside the home. Indeed, British Columbians have, until recently, been more comfortable than residents of the Pacific Northwest with violence inflicted by people of authority—husbands, parents, teachers, and legal officials—upon subordinates. This acceptance of powerful people's violence often served, ironically, to reduce its use: subordinates who concurred with their subordination were disinclined to use physical force against their betters, and their betters did not need to hit them to keep them in their place. The converse is also true. American violence, Lawrence Friedman points out, has been the handmaiden of American liberty—and not just on the battlefield.[43] Changing rates of violence by husbands and parents have therefore reflected both these people's capacity for violence and wives' and children's capacity for resistance. Biological parents apparently used violence rarely during the nineteenth century, for example, not because they were unwilling to hit their sons and daughters, but because they did not need to. The absence of violence may signify extensive dominance, just as its presence may signal a struggle for more egalitarian and respectful relations between parent and child, husband and wife.

We too often condemn or celebrate violence without considering carefully its context, particularly its relation to power and dominance. Privileged people's discussions of violence therefore tend to replicate the status quo, like newspapers' descriptions of violent men of African, Asian, or Italian descent a century ago. Our interpretations tell us what we already know. They confirm, not challenge, our prejudices. Their lessons are patent, their meanings self-evident. This seems particularly so in our own day, when violence has become for many well-to-do women and men alike simply an emblem of vulgarity and cruelty, when condemnations of physical force obscure rather than illuminate relations of power, privilege, and abuse. If violence is, as Emanuel Marx argues, a way to "communicate things which ordinarily are not clearly stated," it then behooves us to listen and attend closely to acts of physical force, to discern what discomforting secrets they have to tell us.[44]

Mikal Gilmore's family biography, *Shot in the Heart,* is a courageous attempt to do just that. The author is best known as the youngest brother of the notorious Gary Gilmore, who cold-bloodedly killed two young men in Utah in 1976 and then successfully insisted on becoming the first person to be executed in the United States in a decade.

The Gilmores were not a typical family. They moved constantly during the three older boys' early years, as Frank Sr. fled real or imagined enemies. Mikal, the fourth and last child, knew a more stable childhood, when the family settled down on the outskirts of Portland. But staying in one place did not much improve the family's emotional state. Frank Sr. and Bessie, his wife, quarreled constantly, and he beat her horribly. He also regularly battered his sons—once they were old enough to have a mind of their own. They enjoyed a good house and good meals. But the boys never knew when their mother might throw the food on the floor or their father might push their faces into it. Mikal identifies many strands that went into creating Gary Gilmore, the killer. But he is certain that his father's cruelties played a decisive role.

Frank Sr. died before he would have turned against his youngest son, and Mikal has many fond memories of him. But he also witnessed countless instances in which his father and mother tried to pit him against each other, of the resentment his brothers harbored toward him (Galen, the next youngest, once wrapped up a piece of dog shit and gave it to young Mikal as a present), and of the deep sense of guilt all of this generated in him. Mikal seldom faced violence; he endured only one beating from his father. But the family's problems went much deeper than those beatings.

Mikal hoped to escape—a hope that his mother in some ways nurtured. During Christmas of 1980—the last time they saw each other—she remarked that he was "wise to go away," to escape the "curse that has devoured us one by one." She wanted him to be "forever safe."[45] Mikal thought that he was. Indeed, he repeatedly told himself "that whatever ran in Gary's blood that turned him into a killer did not also run in my blood, and that whatever turned my family's hopes to wreckage would not also devastate my life."[46] He was not a killer. He was not a violent man. Yet he came to understand that this was a hollow boast, that his childhood has in fact left him deeply scarred, unable to find the courage or confidence to love another fully, to form a family of his own, unable even at times to get back to sleep without the comfort of repeating to himself, time after time: "It will never be all right. Never. It will *never* be all right."[47]

Yet Mikal's book ends in a triumph of sorts, when he finds his only surviving brother, Frank Jr. The two are very different from each other. Frank is the eldest child, Mikal the youngest. Frank suffered horrible physical abuse at the hands of his parents, Mikal very little. Frank stayed with their mother until her death, sacrificing his own chances for happiness. Mikal made good on his determination to escape. Frank became a drifter, a laborer, Mikal a successful writer. But as the two sat together in a northwest Portland apartment, poring over old photographs and picking at old memories, trying to make sense of the senseless, the only two survivors of a tormented family found comfort in each other. Mikal realized that Frank "may be all the family I have left in the world, but it is family enough." He "had never truly understood the depths of this man's heart or the expanse of his loneliness, but maybe it wasn't too late."[48]

Many if not most of us are separated by deeper chasms than those that stand between Gary Gilmore's eldest and youngest brother. Accidents of age, gender, ethnicity, class, and status render our lives largely incomprehensible and threatening to each other. No wonder our acts of and opinions about violence seem so foreign and wrong-headed, so peculiar and mistaken. But there still exists the possibility that we, too, can turn to and learn from each other, can understand each other's wounds and fears so that we may heal and hope. It will require insight as well as courage to discern the causes of and solutions to interpersonal violence and the innumerable indignities and injustices from which such violence springs. But it is not too late—if we care to try.

ABBREVIATIONS

BCAGC British Columbia Attorney General Correspondence, Outward,
GR 419. British Columbia Archives and Records Service,
Victoria
BCHQ *British Columbia Historical Quarterly*
BCS *(Barkerville) Cariboo Sentinel*
BCST *BC Studies*
CC *Colfax Commoner*
CHR *Canadian Historical Review*
CPG *(Colfax) Palouse Gazette*
CRSA *Canadian Review of Sociology and Anthropology*
DBCVC *Daily British Colonist and Victoria Chronicle*
EC *Ellensburg Capital*
EH *Ethnohistory*
GE *Golden Era*
JAH *Journal of American History*
JMF *Journal of Marriage and the Family*
KIS *(Kamloops) Inland Sentinel*
NFP *Nanaimo Free Press*
NWBC *(New Westminster) British Columbian*
OHQ *Oregon Historical Quarterly*
PGC *Prince George Citizen*
PGFP *Prince George Free Press*
PNQ *Pacific Northwest Quarterly*
PO *(Portland) Oregonian*
PODJ *(Portland) Oregon Daily Journal*
PPO *(Portland) People's Observer*
PRDN *(Prince Rupert) Daily News*
PWW *(Portland) Willamette Week*

QOHS	Quarterly of the Oregon Historical Society
SCJ	(Salem) Capital Journal
SDN	Seattle Daily News
SDT	Seattle Daily Times
SH	Sound Heritage
SMH	Seattle Mail and Herald
SNE	(Seattle) Northwest Enterprise
SNH	(Seattle) Northwest Herald
SOS	(Salem) Oregon Statesman
SPI	Seattle Post-Intelligencer
SPSH	(Steilacoom) Puget Sound Herald
SR	Seattle Republican
ST	Seattle Times
SW	Seattle Weekly
UCPAAE	University of California Publications in American Archaeology and Ethnology
UWPA	University of Washington Publications in Anthropology
VBC	(Victoria) British Colonist
VBCR	(Vancouver) British Columbia Report
VC	(Vancouver [WA]) Columbian
VDBC	(Victoria) Daily British Colonist
VDP	(Vancouver) Daily Province
VGS	(Vancouver) Georgia Straight
VS	Vancouver Sun
VTC	(Victoria) Times-Colonist

NOTES

Canadians are extremely cautious about people's privacy (it took an order from the British Columbia Supreme Court for me to view divorce cases from the 1920s), and I was required to sign research agreements stating that I would obscure the identity of twentieth-century people in certain records. Since some of the more notorious cases were from lightly populated areas, I cannot even divulge the jurisdiction in which the criminal acts occurred. In a number of the notes for chapter five and the epilogue, the court or newspaper had to remain unidentified. I have indicated in these cases that further information has been withheld to protect the privacy of individuals involved and their descendants.

INTRODUCTION

1. Sam Churchill, *Big Sam* (Sausalito, California: Comstock, 1973), 97; Churchill, *Don't Call Me Ma* (Garden City, New York: Doubleday, 1977), 57, 63, 75, 95–98, 143–144.

2. Cases 311, 680, 2418, Clatsop County Circuit Court, Clatsop County Courthouse, Astoria.

3. Emma Gene Miller, *Clatsop County, Oregon: A History* (Portland, Oregon: Binfords and Mort, 1958), 176–192, 211–230, 58–59; Kenneth McNaught, "Violence in Canadian History," in *Studies in Canadian Social History*, ed. Michiel Horn and Ronald Sabourin (Toronto: McClelland and Stewart, 1974), 376–391; Carlos A. Schwantes, "Perceptions of Violence on the Wageworkers' Frontier: An American-Canadian Comparison," *PNQ* 77 (April 1986): 52–57; Hugh Davis Graham, "Violence, Social Theory, and the Historians: The Debate over Consensus and Culture in America," in *Violence in America: Protest, Rebellion, Reform*, ed. Ted Robert Gurr (Newbury Park, California: Sage, 1989), 329–351. Treatments of homicide include Roger Lane, *Murder in America: A History;* Clare V. McKanna Jr., *Homicide, Race, and Justice in the American West, 1880–1920;* Angus McLaren, "Males, Migrants, and Murder in British Columbia, 1900–1923," in *On the Case: Explorations in Social History*, ed. Franca Iacovetta and

Wendy Mitchinson (Toronto: University of Toronto Press, 1998), 159–180. Karen Dubinsky, *Improper Advances: Rape and Heterosexual Conflict in Ontario, 1880–1929* (Chicago: University of Chicago Press, 1993), 6, criticizes Canadian historians for over-looking rape and sex.

4. Murray A. Straus, "Measuring Intrafamily Conflict and Violence: The Conflict Tactics (CT) Scales," *JMF* 41 (1979): 75–88; Richard J. Gelles and Murray A. Straus, *Intimate Violence* (New York: Simon and Schuster, 1988). Martin Daly and Margo Wilson, "Evolutionary Psychology of Male Violence," in *Male Violence*, ed. John Archer (London: Routledge, 1994), 263–272, argue against the automatic classification of violence as pathological.

5. Elliott Leyton, *Hunting Humans: The Rise of the Modern Multiple Murderer*, rev. ed. (Toronto: McClelland and Stewart, 1995), 22.

6. Nigel Rapport, *Talking Violence: An Anthropological Interpretation of Conversation in the City* (St. John's, Newfoundland: Institute of Social and Economic Research, Memorial University of Newfoundland, 1987), 165.

7. Emanuel Marx, *The Social Context of Violent Behaviour: A Social Anthropological Study of an Israeli Immigrant Town* (London: Routledge and Kegan Paul, 1976), 87. I have also profited from: Kenneth Colburn Jr., "Honor, Ritual and Violence in Ice Hockey," *Canadian Journal of Sociology* 10 (spring 1985): 153–170; Thomas W. Dunk, *It's a Working Man's Town: Male Working-Class Culture in Northwestern Ontario* (Montreal: McGill-Queen's University Press, 1991). Dunk's study does not address violence per se, but his analysis of how working-class men use sport to compensate for and protest their working lives could, it seems to me, be easily extended to fighting.

8. Clifford Geertz, *The Interpretation of Cultures: Selected Essays* (New York: Basic Books, 1973), 412–453; Linda Gordon, *Heroes of Their Own Lives: The Politics and History of Family Violence, Boston, 1880–1960*.

9. Steven Maynard, "'Horrible Temptations': Sex, Men, and Working-Class Male Youth in Urban Ontario, 1890–1935," *CHR* 78 (June 1997): 191–235; Jonathan Swainger, "American Crime Comics as Villains: An Incident from Northern Canada," *Legal Studies Forum* 22 (1998): 215–231; Steven Lukes, *Power: A Radical View* (Houndmills, Basingstoke, Hampshire: Macmillan Education, 1975); Philip Cassell, ed., *The Giddens Reader* (Stanford, California: Stanford University Press, 1993), 230–232, 242–243; Ted Robert Gurr, foreword to *Violence in Canada: Sociopolitical Perspectives*, ed. Jeffrey Ian Ross (Don Mills, Ontario: Oxford University Press, 1995), viii-xvii; William J. Goode, "Force and Violence in the Family," *JMF* 33 (November 1971): 624–636.

10. Michel Foucault, *Discipline and Punish: The Birth of the Prison,* trans. Alan Sheridan (New York: Vintage, 1995, orig. 1977), 106.

11. I include in this study homicides in which the victim died instantaneously.

12. Richard Maxwell Brown, "The Other Northwest: The Regional Identity of a Canadian Province," in *Many Wests: Place, Culture, and Regional Identity,* ed. David M. Wrobel and Michael C. Steiner (Lawrence: University Press of Kansas, 1997), 279–314; John M. Findlay, "A Fishy Proposition: Regional Identity in the Pacific Northwest," in *Many Wests,* 37–70; Brown, "Rainfall and History: Perspectives on the Pacific Northwest," in *Experiences in a Promised Land: Essays in Pacific Northwest History,* ed. G. Thomas Edwards and Carlos A. Schwantes (Seattle: University of Washington Press, 1986), 13–27; Brown, "The Great Raincoast of North America: Toward a New Regional History of the Pacific Northwest," in *The Changing Pacific Northwest: Interpreting Its Past,* ed. David H. Stratton and George A. Frykman (Pullman: Washington State University Press, 1988), 39–53; David Alan Johnson, *Founding the Far West: California, Oregon, and Nevada, 1840–1890* (Berkeley: University of California Press, 1992), 7–10, 41–70, 269–278; Seymour Martin Lipset, *Continental Divide: The Values and Institutions of the United States and Canada* (New York: Routledge, 1990); W. L. Morton, *The Canadian Identity,* 2nd ed. (Toronto: University of Toronto Press, 1975, orig. 1972); Margaret Atwood, *Survival: A Thematic Guide to Canadian Literature* (Toronto: Anansi, 1972), 31–35; A. P. Thornton, *The Habit of Authority: Paternalism in British History* (Toronto: University of Toronto Press, 1966). David T. Courtwright, *Violent Land: Single Men and Social Disorder from the Frontier to the Inner City,* as its title implies, emphasizes demography as the key causal agent in violence.

13. Roger D. McGrath, *Gunfighters, Highwaymen, and Vigilantes: Violence on the Frontier* (Berkeley: University of California Press, 1984), 251, 164.

14. Yet homicide records are much more treacherous than they appear to be. It is important to know what sort of deaths are counted. Abortions that resulted in the death of pregnant women, infanticides, accidental homicides, and executions may or may not have been counted in any given set of statistics. Homicide rates have also been affected by such extrinsic factors as improved medical technology, which would tend to deflate rates, and improved firearms technology, which would tend to inflate them. Lane, *Murder in America,* 5–6; H. C. Brearley, *Homicide in the United States* (Montclair, New Jersey: Patterson Smith, 1969, orig. 1932), 12–15, 26; Angus McLaren and Arlene Tigar McLaren, "Discoveries and Dissimulations: The Impact of Abortion Deaths on Maternal Mortality in British Columbia," *BCST* 64 (winter 1984–1985): 3–26.

1. W. M. Halliday, *Potlatch and Totem and the Recollections of an Indian Agent* (London: J. M. Dent and Sons, 1935), 135. Peter Murray, *The Devil and Mr. Duncan* (Victoria: Sono Nis Press, 1985), 41; Douglas Cole and Ira Chaikin, *An Iron Hand upon the People: The Law Against the Potlatch on the Northwest Coast* (Vancouver: Douglas and McIntyre; Seattle: University of Washington Press, 1990), 27. Clayton A. Robarchek and Carole J. Robarchek, "Cultures of War and Peace: A Comparative Study of Waorani and Semani," in *Aggression and Peacefulness in Humans and Other Primates*, ed. James Silverberg and J. Patrick Gray (New York: Oxford University Press, 1992), 189–213, argue that the Waorani of the Amazon seized upon missionaries' solutions for ending warfare. See also Richard White, *The Middle Ground: Indians, Empires, and Republics in the Great Lakes Region, 1650–1815* (Cambridge: Cambridge University Press, 1991), 1–49. Aboriginals' use of newcomers' ideas is of course much different from colonizers' simply imposing their ethical and political systems on Native peoples.

2. Chief Justice Allan McEachern's lengthy justification for the British Columbia Supreme Court's 1991 denial of Gitksan and Wet'suwet'en land claims, for example, presented these Native people as primitive unfortunates who had pursued the fruits of civilization offered by European colonizers. Robin Ridington, "Fieldwork in Courtroom 53: A Witness to *Delgamuukw v. B.C.*," *BCST* 95 (autumn 1992): 17–21.

3. The literature on these culture groups is vast. The best surveys are of the Northwest Coast. Wayne Suttles, ed., *Northwest Coast;* Philip Drucker, *Indians of the Northwest Coast* (Garden City, New York: Natural History Press, 1963, orig. 1955). On the Plateau and sub-Arctic see June Helm, ed., *Subarctic* (Washington, D.C.: Smithsonian Institution, 1981) and Deward E. Walker Jr., ed., *Plateau*. On the Paiute see Julian H. Steward, "Basin-Plateau Aboriginal Sociopolitical Groups," *Bulletin of the Bureau of American Ethnology* 120 (1938).

4. George Gibbs, *Tribes of Western Washington and Northwestern Oregon* (Washington, D.C.: Government Printing Office, 1877), 191. Philip Ashton Rollins, ed., *The Discovery of the Oregon Trail* (New York: Charles Scribner's Sons, 1935), 11. See also Gabriel Franchère, *Narrative of a Voyage to the Northwest Coast of America*, trans. and ed. J. V. Huntington (Cleveland: Arthur H. Clark, 1904, orig. 1854), 330; J. C. Beaglehole, ed., *The Voyage of the Resolution and Discovery: 1776–1780* (Cambridge: Cambridge University Press, 1967), part 1: 1092–1094; Edward S. Curtis, *The North American Indian*, ed. Frederick Webb Hodge (New York: Johnson Reprint Corporation, 1978, orig. 1915), vol. 10: 99; Hilary Stewart, annot., *The Adventures and Sufferings of John R. Jewitt, Captive*

of Maquinna (Seattle: University of Washington Press, 1987), 157–158. Warfare also occurred outside the observable world. An ethnologist reported that war chiefs of the Shuswap, a northern Plateau people, were "unable to cope with the enemy except in a material way," whereas shamans could control the weather, prophesy outcomes, throw and repel spells. James Alexander Teit, *The Shuswap*, ed. Franz Boas (Leiden: E. J. Brill; New York: G. E. Stechert, 1909), 542–543. Puget Sound Natives likewise recalled that a landslide killed several residents of a Skagit village a few weeks after two otter spirits sent by a Skokomish shaman had attacked its foundations. W. W. Elmendorf and A. L. Kroeber, *The Structure of Twana Culture, with Comparative Notes on the Structure of Yurok Culture* (Pullman: Washington State University, 1960), 474. Philip Drucker, "Contributions to Alsea Ethnography," *UCPAAE* 35 (1934–1943), (New York: Kraus Reprint Corporation, 1965), 95; Ronald L. Olson, *The Quinault Indians* (Seattle: University of Washington Press, 1967, orig. 1936), 117.

5. W. Kaye Lamb, ed., *Sixteen Years in the Indian Country: The Journal of Daniel Williams Harmon, 1800–1816* (Toronto: Macmillan, 1957), 251–252.

6. Donald Mitchell, "Predatory Warfare, Social Status, and the North Pacific Slave Trade," *Ethnology* 23 (January 1984): 39. Brian Ferguson, "Warfare and Redistributive Exchange on the Northwest Coast," 134; Herbert D. G. Maschner, "The Evolution of Northwest Coast Warfare," in *Troubled Times: Violence and Warfare in the Past*, ed. Debra L. Martin and David W. Frayer (Amsterdam: Gordon and Breach, 1997), 267–302.

7. Teit, *Shuswap*, 548; Leslie Spier and Edward Sapir, "Wishram Ethnography," *UWPA* 3 (1930): 228; James Alexander Teit, "The Salishan Tribes of the Western Plateaus," ed. Franz Boas, in *Forty-Fifth Annual Report of the Bureau of American Ethnography, 1927–1928* (Washington, D. C.: Government Printing Office, 1930), 257–258; Melville Jacobs, "An Historical Event Text from a Galice Athabaskan in Southwestern Oregon," *International Journal of American Linguistics* 34 (July 1968): 184. About 11 percent of burials at a site between fifteen hundred and three thousand years old along the Strait of Georgia had skeletal injuries, nearly 40 percent at a more northern location, in what is now Prince Rupert. More than one half of these fractures in the northern site, moreover, were apparently caused by interpersonal violence. Seventy-five percent of sixteen skeletons from the interior, buried along the Okanogan River between A.D. 330 and 1780, bore evidence of physical violence. Jerome S. Cybulski, "Human Biology," in Suttles, *Northwest Coast*, 55, 58; Robert T. Boyd, "Demographic History Until 1990," in Walker, *Plateau*, 468–470; Suttles, *Northwest Coast*, passim; Philip Drucker, *Cultures of the North Pacific Coast* (San Francisco: Chandler, 1965), 75–76; Drucker, *Indians of the Northwest Coast*, 147–149;

Leland Donald, "Slave Raiding on the North Pacific Coast," in *Native People, Native Lands: Canadian Indians, Inuit and Metis*, ed. Bruce Alden Cox (Ottawa: Carleton University Press, 1991), 164–170; Jacob Herman Van Den Brink, *The Haida Indians: Cultural Change, Mainly Between 1876–1970*, trans. I. Seeger (Leiden: E. J. Brill, 1974), 36–39; Curtis, *North American Indian*, vol. 10: 105; Erna Gunther, "Klallam Ethnography," *UWPA* 1 (1927): 266; Diamond Jenness, *The Sekani Indians of British Columbia* (Ottawa: J. O. Patenaude, 1937), 17–26; David V. Burley, J. Scott Hamilton, and Knut R. Fladmark, *Prophecy of the Swan: The Upper Peace River Fur Trade of 1794–1823*, 31; A. G. Morice, *The History of the Northern Interior of British Columbia* (Smithers, British Columbia: Interior Stationary, 1978, orig. 1906), 10–32; Peter Carstens, *The Queen's People: A Study of Hegemony, Coercion, and Accommodation among the Okanagan of Canada* (Toronto: University of Toronto Press, 1991), 28; Teit, "The Thompson Indians of British Columbia," ed. Boas, *American Museum of Natural History Memoirs* (1900), vol. 2, part 4: 267; Theodore Stern, *The Klamath Tribe: A People and Their Reservation* (Seattle: University of Washington Press, 1965), 23–24, 27–29; Frederick Merk, ed., *Fur Trade and Empire: George Simpson's Journal*, rev. ed. (Cambridge: Harvard University Press 1968), 55; *The Oregon Territory, Consisting of a Brief Description of the Country and Its Productions, and of the Habits and Manners of the Native Indian Tribes* (London: M. A. Nattali, 1846), 58–59; W. Kaye Lamb, ed., *The Journals and Letters of Sir Alexander Mackenzie* (London: Cambridge University Press, 1970), 287; Lamb, *Sixteen Years in the Indian Country*, 250; [Alexander Ross], *The Fur Hunters of the Far West*, ed. Milo Milton Quaife (Chicago: Lakeside Press, 1924, orig. 1855), 222–223; John R. Swanton, *Haida Texts and Myths: Skidegate Dialect* (Brighton, Michigan: Native American Book Publishers, 1991), 364–448.

8. James Alexander Teit, "The Lillooet Indians," in *Memoir of the American Museum of Natural History, New York*, ed. Franz Boas (Leiden: E. J. Brill, New York: G. E. Stechert, 1906), vol. 2, part 5: 236. Teit, *Shuswap*, 540; June McCormick Collins, *Valley of the Spirits: The Upper Skagit Indians of Western Washington* (Seattle: University of Washington Press, 1974), 114–115; Marian W. Smith, *The Puyallup-Nisqually* (New York: Columbia University Press, 1940), 150–151; Elmendorf and Kroeber, *Structure of Twana Culture*, 465–466.

9. Verne F. Ray, *The Sanpoil and Nespelem: Salishan Peoples of Northeastern Washington* (New Haven, Connecticut: Human Relations Area Files, 1954, orig. 1933), 114, 25. James Alexander Teit, "The Middle Columbia Salish: Historical and Geographical," *UWPA* 2 (1928): 123, concludes that groups around the middle Columbia seldom mounted large-scale attacks against each other.

10. Verne F. Ray, *Cultural Relations in the Plateau of Northwestern America* (Los Angeles: n.p., 1939), 35–36, 40–41.

11. Ray, *Sanpoil and Nespelem*, 26. Wayne Suttles, *Coast Salish Essays* (Vancouver: Talonbooks; Seattle: University of Washington Press, 1987), 282–286. Susan Kent, "Pacifism: A Myth of the Plateau," *Northwest Anthropological Research Notes* 14 (fall 1980): 125–134.

12. W. W. Elmendorf, *Twana Narratives: Native Historical Accounts of a Coast Salish Culture* (Seattle: University of Washington Press; Vancouver: University of British Columbia Press, 1993), 128, 131, 145–153.

13. Elmendorf and Kroeber, *Structure of Twana Culture*, 478–479.

14. Ferguson, "A Reexamination of the Causes of Northwest Coast Warfare," 311. Ferguson, "Warfare and Redistributive Exchange"; Morris Swadesh, "Motivations in Nootka Warfare," 76–93.

15. Ferguson, "A Reexamination of the Causes of Northwest Coast Warfare," 308; Viola E. Garfield, "Tsimshian Clan and Society," *UWPA* 7 (February 1939): 267; Rollins, *Discovery of the Oregon Trail*, 12; *Oregon Territory, Consisting of a Brief Description*, 51; Lamb, *Sixteen Years in the Indian Country*, 193.

16. Ross, *Fur Hunters of the Far West*, 171.

17. Franz Boas, *Kwakiutl Ethnography*, ed. Helen Codere (Chicago: University of Chicago Press, 1966), 107. Edward S. Curtis, *The North American Indian*, ed. Frederick Webb Hodge (New York: Johnson Reprint Corporation, 1970, orig. 1913), vol. 9: 75; Curtis, *North American Indian*, vol. 10: 104–105; Bernhard J. Stern, *The Lummi Indians of Northwestern Washington* (New York: AMS Press, 1969, orig. 1934), 98.

18. Swadesh, "Motivations in Nootka Warfare," 93. Smith, *The Puyallup-Nisqually*, 151–153; Homer G. Barnett, *The Coast Salish of British Columbia* (Eugene: University of Oregon, 1955), 267–268.

19. Curtis, *North American Indian*, vol. 10: 124. Ferguson, "Reexamination of the Causes of Northwest Coast Warfare," 308–309; Helen Codere, *Fighting With Property: A Study of Kwakiutl Potlatching and Warfare, 1792–1930* (Seattle: University of Washington Press, 1950), 98–108; Olson, *Quinault Indians*, 117.

20. Franz Boas, *Kwakiutl Ethnography*, 109. Curtis, *North American Indian*, vol. 9: 22; Barnett, *Coast Salish of British Columbia*, 268. Even nonviolent deaths could provoke revenge killings. An early-nineteenth-century fur trader asserted that the Sekani's proclivity toward "murder" arose from their belief that all deaths were caused by someone, a belief that helps to explain why suspicions of witchcraft were so common. Lamb, *Sixteen Years in the Indian Country*, 160.

21. Morice, *History of the Northern Interior of British Columbia*, 14–19, 20–27, 137. Jenness, *Sekani Indians of British Columbia*, 45–46; Charles A. Bishop, "Kwah: A Carrier Chief," in *Old Trails and New Directions: Papers of the Third North American Fur Trade Conference*, ed. Carol M. Judd and Arthur J. Ray (Toronto: University of Toronto Press, 1980), 200–201; Teit, *Lillooet Indians*, 240–246. Native societies created mechanisms for trying to contain the violent rages that death provoked. Among some northern groups, someone from the offending group might volunteer his life to avoid a more general and prolonged conflict. Most Northwest Coast groups used payments of wealth to settle blood feuds, but usually only after blood vengeance had been carried out. Drucker, *Cultures of the North Pacific Coast*, 72–74.

22. Ferguson, "Warfare and Redistributive Exchange," 135. Swadesh, "Motivations in Nootka Warfare," 92; Elmendorf and Kroeber, *Structure of Twana Culture*, 475; Viola E. Garfield, "Tsimshian Clan and Society," *UWPA* 7 (February 1939): 257.

23. Barnett, *Coast Salish of British Columbia*, 267.

24. Collins, *Valley of the Spirits*, 120. Melville Jacobs, "Coos Narrative and Ethnologic Texts," *UWPA* 8 (April 1939): 120.

25. Robin Fisher and J. M. Bumsted, eds., *Account of a Voyage to the North West Coast of America in 1785 and 1786 by Alexander Walker* (Vancouver: Douglas and McIntyre; Seattle: University of Washington Press, 1982), 88, 85. Walker recorded the experiences of John Mackey, a surgeon's mate who lived among the Nootka, as well as his own observations.

26. José Mariano Moziño, *Noticias de Nutka: An Account of Nootka Sound in 1792*, trans. and ed. Iris Higbie Wilson (Seattle: University of Washington Press, 1970), 84. W. Kaye Lamb, ed., *A Voyage of Discovery to the North Pacific Ocean and Round the World, 1791–1795* (London: The Hakluyt Society, 1984), vol. 3: 943. Gilbert Malcolm Sproat, *The Nootka: Scenes and Studies of Savage Life*, ed. Charles Lillard (Victoria: Sono Nis Press, 1987), 39–40; John Meares, *Voyages Made in the Years 1788 and 1789, from China to the North-West Coast of America* (New York: Da Capo Press, 1967, orig. 1790), 255; Drucker, *Cultures of the North Pacific Coast*, 74.

27. The more decentralized peoples of the interior apparently maintained pacific intragroup relations with greater difficulty than did their coastal counterparts. Lamb, *Sixteen Years in the Indian Country*, 252, 250; Lizette Hall, *The Carrier, My People* (Cloverdale, British Columbia: Friesen Printers, 1992), 7; Ross Cox, *Adventures on the Columbia River* (New York: J. and J. Harper, 1832), 230; Morice, *History of the Northern Interior of British Columbia*, 11–13; Herbert Joseph Spinden, "The Nez Percé

Indians," *Memoirs of the American Anthropological Association* 2 (1907–1915): 244; Teit, *Shuswap*, 558–560; Theodore Stern, "Ideal and Expected Behavior as Seen in Klamath Mythology," *Journal of American Folklore* 76 (January-March 1963): 21–30. Slaves were an exception. They constituted as much as 15 percent of some Northwest Coast groups, and slave owners, particularly in the north, not uncommonly killed them to demonstrate their wealth and status. They were, after all, "not members of the society but were outsiders," to quote Drucker, *Cultures of the North Pacific Coast*, 51. Robert H. Ruby and John A. Brown, *Indian Slavery in the Pacific Northwest* (Spokane, Washington: Arthur H. Clark, 1993); Elmendorf and Kroeber, *Structure of Twana Culture*, 345; Herman Haeberlin and Erna Gunther, *The Indians of Puget Sound* (Seattle: University of Washington Press, 1980, orig. 1930), 57. The annual homicide rate for slaves living at Stikine, on the north coast of British Columbia, was roughly 1,329 per hundred thousand from 1840 to 1848, an astronomical figure. Leland Donald, *Aboriginal Slavery on the Northwest Coast of North America* (Berkeley: University of California Press, 1997), 80–81, 165–173, 194. Among Plateau peoples, less wealthy and more egalitarian than their coastal counterparts, slavery was both more rare and less onerous. Ruby and Brown, *Indian Slavery*; Carstens, *Queen's People*, 24. Malevolent or incompetent shamans were also outside of society and might be killed. Indeed, family members of people who became shamans among the Alsea of the southern Northwest Coast reportedly grieved since the relation would in all probability die young. Livingston Farrand, "Notes on the Alsea Indians of Oregon," *American Anthropologist* 3 (April-June 1901): 245. Drucker, *Cultures of the North Pacific Coast*, 74–75; Edward Sapir and Morris Swadesh, *Nootka Texts: Tales and Ethnological Narratives, with Grammatical Notes and Lexical Materials* (New York: AMS Press, 1978, orig. 1939), 209.

28. T. C. Elliott, "The Journal of the Ship *Ruby*," *OHQ* 28 (September 1927): 277. Robert Stuart, one of the Astorians who arrived at the Columbia's mouth in 1811, declared: "Husbands and Fathers are not subject to any punishment for killing their wives or children." Rollins, *Discovery of the Oregon Trail*, 11.

29. A. V. Venkatarama Ayyar, ed., *James Strange's Journal and Narrative of the Commercial Expedition from Bombay to the North-West Coast of America* (Seattle: Shorey Book Store, 1967, orig. 1928), 25.

30. Fisher and Bumsted, *Account of a Voyage to the North West Coast of America*, 85.

31. Camille de Roquefeuil, *Voyage Around the World, 1816–1819, and Trading for Sea Otter Fur on the Northwest Coast of America* (Fairfield, Washington: Ye Galleon Press, 1981), 123. Stewart, *Adventures and Sufferings of John R. Jewitt*, 157.

32. Olson, *Quinault Indians*, 118. Barnett, *Coast Salish of British Columbia*, 194–195. Victor J. Farrar, ed., "The Nisqually Journal," *Washington Historical Quarterly* 10 (July 1919): 212–213.

33. Philip Drucker, "The Tolowa and their Southwest Oregon Kin," *UCPAAE* 36 (1935–1939): 248.

34. Elmendorf and Kroeber, *Structure of Twana Culture*, 359; Collins, *Valley of the Spirits*, 106; James G. Swan, *The Indians of Cape Flattery* (Seattle: Shorey Book Store, 1964, orig. 1870), 11. Walter Cline, Rachel S. Commons, May Mandelbaum, Richard H. Post, and L. V. W. Walters, *The Sinkaietk or Southern Okanagon of Washington*, ed. Leslie Spier (Menasha, Wisconsin: George Banta Publishing Company, 1938), 116; Verne F. Ray, *Primitive Pragmatists: The Modoc Indians of Northern California* (Seattle: University of Washington Press, 1963), 91–92; Jonathan S. Green, *Journal of a Tour on the North West Coast of America in the Year 1829* (New York: Chas. Fred. Heartman, 1915), 44–45; Margaret B. Blackman, "The Changing Status of Haida Women: An Ethnohistorical and Life History Approach," in *The World Is as Sharp as a Knife: An Anthology in Honour of Wilson Duff*, ed. Donald N. Abbot (Victoria: British Columbia Provincial Museum, 1981), 65–77; Loraine Littlefield, "Gender, Class and Community: The History of Sne-nay-muxw Women's Employment" (Ph.D. diss., University of British Columbia, 1995), 51–55; David Peterson del Mar, "Intermarriage and Agency: A Chinookan Case Study," *EH* 42 (winter 1995): 1–30; Mary C. Wright, "Economic Development and Native American Women in the Early Nineteenth Century," *American Quarterly* 33 (winter 1981): 525–536; de Roquefeuil, *Voyage Around the World*, 123–124; Reuben Gold Thwaites, ed., *Original Journals of the Lewis and Clark Expedition, 1804–1806* (New York: Antiquarian Press, 1959, orig. 1904–1905), vol. 3: 315.

35. Moziño, *Noticias de Nutka*, 43; Mark D. Kaplanoff, ed., "Nootka Sound in 1789: Joseph Ingraham's Account," *PNQ* 65 (October 1974): 162; Erna Gunther, "Klallam Ethnography," *UWPA* 1 (January 1927): 247; Olson, *Quinault Indians*, 107–108; Verne F. Ray, "Lower Chinook Ethnographic Notes," *UWPA* 7 (May 1938): 73; Gabriel Franchère, *Adventure at Astoria, 1810–1814*, trans. and ed. Hoyt C. Franchère (Norman: University of Oklahoma Press, 1967), 117; *Message from the President of the United States to the Two Houses of Congress*, 33rd Congress, 2nd session, House of Representatives, Executive Document No. 1, part 1 (Washington, D.C.: A. O. P. Nicholson, 1854), 467; Cora Du Bois, "The Wealth Concept as an Integrative Factor in Tolowa-Tututni Culture," in *Essays in Anthropology: Presented to A. L. Kroeber*, ed. Robert H. Lowie (Berkeley: University of California Press, 1936), 57–60; Drucker, "Tolowa and Their

48. Ferguson, "A Reexamination of the Causes of Northwest Coast Warfare," 312. James P. Ronda, *Lewis and Clark among the Indians* (Lincoln: University of Nebraska Press, 1984), 159–160; Robin Fisher, "Arms and Men on the Northwest Coast, 1774–1825," *BCST* 29 (spring 1976): 3–18; Suttles, "Post-Contact Culture Change," 42, 46; Helen Codere, "Kwakiutl," in *Perspectives in American Indian Culture Change*, 438–440; Morice, *History of the Northern Interior of British Columbia*, 29–32; Elliott, "Journal of the Ship *Ruby*," 269; Meares, *Voyages Made in the Years 1788 and 1789*, 142; Robert Steven Grumet, "Changes in Coast Tsimshian Redistributive Activities in the Fort Simpson Region of British Columbia, 1788–1862," *EH* 22 (fall 1975): 302; Jenness, "Carrier Indians of the Bulkley River," 478; E. Palmer Patterson, "Early Nishga-European Contact to 1860: A People for 'Those Who Talk of the Efficiency of Moral Lectures to Subdue the Obduracy of the Heart,'" *Anthropologica* 25 (1983): 205; Sir George Simpson, *Narrative of a Journey Round the World During the Years 1841 and 1842* (London: Henry Colburn, 1847), vol. 1: 232; Jonathan R. Dean, "'These Rascally Spackaloids': The Rise of Gispaxlots Hegemony at Fort Simpson, 1832–40," *BCST* 101 (spring 1994): 41–78; *Metlahkatlah: Ten Years' Work Among the Tsimsheean Indians* (Salisbury Square: Church Missionary House, 1869), 19–21, 33; Daniel W. Clayton, *Islands of Truth: The Imperial Fashioning of Vancouver Island* (Vancouver: University of British Columbia Press, 2000), 121–126, 143–148, 150–161; Fisher, *Contact and Conflict: Indian-European Relations in British Columbia, 1774–1890*, 2nd ed., 46–47. Increased wealth led to increased demand for slaves, which stimulated slave raiding, itself a very violent activity. Ferguson, "Reexamination of the Causes of Northwest Coast Warfare," 314–315; Donald, *Aboriginal Slavery*, 225–233, 239–240; Donald, "Slave Raiding on the North Pacific Coast," 163, 169–170; Ruby and Brown, *Indian Slavery*, 75–115, 253–276; Spier, *Klamath Ethnography*, 25–26, 313–314; Donald Mitchell, "A Demographic Profile of Northwest Coast Slavery," in *Status, Structure, and Stratification: Current Archaeological Reconstructions*, ed. Marc Thompson, Maria Teresa Garcia, and Francois J. Kense (Calgary: University of Calgary Archaeological Association, 1985), 227–236.

49. Ferguson, "Warfare and Redistributive Exchange," 136.

50. June McCormick Collins, "Growth of Class Distinctions and Political Authority Among the Skagit Indians During the Contact Period," *American Anthropologist* 52 July-September, 1950): 339–340, 331–342. Carstens, *The Queen's People*, 37–41; James Gilbert Movius, "Sagebrush War: White-Paiute Conflicts, 1825–1868" (M.A. thesis, University of Oregon, 1968), 15–18.

Southwest Oregon Kin," 248; Jenness, *Sekani Indians of British Columbia*, 54; Teit, "Thompson Indians of British Columbia," 326; Margaret A. Ormsby, ed., *A Pioneer Gentlewoman in British Columbia: The Recollections of Susan Allison* (Vancouver: University of British Columbia Press, 1976), 74; Ray, *Sanpoil and Nespelem*, 145; Cline et al., *Sinkaietk or Southern Okanagon of Washington*, 116; Spinden, "The Nez Percé Indians," 244; Curtis, *North American Indian*, vol. 8: 50, 89; Gustavus Hines, *Oregon: Its History, Condition, and Prospects* (New York: Arno Press, 1973, orig. 1851), 113; Leslie Spier, *Klamath Ethnography* (Millwood, New York: Kraus Reprint Company, 1976, orig. 1930), 51; Ray, *Primitive Pragmatists*, 91; Elmendorf and Kroeber, *Structure of Twana Culture*, 360–361; Albert S. Gatschet, Leo J. Frachtenberg, and Melville Jacobs, "Kalapuya Texts," *UWPA* 11 (June 1945): 192–193; David French, "Wasco-Wishram," in *Perspectives in American Indian Culture Change*, ed. Edward H. Spicer (Chicago: University of Chicago Press, 1961), 353–354; Peter Skene Ogden, *Traits of American Indian Life* (Fairfield, Washington: Ye Galleon Press, 1986, orig. 1853), 125–127; Stewart, *Adventures and Sufferings of John R. Jewitt*, 149.

36. Spier, *Klamath Ethnography*, 51, 279, 301; "Official Report of the Owyee Reconnaissance Made by Lieut. Colonel C. S. Drew, 1st Oregon Cavalry, in the Summer of 1864," *EH* 2 (spring 1955): 167. Curtis, *North American Indian*, vol. 9: 121; Moziño, *Noticias de Nutka*, 43; Kaplanoff, "Nootka Sound in 1789," 162; Stern, *Lummi Indians of Northwestern Washington*, 99; Gunther, "Klallam Ethnography," 247; Olson, *Quinault Indians*, 107–108, 116; Smith, *Puyallup-Nisqually*, 198; Ray, "Lower Chinook Ethnographic Notes," 73; Spier and Sapir, "Wishram Ethnography," 216; Melville Jacobs, "Santiam Kalapuya Ethnologic Texts," *UWPA* 11 (June 1945): 44; Teit, "Thompson Indians of British Columbia," 326; Ray, *Sanpoil and Nespelem*, 145; Cline et al., *Sinkaietk or Southern Okanagon of Washington*, 116; Spinden, "Nez Percé Indians," 244; Curtis, *North American Indian*, vol. 8: 50, 89; Ray, *Primitive Pragmatists*, 91; Ogden, *Traits of American Indian Life*, 127–128.

37. Lamb, *Sixteen Years in the Indian Country*, 247, 195, 148–149; John M'Lean, *Notes of a Twenty-Five Years' Service in the Hudson's Bay Territory* (London: Richard Bentley, 1849), vol. 1: 256–257. Gatschet, Frachtenberg, and Jacobs, "Kalapuya Texts," 196–197. When Kwah, a Carrier leader, received a beating at the hands of Daniel Harmon, a North West Company employee, in 1811, he reportedly remarked that he had become like Harmon's wife, for Kwah beat his own wives when they misbehaved. Bishop, "Kwah: A Carrier Chief," 193–194.

38. Rebecca Morley, "Wife Beating and Modernization: The Case of Papua New Guinea," *Journal of Comparative Family Studies* 25 (spring 1994): 42.

39. Olson, *Quinault Indians,* 102.

40. Stern, *Lummi Indians of Northwestern Washington,* 17–18; Collins, *Valley of the Spirits,* 222–223; Smith, *Puyallup-Nisqually,* 187–193; June M. Collins, "John Fornsby: The Personal Document of a Coast Salish Indian," in *Indians of the Urban Northwest,* ed. Marian W. Smith (New York: AMS Press, 1969, orig. 1949), 292–293; Curtis, *North American Indian,* vol. 10: 99; Edward Sapir and Morris Swadesh, *Native Accounts of Nootka Ethnography* (New York: AMS Press, 1978, orig. 1955), 381; Margaret Connell Szasz, "Native American Children," in *American Childhood: A Research Guide and Historical Handbook,* ed. Joseph M. Hawes and N. Ray Hiner (Westport, Connecticut: Greenwood Press, 1985), 319–320.

41. Diamond Jenness, "The Carrier Indians of the Bulkley River: Their Social and Religious Life," *Bureau of American Ethnology Bulletin* 133 (1943): 521; Jenness, "The Ancient Education of a Carrier Indian," *National Museum of Canada Annual Report for 1928* 62 (1929): 26. Pamela Brink, "Paviotso Child Training: Notes," *Indian Historian* 4 (spring 1971): 49; Sarah Winnemucca Hopkins, *Life Among the Piutes: Their Wrongs and Claims,* ed. Mrs. Horace Mann (Boston: Cupples, Upham and Co., 1883), 26; Julian H. Steward, "Ethnography of the Owens Valley Paiute," *UCPAAE* 33 (1933): 291.

42. Melville Jacobs, *Northwest Sahaptin Texts* (New York: Columbia University Press, 1935), part 1: 271. Teit, "Lillooet Indians," 266–267; Cline et al., *Sinkaietk or Southern Okanagon of Washington,* 108; Wilson Duff, *The Upper Stalo Indians of the Fraser Valley, British Columbia* (Victoria: British Columbia Provincial Museum, 1952), 91; Spier, *Klamath Ethnography,* 71.

43. Teit, "Thompson Indians of British Columbia," 309–310. According to Teit's description, girls as well as boys received these whippings, but he describes boys as the ones to call for additional blows. Teit, *Shuswap,* 588. Teit, "Salishan Tribes of the Western Plateaus," 168, 281–282. Ray, *Sanpoil and Nespelem,* 131, 112–113, describes more punitive uses of violence toward children and adults. Cross-cultural studies of violence toward children suggest that societies with little stratification have generally not sanctioned extensive corporal punishment. When adults are closely supervised in their economic and political lives, they socialize their children to obey external authorities. Societies in which authority is broadly dispersed place a premium on self-reliance. Parents in these societies raise their children to have an internal locus of control. Larry R. Petersen, Gary R. Lee, and Godfrey J. Ellis, "Social Structure, Socialization Values, and Disciplinary Techniques: A Cross-Cultural Analysis," *JMF* 44 (February 1982): 131–142; David Levinson, *Family Violence in Cross-Cultural Perspective* (Newbury Park, California: Sage, 1989), 62–63, 94–95. Levinson, 55, 94, also suggests that children

raised in extended families have been less apt to suffer from physical punishment because the availability of several caregivers has made for less stress and because grandparents are more likely to be warm caregivers than siblings are.

44. Stern, *Lummi Indians of Northwestern Washington,* 100.

45. Simon Harrison, *The Mask of War: Violence, Ritual and the Self in Melanesia* (Manchester: Manchester University Press, 1993); David D. Gilmore, *Manhood in the Making: Cultural Concepts of Masculinity* (New Haven, Connecticut: Yale University Press, 1990). Despite hydraulic or safety-valve theories of violence, internal and external violence are often associated positively with each other. Marc Howard Ross, "Internal and External Conflict and Violence: Cross-Cultural Evidence and a New Analysis," *Journal of Conflict Resolution* 29 (December 1985): 547–579; Richard G. Sipes, "War, Sports, and Aggression: An Empirical Test of Two Rival Theories," *American Anthropologist* 75 (June 1973): 64–86.

46. Elizabeth Vibert, "'The Natives Were Strong to Live': Reinterpreting Early-Nineteenth-Century Prophetic Movements in the Columbia Plateau," *EH* 42 (spring 1995): 219. Robert T. Boyd, "Another Look at the 'Fever and Ague' of Western Oregon," *EH* 22 (spring 1975): 135–154; Boyd, "Demographic History, 1774–1874," i Suttles, *Northwest Coast,* 135–148; Cole Harris, *The Resettlement of British Columbi Essays on Colonialism and Geographic Change,* 3–30; Boyd, "Smallpox in the Pac Northwest: The First Epidemics," *BCST* 101 (spring 1994): 5–40; James R. Gibs "Smallpox on the Northwest Coast, 1835–1838," *BCST* 56 (winter 1982–1983): 6 Wayne Suttles, "Post-Contact Culture Change Among the Lummi Indians," *B* 18 (January-April 1954): 45–48; Suttles, *Coast Salish Essays,* 152–198; Vibert, *T Tales: Narratives of Cultural Encounters in the Columbia Plateau, 1807–1846* (No University of Oklahoma Press, 1997), 50–83.

47. Christopher L. Miller, *Prophetic Worlds: Indians and Whites on the C Plateau* (New Brunswick, New Jersey: Rutgers University Press, 1985), 23–5 *Traders' Tales,* 211–215, 225–239; Robert H. Ruby and John A. Brown, *The Cayu Imperial Tribesmen of Old Oregon* (Norman: University of Oklahoma Pr 3–14; Carstens, *Queen's People,* 21–22; Teit, "Salishan Tribes of the Western 359–360; David H. Chance, *Influences of the Hudson's Bay Company or Cultures of the Colville District* (Moscow, Idaho: Northwest Anthropologi Notes, 1973), 16; Alvin M. Josephy Jr., *The Nez Perce Indians and the C Northwest* (New Haven, Connecticut: Yale University Press, 1965), 29–3 *The Kalispel Indians* (Norman: University of Oklahoma Press, 1986), Hamilton, and Fladmark, *Prophecy of the Swan,* 130–131.

51. Meares, *Voyages Made in the Years 1788 and 1789*, 196. Lamb, *Journals and Letters of Sir Alexander Mackenzie*, 288.

52. E. E. Rich, ed., *Part of Dispatch from George Simpson Esqr.* (Toronto: Champlain Society, 1947), 235; Duff, *Upper Stalo Indians*, 96. Chance, *Influences of the Hudson's Bay Company on the Native Cultures of the Colvile District*, 87–89; Dean, "'These Rascally Spackaloids,'" 67–68.

53. Ross, *Fur Hunters of the Far West*, 183–186.

54. Lamb, *Sixteen Years in the Indian Country*, 136. L. F. Ramsey, ed., *Joseph Thomas Heath Diary: The Journal of Joseph Thomas Heath from 1845 to 1849, a Settler in the Oregon Country, at Present Fort Steilacoom, Washington* [Tacoma: City Print Shop, 1976], 62; James P. Ronda, *Astoria and Empire* (Lincoln: University of Nebraska Press, 1990), 215; Paul Kane, *Wanderings of an Artist Among the Indians of North America* (London: Longman, Brown, Green, Longman, and Roberts, 1859), 257–259; Burley, Hamilton, and Fladmark, *Prophecy of the Swan*, 150; Dorothy Blakey Smith, ed., *The Reminiscences of Doctor John Sebastian Helmcken* (Vancouver: University of British Columbia Press, 1975), 79.

55. Kane, *Wanderings of an Artist*, 261. Robert F. Jones, ed., *Astorian Adventure: The Journal of Alfred Seton, 1811–1815* (New York: Fordham University Press, 1993), 34, 47–48.

56. Hamar Foster, "Killing Mr. John: Law and Jurisdiction at Fort Stikine, 1842–1846," in *Law for the Elephant, Law for the Beaver: Essays in the Legal History of the North American West*, ed. John McLaren, Hamar Foster, and Chet Orloff, 176–177 (quote), 147–193. Merk, *Fur Trade and Empire*, 144, 143–144; *The Journals of William Fraser Tolmie, Physician and Fur Trader* (Vancouver: Mitchell Press, 1963), 212, 240–241, 268–269; Robert E. McKechnie II, *Strong Medicine: History of Healing on the Northwest Coast* (Vancouver: J. J. Douglas, 1972), 84–85; Foster, "Mutiny on the *Beaver*: Law and Authority in the Fur Trade Navy, 1835–1840," in *Glimpses of Canadian Legal History*, ed. Dale Gibson and W. Wesley Pue (n.p.: Legal Research Institute of the University of Manitoba, 1991): 15–46; Donald A. Harris and George C. Ingram, "New Caledonia and the Fur Trade: A Status Report," *The Western Canadian Journal of Anthropology* 3 (1972): 179–195; Lamb, *Letters and Journals of Simon Fraser*, 166–168; Alexander Ross, *Adventures of the First Settlers on the Oregon or Columbia River*, ed. Milo Milton Quaife (Chicago: Lakeside Press, 1923), 216; "Letters to Mrs. F. F. Victor," *OHQ* 63 (June-September 1962): 199, 216; Elwood Evans, *History of the Pacific Northwest: Oregon and Washington* (Portland, Oregon: North Pacific History

Company, 1889), vol. 1: 117–118; E. Blanche Norcross, ed., *Nanaimo Retrospective: The First Century* (Nanaimo, British Columbia: Nanaimo Historical Society, 1979), 10; Helen Meilleur, *A Pour of Rain: Stories from a West Coast Fort* (Victoria, British Columbia: Sono Nis Press, 1980), 194; Morice, *History of the Northern Interior of British Columbia*, 179, 199–200, 279, 280–282; Fisher, *Contact and Conflict*, 54; Harris, *Resettlement of British Columbia*, 43–46; Tina Loo, *Making Law, Order, and Authority in British Columbia, 1821–1871* (Toronto: University of Toronto Press, 1994), 18–33; Vibert, *Traders' Tales*, 40–42; R. C. Macleod, "Law and Order on the Western-Canadian Frontier," in *Law for the Elephant*, 92.

57. Lamb, *Sixteen Years in the Indian Country*, 136.

58. Simpson, *Narrative of a Journey Round the World*, 240. Nor did Native peoples have any use for European-style dueling. Ross Cox recounted how a burly North West Company employee at Spokane House demanded that a Native with whom he was quarreling meet him on open ground. "Who ever heard of a wise warrior standing before his enemy's gun to be shot at like a dog," the Native retorted. Cox, *Adventures on the Columbia River*, 165.

59. *Journals of William Fraser Tolmie*, 223, 308–309. Anonymous, "Dried Salmon and Rum Again," in *Peace River Chronicles*, ed. Gordon E. Bowes (Vancouver, British Columbia: Prescott Publishing, 1963), 62.

60. Fisher and Bumsted, *Account of a Voyage to the North West Coast of America*, 63–64. French, "Wasco-Wishram," 353–354, argues that the Natives at The Dalles frequently stole from early white traders in order to get the newcomers to pay attention to them, to recognize them. David Peterson del Mar, "Intermarriage and Agency: A Chinookan Case Study," *EH* 42 (winter 1995): 4, argues instead that Natives did not necessarily find successful thievery morally objectionable.

61. Stewart, *Adventures and Sufferings of John R. Jewitt*, 112, 65. Clayton, *Islands of Truth*, 83–97, 106–108; James R. Gibson, *Otter Skins, Boston Ships, and China Goods: The Maritime Fur Trade of the Northwest Coast, 1785–1841* (Montreal: McGill-Queen's University Press, 1992), 160–173; Ferguson, "Reexamination of the Causes of Northwest Coast Warfare," 294–297; Mary Gormly, "Early Culture Contact on the Northwest Coast, 1774–1795: Analysis of Spanish Source Material," *Northwest Anthropological Research Notes* 11 (spring 1977): 1–80; Yvonne Marshall, "Dangerous Liaisons: Maquinna, Quadra, and Vancouver in Nootka Sound, 1790–5," in *From Maps to Metaphors: The Pacific World of George Vancouver*, ed. Robin Fisher and Hugh Johnston (Vancouver: University of British Columbia Press, 1993), 168–169; Erna Gunther, *Indian Life on the Northwest Coast of North America As Seen by the Early*

Explorers and Fur Traders during the Last Decades of the Eighteenth Century (Chicago: University of Chicago Press, 1972), 64; Kenneth N. Owens, ed., *The Wreck of the Sv. Nikolai: Two Narratives of the First Russian Expedition to the Oregon Country, 1808–1810*, trans. Alton S. Donnelly (Portland: Oregon Historical Society, 1985), 41–73; Fisher and Bumsted, *Account of a Voyage to the North West Coast of America*, 181; M'Lean, *Notes of a Twenty-Five Years' Service*, vol. 1: 244–248; Vibert, *Traders' Tales*, 145–160; Moziño, *Noticias de Nutka*, 84; William Ellis, *An Authentic Narrative of a Voyage Performed by Captain Cook and Captain Clerke* (Amsterdam: N-Israel; New York: Da Capo, 1969, orig. 1782), vol. 1: 206; [José Espinosa y Tello, ed.], *A Spanish Voyage to Vancouver and the Northwest Coast of America*, trans. Cecil Jane (New York: AMS Press, 1971, orig. 1930), 83–84; W. Kaye Lamb, ed., *A Voyage of Discovery to the North Pacific Ocean and Round the World, 1791–1795* (London: Hakluyt Society, 1984), vol. 4: 1401.

62. John Dunn, *History of the Oregon Territory* (London: Edwards and Hughes, 1844), 228; Jones, *Astorian Adventure*, 115; Cox, *Adventures on the Columbia River*, 107–108; Franchère, *Narrative of a Voyage to the Northwest Coast of America;* Clifford E. Trafzer and Richard D. Scheuerman, *Renegade Tribe: The Palouse Indians and the Invasion of the Inland Pacific Northwest* (Pullman: Washington State University Press, 1986), 14–16; Ross, *Adventures of the First Settlers on the Oregon or Columbia River*, 213; Merk, *Fur Trade and Empire*, 58–59; Harrison Clifford Dale, ed., *The Ashley-Smith Explorations and the Discovery of a Central Route to the Pacific, 1822–1829*, rev. ed. (Glendale, California: Arthur H. Clark, 1941), 279–280; Rich, *Part of Dispatch from George Simpson*, 60–61; John Kirk Townsend, *Narrative of a Journey Across the Rocky Mountains to the Columbia River* (Lincoln: University of Nebraska Press, 1978, orig. 1839), 244–245; Larry Cebula, "British vs. American Fur Trade Relations in the Pacific Northwest: The Indian Perspective," *The Pacific Northwest Forum*, second series, 9 (winter-fall 1996): 45–46.

63. Merk, *Fur Trade and Empire*, 63.

64. Morice, *History of the Northern Interior of British Columbia*, 204. Rich, *Part of Dispatch from George Simpson*, 42–43; Burley, Hamilton, and Fladmark, *Prophecy of the Swan*, 126–136; Shepard Krech III, "The Beaver Indians and the Hostilities at Fort St. John's," *Arctic Anthropology* 20 (1983): 35–45; M'Lean, *Notes of a Twenty-Five Years' Service*, vol. 1: 235–237; Harris, *Resettlement of British Columbia*, 34–36, 48–57; Jonathan R. Dean, "The Hudson's Bay Company and Its Use of Force, 1828–1829," *OHQ* 98 (fall 1997): 262–295; John Phillip Reid, "Certainty of Vengeance: The Hudson's Bay Company and Retaliation in Kind Against Indian Offenders in New

Caledonia," *Montana: The Magazine of Western History* 43 (winter 1993): 4–17; Reid, "Restraints of Vengeance: Retaliations-in-Kind and the Use of Indian Law in the Old Oregon Country," *OHQ* 95 (spring 1994): 48–92; Reid, "Principles of Vengeance: Fur Trappers, Indians, and Retaliation for Homicide in the Transboundary North American West," *Western Historical Quarterly* 24 (February 1993): 21–43; Hamar Foster, "'The Queen's Law is Better Than Yours': International Homicide in Early British Columbia," in *Essays in the History of Canadian Law: Crime and Criminal Justice,* ed. Jim Phillips, Tina Loo, and Susan Lewthwaite (Toronto: University of Toronto Press, for the Osgoode Society, 1994); John S. Ferrell, "Indians and Criminal Justice in Early Oregon, 1842–1859" (M.A. thesis, Portland State University, 1973), 5–7; Simpson, *Narrative of a Journey Round the World,* vol. 1: 194.

65. Dunn, *History of the Oregon Territory,* 244–250; W. Wymond Walkem, *Stories of Early British Columbia* (Vancouver, British Columbia: News-Advertiser, 1914), 65–73, 86; Dean "'These Rascally Spackaloids,'" 58; Lamb, *Sixteen Years in the Indian Country,* 146; Bishop, "Kwah: A Carrier Chief," 193–194, 199–201. Madge Wolfenden, "John Tod: 'Career of a Scotch Boy,'" *BCHQ* 18 (July-October, 1954): 213–214; Fisher, *Contact and Conflict,* 1–48. The Hudson's Bay Company seemed most oriented toward acculturation on the Plateau, where it actively intervened in Native religious and judicial practices. Chance, *Influences of the Hudson's Bay Company on the Native Cultures of the Colvile District,* 27–29, 71–78, 85–87, 96–98; Theodore Stern, *Chiefs and Change in the Oregon Country: Indian Relations at Fort Nez Percés, 1818–1855* (Corvallis: Oregon State University Press, 1996), vol. 2: 22–27; Douglas Cole and David Darling, "History of the Early Period," in Suttles, *Northwest Coast,* 119–134.

66. Carol Cooper, "Native Women of the Northern Pacific Coast: An Historical Perspective, 1830–1900," *Journal of Canadian Studies* 27 (winter 1992–1993): 55.

67. Samuel Parker, *Journal of an Exploring Tour Beyond the Rocky Mountains Under the Direction of the A.B.C.F.M. Performed in the Years 1835, '36, and '37* (Minneapolis: Ross and Haines, 1967, orig. 1838), 170–171. Peterson del Mar, "Intermarriage and Agency"; Mary C. Wright, "The Circle, Broken: Gender, Family, and Difference in the Pacific Northwest, 1811–1850" (Ph.D. diss., Rutgers University, 1996), 138–143; Morice, *History of the Northern Interior of British Columbia,* 261; Cooper, "Native Women of the Northern Pacific Coast," 56.

68. *Journal Kept By David Douglas During His Travels in North America, 1823–1827* (New York: Antiquarian Press, 1959, orig. 1914), 195.

69. Ramsey, *Joseph Thomas Heath Diary,* 20–21, 26, 29, 66. Richard Somerset Mackie, *Trading Beyond the Mountains: The British Fur Trade on the Pacific, 1793–1843*

(Vancouver: University of British Columbia Press, 1997), 294–301; John S. Galbraith, "The British and Americans at Fort Nisqually, 1846–1859," *PNQ* 41 (April 1950): 117–118.

70. Ronald Spores, "Too Small a Place: The Removal of the Willamette Valley Indians, 1850–1856," *American Indian Quarterly* 17 (spring 1993): 171–191; William G. Robbins, "The Indian Question in Western Oregon: The Making of a Colonial People," in *Experiences in a Promised Land: Essays in Pacific Northwest History*, ed. G. Thomas Edwards and Carlos A. Schwantes (Seattle: University of Washington Press, 1986), 51–67; Brad Asher, "Coming Under the Law: Indian/White Relations and Legal Change in Washington Territory, 1853–1889," 166–168; Mackie, *Trading Beyond the Mountains*, 295, 307–308.

71. Frederick A. Norwood, "Two Contrasting Views of the Indians: Methodist Involvement in the Indian Troubles in Oregon and Washington," *Church History* 49 (June 1980): 179. Carlos Arnaldo Schwantes, *The Pacific Northwest: An Interpretive History*, rev. ed., 147–153.

72. Asher, "Coming Under the Law," 178–183; case 17, box 2, Washington Territorial Supreme Court, Washington State Archives, Olympia; *(Steilacoom) Puget Sound Courier*, 25 April 1856, p. 2. Patrick Henry McLatchy, "The Development of the National Guard of Washington as an Instrument of Social Control, 1854–1916" (Ph.D. diss., University of Washington, 1973), 18–43; *Message from the President of the United States to the Two Houses of Congress*, 33rd Congress, 2nd session, House of Representatives, Executive Document no. 1, part 1 (Washington, D.C.: A. O. P. Nicholson, 1854), 499; H. M. Judah to Major E. D. Townsend, 2 November 1855, 34th Congress, 1st session, House of Representatives, Executive Document no. 93, "Indian Hostilities in Oregon and Washington" (Washington, D.C.: Cornelius Wendell, 1856), 31–32; Alice H. Wooldridge, *Pioneers and Incidents of the Upper Coquille Valley, 1890–1940* (Myrtle Creek, Oregon: Mail Printers, 1971), 276; Nathan Douthit, "Joseph Lane and the Rogue River Indians: Personal Relations Across a Cultural Divide," *OHQ* 95 (winter 1994–1995): 472–515; *The Diary of Philip Leget Edwards: The Great Cattle Drive from California to Oregon in 1837* (Fairfield, Washington: Ye Galleon Press, 1989, orig. 1860), 52–53; [Ida Pfeiffer], *A Lady's Visit to California, 1853* (Oakland, California: Biobooks, 1950, orig. 1856), 50–52; Martin F. Schmitt, ed., *General George Crook: His Autobiography*, 2nd ed. (Norman: University of Oklahoma Press, 1960), 16; Stephen Dow Beckham, *Requiem for a People: The Rogue Indians and the Frontiersmen* (Norman: University of Oklahoma Press, 1971); Herbert B. Nelson and Preston E. Onstad, eds., *A Webfoot Volunteer: The Diary of William M. Hilleary, 1864–1866* (Corvallis: Oregon State University Press, 1965), 2–4; Kent D. Richards, *Isaac I. Stevens: Young Man in a*

Hurry (Provo, Utah: Brigham Young University Press, 1979), 297–298, 303–307; John Robert Finger, "Henry L. Yesler's Seattle Years, 1852–1892" (Ph.D. diss., University of Washington, 1968), 38–39; William B. Skelton, "Army Officers' Attitudes Toward Indians, 1830–1860," *PNQ* 67 (July 1976): 113–125.

73. Lancaster Pollard, ed., "Journal of a Voyage on Puget Sound in 1853 by William Petit Trowbridge," *PNQ* 33 (October 1942): 395. Gunter Barth, ed., *All Quiet on the Yamhill: The Civil War in Oregon* (Eugene: University of Oregon Books, 1959), 75, 79, describes Native peoples being punished with whippings by army personnel in the Willamette Valley during the Civil War.

74. Finger, "Henry L. Yesler's Seattle Years," 29. Ferrell, "Indians and Criminal Justice in Early Oregon," 8–12.

75. *(Portland) Weekly Oregonian*, 18 August 1855, p. 2. *(Portland) Weekly Oregonian*, 25 August 1855, p. 2; *SPSH*, 10 July 1862, p. 2; *VDBC*, 21 December 1864, p. 3.

76. *SPSH*, 24 September 1858, p. 2. James G. Swan, *The Northwest Coast: Or, Three Years' Residence in Washington Territory* (Seattle: University of Washington Press, 1972, orig. 1857), 381; *Message from the President of the United States to the Two Houses of Congress*, 33rd Congress, 2nd session, House of Representatives, Executive Document no. 1, part 1 (Washington, D.C.: A. O. P. Nicholson, 1854), 467; A. B. Meacham, *Wigwam and War-Path; or the Royal Chief in Chains* (Boston: John P. Dale and Company, 1875), 41; *Message of the President of the United States and Accompanying Documents, to the Two Houses of Congress*, 38th Congress, 2nd session, House of Representatives, Executive Document no. 1 (Washington, D.C.: Government Printing Office, 1865), 206, 213–214; *Message of the President of the United States and Accompanying Documents, to the Two Houses of Congress, at the Commencement of the First Session of the Thirty-ninth Congress, Reports of the Secretary of the Interior and Post Master General* (Washington, D.C.: Government Printing Office, 1865), 240. Yet convictions against whites who murdered Natives were not unheard of: Charles H. Carey, ed., *The Journals of Theodore Talbot, 1843 and 1849–52* (Portland, Oregon: Metropolitan Press, 1931), 112.

77. Asher, "Coming Under the Law," 163, 171-196, 91–119. The exclusion of Native testimony from Oregon territorial courts contributed to the difficulty in convicting whites accused of killing or attacking Natives. In 1851, for example, the Oregon Supreme Court refused to hear the testimony of a Native woman who claimed to have witnessed William and Ezra Johnson's assault and battery on a Clackamas Native. This law did not change until Oregon became a state, in 1859. Not until 1869 did Washington Territory law allow Native peoples to testify against non-Natives, and then it was only in cases involving whites accused of giving or selling liquor to Natives. Ferrell,

"Indians and Criminal Justice in Early Oregon," 37–38, 51–53; Greg Russell Hubbard, "The Indian Under the White Man's Law in Washington Territory, 1853–1889" (M.A. thesis, University of Washington, 1972), 42; Charles Prosch, *Reminiscences of Washington Territory* (Fairfield, Washington: Ye Galleon Press, 1969, orig. 1904), 69.

78. Gustavas Hines, *Oregon: Its History, Condition, and Prospects* (New York: Arno Press, 1973, orig. 1851), 435.

79. Case 23, series 1, Walla Walla County District Court, Washington State Archives. Theft constituted a less direct form of resistance. *(Walla Walla) Washington Statesman,* 2 April 1864, p. 9. T. W. Davenport, "Recollections of an Indian Agent," *QOHS* 8 (March 1907): 24. Whites also stole goods from Native peoples, although settlers of course did not typically comment on it. James Strong, who was much more sympathetic to Native peoples than most of his counterparts, recalled coming across a dying Native somewhere on the West Coast who had been shot and robbed by a white man for refusing to trade a good horse for a bad one. James C. Strong, *Wah-Kee-Nah and Her People: The Curious Customs, Traditions and Legends of the North American Indians* (New York: G. P. Putnam's Sons, 1893), 164–166.

80. *SOS*, 13 May 1861, p. 2.

81. *SOS*, 13 January 1862, p. 1. The Coos Bay correspondent noted that two of the men were discharged by the local judge for want of testimony, but that a group of local citizens tarred and feathered them before turning them out of town. Beckham, *Requiem for a People,* 134, 140, 151; Douthit, "Joseph Lane and the Rogue River Indians," 502; Trafzer and Scheuerman, *Renegade Tribe,* 61–62; Strong, *Wah-Kee-Nah and Her People,* 163–164; Robert L. Hall, *Oral Traditions of the Coquille Indians* (Corvallis: Oregon State University Department of Anthropology, 1978), 29. See also: Barth, ed., *All Quiet on the Yamhill,* 37; *Message of the President of the United States and Accompanying Documents, to the Two Houses of Congress, at the Commencement of the First Session of the Thirty-ninth Congress, Reports of the Secretary of the Interior and Post Master General* (Washington, D.C.: Government Printing Office, 1865), 240; case 93, Jefferson County District Court, Washington State Archives.

82. *Message from the President of the United States to the Two Houses of Congress,* 35th Congress, 2nd session, House of Representatives, Executive Document no. 2 (Washington, D.C.: James B. Steadman, 1858), vol. 1: 600. On punishment see also: *(Olympia) Washington Standard,* 28 March 1863, p. 2; Howard M. List and Edith M. List, eds., "John M. Shively's Memoir, Part I," *OHQ* 81 (spring 1980): 23; *NWBC,* 25 May 1869, p. 3. Asher, "Coming Under the Law," 188–192; John Lutz, "Inventing an Indian War: Canadian-Indians and American Settlers in the Pacific West, 1854–1864,"

Journal of the West 38 (July 1999): 7–13; *SOS*, 14 December 1863, p. 3. Phoebe Goodell Judson, *A Pioneer's Search for an Ideal Home* (Lincoln: University of Nebraska Press, 1984, orig. 1925), 100; Egbert Noyes Foster interview, vol. 18, J. L. Osburn interview, vol. 40, and Mrs. H. L. Rann interview, vol. 43, Fred Lockley Collection, University of Oregon Special Collections, Eugene; Mace case, box 61A-97/1, Clackamas County Circuit Court case files, Oregon State Archives, Salem; Charlotte Matheny Kirkwood, *Into the Eye of the Setting Sun: A Story of the West When It Was New*, 2nd ed., (McMinnville, Oregon: The Family Association of Matheny, Cooper, Hewitt, Kirkwood, and Bailey, 1991), 46, 113; *Pioneer Stories of Linn County, Oregon* (Albany, Oregon: Linn Benton Genealogical Services, n.d.), vol. 3: 12; Joseph Williams, *Narrative of a Tour from the State of Indiana to the Oregon Territory in the Years 1841–2* (New York: Cadmus Book Shop, 1921, orig. 1843), 60; Tess E. Jennings, trans., *Mission of the Columbia: Second Letter and Journal of Father J. B. Z. Bolduc* (Seattle: Works Progress Administration, 1937), 33; *(Oregon City) Spectator*, 11 November 1847, p. 2; 23 March 1848, p. 2; 1 June 1848, p. 2; *PO*, 17 December 1853, p. 2.

83. *(Olympia) Washington Standard*, 12 October 1861, p. 3.

84. Swan, *Northwest Coast*, 282. A. J. Splawn, *Ka-mi-akin: Last Hero of the Yakimas* (Portland: Binfords and Mort for the Oregon Historical Society, 1944, orig. 1917), 157–158, 149, 166–167, 217–218; L. L. Langness, "Individual Psychology and Cultural Change: An Ethnohistorical Case from the Klallam," in *The Tsimshian and Their Neighbors of the North Pacific Coast*, ed. Jay Miller and Carol M. Eastman (Seattle: University of Washington Press, 1984), 273; *SOS*, 2 June 1855, p. 1.

85. Roberta L. Bagshaw, ed., *No Better Land: The 1860 Diaries of the Anglican Colonial Bishop George Hills* (Victoria: Sono Nis Press, 1996), 197, 185, 168. Loo, *Making Law, Order, and Authority in British Columbia*, 149–154; Jennings, *Mission of the Columbia*, 32.

86. *NWBC*, 18 May 1864, p. 2; 27 August 1864, p. 2. *Daily Victoria Gazette*, 12 October 1858, p. 2; *VBC*, 26 January 1860, p. 2; *VDBC*, 5 September 1862, p. 3; *NWBC*, 20 May 1863, p. 1; 14 May 1864, p. 3.

87. Victoria Charge Book, vol. 5, 15 July 1868 to 15 January 1869, GR 848, British Columbia Archives and Records Service, Victoria.

88. Foster, "'The Queen's Law Is Better Than Yours,'" 84, 103–104. This is not a complete listing of all homicides from the colonial period, or even for these years. A few whites were executed. Killings of Natives were less apt to be investigated than killings of whites. Duncan Duane Thomson, "A History of the Okanagan: Indians and Whites in the Settlement Era, 1860–1920" (Ph.D. diss., University of British Columbia,

1985), 83–84. Nancy Parker, "Swift Justice and the Decline of the Criminal Trial Jury: The Dynamics of Law and Authority in Victoria, B.C., 1858–1905," in *British Columbia and the Yukon,* ed. Hamar Foster and John McLaren (Toronto: University of Toronto Press, for The Osgoode Society, 1995), 174–175; William Swanton Thackray, "Keeping the Peace on Vancouver Island: The Colonial Police and the Royal Navy, 1850–1866" (M.A. thesis, University of Victoria, 1980), 59–60, 143–144; *VDBC,* 6 April 1866, p. 3; 10 May 1859, p. 2; 9 May 1864, p. 3; 18 July 1861, p. 3; 28 April 1864, p. 3; 19 July 1864, p. 3; 5 September 1862, p. 3; 30 July 1864, p. 3; Bagshaw, *No Better Land,* 240; Gough, *Gunboat Frontier: British Maritime Authority and Northwest Coast Indians, 1846–90,* 106, 197, passim; Robin Fisher, "Indian Warfare and Two Frontiers: A Comparison of British Columbia and Washington Territory During the Early Years of Settlement," *Pacific Historical Review* 50 (1981): 31–51.

89. *VDBC,* 5 January 1866, p. 3. South of the line, by way of contrast, legal officials often ignored intra-Native violence. In 1854 Oregon's Superintendent of Indian Affairs Joel Palmer informed a coastal sub-agent with no police force and no jail to let his charges manage "their criminal code in their own way." Ferrell, "Indians and Criminal Justice in Early Oregon," 40. *(Olympia) Washington Standard,* 11 November 1865, p. 2; *PO,* 20 April 1863, p. 3; 30 January 1863, p. 3; 5 December 1864, p. 3; Asher, "'Their Own Domestic Difficulties': Intra-Indian Crime and White Law in Western Washington Territory, 1873–1889," *Western Historical Quarterly* 27 (summer 1996): 189–209; Brad Asher, "A Shaman-Killing Case on Puget Sound, 1873–1874: American Law and Salish Culture," *PNQ* 86 (winter 1994–1995): 17–24; Langness, "Individual Psychology and Cultural Change," 263; John Lutz, "A Border That Does Not Hold People Back: Annual Migrations of Canadian Indians to the American Pacific Northwest" (paper presented at "On Brotherly Terms": Canadian-American Relations West of the Rockies, Seattle, 14 September 1996), 25.

90. *Nanaimo Gazette,* 21 April 1866, p. 1; 19 May 1866, p. 2. D. G. Forbes MacDonald, *British Columbia and Vancouver's Island,* 3rd ed. (London: Longman, Green, Longman, Roberts and Green, 1863), 357–358; *VBC,* 13 June 1859, p. 1; 15 June 1859, p. 3; *(Victoria) Gazette,* 4 August 1859, p. 3; *(Yale) British Columbia Tribune,* 16 July 1866, p. 2.

91. Gary Fuller Reese, ed., *The Northwest Was Their Goal: A Collection of Pioneer Reminiscences Published in Clinton Snowden's* Tacoma Daily *and* Weekly Ledger *in 1892–1893* (Tacoma, Washington: Tacoma Public Library, 1984), vol. 2: 279, 281. Daniel P. Marshall, "Rickard Revisited: Native 'Participation' in the Gold Discoveries of British Columbia," *Native Studies Review* 11 (1997): 91–108; Harris, *Resettlement of British Columbia,* 110–114; Patricia Elizabeth Vaughan, "Co-operation and Resistance:

Indian-European Relations on the Mining Frontier in British Columbia, 1835–1858" (M.A. thesis, University of British Columbia, 1978), 45–55.

92. Case 16/1857–1859, BCAGC.

93. Peter Murray, *The Devil and Mr. Duncan* (Victoria: Sono Nis Press, 1985), 34; *VDBC*, 12 September 1865, p. 3. Lutz, "A Border That Does Not Hold People Back," p. 11; Jean Usher, *William Duncan of Metlakatla: A Victorian Missionary in British Columbia* (Ottawa: National Museums of Canada, 1974), 57–58; *DBCVC*, 12 March 1867, p. 2; 27 December 1866, p. 3; 2 November 1866, p. 3; 22 May 1867, p. 3; 12 December 1867, p. 3; *VDBC*, 13 February 1862, p. 3; 27 April 1864, p. 3; 31 July 1866, p. 3; cases 24/1860, 30/1866, BCAGC; Gough, *Gunboat Frontier*, 76–80.

94. Cases 36/1864, 16/1864, BCAGC.

95. Fenton Aylmer, ed., *A Cruise in the Pacific* (London: Hurst and Blackett, 1860), vol. 2: 89. *VDBC*, 11 June 1864, p. 3.

96. John Hayman, ed., *Robert Brown and the Vancouver Island Exploring Expedition* (Vancouver: University of British Columbia Press, 1989), 94. Jean Barman, *The West Beyond the West: A History of British Columbia*, rev. ed., 379; *Ninth Census of the United States: Statistics of Population* (Washington, D.C.: Government Printing Office, 1879), 57; *VBC*, 23 May 1859, p. 1. Fisher, *Contact and Conflict*, 95–118; J. E. Michael Kew, "History of Coastal British Columbia Since 1846," in Suttles, *Northwest Coast*, 159–164.

97. Case 1/1866, BCAGC. *VDBC*, 6 February 1865, p. 3; *DBCVC*, 5 December 1869, p. 3.

98. Bagshaw, ed., *No Better Land*, 156, 195. Gough, *Gunboat Frontier*, 138–139. *VBC*, 10 April 1860, p. 2; *VDBC*, 25 January 1861, p. 3; 27 June 1861, p. 3; 18 March 1863, p. 3; 24 December 1863, p. 3; 9 February 1864, p. 3; 17 July 1865, p. 3; 5 August 1865, p. 3; 12 June 1866, p. 3; *DBCVC*, 27 November 1866, p. 3; 24 December 1866, p. 3; 9 April 1867, p. 3; 6 August 1867, p. 3; 19 September 1871, p. 3. See also *PO*, 21 August 1865, p. 3.

99. Case 18/1868, BCAGC. Fisher, *Contact and Conflict*, 90–91; Gillian Marie, "Attitudes Toward Chinese Immigrants to British Columbia, 1858–1885" (M.A. thesis, Simon Fraser University, 1976), 20–21; Robert Edward Wynne, *Reaction to the Chinese in the Pacific Northwest and British Columbia, 1850 to 1910* (New York: Arno Press, 1978), 108–109, 114–115; Lorraine Barker Hildebrand, *Straw Hats, Sandals and Steel: The Chinese in Washington State* (Tacoma: Washington State American Revolution Bicentennial Commission, 1977), 16–17.

100. *Message from the President of the United States to the Two Houses of Congress,* 35th Congress, 1st session, House of Representatives, Executive Document no. 2

(Washington: Cornelius Wendell, 1857), 631. Robert Bunting, *The Pacific Raincoast: Environment and Culture in an American Eden, 1778–1900*, 63–67; Cesare Marino, "History of Western Washington Since 1846," in Suttles, *Northwest Coast*, 169–175; Stephen Dow Beckham, "History of Western Oregon Since 1846," in Suttles, *Northwest Coast*, 180–187; Asher, "Coming Under the Law," 58–80, notes that many Washington Natives either stayed off their reservation altogether or used it as one stop in a seasonal round of economic activities that usually included wage labor for whites.

101. Gilbert Malcolm Sproat, "The West Coast Indians in Vancouver Island," *Transactions of the Ethnological Society of London* 5 (1867): 245.

102. Fisher, *Contact and Conflict*, 96.

103. Fisher, *Contact and Conflict*, 146–174; Harris, *Resettlement of British Columbia*, 126–127; Paul Tennant, *Aboriginal Peoples and Politics: The Indian Land Question in British Columbia, 1849–1989* (Vancouver: University of British Columbia Press, 1990), 39–52.

104. Hines, *Oregon*, 157.

105. Zacharia Atwell Mudge, *Sketches of Mission Life Among the Indians of Oregon* (Fairfield, Washington: Ye Galleon Press, [1983], orig. 1854), 47. Stern, *Chiefs and Change in the Oregon Country*, 134–155; Ferrell, "Indians and Criminal Justice in Early Oregon," 12–16.

106. William Barnhart to C. H. Hale, 13 June 1862, reel 20, Records of the Superintendency of Indian Affairs. *Message of the President of the United States, and Accompanying Documents, to the Two Houses of Congress*, 38th Congress, 2nd session, House of Representatives, Executive Document no. 1 (Washington, D.C.: Government Printing Office, 1865), 219; E. A. Schwartz, *The Rogue River Indian War and Its Aftermath, 1850–1980* (Norman: University of Oklahoma Press, 1997), 174; Lionel Youst, *She's Tricky Like Coyote: Annie Miner Peterson, an Oregon Coast Indian Woman* (Norman: University of Oklahoma Press, 1997), 50, 53. Asher, "Coming Under the Law," 252–265.

107. T. W. Davenport, "Recollections of an Indian Agent—III," *QOHS* 8 (September 1907): 232–233. *Message of the President of the United States, and Accompanying Documents, to the Two Houses of Congress*, 38th Congress, 1st session, House of Representatives, Executive Document no. 1 (Washington, D.C.: Government Printing Office, 1863), 178.

108. Clifford M. Drury, *Nine Years With the Spokane Indians: The Diary, 1838–1848, of Elkanah Walker* (Glendale, California: Arthur H. Clark, 1976), 229, 277. Vibert, *Traders' Tales*, 58–83; Robert T. Boyd, *People of the Dalles, The Indians of*

Wascopam Mission: A Historical Ethnography Based on the Papers of the Methodist Missionaries (Lincoln: University of Nebraska Press, 1996), 175–185, 209–210; Asher, "Coming Under the Law," 262–263; Antonia Curtze Mills, "The Beaver Indian Prophet Dance and Related Movements Among North American Indians" (Ph.D. diss., Harvard University, 1981), 44–69; Mills, *Eagle Down Is Our Law: Witsuwit'en Law, Feasts, and Land Claims* (Vancouver: University of British Columbia Press, 1994), 166–175; Erik Anderson, "'Ready for the Religious Relationship': Carrier Negotiations with Christianity Through Fur Traders, Prophets, and Missionaries to 1885" (M.A. thesis, University of Northern British Columbia, 1996); Stern, *Chiefs and Change in the Oregon Country*, 26–27; Thomas R. Garth, "The Plateau Whipping Complex and Its Relationship to Plateau-Southwest Contacts," *EH* 12 (spring 1965): 141–170; Elizabeth Furniss, "Resistance, Coercion, and Revitalization: The Shuswap Encounter with Roman Catholic Missionaries, 1860–1900," *EH* 42 (spring 1995): 237–244; Tina Loo, "Tonto's Due: Law, Culture, and Colonization in British Columbia," in Foster and McLaren, *British Columbia and the Yukon*, 128–170; Jacqueline Gresko, "Roman Catholic Missions to the Indians of British Columbia: A Reappraisal of the Lemert Thesis," *Journal of the Canadian Church Historical Society* 24 (October 1982): 51–62; Usher, *William Duncan of Metlakatla*, 57–58; Michael Harkin, "The Evangelic Dialogue Among the Heiltsuk," *EH* 40 (winter 1993): 1–33; Ruth Karr McKee, *Mary Richardson Walker: Her Book* (Caldwell: Idaho: Caxton Printers, 1945), 242, 264–265; Nellie B. Pipes, ed., "Journal of John H. Frost, 1840–43," *OHQ* 35 (December 1934): 350.

109. Clifford M. Drury, *The Diaries and Letters of Henry H. Spalding and Asa Bowen Smith Relating to the Nez Perce Mission, 1838–1842* (Glendale, California: Arthur H. Clark, 1958), 172–173, 252. Deborah Lynn Dawson, "'Laboring in My Savior's Vineyard': The Mission of Eliza Hart Spalding" (Ph.D. diss., Bowling Green State University, 1988), 74–75, 82–83, 94; Chance, *Influences of the Hudson's Bay Company on the Native Cultures of the Colvile District*, 98; Trafzer and Scheuerman, *Renegade Tribe*, 25. Charles Henry Carey, ed., "Diary of Rev. George Gary," *QOHS* 24 (March 1923): 84.

110. Usher, *William Duncan of Metlakatla*, 77, 83; Murray, *The Devil and Mr. Duncan*, 53; Douglas Hudson, "Internal Colonialism and Industrial Capitalism," in *Sa Ts'e: Historical Perspectives on Northern British Columbia*, ed. Thomas Turner (Prince George: College of New Caledonia Press, 1989), 183; Duane Duncan Thomson, "A History of the Okanagan: Indians and Whites in the Settlement Era, 1860–1920" (Ph.D. diss., University of British Columbia, 1985), 37–61, 84–91; Fisher, *Contact and Conflict*, 119–145.

111. Case 12/1857–1859, BCAGC. Meacham, *Wigwam and War-Path*, 262–265; Stern, *Klamath Tribe*, 96–99.

112. *VDBC*, 18 March 1863, p. 3.

113. Case 3/1859, British Columbia Attorney General Inquisitions, GR 1328, British Columbia Archives and Records Service. Asher, "Coming Under the Law," 81–89; Brad Asher, *Beyond the Reservation: Indians, Settlers, and the Law in Washington Territory, 1853–1889* (Norman: University of Oklahoma Press, 1999), 64–66; Jean Barman, "Invisible Women: Aboriginal Mothers and Mixed-Race Daughters in Rural Pioneer British Columbia," in *Beyond the City Limits: Rural History in British Columbia,* ed. R. W. Sandwell, 159–179; Peterson del Mar, "Intermarriage and Agency"; Peterson del Mar, *What Trouble I Have Seen: A History of Violence against Wives,* 27–28; Elizabeth Lord, *Reminiscences of Eastern Oregon* (Portland, Oregon: Irwin-Hodson, 1903), 145; Edward Cridge Diary, 105–106, MS 320, British Columbia Archives and Records Service; Harriet Duncan Munnick, annot., *Catholic Church Records of the Pacific Northwest: Vancouver,* trans. Mikell De Lores Wormell Warner (St. Paul, Oregon: French Prairie Press, 1972), A-36; case 12/1865, British Columbia Attorney General's Correspondence; *PO*, 16 July 1856, p. 2; *SOS*, 15 February 1859, p. 2; 22 February 1859, p. 2; *VDBC*, 4 November 1862, p. 3; *DBCVC*, 21 February 1867, p. 3.

114. Case 169, Jefferson County District Court, Washington State Archives. Peterson del Mar, *What Trouble I Have Seen,* 33–35.

115. Lutz, "A Border That Does Not Hold People Back," 17. Gough, *Gunboat Frontier,* 129; Fisher, *Contact and Conflict,* 112–113.

116. Littlefield, "Gender, Class and Community," 99–100; Gough, *Gunboat Frontier,* 86, 106; Codere, "Kwakiutl," 473; Langness, "Individual Psychology and Cultural Change," 263; Swan, *Indians of Cape Flattery,* 51; James G. Swan, *Almost Out of the World: Scenes from Washington Territory,* ed. William A. Katz (Tacoma: Washington State Historical Society, 1971), 107; Asher, "Coming Under the Law," 197–204; Lutz, "A Border That Does Not Hold People Back," 25–26.

117. Bagshaw, *No Better Land,* 56, 55, 215–216, 225. Clarence Bolt, *Thomas Crosby and the Tsimshian: Small Shoes for Feet Too Large* (Vancouver: University of British Columbia Press, 1992), 21; *DBCVC*, 10 November 1868, p. 3; *VDBC*, 13 May 1861, p. 3.

118. *DBCVC*, 15 January 1867, p. 3. *VDBC*, 15 April 1861, p. 3; 12 August 1861, p. 3; 4 May 1863, p. 3; 5 May 1863, p. 3; 13 July 1863, p. 3; 2 February 1864, p. 3; 4 March 1864, p. 3; 21 May 1864, p. 3; 25 July 1864, p. 3; 3 April 1865, p. 3; 24 April 1866, p. 3; 18 May 1866, p. 3; *DBCVC*, 30 July 1866, p. 3; 18 September 1866, p. 3; 20 February 1867, p. 3; 22 February 1867, p. 3; 19 November 1867, p. 3; 27 December 1867, p. 1; 18 January 1869,

p. 3. Victoria's charge books identified the membership of fourteen of the sixteen Natives charged with simple assault during six months ending in mid-January 1869. Ten were Haida, two Tsimshian, one Songhish, and one Fort Rupert. This of course does not prove that Haida were more prone to violence, as the police may have been more prone to arrest them than other Natives. Victoria Charge Book, vol. 5, 15 July 1868 to 15 January 1869.

119. *PO,* 20 April 1863, p. 3; 30 May 1864, p. 3, emphasis in the original. *(Olympia) Washington Standard,* 11 November 1865, p. 2; *SOS,* 26 June 1860, p. 2; 21 March 1864, p. 2; *PO,* 29 January 1863, p. 3; 30 January 1863, p. 3; 9 February 1864, p. 3; 20 May 1864, p. 3; 31 May 1864, p. 3.

120. Curtis, *North American Indian* (New York: Johnson Reprint Corporation, 1970, orig. 1924), vol. 13: 95.

121. *Message of the President of the United States, and Accompanying Documents, to the Two Houses of Congress,* 38th Congress, 1st session, House of Representatives, Executive Document no. 1 (Washington, D.C.: Government Printing Office, 1863), 184; Bunting, *The Pacific Raincoast,* 65.

122. Cooper, "To Be Free on Our Lands: Coast Tsimshian and Nisga'a Societies in Historical Perspective, 1830–1900" (Ph.D. diss., University of Waterloo, 1993), 190–193; Cooper, "Native Women of the Northern Pacific Coast," 57.

123. Boyd, *People of the Dalles,* 79–82. Stephen Dow Beckham, *The Indians of Western Oregon: This Land Was Theirs* (Coos Bay, Oregon: Arago Books, 1977), 155; cases 10/1869, 19/1871, BCAGC.

124. Fred Lockley, "Reminiscences of Mrs. Frank Collins, Nee Martha Elizabeth Gilliam," *QOHS* 17 (December 1916): 369. *SPSH,* 18 February 1859, p. 2; *VDBC,* 13 May 1861, p. 3; *DBCVC,* 28 December 1867, p. 1.

125. Jacobs, "Santiam Kalapuya Ethnologic Texts," 66; *Message from the President of the United States to the Two Houses of Congress,* 35th Congress, 1st session, House of Representatives, Executive Document no. 2 (Washington, D.C.: Cornelius Wendell, 1857), 649; *Message of the President of the United States to the Two Houses of Congress,* House of Representatives, 3rd session, 37th Congress, Executive Document no. 1 (Washington, D.C.: Government Printing Office, 1863), vol. 2: 405–406; Sapir and Swadesh, *Nootka Texts,* 209; vol. 1409, Capital Cases, RG 13, National Archives of Canada, Ottawa; Jacobs, "An Historical Event Text from a Galice Athabaskan," 187; Asher, "A Shaman-Killing Case on Puget Sound," 17–24.

126. Swan, *Northwest Coast,* 167. U. E. Fries, with the assistance of Emil B. Fries, *From Copenhagen to Okanogan: The Autobiography of a Pioneer,* ed. Grace V. Stearns

and Eugene F. Hoy (Caldwell, Idaho: Caxton Printers, 1949), 299–300; A. F. Chamberlain, "Report on the Kootenay Indians of South-eastern British Columbia," *Report on the North-Western Tribes of Canada* 1 (1892): 13; Elmendorf and Kroeber, *Structure of Twana Culture*, 430. Suttles, *Coast Salish Essays*, 189–190, says that corporal punishment among the Upper Skagit was probably due to the influence of Christianity.

127. Kirkwood, *Into the Eye of the Setting Sun*, 113. Melville Jacobs, "Coos Narrative and Ethnologic Texts," *UWPA* 8 (April 1939): 104, 107–108, 116; *Pioneer Stories of Linn County, Oregon* (Albany, Oregon: Linn Benton Genealogical Services, n.d.), vol. 3: 13; *SOS*, 14 August 1860, p. 2; Herndon Smith, comp., *Centralia: The First Fifty Years, 1845–1900* (Centralia, Washington: The Daily Chronicle and F. H. Cole Printing Company, 1942), 163; case 261, Thurston County District Court, Washington State Archives; Meacham, *Wigwam and War-Path*, 45; Daniel Lee and John H. Frost, *Ten Years in Oregon* (New York: J. Collard, 1844), 314; Cooper, "Native Women of the Northern Pacific Coast," 57; *VDBC*, 21 June 1865, p. 3; 23 April 1866, p. 3.

128. Bagshaw, *No Better Land*, 185. *Victoria Gazette*, 3 September 1859, p. 3; *Nanaimo Gazette*, 4 December 1865, p. 2; David R. Williams, ". . . *The Man for a New Country*": *Sir Matthew Baillie Begbie* (Sidney, British Columbia: Grays Publishing, 1977), 101.

129. *Report of the Secretary of the Interior*, 52nd Congress, 1st session, House of Representatives, Executive Document no. 1, part 5 (Washington, D.C.: Government Printing Office, 1892), vol. 2: 375. Barman, *West Beyond the West*, 379; Johansen and Gates, *Empire of the Columbia: A History of the Pacific Northwest*, 2nd ed., 608–609; *Dominion of Canada Annual Report of the Department of Indian Affairs for the Year Ended June 30, 1899* (Ottawa: S. E. Dawson, 1900), 566, 436–437, 546; Douglas R. Hudson, "Traplines and Timber: Social and Economic Change Among the Carrier Indians of Northern British Columbia" (Ph.D. diss., University of Alberta, 1983), 118, 122–130; James A. McDonald, "Bleeding Day and Night: The Construction of the Grand Trunk Pacific Railway Across Tsimshian Reserve Lands," *Canadian Journal of Native Studies* 10 (1990): 33–69; James Redford, "Attendance at Indian Residential Schools in British Columbia, 1890–1920," *BCST* 44 (winter 1979–1980): 41–56; McDonald, "Social Change and the Creation of Underdevelopment: A Northwest Coast Case," *American Ethnologist* 21 (1994): 152–175; Cary C. Collins, "Subsistence and Survival: The Makah Indian Reservation, 1855–1933," *PNQ* 87 (fall 1996): 180–193; *Annual Reports of the Department of the Interior for the Fiscal Year Ended June 30, 1900, Indian Affairs: Report of Commissioner and Appendixes*, 56th Congress, 2nd session, House of Representatives, House Document no. 5 (Washington, D.C.: Government Printing Office, 1900), vol. 27: 369. Jay Miller, ed., *Mourning Dove: A Salishan Autobiography* (Lincoln: University

of Nebraska Press, 1990), illustrates that some Plateau peoples maintained much of their traditional culture into the 1890s.

130. *Annual Reports of the Department of the Interior for the Fiscal Year Ended June 30, 1898, Indian Affairs*, 55th Congress, 3rd session, House of Representatives, House Document no. 5 (Washington, D.C.: Government Printing Office, 1898), vol. 15: 298. Josephy, *Nez Perce Indians*, 386–515.

131. Fisher, *Contact and Conflict*, 175–211; Duncan Duane Thomson, "The Response of Okanagan Indians to European Settlement," *BCST* 101 (spring 1994): 96–117; Clarence Bolt, "The Conversion of the Port Simpson Tsimshian: Indian Control or Missionary Manipulation?" *BCST* 57 (spring 1983): 38–56; James K. Burrows, "'A Much-Needed Class of Labour': The Economy and Income of the Southern Interior Plateau Indians, 1897–1910," *BCST* 71 (autumn 1986): 27–46; Daniel L. Boxberger, "In and Out of the Labor Force: The Lummi Indians and the Development of the Commercial Salmon Fishery of North Puget Sound, 1880–1900," *EH* 35 (spring 1988): 161–190; Russel Lawrence Barsh, "Puget Sound Indian Demography, 1900–1920: Migration and Economic Integration," *EH* 43 (winter 1996): 65–97; Trafzer and Scheuerman, *Renegade Tribe*, 98–135; John Lutz, "'Relating to the Country': The Lekwammen and the Extension of European Settlement, 1843–1911," in Sandwell, *Beyond the City Limits*, 17–32.

132. W. M. Halliday, *Potlatch and Totem and the Recollections of an Indian Agent* (London: J. M. Dent and Sons, 1935), 129–132, 173–177. *KIS*, 4 January 1895, p. 4; *CPG*, 22 August 1890, p. 1; 30 June 1893, p. 4; *(Colfax) Weekly Commoner*, 1 June 1894, p. 1; case 651, box 12, Skagit County Superior Court, Washington State Archives, Northwest Region, Bellingham.

133. *Report of the Secretary of the Interior*, 52nd Congress, 1st session, House of Representatives, Executive Document no. 1, part 5 (Washington, D.C.: Government Printing Office, 1892), vol. 2: 381; James Alan Smith, "To Assimilate the Children: The Boarding School at Chemawa, Oregon, 1880–1930" (M.A. thesis, Central Washington University, 1993), 40–41; Mary Ashworth, *The Forces Which Shaped Them: A History of the Education of Minority Group Children in British Columbia* (Vancouver: New Star Books, 1979), 15–16; Cooper, "'To Be Free on Our Lands,'" 261; David Mulhall, *Will to Power: The Missionary Career of Father Morice* (Vancouver: University of British Columbia Press, 1986), 23–24, 80–82, 123, 134–135, 157; Margaret Whitehead, ed., *They Call Me Father: Memoirs of Father Nicolas Coccola* (Vancouver: University of British Columbia Press, 1988), 58–59, 71.

134. Chamberlain, "Report on the Kootenay Indians," 10. British Columbia

Registers and Indexes to Coroners' Inquiries and Inquests, 1893 to 1899, GR 432, British Columbia Archives and Records Service. These records indicate that Natives killed about one half of the fourteen Natives victimized by homicide but only one of the forty-five non-Natives. These fourteen killings work out to a homicide rate of 7.11 per hundred thousand per year, roughly the same rate as for British Columbia's non-Native population. Native homicides often occurred in remote areas, however, and it appears that one-third or more went unreported to the coroner. In early 1893 an Indian agent on the northern coast had heard that a group of Natives had murdered "a number" of Natives belonging to a rival group. Case 382/1893, British Columbia Attorney General's Correspondence, Inward, GR 429, British Columbia Archives and Records Service. I found references to several other unreported intra-Native killings between 1893 and 1899: cases 27/1897, 9/1898, 6/1899, BCAGC; case 1457/1896, British Columbia Attorney General's Correspondence, Inward. There are no coroner's records for the United States, but anecdotal evidence suggests that the Native homicide rate there was high. The head of the Tulalip Agency in western Washington reported in 1900 that "many murders" had "been committed within the jurisdiction of this reservation," and not a single one of the murderers had been killed. *Annual Reports of the Department of the Interior for the Fiscal Year Ended June 30, 1900, Indian Affairs: Report of Commissioner and Appendixes*, 56th Congress, 2nd session, House of Representatives, House Document no. 5 (Washington, D.C.: Government Printing Office, 1900), vol. 27: 400. Less extreme forms of intra-Native violence near the century's close are difficult to measure. Many reservations had Native judicial systems in the 1880s, but the government phased out many of these Native courts in the 1890s. The agent at Grand Ronde in western Oregon complained in 1895 that this created a void, as county courts remained reluctant to assume the responsibility and costs of prosecuting Native criminals. Hence crimes such as larceny, adultery, and assault were going unpunished. *Report to the Secretary of the Interior*, 54th Congress, 1st session, House of Representatives, Document no. 5 (Washington, D.C.: Government Printing Office, 1896), vol 2: 267; *Report of the Secretary of the Interior*, 54th Congress, 2nd session, House of Representatives, House Document no. 5 (Washington, D.C.: Government Printing Office, 1897), vol. 2: 277; William T. Hagan, *Indian Police and Judges: Experiments in Acculturation and Control* (New Haven: Yale University Press, 1966). Case 262/1891, British Columbia Attorney General's Correspondence, Inward; case 69/1892, BCAGC; *KIS*, 14 May 1892, p. 4; 21 May 1892, p. 1; Kenneth Wiggins Porter, " 'The Boy's War': A Study in Frontier Racial Conflict, Journalism, and Folk History," *PNQ* 68 (October 1977): 175–190; *KIS*, 6 October 1894, p. 4.

135. Case 9/1898, BCAGC; case 9/1898, British Columbia Attorney General's Correspondence, Inward. Cases 10/1898, 50/1899, BCAGC.

136. *NFP*, 9 August 1894, p. 1. *(Colfax) Weekly Commoner*, 29 January 1892, p. 1; *NFP*, 11 September 1894, p. 4; 3 January 1898, p. 4.

137. *KIS*, 29 May 1896, p. 1.

138. Case 75/1895, BCAGC. Case 2484/1898, British Columbia Attorney General's Correspondence, Inward; cases 27/1892, 46/1896, 37/1897, BCAGC; *Kamloops Standard*, 2 June 1898, pp. 1, 8; *Vernon News*, 2 July 1891, p. 1.

139. *Vernon News*, 18 October 1894, p. 5; *Chilliwack Progress*, 29 August 1900, p. 1.

140. *KIS*, 18 April 1891, p. 7. *Report of the Secretary of the Interior*, 52nd Congress, 1st session, House of Representatives, Executive Document no. 1, part 5 (Washington, D.C.: Government Printing Office, 1892), vol. 2: 444; *Anacortes American*, 24 July 1890, p. 1; *NFP*, 11 November 1892, p. 1; *KIS*, 18 July 1891, p. 8; 10 July 1896, p. 6; 28 May 1897, p. 1. *(Burns) East Oregon Herald*, 15 January 1896, p. 7; *EC*, 8 May 1890, p. 3; *(Lakeview) Lake County Examiner*, 2 December 1897, p. 3; *(McMinnville) Telephone Register*, 21 October 1897, p. 3; *CPG*, 25 July 1890, p. 6; *Chilliwack Progress*, 3 January 1900, p. 1.

141. Slim Jackson, "How Civilization Affected the Lillooet People," *SH* 6 (1977): 48–49.

142. Craig MacAndrew and Robert B. Edgerton, *Drunken Comportment: A Social Explanation* (Chicago: Aldine, 1969); Gerald Mohatt, "The Sacred Water: The Quest for Personal Power Through Drinking Among the Teton Sioux," in *The Drinking Man*, ed. David C. McClelland, William N. Davis, Rudolf Kalin, and Eric Wanner (New York: Free Press, 1972), 261–275; David Riches, "The Phenomenon of Violence," in *The Anthropology of Violence*, ed. Riches (Oxford: Basil Blackwell, 1986), 1–27; Yngve Georg Lithman, "Feeling Good and Getting Smashed: On the Symbolism of Alcohol and Drunkenness among Canadian Indians," *Ethnos* 44 (1979): 119–133; A. D. Fisher, "Alcoholism and Race: the Misapplication of Both Concepts to North American Indians," *CRSA* 24 (February 1987): 81–98; James J. Collins, "Alcohol and Interpersonal Violence: Less Than Meets the Eye," in *Pathways to Criminal Violence*, ed. Neil Alan Weiner and Marvin E. Wolfgang (Newbury Park, California: Sage, 1989), 49–67; Peter C. Mancall, *Deadly Medicine: Indians and Alcohol in Early America* (Ithaca, New York: Cornell University Press, 1995); Edwin M. Lemert, "Alcohol and the Northwest Coast Indians," *University of California Publications in Culture and Society* 2 (1954): 303–406; Lemert, "The Use of Alcohol in Three Salish Indian Tribes," *Quarterly Journal of Studies on Alcohol* 19 (March 1958): 90–107; Adele Perry, "Bachelors in the Backwoods: White Men and Homosocial Culture in Up-Country British Columbia, 1858–1871," in Sandwell, *Beyond the City Limits*, 187–188.

143. *KIS*, 18 April 1891, p. 7.

144. *Message of the President of the United States to the Two Houses of Congress*, House of Representatives, 37th Congress, 3rd session, Executive Document no. 1 (Washington, D. C.: Government Printing Office, 1863), vol. 2: 406. Ruby and Brown, *Cayuse Indians*, 81.

145. Jay Connolly, *Rough Diamond: An Oral History of Shawnigan Lake School* (Shawnigan Lake, British Columbia: Shawnigan Lake School, 1992), 284–285, 333–334; Hilda Mortimer, with Chief Dan George, *You Call Me Chief: Impressions of the Life of Chief Dan George* (Toronto: Doubleday Canada, 1981), 139–146; Rosemary Gartner, "Homicide in Canada," in *Violence in Canada: Sociopolitical Perspectives*, ed. Jeffrey Ian Ross (Don Mills, Ontario: Oxford University Press, 1995), 205–206; Joan Ryan, "Squamish Socialization" (Ph.D. diss., University of British Columbia, 1973), 172–174; Claudia Lewis, *Indian Families of the Northwest Coast: The Impact of Change* (Chicago: University of Chicago Press, 1970), 123, 144, 171–175; Pamela Thorsen Amoss, "Persistence of Aboriginal Beliefs and Practices Among the Nooksack Coast Salish" (Ph.D. diss., University of Washington, 1972), 49–50; N. Rosalyn Ing, "The Effects of Residential Schools on Native Child-Rearing Practices," *Canadian Journal of Native Education* 18, supplement (1991): 82, 100–105; Margaret Craven, *Again Calls the Owl* (New York: G. P. Putnam's Sons, 1980), 104; Janet Campbell Hale, *Bloodlines: Odyssey of a Native Daughter* (New York: Random House, 1993), 42; Lee Maracle, *Bobbi Lee: Indian Rebel* (Toronto: Women's Press, 1990); John Gibson, *A Small and Charming World* (Toronto: Collins, 1972), 39–41, 109, 112, 199–202; Ronald P. Rohner, *The People of Gilford: A Contemporary Kwakiutl Village* (Ottawa: National Museum of Canada, 1967), 89, 92–99, 122, 124–126; Ronald P. Rohner and Evelyn C. Rohner, *The Kwakiutl: Indians of British Columbia* (New York: Holt, Rinehart and Winston, 1970), 42–52, 65–68; Mary Lee Stearns, *Haida Culture in Custody: The Masset Band* (Vancouver: Douglas and McIntyre; Seattle: University of Washington Press, 1981), 138; Guy Lanoue, *Brothers: The Politics of Violence Among the Sekani of Northern British Columbia* (New York: Berg, 1992); Robert Silverman and Leslie Kennedy, *Deadly Deeds: Murder in Canada* (Scarborough, Ontario: Nelson, 1993), 211–230; Sharon Moyer, "Race, Gender, and Homicide: Comparisons Between Aboriginals and Other Canadians," *Canadian Journal of Criminology* 34 (July-October 1992): 387–402; Wolfgang Jilek and Chunilal Roy, "Homicide Committed by Canadian Indians and Non-Indians," *International Journal of Offender Therapy and Comparative Criminology* 20 (1976): 201–216; Carol LaPrairie, "Native Women and Crime: a Theoretical Model," *Canadian Journal of Native Studies* 7 (1987): 121–137; Ronet Bachman, *Death and*

Violence on the Reservation: Homicide, Family Violence, and Suicide in American Indian Populations (New York: Auburn House, 1992); Robin Ridington, *Trail to Heaven: Knowledge and Narrative in a Northern Native Community* (Vancouver: Douglas and McIntyre, 1988), 43–44; *ST*, 7 March 1993, p. B8; *SPI*, 19 September 1997, p. C2; *PO*, 26 December 1987, p. B5. Washington's Native people have been the victims of homicide at a bit less than three times the rate of their non-Native counterparts. *Crime in Washington State Annual Reports* (Olympia: Washington Association of Sheriffs and Police Chiefs, n.d.); Clifford E. Trafzer, *Death Stalks the Yakima: Epidemiological Transitions and Mortality on the Yakima Indian Reservation, 1888–1964* (East Lansing: Michigan State University Press, 1997), 179, 199, 201; John L. Hall, "Ethnic Tensions and Economics: Indian-White Interaction in a British Columbia Ranching Community," *Canadian Journal of Anthropology* 1 (winter 1980): 185; Lithman, "Feeling Good and Getting Smashed," 129–131.

146. *PGC*, 26 May 1960, p. 1.

147. Sherman Alexie, *The Lone Ranger and Tonto Fistfight in Heaven* (New York: Atlantic Monthly Press, 1993), 2; Alexie, *Reservation Blues* (New York: Warner Books, 1995), 13–15. Several Native characters in *Indian Killer*, a 1996 novel, express a desire to intimidate whites. Alexie, *Indian Killer* (New York: Warner Books, 1996), 30, 188–189, 219–220, 313–314. *VDP*, 13 March 1968, p. 7; 20 November 1968, p. 36; *Vancouver Daily Times*, 29 January 1970, p. 21.

148. Alexie, *The Lone Ranger and Tonto Fistfight in Heaven,* 10.

149. Alexie, *Reservation Blues,* 12.

150. Alexie, *The Lone Ranger and Tonto Fistfight in Heaven,* 223. Lee Maracle, a British Columbia writer, treats some of these same themes. Maracle, *Sundogs* (Penticton, British Columbia: Theytus, 1992), 86, 150. Laurence French and Jim Hornbuckle, "An Analysis of Indian Violence: the Cherokee Example," *American Indian Quarterly* 3 (1977): 335–356.

2 / TO TAKE YOUR OWN PART

1. *The Journals of William Fraser Tolmie: Physician and Fur Trader* (Vancouver, British Columbia: Mitchell Press, 1963), 268–269.

2. Hugh J. M. Johnston, ed., *The Pacific Province: A History of British Columbia*, 68–132; Jean Barman, *The West Beyond the West: A History of British Columbia*, rev. ed., 52–98; Margaret A. Ormsby, *British Columbia: A History* (Vancouver, British

Columbia: Macmillan, 1958), 110–257; Carlos Arnaldo Schwantes, *The Pacific Northwest: An Interpretive History,* rev. ed., 91–142; Dorothy Johansen and Charles M. Gates, *Empire of the Columbia: A History of the Pacific Northwest,* 2nd ed., 151–299; Gordon B. Dodds, *The American Northwest: A History of Oregon and Washington,* 64–109; Robert Bunting, *The Pacific Raincoast: Environment and Culture in an American Eden, 1778–1900,* 91–96, 126–133; Dean L. May, *Three Frontiers: Family, Land, and Society in the American West, 1850–1900* (Cambridge: Cambridge University Press, 1994), 107–184; *Population of the United States in 1860* (Washington, D.C.: Government Printing Office, 1864), 401; *Censuses of Canada: 1665 to 1871* (Ottawa: I. B. Taylor, 1876), vol. 4: 376.

3. Barry M. Gough, "The Character of the British Columbia Frontier," in *A History of British Columbia: Selected Readings,* ed. Patricia E. Roy (Toronto: Copp Clark Pitman, 1989), 17. Walter N. Sage, "British Columbia Becomes Canadian (1871–1901)," in *Readings in Canadian History: Post-Confederation,* 3rd ed., ed. R. Douglass Francis and Donald B. Smith (Toronto: Holt, Rinehart and Winston of Canada, 1990), 12–22; R. C. Lundin Brown, *British Columbia: An Essay* (New Westminster, British Columbia: Royal Engineer Press, 1863), 52. Hamar Foster, "Shooting the Elephant: Historians and the Problem of Frontier Lawlessness," in *The Political Context of Law: Proceedings of the Seventh British Legal History Conference, Canterbury, 1985,* ed. Richard Eales and David Sullivan (London: Hambledon Press, 1987), 135–144; Rodman W. Paul, "'Old Californians' in British Gold Fields," *Huntington Library Quarterly* 17 (February 1954): 161–172; S. D. Clark, *The Social Development of Canada: An Introductory Study with Select Documents* (Toronto: University of Toronto Press, 1942), 4; Gough, "Keeping British Columbia British: The Law-and-Order Question on a Gold Mining Frontier," *Huntington Library Quarterly* 38 (May 1975): 279–280; Matthew Macfie, *Vancouver Island and British Columbia: Their History, Resources, and Prospects* (Toronto: Coles Publishing, 1972, orig. 1865), 511–513.

4. Orange Jacobs, *Memoirs of Orange Jacobs* (Seattle: Lowman and Hanford, 1908), 30.

5. Verne Bright, "Blue Mountain Eldorados: Auburn, 1861," *OHQ* 62 (September 1961): 229–230; Harry N. M. Winton, ed., "The Powder River and John Day Mines in 1862: Diary of Winfield Scott Ebey," *PNQ* 33 (October 1942): 429–430; Thomas A. McBride interview, Lockley collection, vol. 34, Special Collections, University of Oregon, Eugene; "Uncle Dan" Drumheller, *"Uncle Dan" Drumheller Tells Thrills of Western Trails in 1854* (Fairfield, Washington: Ye Galleon Press, 1985, orig. 1925), 97–98; George F. G. Stanley, *Mapping the Frontier: Charles Wilson's Diary of the Survey of the*

49th Parallel, 1858–1862, While Secretary of the British Boundary Commission (Seattle: University of Washington Press, 1970), 126; "Letter from Peter H. Burnett, Esq.," *QOHS* 24 (March 1923): 106.

6. Allan Pritchard, ed., *Vancouver Island Letters of Edmund Hope Verney, 1862–65* (Vancouver: University of British Columbia Press, 1996), 76.

7. Alan Hughes, "Charles Kean in Victoria: Touring Actors and Local Politicians in 1864," *BCST* 74 (autumn 1987): 27. Dorothy Blakey Smith, ed., *The Reminiscences of Doctor John Sebastian Helmcken* (Vancouver: University of British Columbia Press, 1975), 164; Roberta L. Bagshaw, ed., *No Better Land: The 1860 Diaries of the Anglican Colonial Bishop George Hills* (Victoria: Sono Nis Press, 1996), 208; Walter B. Cheadle, *Cheadle's Journal of Trip Across Canada, 1862–1863* (Edmonton: M. G. Hurtig, 1971, orig. 1931), 281.

8. Stanley, *Mapping the Frontier*, 97, 170. Hamar Foster, "Law Enforcement in Nineteenth-Century British Columbia: A Brief and Comparative Overview," *BCST* 63 (autumn 1984): 4–5; Allan Smith, "The Writing of British Columbia History," *BCST* 45 (spring 1980): 75–76; W. Champness, *To Cariboo and Back in 1862* (Fairfield, Washington: Ye Galleon Press, 1972), 28–29, 98; *VDBC*, 2 September 1862, p. 3; 16 January 1864, p. 3; 29 March 1866, p. 3; *DBCVC*, 6 October 1871, p. 3.

9. *BCS*, 14 October 1866, p. 2.

10. *BCS*, 4 July 1867, p. 2.

11. W. Wymond Walkem, *Stories of Early British Columbia* (Vancouver: News-Advertiser, 1914), 33–34. J. Despard Pemberton, *Facts and Figures Relating to Vancouver Island and British Columbia* (London: Longman, Green, Longman, and Roberts, 1860), 128–130; A. J. Splawn, *Ka-mi-akin: Last Hero of the Yakimas* (Portland: Binfords and Mort for the Oregon Historical Society, 1944, orig. 1917), 179; *NWBC*, 9 August 1862, p. 2.

12. William Thompson, *Reminiscences of a Pioneer* (San Francisco: n.p., 1912), 177.

13. *PO*, 15 October 1853, p. 2.

14. David R. Williams, ". . . *The Man for a New Country": Sir Matthew Baillie Begbie* (Sidney, British Columbia: Gray's Publishing, 1977), 97–98. SOS index, Oregon Historical Society, Portland; Hamar Foster, "'The Queen's Law is Better Than Yours': International Homicide in Early British Columbia," in *Crime and Criminal Justice,* ed. Jim Phillips, Tina Loo, and Susan Lewthwaite (Toronto: University of Toronto Press, for the Osgoode Society, 1994), 84–85; Doyce B. Nunis Jr., ed., *The Golden Frontier: The Recollections of Herman Francis Reinhart, 1851–1869* (Austin: University of Texas Press, 1962), 168–169. The index for the *SOS* indicates that Oregon executed

twelve men from 1850 to 1865. Unlike British Columbia, the majority of these men were white. Richard Maxwell Brown, *No Duty to Retreat: Violence and Values in American History and Society*, 3–37; Clare V. McKanna Jr., "Alcohol, Handguns, and Homicide in the American West: A Tale of Three Counties, 1880–1920," *Western Historical Quarterly* 26 (winter 1995): 472; Dorothy Blakey Smith, ed., "The Journal of Arthur Thomas Bushby, 1858–1859," *BCHQ* 21 (1957–1958): 144–145.

15. D. W. Higgins, *The Mystic Spring and Other Tales of Western Life* (Toronto: William Briggs, 1904), 371, 197. *(Olympia) Washington Standard*, 19 October 1861, p. 2. *SOS*, 26 November 1860, p. 2; *BCS*, 30 September 1865, p. 3; Bagshaw, *No Better Land*, 68. This is not to say that Oregon and Washington courts never concerned themselves about the details of a self-defense plea. For example, an eastern Washington court allowed the defense for a man accused of an 1864 murder to instruct the jury to find the defendant not guilty if it believed "that the deceased made the first assault and that def[endan]t used no more force than was necessary to protect himself" and if "the Def[endan]t believed that his life was in imminent danger . . . when he fired upon deceased." Case 217, series 1, Walla Walla County District Court, Washington State Archives, Olympia. Nunis, *Golden Frontier*, 242–243; James W. Watt, *Journal of Mule Train Packing in Eastern Washington in the 1860's* (Fairfield, Washington: Ye Galleon Press, 1978), 30. Juries often ignored such instructions, however. British Columbia jurists, furthermore, went beyond such definitions of self-defense and at least occasionally indicated that they expected men to retreat rather than to use force. In Victoria in 1862 James Clark Chafa went to the store of one Ibbotson and accused him of stealing his canoe. Chafa had reportedly hit Ibbotson, and Ibbotson threw some weights at Chafa to drive him from his store. Chafa then returned with a rifle, called Ibbotson out to shoot, and was hit in the hand by a pistol shot fired by Ibbotson. Two men testified that Ibbotson could have avoided the armed confrontation by going out the back door of his store. "I am not aware that there was any circumstance in the way to prevent Ibbotson retreating by that way if he thought Chafa intended to shoot him," explained one witness. Case 19/1862, BCAGC. *VBC*, 19 March 1859, p. 2.

16. Myron Eells, *Father Eells, or the Results of Fifty-Five Years of Missionary Labors in Washington and Oregon* (Boston: Congregational Sunday School and Publishing Society, 1894), 185–186. Richard Maxwell Brown, *Strain of Violence: Historical Studies of American Violence and Vigilantism* (New York: Oxford University Press, 1975), 93–179, 318; John R. Wunder, *Inferior Courts, Superior Justice: A History of the Justices of the Peace on the Northwest Frontier, 1853–1889* (Westport, Connecticut: Greenwood Press, 1979), 162–163; W. D. Lyman, *Lyman's History of Old Walla Walla County* (Chicago:

S. J. Clarke, 1918), vol. 1: 132–134; Hubert Howe Bancroft, *Popular Tribunals* (San Francisco: History Company, 1887), vol. 1: 636–640; Drumheller, *"Uncle Dan"* *Drumheller*, 69–70, 76; Andrew Dominique Pambrum, *Sixty Years on the Frontier in the Pacific Northwest* (Fairfield, Washington: Ye Galleon Press, 1978), 119; Nunis, ed., *Golden Frontier*, 73–75, 91–93, 178, 230–231; *(Walla Walla) Washington Statesman,* 15 November 1862, p. 2; 10 February 1865, p. 2; 21 April 1865, p. 3; 26 May 1865, p. 2; James Joseph Poth, "A History of Crime and Violence in Washington Territory, 1851–60" (M. A. thesis, University of Washington, 1969), 27–32; case 400, Jefferson County District Court, Washington State Archives; *(Olympia) Washington Standard,* 16 July 1864, p. 1; 30 July 1864, p. 2.

17. B. F. Manring, "Recollections of a Pioneer of 1859, Lawson Stockman," *QOHS* 11 (June 1910): 171.

18. Virginia Duffy McLoughlin, "Cynthia Stafford and the Lost Mining Town of Auburn," *OHQ* 98 (spring 1997): 38–39; Charles Prosch, *Reminiscences of Washington Territory* (Fairfield, Washington: Ye Galleon Press, 1969, orig. 1904), 69–70; Nunis, *Golden Frontier*, 134–135, 157; Mrs. William Kersey interview, Lockley collection, vol. 30; Ned Wicks interview, Lockley collection, vol. 56; *(Walla Walla) Washington Statesman,* 29 November 1862, p. 2; 21 July 1865, p. 2; *SPSH*, 24 January 1861, p. 2; 29 August 1861, p. 2; 17 October 1861, p. 2; 10 July 1862, p. 2; 29 January 1863, p. 2; 5 March 1863, p. 2; *(Oregon City) Oregon Spectator,* 11 November 1847, p. 2; *SOS*, 17 February 1857, p. 2; 20 December 1859, p. 2; 13 January 1862, p. 1; 6 April 1863, p. 3; Williams, ". . . *The Man for a New Country,"* 88–89; *NWBC*, 9 August 1862, p. 2; 8 September 1862, p. 3; Roger D. McGrath, *Gunfighters, Highwaymen, and Vigilantes: Violence on the Frontier* (Berkeley: University of California Press, 1984), 70–101. Most newspaper accounts of lynchings reported on them without criticizing or approving them.

19. Drumheller, *"Uncle Dan" Drumheller*, 76.

20. D. W. Higgins, *The Passing of a Race, and More Tales of Western Life* (Toronto: William Briggs, 1905), 236. Robert E. Ficken and Charles P. LeWarne, *Washington: A Centennial History* (Seattle: University of Washington Press, 1988), 23, remark that Port Townsend "teemed with liquor, gambling, thievery, smuggling, prostitution, and violence."

21. Stanley, *Mapping the Frontier*, 170.

22. Wunder, *Inferior Courts, Superior Justice*, 173. Poth, "History of Crime and Violence in Washington Territory," 57–65.

23. Research assistants examined nearly all of the extant newspapers on the north Pacific slope for this period. The *SOS*, one of the era's major newspapers, has a very

useful and detailed index at the Oregon Historical Society. I also used the 1860 Manuscript Census, Mortality Schedule, Oregon and Washington, and the Attorney General Inquisitions, GR 1328, British Columbia Archives and Records Service. I did not count executions or lynchings of murderers. I cut off Oregon and Washington's settlement period in 1865, British Columbia's six years later. British Columbia's non-Native population fluctuated considerably during this time. I put its average at twenty thousand.

24. Clare V. McKanna Jr., *Homicide, Race, and Justice in the American West, 1880–1920*, 44, 163.

25. Robie L. Reed, ed., "Two Narratives of the Fraser River Gold-Rush," *BCHQ* 5 (July 1941): 227. John Hope Franklin, *The Militant South, 1800–1861* (Cambridge: Harvard University Press, 1956), 34–58; Raymond D. Gastil, *Cultural Regions of the United States* (Seattle: University of Washington Press, 1975), 103–116; Bertram Wyatt-Brown, *Southern Honor: Ethics and Behavior in the Old South* (New York: Oxford University Press, 1982), 25–61; David T. Courtwright, *Violent Land: Single Men and Social Disorder from the Frontier to the Inner City*, 1–197; McKanna, *Homicide, Race, and Justice*; McKanna, "Alcohol, Handguns, and Homicide," 455–482; Roger Lane, *Murder in America: A History*, 124, 126–129; McLoughlin, "Cynthia Stafford," 29.

26. Thompson, *Reminiscences of a Pioneer*, 59. Interview regarding Ferd Patterson, Lockley collection, vol. 41.

27. Fred Lockley, "Reminiscences of Colonel Henry Ernst Dosch," *QOHS* 25 (March 1924): 61. Frederic Trautman, ed. and trans., *Oregon East, Oregon West: Travels and Memoirs by Theodor Kirchhoff, 1863–1872* (Portland: Oregon Historical Society Press, 1987), 31; Splawn, *Ka-mi-akin*, 199; Elizabeth Lord, *Reminiscences of Eastern Oregon* (Portland, Oregon: Irwin-Hodson, 1903), 141; James D. Miller, "Early Oregon Scenes: A Pioneer Narrative," *OHQ* 31 (June 1930): 165; Louis Albert Banks, *Live Boys in Oregon or An Oregon Boyhood* (Boston: Lothrop, Lee and Shepard, 1900, orig. 1897), 95; Harry N. M. Winton, "The Powder River and John Day Mines in 1862: Diary of Winfield Scott Ebey," *PNQ* 34 (January 1943): 41, 76, 85–86; G. W. Kennedy, *The Pioneer Campfire* (Portland, Oregon: Marsh Printing, 1913), 137–138; Manring, "Recollections of a Pioneer of 1859," 168–171; *(Walla Walla) Washington Statesman*, 24 October 1863, p. 2.

28. Splawn, *Ka-mi-akin*, 208. Clark, *The Social Development of Canada*, 312; Walkem, *Stories of Early British Columbia*, 25, 255; Stanley, *Mapping the Frontier*, 25; Smith, "Journal of Arthur Thomas Bushby," 127; *SOS*, 23 November 1863, p. 3; *VDBC*, 8 September 1862, p. 3; Drumheller, *"Uncle Dan" Drumheller*, 66.

29. Lane, *Violent Death in the City: Suicide, Accident, and Murder in Nineteenth-Century Philadelphia*, 61.

30. Smith, "Journal of Arthur Thomas Bushby," 127. *VDBC*, 1 November 1864, p. 3; Bagshaw, *No Better Land*, 165, 196; John Willis Christian, "The Kootenay Gold Rush: The Placer Decade, 1863–1872" (Ph.D. diss., Washington State University, 1967), 59; Walkem, *Stories of Early British Columbia*, 27; David Ricardo Williams, "The Administration of Criminal and Civil Justice in the Mining Camps and Frontier Communities of British Columbia," in *Law and Justice in a New Land: Essays in Western Canadian Legal History*, ed. Louis A. Knafla (Toronto: Carswell, 1986), 230–231; *VDBC*, 15 November 1860, p. 3; Hubert Howe Bancroft, *History of British Columbia, 1792–1887* (San Francisco: History Company, 1887), 517–518.

31. Michael A. Bellesîles, "The Origins of Gun Culture in the United States, 1760–1865," *JAH* 83 (September 1996): 442. Foster, "Shooting the Elephant," 142.

32. Matthew B. Begbie, "Journey into the Interior of British Columbia," in *Excerpt from the Journal and Proceedings of the Royal Geographical Society*, 247, University of British Columbia Special Collections, Vancouver.

33. Lawrence M. Friedman, *Crime and Punishment in American History*, 463–465. Robert R. Dykstra, *The Cattle Towns* (New York: Atheneum, 1976), 112–148, argues that resolute law enforcement succeeded in minimizing homicides in several Kansas cattle towns in the late nineteenth century.

34. R. Byron Johnson, *Very Far West Indeed: A Few Rough Experiences on the North-West Pacific Coast* (n.p.: n.p., 1985, orig. 1872), 39–40; *VDBC*, 5 April 1861, p. 2; *SOS*, 9 November 1863, p. 2.

35. *BCS*, 6 June 1865, p. 3. *BCS*, 24 June 1865, p. 3.

36. *BCS*, 7 October 1865, p. 3. *BCS*, 1 July 1865, supplement, p. 2.

37. *VDBC*, 17 October 1861, p. 3. This is not to say that men's fights with each other served no immediate or tangible ends, that the participants were only jockeying for status with those outside their peer group. Murders that occurred in the course of robberies were the most obvious type of instrumental violence. Mining regions, in particular, offered tempting payoffs for successful thieves, and dead men told no tales. Other violent acts arose from disputes over property. Strong, an early judge in Oregon and Washington, estimated that most of the roughly eighteen homicides he tried "arose from disputes about land under the donation [land] law." "Knickerbocker Views of the Oregon Country: Judge William Strong's Narrative," *OHQ* 62 (March 1961): 66. Lawrence A. McNary, "Oregon's First Reported Murder Case," *OHQ* 36 (December 1935): 359; E. A. Garrison, *Life and Labour of Rev. A. E. Garrison: Forty Years in Oregon*

([Salem, Oregon: Elliott Printing House], 1887), 47–48; Mrs. George Hoeye interview, Lockley collection, vol. 25; *PO,* 5 June 1852, p. 1; *(Walla Walla) Washington Statesman,* 12 September 1863, p. 2; *BCS,* 5 December 1868, p. 3; Drumheller, *"Uncle Dan" Drumheller,* 66. Political disagreements also led to fights. A man born in 1852 recalled that his father's resolute agitation against Oregon City's drinking establishments required him to demonstrate that he "was quick as a cat and a hard hitter." Interview regarding Peter H. Hatch, Lockley collection, vol. 23. Smith, *Reminiscences of Doctor John Sebastian Helmcken,* 192–193; James E. Hendrickson, *Joe Lane of Oregon: Machine Politics and the Sectional Crises, 1849–1861* (New Haven: Yale University Press, 1967), 112–113; James T. Hunt interview, Lockley collection, vol. 27; Stanley, *Mapping the Frontier,* 96–97; *SOS,* 5 July 1859, p. 2; 28 July 1862, p. 2; 27 November 1865, p. 1; *(Olympia) Washington Standard,* 19 October 1861, p. 2; case 361, Jefferson County District Court; George Harkleroad interview, Lockley collection, vol. 22; Henry Buckle Luce interview, Lockley collection, vol. 32; Mrs. Susan Whitwell interview, Lockley collection, vol. 56; *PO,* 6 January 1862, p. 3; 27 January 1864, p. 2; James C. Williams, "The Long Tom Rebellion," *OHQ* 67 (March 1966): 54–60; Lyle Allen Schwarz, "Theatre on the Gold Frontier: A Cultural Study of Five Northwest Mining Towns, 1860–1870" (Ph.D. diss., Washington State University, 1975), 82–84; Lyman, *Lyman's History of Old Walla Walla County,* vol. 1: 130–135; Nunis, *Golden Frontier,* 204–207; Higgins, *Mystic Spring,* 149–163.

38. *VDBC,* 29 March 1866, p. 3. Gaston's attachment to principle cost him: the court required him to find bonds adding up to nine hundred dollars to keep the peace.

39. *SOS,* 25 May 1852, p. 1.

40. Orange Jacobs, *Memoirs of Orange Jacobs* (Seattle: Lowman and Hanford, 1908), 70.

41. *SOS,* 1 June 1852, p. 2.

42. *Beauchamp vs. Roland and Pike,* December 1854, David Cameron's Bench Book, 1853–1856, Vancouver Island Supreme Court of Civil Justice, GR 2032, British Columbia Archives and Records Service; cases 161, 165, and 217, series 1, Walla Walla County District Court; *BCS,* 20 March 1869, p. 3; *DBCVC,* 13 August 1867; Kenneth S. Greenburg, *Honor and Slavery: Lies, Duels, Noses, Masks, Dressing as a Woman, Gifts, Strangers, Humanitarianism, Death, Slave Rebellions, the Pro-Slavery Argument, Baseball, Hunting, and Gambling in the Old South,* 7–9; Elliott J. Gorn, "Gouge and Bite, Pull Hair and Scratch: The Social Significance of Fighting in the Southern Backcountry," *American Historical Review* 90 (February 1985): 40.

43. James G. Swan, *The Northwest Coast: Or, Three Years' Residence in Washington*

Territory (Seattle: University of Washington Press, 1972, orig. 1857), 278. Dr. [Bethenia] Owen-Adair, *Some of Her Life Experiences* (Portland, Oregon: Mann and Beach Printers, [1906]), 22; case 581, Thurston County District Court, Washington State Archives; Joseph H. Hunt interview, Lockley collection, vol. 27. Pieter Spierenburg, "Knife Fighting and Popular Codes of Honor in Early Modern Amsterdam," in *Men and Violence: Gender, Honor, and Rituals in Modern Europe and America*, ed. Spierenburg (Columbus: Ohio State University Press, 1988), 111–114, points out that even men fighting with knives might observe rules. *VDBC*, 16 January 1864, p. 3; 22 January 1964, p. 3; 29 July 1864, p. 3; 11 November 1865, p. 3.

44. Case 161, series 1, Walla Walla County District Court.

45. *VDBC*, 23 November 1865, p. 3. *VDBC*, 15 December 1863, p. 3; 23 December 1864, p. 2; 16 December 1865, p. 3; 20 December 1865, p. 3; *SOS*, 3 July 1860, p. 2; *BCS*, 9 August 1866; "Uncle Sam" Handsaker, *Pioneer Life* (Eugene, Oregon: Samuel Handsaker, 1908), 37; Higgins, *Passing of a Race*, 258–259; Derek Anthony Swain, "A History of Sport in British Columbia to 1885: A Chronicle of Significant Developments and Events" (M.A. thesis, University of British Columbia, 1977), 106–117.

46. Kinahan Cornwallis, *The New El Dorado; or, British Columbia* (New York: Arno Press, 1973, orig. 1858), 266–267. Elliott West, *The Saloon on the Rocky Mountain Mining Frontier* (Lincoln: University of Nebraska Press, 1979), 73–96.

47. *SPSH*, 13 August 1858, p. 2. *VDBC*, 8 April 1864, p. 3; *SPSH*, 9 September 1859, p. 2. Champness, *To Cariboo and Back in 1862*, 86; *(Oregon City) Oregon Spectator*, 17 April 1851, p. 2; *(Olympia) Washington Standard*, 19 October 1861, p. 2; Courtwright, *Violent Land*, 33–34; West, *Saloon on the Rocky Mountain Mining Frontier*, 19–21.

48. *DBCVC*, 16 April 1869, p. 3.

49. *VDBC*, 16 August 1860, p. 3.

50. Case 5/1863, box 2, BCAGC. Greenburg, *Honor and Slavery*, 74, 51–86.

51. Greenburg, *Honor and Slavery*, 70–74. Edward L. Ayers, *Vengeance and Justice: Crime and Punishment in the Nineteenth-Century American South* (New York: Oxford University Press, 1984), 9–33; Cecilia Morgan, "'In Search of the Phantom Misnamed Honour': Duelling in Upper Canada," *CHR* 76 (December 1995): 529–562; V. G. Kiernan, *The Duel in European History: Honour and the Reign of Aristocracy* (Oxford: Oxford University Press, 1988), 152–164.

52. *NWBC*, 27 May 1863, p. 1. Poth, "History of Crime and Violence in Washington Territory," 65; Charlotte Matheny Kirkwood, *Into the Eye of the Setting Sun: A Story of the West When It Was New*, 2nd ed. (McMinnville, Oregon: Family Association of Matheny, Cooper, Hewitt, Kirkwood, and Bailey, 1991), 22; Gustavas Hines, *Wild Life*

in Oregon (New York: Hurst and Co., 1881), 435; case 125, Thurston County Circuit Court; Higgins, *Mystic Spring*, 240–244; Smith, *Reminiscences of Doctor John Sebastian Helmcken*, 176; Walkem, *Stories of Early British Columbia*, 279–281; VDBC, 12 June 1861, p. 3; 20 June 1861, p. 3.

53. Pritchard, *Vancouver Island Letters of Edmund Hope Verney*, 101. Men of standing found it more difficult to ignore their inferiors south of the line, in part because virtually all white men enjoyed the franchise. Orville C. Pratt, a former judge, learned this while electioneering in southern Oregon's mining districts in 1854. An observer recalled that the hopeful candidate "was very proud and dignified" and wore "a faultless suit, including a silk hat and a high shirt collar." The miners backed General Joseph Lane, a popular Indian-fighter with southern roots. As Pratt began holding forth in a drinking establishment, one of his listeners drew a long knife out of his boot, remarked that Pratt's "stove-pipe is too high by a j'int," and cut it in two. The former judge "took this all in good part" and ordered a round of drinks. The miner then turned his attention to Pratt's long, glossy hair and "cut off a lock, saying as he did so that it was the 'puttiest ha'r he had ever seed,' that he must have just one lock for a keepsake." He then embraced Pratt. The aspiring politician passed this test of democracy "with a wonderful exhibition of good nature and tact." George E. Cole, *Early Oregon* (Spokane, Washington: Shaw and Borden, 1905), 66–68.

54. SPSH, 13 August 1858, p. 2. Stanley, *Mapping the Frontier*, 167, 174; *(Oregon City) Oregon Spectator*, 17 April 1851, p. 2; VDBC, 7 July 1864, p. 3; 6 February 1866, p. 3; DBCVC, 27 November 1867, p. 3.

55. Herbert B. Nelson and Preston E. Onstad, eds., *A Webfoot Volunteer: The Diary of William M. Hilleary, 1864–1866* (Corvallis: Oregon State University Press, 1965), 36. William A. Peck Jr., *The Pig War, and Other Experiences of William Peck* (Medford, Oregon: Webb Research Group, 1993), 52; Gunter Barth, ed., *All Quiet on the Yamhill: The Civil War in Oregon* (Eugene: University of Oregon Books, 1959), 58, 90.

56. PO, 31 October 1857, p. 2, emphasis in the original. The PO objected not simply to the fight, however, but to the unfair manner in which it was carried out.

57. SPSH, 13 August 1858, p. 2.

58. SPSH, 25 April 1861, p. 2. BCS, 8 July 1865, p. 3.

59. VDBC, 12 December 1861, p. 3.

60. BCS, 13 November 1869, p. 3. Ruth Bleasdale, "Class Conflict on the Canals of Upper Canada in the 1840s," in *Pre-Industrial Canada, 1760–1849: Readings in Canadian Social History*, ed. Michael S. Cross and Gregory S. Kealey (Toronto: McClelland and Stewart, 1982), vol. 2: 100–138; Michael Kaplan, "New York City Tavern

Violence and the Creation of a Working-Class Male Identity," *Journal of the Early Republic* 15 (winter 1995): 597. Ethnic rivalries could provoke violence between Caucasian men. A quarrel that culminated in a nonlethal shooting in western Washington began when one of the principals "began to cursing Germans, Dutch, Welsh" over dinner at a boardinghouse. Case 581, Thurston County District Court.

61. *SPSH*, 25 April 1861, p. 2.

62. Gorn, "'Gouge and Bite,'" 36, 41. Adele Perry, "Bachelors in the Backwoods: White Men and Homosocial Culture in Up-Country British Columbia, 1858–71," in *Beyond the City Limits: Rural History in British Columbia*, ed. R. W. Sandwell, 180–194; Gunther Peck, "Manly Gambles: The Politics of Risk on the Comstock Lode, 1860–1880," *Journal of Social History* 26 (summer 1993): 701–723; David Philips, *Crime and Authority in Victorian England: The Black Country, 1835–1860* (London: Croom Helm, 1977), 259–260.

63. Kaplan, "New York City Tavern Violence," 614.

64. Case 19/1869, BCAGC. Robert Edward Wynne, *Reaction to the Chinese in the Pacific Northwest and British Columbia, 1850 to 1910* (New York: Arno Press, 1978), 43–147; Courtwright, *Violent Land*, 152–169; Lorraine Barker Hildebrand, *Straw Hats, Sandals, and Steel: The Chinese in Washington State* (Tacoma: The Washington State American Revolution Bicentennial Commission, 1977), 12–15; Christopher Howard Edson, *The Chinese in Eastern Oregon, 1860–1890* (San Francisco: R and E Research Associates, 1974), 44–45; Patricia E. Roy, *A White Man's Province: British Columbia Politicians and Chinese and Japanese Immigrants, 1858–1914* (Vancouver: University of British Columbia Press, 1989), 3–11; Tamara Adilman, "A Preliminary Sketch of Chinese Women and Work in British Columbia, 1858–1950," in *Not Just Pin Money: Selected Essays on the History of Women's Work in British Columbia*, ed. Barbara K. Latham and Roberta J. Pazdro, 55; Peter S. Li, *The Chinese in Canada* (Toronto: Oxford University Press, 1988), 11–40, 71, 79–82; David Chuenyan Lai, *Chinatowns: Towns Within Cities in Canada* (Vancouver: University of British Columbia Press, 1988), 183–186; W. Peter Ward, *White Canada Forever: Popular Attitudes and Public Policy Toward Orientals in British Columbia*, 3–22; Stanford M. Lyman, W. E. Willmott, and Berching Ho, "Rules of a Chinese Secret Society in British Columbia," *Bulletin of the School of Oriental and African Studies, University of London* 27 (1964): 530–539; *VDBC*, 15 June 1865, p. 3; *DBCVC*, 19 May 1871, p. 3; 10 September 1866, p. 3; 23 June 1870, p. 3; 24 June 1870, p. 3; *NWBC*, 11 October 1865, p. 3; *PO*, 30 November 1864, p. 3.

65. *DBCVC,* 11 February 1871, p. 3; 18 May 1871, p. 3; 19 May 1871, p. 3; 13 October 1870, p. 3; 12 October 1870, p. 3; 19 September 1871, p. 3; *BCS,* 12 December 1868, p. 3; *PO,* 13 April 1864, p. 3; Lai, *Chinatowns,* 195.

66. Johnson, *Very Far West Indeed,* 78.

67. Pritchard, *Vancouver Island Letters of Edmund Hope Verney,* 148. R. C. Mayne, *Four Years in British Columbia and Vancouver Island* (London: John Murray, 1862), 352; D. G. Forbes MacDonald, *British Columbia and Vancouver's Island,* 3rd ed. (London: Longman, Green, Longman, Roberts, and Green, 1863), 299–304.

68. *VDBC,* 13 December 1860, p. 3.

69. Johnson, *Very Far West Indeed,* 78. See note 23 for the sources on homicides. Ward, *White Canada Forever,* 24–25. *VDBC,* 2 April 1863, p. 3; 1 March 1864, p. 3; *NWBC,* 22 April 1865, p. 3; *DBCVC,* 28 January 1867, p. 3; 6 August 1869, p. 3; 1 January 1871, p. 3. Gillian Marie, "Attitudes Toward Chinese Immigrants to British Columbia, 1858–1885" (M. A. thesis, Simon Fraser University, 1976), 18, asserts that the Chinese were the victims of a number of killings and shootings by whites from 1858 to 1865 and that their killers often went undiscovered and unpunished.

70. John Mullan, "From Walla Walla to San Francisco," *QOHS* 4 (September 1903): 219.

71. *VDBC,* 15 June 1865, p. 3. *BCS,* 2 September 1865, p. 1.

72. *DBCVC,* 7 August 1867, p. 3. *DBCVC,* 6 October 1869, p. 3.

73. *VDBC,* 18 December 1861, p. 3.

74. *VDBC,* 20 September 1862, p. 3; 9 August 1862, p. 3; 15 August 1861, p. 3; 18 December 1861, p. 3.

75. Peterson del Mar, *What Trouble I Have Seen: A History of Violence Against Wives,* 23. A. James Hammerton, *Cruelty and Companionship: Conflict in Nineteenth-Century Married Life* (London: Routledge, 1992), 15–33; Anna Clark, "Humanity or Justice? Wifebeating and the Law in the Eighteenth and Nineteenth Centuries," in *Regulating Womanhood: Historical Essays on Marriage, Motherhood and Sexuality,* ed. Carol Smart (London: Routledge, 1992), 187–206; Martin J. Wiener, *Reconstructing the Criminal: Culture, Law, and Policy in England, 1830–1914* (Cambridge: Cambridge University Press, 1990), 82–83; Wiener, "The Victorian Criminalization of Men," in Spierenburg, *Men and Violence,* 197–212; Elizabeth Pleck, "Wife Beating in Nineteenth-Century America," *Victimology* 4 (1979): 60–74; E. Anthony Rotundo, *American Manhood: Transformations in Masculinity from the Revolution to the Modern Era,* 10–30.

76. "Diary of Reverend Jason Lee," *QOHS* 17 (December 1916): 406.

77. *SOS*, 6 April 1863, p. 3. *SPSH*, 24 January 1861, p. 2; 29 August 1861, p. 2; 30 January 1864, p. 2; *SOS*, 22 July 1861, p. 2; 10 February 1862, p. 3; Mrs. Lewis T. Thompson interview, Lockley collection, vol. 52.

78. *VDBC*, 8 December 1863, p. 3. *VDBC*, 24 May 1864, p. 3; 13 July 1865, p. 3; *BCS*, 13 November 1867, p. 3.

79. Hendrik Hartog, "Lawyering, Husbands' Rights, and 'the Unwritten Law' in Nineteenth-Century America," *JAH* 84 (June 1997): 67–96; Friedman, *Crime and Punishment in American History*, 121–122.

80. Case 471, Jefferson County Circuit Court. *VDBC*, 3 March 1863, p. 3.

81. Margaret Hunt, "Wife Beating, Domesticity, and Women's Independence in Eighteenth-Century London," *Gender and History* 4 (spring 1992): 14. Constance Backhouse, " 'Pure Patriarchy': Nineteenth-Century Canadian Marriage," *McGill Law Journal* 31 (March 1986): 264–312; Annalee E. Gölz, "If a Man's Wife Does Not Obey Him, What Can He Do? Marital Breakdown and Wife Abuse in Late Nineteenth-Century and Early Twentieth-Century Ontario," in *Law, Society, and the State: Essays in Modern Legal History*, ed. Louis A. Knafla and Susan W. S. Binnie (Toronto: University of Toronto Press, 1995), 342–343; Peterson del Mar, *What Trouble I Have Seen*, 18–19; Clark, "Humanity or Justice?" 191; Hammerton, *Cruelty and Companionship*, 27.

82. Case L-19, Wasco County Circuit Court, Oregon State Archives, Salem.

83. Case 1409, Marion County Circuit Court, Oregon State Archives, Salem.

84. Case 467, Walla Walla County District Court.

85. Peterson del Mar, *What Trouble I Have Seen*, 24–25, 28–31; Kaplan, "New York City Tavern Violence," 610–614.

86. Case 1, Thurston County District Court. Indeed, George had physical custody of their only child, and Harriet's complaint did not seek custody. Peterson del Mar, *What Trouble I Have Seen*, 31–35; Steven J. Stern, *The Secret History of Gender: Women, Men, and Power in Late Colonial Mexico* (Chapel Hill: University of North Carolina Press, 1995).

87. *SPSH*, 22 May 1862, p. 2. See note 23 on sources for homicides. *SOS*, 6 March 1860, p. 2; case 8A, box 1, Washington Territorial Supreme Court, Washington State Archives; *PO*, 11 February 1864, p. 3; 6 June 1864, p. 3; Owen-Adair, *Some of Her Life Experiences*, 20–21; Mary Hayden, *Pioneer Days* (Fairfield, Washington: Ye Galleon Press, 1979), 55.

88. *SOS*, 9 June 1862, p. 3.

89. Case 25/1866, BCAGC; *VDBC*, 15 July 1861, p. 3; 17 May 1866, p. 3; *BCS*, 13 July

1868, p. 3. Only 2 of the 115 homicides for Oregon between 1850 and 1865 were attributed to women, and none of the 43 in British Columbia from 1860 to 1871. See note 23.

90. *VDBC*, 30 May 1865, p. 3. *VDBC*, 26 January 1863, p. 3; 23 January 1863, p. 3; 15 June 1865, p. 3; 4 December 1865, p. 2; *BCS*, 26 July 1868, p. 3; Sylvia Van Kirk, "A Vital Presence: Women in the Cariboo Gold Rush, 1862–1875," in *British Columbia Reconsidered: Essays on Women,* ed. Gillian Creese and Veronica Strong-Boag (Vancouver: Press Gang Publishers, 1992), 31; Higgins, *Mystic Spring,* 70.

91. *VDBC*, 10 February 1865, p. 3; 31 May 1865, p. 3; 17 May 1866, p. 3.

92. *VDBC*, 22 February 1865, p. 3.

93. *BCS*, 26 July 1868, p. 3.

94. *DBCVC*, 26 May 1868, p. 3. Terence O'Donnell, *An Arrow in the Earth: General Joel Palmer and the Indians of Oregon* (Portland: Oregon Historical Society Press, 1991), 154–155.

95. George Melvin Miller interview, Lockley collection, vol. 37.

96. Case D-7, Wasco County Circuit Court.

97. Appended to Mrs. S. J. Perry interview, Lockley collection, vol. 41. Splawn, *Ka-mi-akin,* 331; Kirkwood, *Into the Eye of the Setting Sun,* 105, 77.

98. Matilda Jane Sager Delaney interview, Lockley collection, vol. 14. *PO*, 29 April 1864, p. 3. Mary P. Sawtelle, *The Heroine of '49: A Story of the Pacific Coast,* 2nd ed (n.p.: n.p., 1891), 191; Pleck, *Domestic Tyranny: The Making of American Social Policy Against Family Violence from Colonial Times to the Present,* 34–47.

99. Appended to Perry interview. Banks, *Live Boys in Oregon,* 29; Elliott West, *Growing Up with the Country: Childhood on the Far Western Frontier* (Albuquerque: University of New Mexico Press, 1989), 158–169; Stephen M. Frank, *Life with Father: Parenthood and Masculinity in the Nineteenth-Century American North* (Baltimore: Johns Hopkins University Press, 1998), 115–116, 119. Daniel Blake Smith, *Inside the Great House: Planter Family Life in Eighteenth-Century Chesapeake Society* (Ithaca: Cornell University Press, 1980), 51–52, 111–112, asserts that well-to-do southern parents of the eighteenth century were not very violent toward their children. J. B. Hoss interview, Lockley collection, vol. 26; Frank Langlois interview, Lockley collection, vol. 32.

100. Case 2964, Multnomah County Circuit Court, Multnomah County Court House, Portland.

101. John W. Cullen interviews, Lockley collection, vol. 13.

102. Mrs. Monterey Ann Pugh interview, Lockley collection, vol. 42.

103. Thomas C. Watts interview, Lockley collection, vol. 54. David Arba Carter inter-

view, Lockley collection, vol. 9; John William Craig interview, Lockley collection, vol. 12; *SOS*, 27 June 1864, p. 3; R. E. Mather, *Scandal of the West: Domestic Violence on the Frontier* (Oklahoma City: History West Publishing, 1998), 36–38. Brutal stepparents drew on long-held and widely accepted religious beliefs to sanction their violence. Ian Gibson notes that well-to-do Victorians in England "never tired of reminding themselves that the beating of naughty children had been strictly enjoined upon them by God." Ian Gibson, *The English Vice: Beating, Sex, and Shame in Victorian England and After* (London: Duckworth, 1978), 48. Pugh interview; Delaney interview. One of the few biological fathers reported to have treated his children brutally was a former Methodist missionary, William Raymond. David Peterson del Mar, "Violence against Wives by Prominent Men in Clatsop County," *OHQ* 100 (winter 1999): 438–439.

104. F. Henry Johnson, "Changing Conceptions of Discipline and Pupil-Teacher Relations in Canadian Schools," 40–42. "Punishment, Corporal," in *A Cyclopedia of Education*, ed. Paul Monroe (New York: Macmillan, 1925, orig. 1913), vol. 5: 83–88. Alison Prentice, *The School Promoters: Education and Social Class in Mid-Nineteenth Century Upper Canada* (Toronto: McClelland and Stewart, 1977), 35; Donald R. Raichle, "The Abolition of Corporal Punishment in New Jersey Schools," in *Corporal Punishment in American Education: Readings in History, Practice, and Alternatives*, ed. Irwin A. Hyman and James H. Wise (Philadelphia: Temple University Press, 1979), 62–88; Barbara Finkelstein, "Casting Networks of Good Influence: The Reconstruction of Childhood in the United States, 1790–1870," in *American Childhood: A Research Guide and Historical Handbook*, ed. Joseph M. Hawes and N. Ray Hiner (Westport, Connecticut: Greenwood Press, 1985), 133.

105. *VBC*, 10 July 1860, p. 2.

106. *VBC*, 12 July 1860, p. 2.

107. *VDBC*, 21 November 1862, p. 3.

108. David Tyack, "The Tribe and the Common School: The District School in Ashland, Oregon in the 1860s," *Call Number* 27 (spring 1966): 18.

109. Interview under George B. Wagnon, Lockley collection, vol. 53. J. D. Matlock interview, Lockley collection, vol. 36; H. S. Lyman, "Recollections of Grandma Brown," *QOHS* 3 (September 1902): 293; Fred Lockley, "Reminiscences of Captain William P. Gray," *QOHS* 14 (December 1913): 323; Kate Morris interview, Lockley collection, vol. 38; Thompson, *Reminiscences of a Pioneer*, 15; West, *Growing Up with the Country*, 203–204.

110. L. F. Hall interview, Lockley collection, vol. 22. Sarah Iola Lyman interview, Lockley collection, vol. 32; A. J. McNemee interview, Lockley collection, vol. 35; Joseph

Lane Meek interview, Lockley collection, vol. 36; John F. Roberts interview, Lockley collection, vol. 44; Marianne Hunsaker D'Arcy interview, Lockley collection, vol. 14; Fred Lockley, "Recollections of Benjamin Franklin Bonney," *QOHS* 24 (March 1923): 54.

111. Mrs. William M. Blakley interview, Lockley collection, vol. 4.

112. William M. Colvig interview, Lockley collection, vol. 11. Robert C. Bouser interview, Lockley collection, vol. 6; Hall interview.

113. Kennedy, *Pioneer Campfire*, 65.

114. Banks, *Live Boys in Oregon*, 33–34 (quote), 33–61, 123.

115. *VDBC*, 28 January 1865, p. 3. *DBCVC*, 19 March 1870, p. 3.

116. J. C. Mason interview, Lockley collection, vol. 36. *VDBC*, 12 June 1861, p. 3. T. T. Geer, *Fifty Years in Oregon* (New York: Neale Publishing, 1912), 240–242; Edgar Fawcett, *Some Reminiscences of Old Victoria* (Toronto: William Briggs, 1912), 29; *PO*, 4 June 1864, p. 3; 4 August 1865, p. 3; Alvin Clinton Going interview, Lockley collection, vol. 21.

117. Thomas Harrison Cooper interview, Lockley collection, vol. 11.

118. Langlois interview.

119. James R. Perry, Richard H. Chused, and Mary DeLano, eds., "The Spousal Letters of Samuel R. Thurston, Oregon's First Territorial Delegate to Congress: 1849–1851," *OHQ* 96 (spring 1995): 41–43, emphasis in the original.

120. William Barnet Simpson interview, Lockley collection, vol. 47.

121. Karin Calvert, *Children in the House: The Material Culture of Early Childhood, 1600–1900* (Boston: Northeastern University Press, 1992), 111–113. Rotundo, *American Manhood*, 31–55.

3 / I WAS NOT THERE TO FIGHT

1. Case 27/1896, BCAGC.

2. Case 36/1899, BCAGC.

3. David Alan Johnson, *Founding the Far West: California, Oregon, and Nevada, 1840–1890* (Berkeley: University of California Press, 1992), 269–278; Peter G. Boag, *Environment and Experience: Settlement Culture in Nineteenth-Century Oregon* (Berkeley: University of California Press, 1992), 113–154; David Peterson del Mar, *What Trouble I Have Seen: A History of Violence Against Wives*, 47–51; Dean L. May, *Three Frontiers: Family, Land, and Society in the American West, 1850–1900* (Cambridge: Cambridge University Press, 1994), 185–243; Peter K. Simpson, *A Social History of the*

Cattle Industry in Southeastern Oregon, 1869–1912 (Moscow: University of Idaho Press, 1987), 42–44; Carlos Arnaldo Schwantes, *The Pacific Northwest: An Interpretive History*, rev. ed., 179–250; Dorothy O. Johansen and Charles M. Gates, *Empire of the Columbia: A History of the Pacific Northwest*, 2nd ed., 316–332; Gordon B. Dodds, *The American Northwest: A History of Oregon and Washington*, 137–154; Marilyn P. Watkins, *Rural Democracy: Family Farmers and Politics in Western Washington, 1890–1925* (Ithaca, New York: Cornell University Press, 1995), 16–47; Wayne D. Rasmussen, "A Century of Farming in the Inland Empire," in *Spokane and the Inland Empire: An Interior Pacific Northwest Anthology*, ed. David H. Stratton (Pullman: Washington State University Press, 1991), 32–51; Schwantes, *Radical Heritage: Labor, Socialism, and Reform in Washington and British Columbia, 1885–1917* (Seattle: University of Washington Press, 1979), 3–21; Rennie Warburton and David Coburn, "The Rise of Non-Manual Work in British Columbia," *BCST* 59 (autumn 1983): 5–27; John Malcolmson, "Politics and the State in the Nineteenth Century," in *Workers, Capital, and the State in British Columbia: Selected Papers*, ed. Warburton and Coburn (Vancouver: University of British Columbia Press, 1988), 9–23; Martin Robin, *The Rush for Spoils: The Company Province, 1871–1933* (Toronto: McClelland and Stewart, 1972), 11–48; Jean Barman, *The West Beyond the West: A History of British Columbia*, rev. ed., 129–150; Hugh J. M. Johnston, ed., *The Pacific Province: A History of British Columbia*, 205–252; Margaret A. Ormsby, *British Columbia: A History* (Vancouver: Macmillans, 1958), 295–325.

4. Roger Lane, *Murder in America: A History*, 184 (quote), 181–188.

5. Case 44/1894, BCAGC. Carolyn Strange and Tina Loo, *Making Good: Law and Moral Regulation in Canada, 1867–1939* (Toronto: University of Toronto Press, 1997).

6. *CPG*, 20 June 1890, p. 1.

7. *CPG*, 6 May 1892, p. 4.

8. *CC*, 2 December 1892, p. 3. *NFP*, 14 January 1897, p. 3; Joe Smith, *Bunch Grass Pioneer* (Fairfield, Washington: Ye Galleon Press, 1986), 63–70; *PO*, 3 January 1891, p. 5; *CPG*, 26 December 1890, p. 1; 17 April 1891, p. 1; 1 May 1891, pp. 1, 4; 28 July 1893, p. 2; *Palouse Republic*, 12 November 1892, p. 2; *(Colfax) Weekly Commoner*, 19 August 1892, p. 1; *(Ritzville) Adams County News*, 2 February 1898, p. 2; *EC*, 30 April 1891, pp. 2, 3; 5 May 1892, p. 3; Joseph Willard Laythe, "Bandits and Badges: Crime and Punishment in Oregon, 1875–1915" (Ph.D. diss., University of Oregon, 1996), 175; John Fahey, *The Inland Empire: Unfolding Years, 1879–1929* (Seattle: University of Washington Press, 1986), 7–8. British Columbians occasionally took extralegal but nonlethal measures against people deemed criminal. In 1892 a group of men on Vancouver Island

apparently came near to drowning a Chinese man they had reportedly "caught committing an unnatural offence with an animal." *NFP*, 7 December 1892, p. 4. Laborers occasionally organized to drive out workers from Asia around the century's turn. W. Peter Ward, *White Canada Forever: Popular Attitudes and Public Policy Toward Orientals in British Columbia*, 64; case 68/1899, BCAGC.

9. *GE*, 10 December 1897, p. 1. Cases 11/1895, 19/1897, BCAGC.

10. *Cases Determined in the Supreme Court of Washington* (Seattle: Bancroft-Whitney, 1906), vol. 11: 486–487.

11. Ibid., vol. 15: 123, emphasis in the original. Ibid., vol. 14: 600; case 32, box 75, Criminal Case Files, Adams County Superior Court, Washington State Archives, Eastern Region, Eastern Washington University, Cheney.

12. *Cases Determined in the Supreme Court of Washington*, vol. 14: 530. Case 1801, box 21, Jefferson County Superior Court, Washington State Archives, Northwest Region, Western Washington University, Bellingham; *Cases Determined in the Supreme Court of Washington*, vol. 16: 265–267; cases 32, 53, box 75, Adams County Superior Court criminal cases; case 33, box 1, Criminal Case Files, Clallam County Superior Court, Washington State Archives Northwest Region; case 1042, box 13, Stevens County Superior Court, Washington State Archives Eastern Region; case 939, box 17, Skagit County Superior Court, Washington State Archives, Northwest Region. See Richard Maxwell Brown, *No Duty to Retreat: Violence and Values in American History and Society*, 3–37, on the strength and persistence of the "no duty to retreat" legal doctrine on the national level in the United States.

13. Pieter Spierenburg, "Masculinity, Violence, and Honor: An Introduction," in *Men and Violence: Gender, Honor, and Rituals in Modern Europe and America*, ed. Spierenburg (Columbus: Ohio State University Press, 1998), 23–25; Allen Steinberg, *The Transformation of Criminal Justice: Philadelphia, 1800–1880* (Chapel Hill: University of North Carolina Press, 1989).

14. *(Victoria) Colonist*, 15 March 1896, p. 4.

15. Vol. 1428, Capital Cases, RG 13, National Archives of Canada, Ottawa.

16. *NFP*, 14 December 1892, p. 1.

17. Ralph Connor, *Black Rock: A Tale of the Selkirks* (New York: Fleming H. Revell, 1900), 158–160.

18. *Rossland Miner*, 2 September 1897, p. 1. *Chilliwack Progress*, 18 May 1898, p. 4; *Rossland Miner*, 3 March 1897, p. 3.

19. R. M. Middleton, ed., *The Journal of Lady Aberdeen: The Okanagan Valley in the Nineties* (Victoria, British Columbia: Morriss Publishing, 1986), 69.

20. Frances Macnab, *British Columbia for Settlers: Its Mines, Trade, and Agriculture* (London: Chapman and Hall, 1898), 279–280.

21. M. Allerdale Grainger, *Woodsmen of the West* (Victoria: Horsdal and Schubart, 1994, orig. 1908), 23–24, 49, 139–140, 147, 195–197. Although the book was not published until 1908, Grainger, a well-educated Englishman, based his novel on work and travel in British Columbia that began in the late 1890s. George Bowering, "Home Away: A Thematic Study of Some British Columbia Novels," *BCST* 62 (summer 1984): 11. Connor, *Black Rock*. Gordon's work is assessed in Jeremy Mouat, *Roaring Days: Rossland's Mines and the History of British Columbia* (Vancouver: University of British Columbia Press, 1995), 112–114, and in Robin W. Winks's introduction to Ralph Connor, *The Sky Pilot: A Tale of the Foothills* (Lexington: University Press of Kentucky, 1970, orig. 1899), v–x.

22. F. H. Balch, *The Bridge of the Gods: A Romance of Indian Oregon* (Portland, Oregon: Binfords and Mort, n.d., orig. 1890). Stephen L. Harris, "Frederic Homer Balch and the Romance of Oregon History," *OHQ* 97 (winter 1996–1997): 390–427; Leonard Wiley, *The Granite Boulder: A Biography of Frederic Homer Balch, Author of the Bridge of the Gods* (Portland, Oregon: Dunham, 1970).

23. Register to Coroners' Inquiries, GR 432/B7894, British Columbia Archives and Records Service, Victoria; *PO*, 1 January 1896, p. 36; *Seventh Census of the United States, 1850: An Appendix* (Washington, D.C.: Robert Armstrong, 1853), 998, 993; *Twelfth Census of the United States, Taken in the Year 1900: Population, Part 2* (Washington, D.C.: United States Census Office, 1902), 82. Clare V. McKanna Jr., *Homicide, Race, and Justice in the American West, 1880–1920*, 40–41. Historians of violent crime in North America are generally agreed that it fell during the nineteenth century, particularly the homicide rate. Lane, *Murder in America*, 181–188; Lane, *Violent Death in the City: Suicide, Accident, and Murder in Nineteenth-Century Philadelphia*, 70–76; Lawrence M. Friedman, *Crime and Punishment in American History*, 209–210; Helen Boritch, "Crime and Punishment in Middlesex County, Ontario, 1871–1920," in *Crime and Criminal Justice*, ed. Jim Phillips, Tina Loo, and Susan Lewthwaite (Toronto: University of Toronto Press, for the Osgoode Society, 1994), 387–438; John C. Weaver, *Crimes, Constables, and Courts: Order and Transgression in a Canadian City, 1816–1970* (Montreal: McGill-Queen's University Press, 1995), 188–224.

24. *NFP*, 13 June 1890, p. 1. *NFP*, 30 June 1892, p. 1; Hulet M. Wells, "I Wanted to Work," box 2, Hulet Wells Papers, University of Washington Manuscripts and University Archives, Seattle.

25. *NFP*, 2 December 1890, p. 3. *NFP*, 9 December 1890, p. 3.

26. Case 370/1891, British Columbia Attorney General Correspondence, Inward,

British Columbia Archives and Records Service. *NFP*, 15 January 1891, p. 4; 12 February 1891, p. 4; *Rossland Miner*, 3 July 1896, p. 2; David Mitchell and Dennis Duffy, eds., "Bright Sunshine and a Brand New Country: Recollections of the Okanagan Valley, 1890–1914," *SH* 8 (1979): 51; S. D. Clark, *The Social Development of Canada: An Introductory Study with Select Documents* (Toronto: University of Toronto Press, 1942), 406–408; Mouat, *Roaring Days*, 39–40, 125–129.

27. Harold Douglas Langille, "Across Oregon's 'Desert' by Buckboard," *OHQ* 59 (December 1958): 328–329. Laythe, "Bandits and Badges," 151–152. Grace and Rufus Matthews to Mrs. B. T. Matthews, 19 June 1895, in *Talking on Paper: An Anthology of Oregon Letters and Diaries*, ed. Shannon Applegate and Terence O'Donnell (Corvallis: Oregon State University Press, 1994), 89; Harriet L. Adams, *A Woman's Journeyings in the New Northwest* (Cleveland: B-P Printing, 1892), 22–23; Thomas W. Riddle, "Populism in the Palouse: Old Ideals and New Realities," *PNQ* 65 (July 1974): 99; B. J. Lyons, *Thrills and Spills of a Cowboy Rancher* (New York: Vantage Press, 1959), 158; Garret D. Kincaid [and A. H. Harris], *Palouse in the Making* ([Rosalia: *Rosalia Citizen Journal*, 1979, orig. 1947]), 43; Earl A. Kessler and Sylba O. Kahler interview, Lockley collection, vol. 30, Special Collections, University of Oregon, Eugene; U. E. Fries with the assistance of Emil B. Fries, *From Copenhagen to Okanagan: The Autobiography of a Pioneer*, ed. Grace V. Stearns and Eugene F. Hoy (Caldwell, Idaho: Caxton Printers, 1949), 293. Occasionally violence flared because of sustained economic disagreements between cattle and farming or sheep interests. Simpson, *A Social History of the Cattle Industry*, 81; Margaret L. Sullivan, "Conflict on the Frontier: The Case of Harney County, Oregon, 1870–1900," *PNQ* 66 (October 1975): 174–181; George A. Wallis, *J. P. Housman in Oregon's Wild West* (Bend, Oregon: Maverick Publications, 1977, orig. 1966), 11; *(Ritzville) Adams County News*, 30 March 1898, p. 3; 5 July 1899, p. 2; *CPG*, 27 June 1890, p. 1.

28. *Palouse Republic*, 12 November 1892, pp. 2, 4. *CPG*, 20 March 1891, p. 1. *Colfax Gazette*, 2 March 1894, p. 5.

29. *CPG*, 25 November 1892, p. 1.

30. *Colfax Weekly Commoner*, 1 September 1899, p. 1. Brown, *No Duty to Retreat*, 39–86, points out that western gunfights were not necessarily strictly personal affairs or the result of blowing off steam, but that they sometimes pitted liberty-loving Democrats against order-loving and corporation-oriented Republicans in a struggle over which political culture would rule a given area.

31. Case 333/1891, British Columbia Attorney General Correspondence, Inward.

32. Case 561/1891, British Columbia Attorney General Correspondence, Inward.

33. Case 17, box 13, Victoria County Court, GR 1567, British Columbia Archives and Records Service. See also cases 134/1892, 9/1898, BCAGC; case 1897–Cooper/ 1897, Revelstoke Police Court, GR 2355, British Columbia Archives and Records Service; case 1501, box 43, Lewis County Superior Court, Washington State Archives, Southwest Region, Olympia; *EC,* 10 July 1890, p. 3.

34. *CPG,* 14 April 1893, p. 1.

35. *Snohomish Tribune,* 25 February 1896, p. 1. Case 37, box 1, San Juan County Superior Court, Washington State Archives, Northwest Region; case 764, box 21, Lewis County Superior Court, Washington State Archives, Southwest Region; case 933, box 11, Clark County Superior Court; *Medford Mail,* 11 October 1895, p. 5; *CPG,* 6 November 1891, p. 1; Harry E. Rice, "Columbia River Kid," *OHQ* 74 (December 1973): 323–325; case 27/1896, BCAGC.

36. Case 2159, box 29, Thurston County Superior Court, Washington State Archives, Southwestern Regional Branch.

37. *CPG,* 21 October 1892, p. 1.

38. *GE,* 28 October 1893, p. 1.

39. *NFP,* 1 April 1891, p. 4.

40. Case 719, box 573, Thurston County Superior Court.

41. *NFP,* 11 July 1890, p. 1; [Bert Williams], "The Blue Jays of Langley," *SH* 40 (1983): 14.

42. *Snohomish Tribune,* 25 February 1896, p. 1.

43. *EC,* 3 July 1890, p. 2.

44. *CPG,* 29 January 1892, p. 1. Case 145, box 2, Okanogan County Superior Court, Washington State Archives, Central Region, Central Washington University, Ellensburg.

45. *Vernon News,* 9 August 1894, p. 1. *Vernon News,* 12 December 1895, p. 8; *NFP,* 11 February 1890, p. 1; *Snohomish Tribune,* 15 February 1896, p. 1.

46. *CPG,* 30 September 1892, p. 1.

47. Case 80, box 2, Clallam County Superior Court, criminal cases.

48. Case 1294, box 564, Thurston County Superior Court. Case 860, box 575, Thurston County Superior Court.

49. Case 3/1892, BCAGC.

50. Case 38/1894, BCAGC.

51. Case 74/1899, BCAGC.

52. Case 9/1898, BCAGC.

53. Hulet M. Wells, "I Wanted to Work," box 2, Wells papers.

54. Case 38/1894, BCAGC.

55. Case 1100, box 32, Lewis County Superior Court.

56. Case 27/1896, BCAGC.

57. Case 27/1896, BCAGC.

58. Case 27/1896, BCAGC.

59. *Chilliwack Progress*, 15 September 1892, p. 1. Case 699, box 9, Stevens County Superior Court; *NFP*, 12 February 1890, p. 1; 2 September 1890, p. 1; cases 11/1895, 32/1896, 65/1899, BCAGC; case 1848, box 1, Kittitas County Superior Court, Washington State Archives, Central Region; case file 1897/Cooper, box 1, Revelstoke Police Court; *(Colfax) Weekly Commoner*, 10 November 1893, p. 1; case 80, box 2, Clallam County Superior Court, criminal cases; case 145, box 2, Okanogan County Superior Court; case 61, box 2, Douglas County Superior Court, criminal cases, Washington State Archives, Central Region. As during the settlement period, participants might agree to the mutual use of weapons, or to a "free fight" in which the combatants tried to injure or maim each other. But free fights, in which large numbers of men attacked each other indiscriminately, with whatever weapons happened to be at hand, had become more infrequent by the 1890s.

60. Case 540, box 7, Clark County Superior Court. Case 1001, box 28, Lewis County Superior Court; case 319, box 4, Stevens County Superior Court.

61. Case 982, box 28, Lewis County Superior Court.

62. Case 38/1894, BCAGC. Case 67/1893, BCAGC; case 53, box 75, Adams County Superior Court, criminal cases; case 1014, box 10, Jefferson County Superior Court; *NFP*, 2 December 1890, p. 2.

63. Viviana A. Zelizer, *Pricing the Priceless Child: The Changing Social Value of Children* (Princeton: Princeton University Press, 1994, orig. 1985); Neil Sutherland, *Children in English-Canadian Society: Framing the Twentieth-Century Consensus* (Toronto: University of Toronto Press, 1976), 13–36; Neil Semple, "'The Nurture and Admonition of the Lord': Nineteenth-Century Canadian Methodism's Response to 'Childhood,'" *Social History* 14 (May 1981): 157–175; Elizabeth Pleck, *Domestic Tyranny: The Making of American Social Policy Against Family Violence from Colonial Times to the Present*, 34–44; Jill Beth Schlessinger, "'Such Inhuman Treatment': Family Violence in the Chicago Middle Class, 1871–1920" (Ph.D. diss., University of California, Berkeley, 1998), 28–41; Donald R. Raichle, "The Abolition of Corporal Punishment in New Jersey Schools," in *Corporal Punishment in American Education: Readings in History, Practice, and Alternatives*, ed. Irwin A. Hyman and James H. Wise (Philadelphia: Temple University Press, 1979), 62–88; Herbert Arnold Falk, *Corporal Punishment: A*

Social Interpretation of Its Theory and Practice in the Schools of the United States (New York: Columbia University, 1941), 78–80; LeRoy Ashby, *Endangered Children: Dependency, Neglect, and Abuse in American History* (New York: Twayne, 1997), 58–59; F. Henry Johnson, "Changing Conceptions of Discipline and Pupil-Teacher Relations in Canadian Schools," 40–45; John Adams and Becky Thomas, *Floating Schools and Frozen Inkwells: The One-Room Schools of British Columbia* (Madeira Park, British Columbia: Harbour Publishing, 1985), 71.

64. Case 7629, Whitman County Superior Court, Whitman County Courthouse, Colfax.

65. Case 439, box 6, Clark County Superior Court. Case 226, box 3, Clark County Superior Court. Case 1659, box 49, Lewis County Superior Court; case 441, box 6, Klickitat County Superior Court civil cases, Washington State Archives, Central Region; case 218, box 2, Asotin County Superior Court, Washington State Archives, Eastern Region.

66. Case 21, box 1, Walla Walla County Superior Court, Washington State Archives, Eastern Region.

67. Case 1830, box 18, Clark County Superior Court. Nineteenth- and early-twentieth-century people used the term "whipping" to refer to a broad range of violent acts, some of them relatively mild, such as striking children's legs with switches or their hands with rulers.

68. Case 45, box 4, Walla Walla County Superior Court. Case 1096, box 560, Thurston County Superior Court; case 44, box 3, Walla Walla County Superior Court; Peterson del Mar, *What Trouble I Have Seen*, 57.

69. Case 647, box 8, Stevens County Superior Court.

70. Case 805, Boys' Case Record Book 1, Boys and Girls Aid Society, Portland. Case 1047, box 30, Lewis County Superior Court; case 1534¹/₂, box 560, Thurston County Superior Court.

71. Impert Orchard, "Martin: The Story of a Young Fur Trader," *SH* 30 (1981): 14.

72. Lillian Scott, *Lilly: Early Years on Puget Sound* (Seattle: Trick and Murray, 1975), 10, 13, 15–16. [Williams], "The Blue Jays of Langley," 12–14; Bessie Wilson Craine, *Squak Valley (Issaquah)* (Issaquah, Washington: Issaquah Historical Society, 1976), 39; J. B. West, *Growing Up in the Palouse* (n.p.: n.p., 1980), 62–63. Laurence Pratt recalled that a neighbor woman in the Willamette Valley would tell her children to bring her a switch and that the air would then be filled with "the screams of the punished boy or girl." But Pratt, whose father was an attorney and newspaperman, added that his fam-

ily viewed these neighbors as "crude or something." Dowrick [Laurence Pratt], *An Oregon Boyhood* (Portland, Oregon: Worthylake Press, 1969), 45.

73. Case 43/1899, BCAGC. Files 90/1895, 75/1899, BCAGC.

74. Case 59/1899, BCAGC.

75. Case file 738, Boys and Girls Aid Society, emphasis in the original.

76. Case file 814, Boys and Girls Aid Society. Case files 190, 330, 608, 660, 732, 748, 817, 825, 936, 943, Boys and Girls Aid Society.

77. *CPG,* 27 November 1891, p. 1; 20 November 1891, p. 1. *(McMinnville) Telephone Register,* 13 August 1896, p. 3; *SOS,* 28 May 1891, p. 4; *SCJ,* 28 May 1891, p. 3.

78. Kincaid [and Harris], *Palouse in the Making,* 12–13; *CC,* 4 January 1895, p. 3; Bill Bighill interview, file PAC 75–1dm, Pacific County Oral History Project, Washington State Archives, Olympia; Walter L. Scott, *Pan Bread 'n Jerky* (Caldwell, Idaho: Caxton, 1968), 151.

79. *(Nelson) Miner,* 26 November 1898, p. 1. Johnson, "Changing Conceptions of Discipline," 49. David W. Brown, "Social Darwinism, Private Schooling, and Sport in Victorian and Edwardian Canada," in *Pleasure, Profit, Proselytism: British Culture and Sport at Home and Abroad, 1700–1914,* ed. J. A. Mangan (London: Frank Cass, 1988), 220–221; Adams and Thomas, *Floating Schools and Frozen Inkwells,* 70–71; [Peter Legacé], "Little Pete," *SH* 40 (1983): 29; Edward L. Affleck, *Kootenay Yesterdays: Three First Hand Accounts of Mining, Prospecting, Ranching, Teaching, and Trapping in the Kootenay District in Pre–World War I Times* (Vancouver, British Columbia: Alexander Nicolls Press, 1976), 14.

80. Linda Louise Hale, "The British Columbia Woman Suffrage Movement, 1890–1917" (M.A. thesis, University of British Columbia, 1977), 17–30; Michael H. Cramer, "Public and Political: Documents of the Woman's Suffrage Campaign in British Columbia, 1871–1917: The View from Victoria," in *In Her Own Right: Selected Essays on Women's History in B.C.,* ed. Barbara Latham and Cathy Kess (Victoria: Camosum College, 1980), 79–100; Mimi Ajzenstadt, "Cycles of Control: Alcohol Regulation and the Construction of Gender Role, British Columbia, 1870–1925," *International Journal of Canadian Studies* 11 (spring 1995): 101–120; E. Anthony Rotundo, *American Manhood: Transformations in Masculinity from the Revolution to the Modern Era;* Robert L. Griswold, *Fatherhood in America: A History* (New York: Basic Books, 1993), 10–33; Karen Lystra, *Searching the Heart: Women, Men, and Romantic Love in Nineteenth-Century America* (New York: Oxford University Press, 1989); Carl Degler, *At Odds: Women and the Family in America from the Revolution to*

the Present (Oxford: Oxford University Press, 1980), 26–51; Mary P. Ryan, *Cradle of the Middle Class: The Family in Oneida County, New York, 1790–1865* (Cambridge: Cambridge University Press, 1981); Peterson del Mar, *What Trouble I Have Seen*, 49–53; *Twelfth Census of the United States, Taken in the Year 1900: Population, Part 2*, 294, 304; Adele Perry, "'Oh I'm Just Sick of the Faces of Men': Gender Imbalance, Race, Sexuality, and Sociability in Nineteenth-Century British Columbia," *BCST* 105–106 (spring/summer 1995): 27–43; John Douglas Belshaw, "Cradle to Grave: An Examination of Demographic Behaviour on Two British Columbia Frontiers," *Journal of the Canadian Historical Association* 5 (1994): 41–62; Barman, *West Beyond the West*, 385; Ellen M. Thomas Gee, "Marriage in Nineteenth-Century Canada," *CRSA* 19 (August 1982): 320; Sandra Haarsager, *Organized Womanhood: Cultural Politics in the Pacific Northwest, 1840–1920* (Norman: University of Oklahoma Press, 1997); Marilyn P. Watkins, "Political Activism and Community-Building among Alliance and Grange Women in Western Washington, 1892–1925," *Agricultural History* 67 (spring 1993): 197–213.

81. Bureau of the Census, *Marriage and Divorce, 1867–1906*, part 1 (Washington, D.C.: Government Printing Office, 1909), 72.

82. *Reports of Cases Determined in the Supreme Court of the State of Washington* (Olympia, Washington: O. C. White, 1893), vol. 4: 709–710.

83. James G. Snell, *In the Shadow of the Law: Divorce in Canada, 1900–1939* (Toronto: University of Toronto Press, 1991), 22 (quote), 10, 21–47. Robert Pike, "Legal Access and the Incidence of Divorce in Canada: A Sociohistorical Analysis," *CRSA* 12 (May 1975): 128.

84. Case 7629, Whitman County Superior Court. Elaine Tyler May, *Great Expectations: Marriage and Divorce in Post-Victorian America* (Chicago: University of Chicago Press, 1980).

85. Case 45, box 4, Walla Walla Superior Court. Case 1649, box 48, Lewis County Superior Court.

86. Case 1433, box 14, Clark County Superior Court.

87. Box 15, file 1545, Clark County Superior Court. Linda Gordon, *Heroes of Their Own Lives: The Politics and History of Family Violence, Boston, 1880–1960*, 255, 257; Martin J. Wiener, "The Victorian Criminalization of Men," in Spierenburg, *Men and Violence*, 197–212.

88. Peterson del Mar, *What Trouble I Have Seen*, 55–57.

89. *NFP*, 22 July 1890, pp. 1, 2.

90. *NFP*, 11 April 1891, p. 4.

91. Linda Gordon, "A Right Not to Be Beaten: The Agency of Battered Women,

1880–1960," in *Gendered Domains: Rethinking Public and Private in Women's History,* ed. Dorothy O. Helly and Susan M. Reverby (Ithaca, New York: Cornell University Press, 1992), 239–240.

92. *CPG,* 9 December 1892, p. 3; *NFP,* 6 August 1890, p. 1; Peterson del Mar, *What Trouble I Have Seen,* 63–64. Anne M. Butler, *Gendered Justice in the American West: Women Prisoners in Men's Penitentiaries* (Urbana: University of Illinois Press, 1997), 113–133, points out that women sentenced to western penitentiaries for violent offenses were often reacting to chronic verbal or physical abuse at home or at work.

93. Case 536, box 16, Lewis County Superior Court. Case 226, box 3, Clark County Superior Court. Case 1598, box 46, Lewis County Superior Court. Anne M. Butler, *Daughters of Joy, Sisters of Misery: Prostitutes in the American West, 1865–90* (Urbana: University of Illinois Press, 1985), 41–46, 61–62, 111–112, points out that prostitutes were apt to both use and be the victims of violence.

94. Case 13, box 12, Victoria County Court. A twenty-year-old son who blamed his father for such quarrels admitted that he had seen his father's "face scratched a little at different times."

95. Case 1096, box 560, Thurston County Superior Court. See also: case 44, box 3 and case 45, box 4, Walla Walla County Superior Court; case 31, box 28, Wahkiakum County Superior Court, Washington State Archives, Southwest Region.

96. Case 2742, box 12, Columbia County Superior Court, Washington State Archives, Eastern Region.

97. Case 58A, box 2, Douglas County Superior Court, criminal case files, Washington State Archives, Central Region. See also: case 1492, box 1, Kittitas County Superior Court, Washington State Archives, Central Region; case 1500, box 43, Lewis County Superior Court; case 90/1895, BCAGC. Schlessinger, "'Such Inhuman Treatment,'" 106–163.

98. Case 2953, box 18, Columbia County Superior Court. Case 1659, box 49, Lewis County Superior Court.

99. Case 427, box 13, Lewis County Superior Court. Case 83, box 7, Walla Walla Superior Court; case 1490, box 15 and case 518, box 7, Clark County Superior Court. Case 2725, Lane County Circuit Court, Oregon State Archives; CPG, 29 January 1892, p. 6.

100. Case 1638, box 48, Lewis County Superior Court. Annalee Golz, "Uncovering and Reconstructing Family Violence: Ontario Criminal Case Files," in *On the Case: Explorations in Social History,* ed. Franca Iacovetta and Wendy Mitchinson (Toronto: University of Toronto Press, 1998), 297–298.

101. *CC,* 13 June 1890, p. 1; case 1638, box 48, Lewis County Superior Court.

102. Case 21, box 1, Walla Walla County Superior Court. Case 44, box 3, Walla Walla County Superior Court. Sex that did not entail intercourse was frowned upon, however. Case H-128, Wasco County Circuit Court, Oregon State Archives. Wives might also complain that their husbands withheld sexual intercourse from them. Case 4087, Benton County Circuit Court, Oregon State Archives; case D-174, Wasco County Circuit Court.

103. Case 2953, box 18, Columbia County Superior Court. Case 1659, box 49, Lewis County Superior Court.

104. Case 9, Lincoln County Circuit Court, Lincoln County Courthouse, Newport, Oregon. The couple had married in 1877, had a child about two years later, and Felanise filed for divorce in 1893. Cases K87, J54, L (Little), Wasco County Circuit Court, Oregon State Archives; cases 4869, 6521, 7234, Marion County Circuit Court civil cases, Oregon State Archives; cases 3099, 3398, Lane County Circuit Court; case 3402, Benton County Circuit Court; case 506, box 6, case 1686, box 16, and case 1209, box 13, Clark County Superior Court.

105. Case 1814, Coos County Circuit Court, Coos County Courthouse, Coquille, Oregon. May, *Great Expectations*, 34–38.

4 / PLUCKY WOMEN AND CRAZED ITALIANS

1. *SDT*, 22 January 1905, p. 12.

2. Edward W. Said, *Orientalism* (New York: Vintage, 1979), p. 40, emphasis in the original. Said, *Culture and Imperialism* (New York: Alfred A. Knopf, 1993), xiii.

3. On the social context of these three cities see Robert A. J. McDonald, *Making Vancouver: Class, Status, and Social Boundaries, 1863–1913*, esp. 104–105, 126–128, 186–191, 202–215; Mark Leier, "Ethnicity, Urbanism, and the Labour Aristocracy: Rethinking Vancouver Trade Unionism, 1889–1909," *CHR* 74 (December 1993): 510–534; David Jay Bercuson, "Labour Radicalism and the Western Industrial Frontier: 1897–1919," *CHR* 58 (June 1977): 166–170; Norbert MacDonald, *Distant Neighbors: A Comparative History of Seattle and Vancouver* (Lincoln: University of Nebraska Press, 1987), 44–77; Gordon B. Dodds, *The American Northwest: A History of Oregon and Washington*, 190–195; Janice L. Reiff, "Urbanization and the Social Structure: Seattle, Washington, 1852–1910" (Ph.D. diss., University of Washington, 1981), 84–87, 109–114, 161–169, 196–220, 225–226; Richard C. Berner, *Seattle, 1900–1920: From Boomtown, Urban Turbulence, to Restoration* (Seattle: Charles Press, 1991), 22–77; Warren B. Johnson, "Muckraking in the Northwest: Joe Smith and Seattle Reform," *Pacific*

Historical Review 40 (1971): 478–500; David Peterson del Mar, *What Trouble I Have Seen: A History of Violence Against Wives*, 72–96; Robert Douglas Johnston, "Middle-Class Political Ideology in a Corporate Society: The Persistence of Small-Propertied Radicalism in Portland, Oregon, 1883–1926" (Ph.D. diss., Rutgers University, 1993); Carl Abbott, *Portland: Planning, Politics, and Growth in a Twentieth-Century City* (Lincoln; University of Nebraska Press, 1983), 49–57; William Toll, *Women, Men, and Ethnicity: Essays on the Structure and Thought of American Jewry* (Lanham, Maryland: University Press of America and American Jewish Archives, 1991), 85–106; *Fourth Census of Canada, 1901: Volume 1, Population* (Ottawa: S. E Dawson, 1902), 284–285; *Fifth Census of Canada, 1911: Religions, Origins, Birthplace, Citizenship, Literacy, and Infirmities, by Provinces, Districts, and Sub-Districts, Volume 2* (Ottawa: C. H. Parmelee, 1913), 170–171; U.S. Bureau of the Census, *Thirteenth Census of the United States Taken in the Year 1910, Abstract of the Census: Statistics of Population, Agriculture, Manufactures, and Mining for the United States, the States, and Principal Cities with Supplement for Oregon* (Washington, D.C.: Government Printing Office, 1913), 592–593; ibid., *Supplement for Washington*, 592–593; Alan Sykes, ed., "Harold Farrow's Splendid Portland, 1910," *OHQ* 99 (spring 1998): 48–61; Star Rosenthal, "Union Maids: Organized Women Workers in Vancouver, 1900–1915," *BCST* 41 (spring 1979): 36–55; Angus McLaren, *Our Own Master Race: Eugenics in Canada, 1885–1945* (Toronto: McClelland and Stewart, 1990), 46–67; W. Peter Ward, *White Canada Forever: Popular Attitudes and Public Policy Toward Orientals in British Columbia*, 97–117; Gloria E. Myers, *A Municipal Mother: Portland's Lola Greene Baldwin, America's First Policewoman* (Corvallis: Oregon State University Press, 1995), 25–47.

4. Jay Ellis Ransom, ed., "Country Schoolma'am," *OHQ* 86 (summer 1985): 130.

5. *PODJ*, 14 November 1904, p. 4. *PODJ*, 22 January 1910, p. 4; 16 December 1906, p. 15. Vancouver reformers were more concerned with nonviolent crimes like prostitution and gambling than with violent crime during these years. Deborah Nilsen, "The 'Social Evil': Prostitution in Vancouver, 1900–1920," in *In Her Own Right: Selected Essays on Women's History in B.C.*, ed. Barbara Latham and Cathy Kess (Victoria, British Columbia: Camosun College, 1980), 205–228; Greg Marquis, "Vancouver Vice: The Police and the Negotiation of Morality, 1904–1935," in *British Columbia and the Yukon*, ed. Hamar Foster and John McLaren (Toronto: University of Toronto Press, for the Osgoode Society, 1995), 242–273.

6. *VDP*, 29 August 1905, p. 6. *VDP*, 21 November 1905, p. 6.

7. *VDP*, 2 September 1905, p. 24.

8. Police Court Calendar, 1901 and 1910, Series 182, City of Vancouver Archives.

9. *SR*, 14 December 1900, p. 1. *SR*, 21 December 1900, p. 1; 28 June 1901, p. 1. *SMH*, 28 July 1906, p. 3; 13 October 1906, p. 3; *SDN*, 16 July 1906, p. 1; *SPI*, 11 July 1910, p. 6.

10. *(Seattle) Patriarch*, 27 November 1909, p. 2; 30 October 1909, p. 2.

11. Berner, *Seattle, 1900–1920*, 6–7.

12. *VDP*, 8 January 1908, p. 15. *VDP*, 22 October 1904, p. 1; 3 December 1904, p. 1; 2 March 1905, p. 6; 4 March 1905, p. 4; 6 March 1905, p. 5; 21 November 1905, p. 6; 17 July 1902, p. 4; 8 June 1905, p. 8. Indiana Matters, "The Boys' Industrial School: Education for Juvenile Offenders," in *Schooling and Society in Twentieth Century British Columbia*, ed. J. Donald Wilson and David C. Jones (Calgary: Detselig Enterprises, 1980), 58.

13. *PO*, 7 September 1909, p. 8.

14. *PO*, 15 February 1908, p. 8; 13 July 1910, p. 8. The *PO*'s view was not as singular as it claimed to be. An account of punishments at the Boys and Girls Aid Society of Portland, one of the state's leading organizations for institutionalized children, noted thirty-eight instances of corporal punishments by staff members in 1908, nearly one-half of the punishments recorded. "Punishments, Accidents, or Incidents from Supervisors' Daily Reports, for 1908," Boys and Girls Aid Society, Portland. Prisoners at Oregon's state penitentiary were subject to beatings, and in 1905 Oregon became the third and last state to make wife beating punishable with a flogging. Ward M. McAfee, "The Formation of Prison-Management Philosophy in Oregon, 1843–1915," *OHQ* 91 (fall 1990): 272, 274; Joseph Willard Laythe, "Bandits and Badges: Crime and Punishment in Oregon, 1875–1915" (Ph.D. diss., University of Oregon, 1996), 77–78, 85; Joseph (Bunko) Kelley, *Thirteen Years in the Oregon Penitentiary* (Portland: n.p., 1908); Peterson del Mar, *What Trouble I Have Seen*, 72–96. Apparently only four wife beaters—three of them from Portland—were whipped under this law, which the legislature overturned in 1911.

15. *PODJ*, 29 August 1907, p. 6. *PODJ*, 2 April 1907, p. 6; 21 June 1907, p. 8; 24 June 1907, p. 6; 4 July 1907, p. 8; 6 July 1907, p. 6; 13 December 1907, p. 8; 20 December 1907, p. 8; 12 May 1909, p. 8; 25 May 1909, p. 8; 27 May 1909, p. 8; 12 June 1907, p. 8; 17 July 1907, p. 1; 10 August 1907, p. 6; 29 August 1907, p. 6; 29 August 1907, p. 6; 25 December 1907, p. 4; 6 January 1909, p. 10. Those who wrote letters to the *PODJ* about revolvers were generally less sanguine about the benefits of outlawing them. *PODJ*, 12 January 1907, p. 8; 15 January 1907, p. 8; 17 January 1907, p. 6; 18 January 1907, p. 8; 25 December 1907, p. 4.

16. Both Portland and Vancouver have coroner's registers that cover 1900 to 1910. Vancouver's are part of the records for British Columbia as a whole. Portland's are

included in Multnomah County. Portland constituted about 90 percent of the county's population at this time, so the city and the county were close to being one and the same. A comparison of the registers with the cities' newspapers reveals that Portland's registers are more complete than Vancouver's. I found five Vancouver murders described in newspapers that did not appear in the coroner's register, which had a total of nineteen. Furthermore, the cause of death listed in Vancouver's registers is often unclear. "Died from gunshot wounds," for example, could indicate death by suicide, accident, or murder. I used newspaper research, together with extant coroner's inquests, to clarify the cause of death in cases that were not clear-cut. I was unable to check as thoroughly for homicides that occurred outside of Vancouver, however. Hence the homicide rate given here for British Columbians who lived outside of Vancouver is probably an underestimate. As in previous chapters, I did not count legal executions, botched abortions, or infanticides as murders. Registers and Indexes to Coroners' Inquiries and Inquests, 1889–1937, GR 432/B7894, British Columbia Archives and Records Service, Victoria; Multnomah County Record of Coroner's Investigations, 1894 to 1923, Multnomah County Medical Examiner's Office, Portland. Washington's urban rate was much higher: 9.3. *Mortality Statistics, 1910* (Washington, D.C.: Government Printing Office, 1913), 157. These statistics for Washington did not differentiate between cities.

17. *VDP*, 27 January 1905, p. 1.

18. *PODJ*, 13 March 1910, p. 1. *PO*, 2 April 1909, p. 6; 1 October 1909, p. 1; *PODJ*, 31 July 1904, p. 2; 29 August 1907, p. 1; 16 July 1910, p. 1; 25 October 1910, p. 1; 28 October 1910, p. 6; 1 July 1910, p. 7; 26 January 1907, p. 2; 14 June 1910, p. 14; 18 October 1906, p. 4; 9 June 1909, p. 2; *VDP*, 24 April 1909, p. 1; 2 August 1905, p. 6.

19. *PO*, 30 March 1907, p. 12. *PODJ*, 6 July 1910, p. 6; *VDP*, 3 July 1903, p. 10; 7 October 1905, p. 15; *SDT*, 22 January 1905, p. 8; *SDN*, 19 December 1906, p. 1.

20. *SDT*, 13 February 1905, p. 7. *SPI*, 3 June 1910, pp. 1, 11.

21. *PODJ*, 2 August 1910, p. 3.

22. *PODJ*, 4 August 1910, p. 10.

23. *PODJ*, 5 October 1906, p. 8. *PODJ*, 1 September 1906, p. 1; 3 July 1904, p. 3; 20 January 1905, p. 2; *SPI*, 3 April 1910, p. 1; *VDP*, 19 December 1900, p. 2.

24. *VDP*, 11 March 1905, p. 1. Portland established a separate court for juveniles around the turn of the century. Canada passed the Juvenile Delinquents Act in 1908 and instituted juvenile courts across the country. These steps indicated both a concern over crimes by juveniles and a desire to rehabilitate and reform them by creating alternatives to the largely punitive mainstream criminal justice system. Laythe,

"Bandits and Badges," 63; Indiana Matters, "Sinners or Sinned Against? Historical Aspects of Female Juvenile Delinquency in British Columbia," in *Not Just Pin Money: Selected Essays on the History of Women's Work in British Columbia,* ed. Barbara K. Latham and Roberta J. Pazdro, 266–268; T. C. Caputo, "The Young Offenders Act: Children's Rights, Children's Wrongs," in *Youth Injustice: Canadian Perspectives,* ed. Thomas O'Reilly-Fleming and Barry Clark (Toronto: Canadian Scholars' Press, 1993), 4–6.

25. *VDP,* 5 May 1905, p. 1.

26. *VDP,* 23 June 1904, p. 1. The *VDP* most commonly mentioned boys' violence toward Chinese Canadians, people widely regarded as physically weak. *VDP,* 3 February 1905, p. 3; 4 February 1905, p. 1; 18 February 1905, p. 1; 23 February 1905, p. 3; 2 March 1905, p. 6; 4 March 1905, p. 4; 6 March 1905, p. 5; 10 February 1908, p. 1. A man who grew up in Vancouver early in the twentieth century recalled that he and his friends used to tie Chinese Canadian men to telephone poles. They did this, iron-ically, while waiting to deliver issues of the *VDP.* Daphne Marlatt and Carole Itter, "Opening Doors: Vancouver's East End," *SH* 8, (1979): 15.

27. *PO,* 19 December 1901, p. 7. *PODJ,* 15 July 1905, p. 24.

28. *(Seattle) Patriarch,* 1 December 1906, p. 1. *(Seattle) Patriarch,* 26 August 1905, p. 2; 30 September 1905, p. 1; 23 December 1905, p. 1; 17 November 1906, p. 1.

29. *(Seattle) Patriarch,* 20 August 1910, p. 2.

30. *VDP,* 22 August 1910, p. 7. *VDP,* 4 April 1902, p. 1; 15 September 1904, p. 1; *PODJ,* 15 November 1904, p. 9.

31. *SMH,* 29 November 1902, p. 6. *SDT,* 8 May 1905, p. 7.

32. *PODJ,* 9 March 1908, p. 6. *PO,* 11 January 1906, p. 1; Multnomah County Record of Coroner's Investigations. *SPI,* 16 November 1910, p. 3; 17 November 1910, p. 7.

33. *PODJ,* 20 February 1905, p. 3.

34. *PODJ,* 16 February, 1905, p. 3. *PODJ,* 11 July 1904, p. 2.

35. *PODJ,* 21 February 1909, p. 2; *VDP,* 7 November 1903, p. 1; *PODJ,* 19 February 1905, p. 6. *PODJ,* 7 September 1904, p. 8; *VDP,* 2 December 1903, p. 1.

36. *VDP,* 30 November 1903, p. 1. *VDP,* 5 October 1903, p. 2; 6 October 1903, p. 1; 7 November 1903, p. 1; 18 November 1903, p. 1; 19 November 1903, p. 1.

37. *PO,* 9 March 1907, p. 18. *Vancouver Daily World,* 5 August 1909, p. 6; *PODJ,* 9 September 1904, p. 4; *PO,* 10 April 1900, p. 7; *VDP,* 4 February 1905, p. 1; 18 February 1905, p. 1; 22 February 1905, p. 3; 23 February 1905, p. 3; 2 March 1905, p. 6; 6 March 1905, p. 5. Some of the young men who assaulted Chinese men were fined, but the criminal justice systems of these cities did not appear to make the apprehension and

prosecution of the offenders in such cases a priority. Timothy J. Stanley, "Schooling, White Supremacy, and the Formation of a Chinese Merchant Public in British Columbia," in *Making Western Canada: Essays on European Colonization and Settlement,* ed. Catherine Cavanaugh and Jeremy Mouat (Toronto: Garamond, 1996), 220.

38. *SDT,* 5 June 1900, p. 5.

39. *PODJ,* 18 January 1905, p. 10. These attitudes prevailed outside of the press, as well. A white man, asked in a Vancouver court to recount a physical confrontation between one of his friends and a Chinese man, remarked: "No one would like the idea of getting hit by a Chinaman." Case 107/1907, BCAGC.

40. *VDP,* 9 July 1907, p. 15.

41. Vancouver Police Scrapbook, 1908–1909, p. 62, series 204, City of Vancouver Archives.

42. *PODJ,* 30 March 1906, p. 1. *VDP,* 2 October 1903, p. 1.

43. *VDP,* 15 February 1905, p. 3.

44. *(Vancouver) British Columbia Saturday Sunset,* 6 July 1907, p. 1.

45. Ibid., 21 September 1907, p. 1. *VDP,* 25 July 1907, p. 1; 3 January 1908, p. 1.

46. *(Vancouver) British Columbia Saturday Sunset,* 29 June 1907, p. 1.

47. *SMH,* 31 October 1903, p. 3.

48. *PODJ,* 27 January 1908, p. 6.

49. *PODJ,* 19 February 1907, p. 8.

50. *PO,* 11 April 1909, p. 5. *VDP,* 8 July 1901, p. 1.

51. *PODJ,* 24 September 1907, p. 1; *VDP,* 12 March 1908, p. 1.

52. *VDP,* 14 January 1901, p. 2.

53. *VDP,* 9 August 1909, p. 2. *VDP,* 23 December 1902, p. 1; 28 December 1903, p. 1; 2 January 1908, p. 1; 25 February 1908, p. 1; *PODJ,* 20 March 1905, p, 8; 26 March 1905, p. 2; 15 April 1910, p. 10.

54. *PODJ,* 9 September 1907, p. 1; 11 September 1907, p. 1; 14 September 1907, p. 3. *PO,* 10 September 1907, p. 1; 11 September 1907, p. 1. Vancouver's Japanese Canadians did in fact resist the rioters while its Chinese Canadians simply withdrew behind closed doors. Ken Adachi, *The Enemy That Never Was: A History of the Japanese Canadians,* 63–85; Howard H. Sugioto, "The Vancouver Riots of 1907: A Canadian Episode," in *East Across the Pacific: Historical and Sociological Studies of Japanese Immigration and Assimilation,* ed. Hilary Conroy and T. Scott Miyakawa (Santa Barbara, California: ABC-Clio Press, 1972), 92–126; Patricia E. Roy, *A White Man's Province: British Columbia Politicians and Chinese and Japanese Immigrants, 1858–1914*

(Vancouver: University of British Columbia Press, 1989), 184–226; Ward, *White Canada Forever*, 68–70.

55. *SPI*, 23 January 1910, p. 5.

56. *VDP*, 22 October 1910, p. 2.

57. *VDP*, 22 April 1907, p. 1; 15 August 1904, p. 10; 2 June 1904, p. 1. *VDP*, 25 July 1904, p. 1; 18 November 1905, p. 1; 2 July 1907, p. 1; 17 March 1909, p. 1; *PODJ*, 6 April 1907, p. 1; 24 December 1907, p. 2; 24 January 1910, p. 4.

58. *VDP*, 10 January 1910, p. 2.

59. *SPI*, 28 March 1910, pp. 1–2. *SPI*, 23 May 1910, p. 1.

60. *SPI*, 7 August 1910, p. 4.

61. *PO*, 26 December 1909, p. 4.

62. *PODJ*, 14 July 1904, p. 12.

63. *VDP*, 20 February 1905, p. 1.

64. *VDP*, 19 September 1904, p. 1. *PODJ*, 1 August 1906, p. 3; 5 February 1907, pp. 1, 7; *SDN*, 27 August 1905, p. 1.

65. *VDP*, 24 April 1909, p. 4. *VDP*, 6 March 1908, p. 1; 27 March 1909, p. 20.

66. *VDP*, 17 May 1910, p. 6; 6 December 1910, p. 2. Such stories also occasionally turned up south of the line: *PODJ*, 24 January 1910, p. 4; 5 February 1910, p. 1; *PO*, 19 December 1907, p. 8. On popular images of Italian immigrants' violence in the early twentieth century see: McDonald, *Making Vancouver*, 212–213; Nellie Virginia Roe, "The Italian Immigrant in Seattle" (M.A. thesis, University of Washington, 1915), 56–57; Karen Dubinsky and Franca Iacovetta, "Murder, Womanly Virtue, and Motherhood: The Case of Angelina Napolitano, 1911–1922," *CHR* 72 (December 1991): 517–518; Andrew F. Rolle, *The Immigrant Upraised: Italian Adventurers and Colonists in an Expanding America* (Norman: University of Oklahoma Press, 1968), 96.

67. *(Vancouver) Western Call*, 22 July 1910, p. 1.

68. *(Vancouver) Saturday Sunset*, 16 April 1910, p. 1. The editorial went on to complain that "Japs or Chinks" were also endangering lives and property by their careless blasting practices.

69. *VDP*, 14 April 1910, p. 1.

70. *VDP*, 25 October 1905, p. 10; 15 August 1905, p. 1. *PODJ*, 23 May 1904, p. 2; 26 May 1904, p. 2; 2 November 1910, p. 5; *PO*, 12 July 1907, p. 12; 7 December 1909, p. 4; *VDP*, 4 April 1902, p. 1; 25 October 1902, p. 1; 21 November 1903, p. 1; 19 February 1906, p. 1.

71. *VDP*, 16 April 1901, p. 8; 12 October 1901, p. 11. *SDT*, 24 October 1905, p. 1.

72. *PODJ*, 16 May 1904, p. 2.

73. *PO*, 12 July 1907, p. 12. *Vancouver Daily News Advertiser*, 1 June 1909, p. 7; *PODJ*, 5 April 1910, p. 1.

74. *VDP*, 10 April 1909, p. 7. *VDP*, 19 February 1906, p. 1.

75. *VDP*, 19 August 1904, p. 1.

76. *Vancouver Daily News Advertiser*, 16 June 1909, p. 7.

77. *SMH*, 21 March 1903, p. 5.

78. *VDP*, 25 October 1902, p. 1. *PO*, 27 February 1909, p. 8. On the growing acceptance of Irish Americans see David R. Roediger, *Towards the Abolition of Whiteness: Essays on Race, Politics, and Working Class History* (London: Verso, 1994), 184–190.

79. *SDN*, 15 July 1907, p. 8. *SDN*, 25 March 1905, p. 4; 20 September 1907, p. 1.

80. *PODJ*, 12 June 1907, p. 1. *Vancouver Daily News Advertiser*, 1 June 1909, p. 7; *VDP*, 17 July 1902, p. 1; 13 June 1908, p. 1; 10 December 1909, p. 5; *PODJ*, 14 November 1907, p. 1; 7 June 1909, p. 2; *PO*, 16 March 1902, p. 5; 23 August 1902, p. 11.

81. *SMH*, 26 August 1905, p. 3.

82. *SMH*, 21 February 1903, p. 2.

83. *(Vancouver) Saturday Sunset*, 6 July 1907, p. 1. *Vancouver Daily News Advertiser*, 5 May 1909, p. 7; *VDP*, 22 April 1909, p. 2.

84. *VDP*, 12 August 1907, p. 6.

85. *VDP*, 10 August 1904, p. 1. *VDP*, 9 September 1904, p. 1; 4 December 1909, p. 1; *PO*, 17 April 1902, p. 7.

86. *VDP*, 10 November 1909, p. 1. *PO*, 23 April 1907, p. 10.

87. *PODJ*, 5 September 1907, p. 2. *VDP*, 20 August 1901, p. 10; 10 July 1902, p. 3; 14 February 1903, p. 1; *PO*, 8 January 1900, p. 8; 5 August 1902, p. 14; 6 September 1907, p. 1; 7 September 1907, p. 16; 5 February 1909, p. 11; *PODJ*, 13 June 1905, p. 8; 21 January 1910, p. 2; 18 May 1910, p. 10; 1 July 1910, p. 1. *VDP*, 4 April 1903, p. 1; 14 April 1903, p. 1; 15 April 1903, p. 1; 16 April 1903, p. 1; 18 April 1903, p. 1; 15 May 1903, p. 1; 2 December 1910, p. 32; *PODJ*, 22 April 1904, p. 14; 30 April 1904, p. 14; 17 March 1905, p. 1; 20 March 1905, p. 3; 21 July 1910, pp. 1, 5; 7 December 1910, p. 6; *SDN*, 7 March 1905, p. 4; 23 April 1906, p. 8.

88. *VDP*, 27 August 1907, p. 10.

89. *VDP*, 30 August 1905, p. 15.

90. *SMH*, 28 July 1906, p. 3.

91. *PO*, 1 April 1907, pp. 1, 5. *SDN*, 30 June 1906, p. 1; *PODJ*, 3 January 1905, p. 5; *PO*, 16 February 1909, p. 9; *VDP*, 10 December 1903, p. 1; 11 May 1904, p. 1.

92. *PO*, 2 April 1907, p. 10.

93. *PODJ*, 1 April 1907, p. 1.

94. *PO*, 9 August 1907, pp. 1, 3.

95. *SPI*, 31 May 1910, pp. 1–2. *SPI*, 9 May 1910, p. 1.

96. The *VDP*, for example, noted in 1905 that an officer called to a Vancouver residence one night "because a man was beating his wife and daughter" found that the wife refused to charge her husband but said that she would go to the police station the next day and "lay an information." She did not. *VDP*, 23 March 1905, p. 3.

97. Letter to Police Commissioners, 25 November 1910, file 14, 75–A-6, series 181, Vancouver Police Board General Files, City of Vancouver Archives.

98. *PO*, 9 May 1907, p. 10.

99. Record of Arrests, March 1905 to 1910, City of Portland Archives and Records Center. City of Vancouver, Police Court Calendar, 1900 to 1910, City of Vancouver Archives; Police Court Reports, Cases Disposed of in Police Court, 1906, file 2, 75–A-5, series 181, City of Vancouver Archives; Vancouver Police Board General Files. *VDP*, 1 February 1901, p. 2; 31 August 1911, p. 11. One should not assume that the arrest records are an exhaustive account of arrests made in these two cities. The *VDP* commonly reported on assaults, and the great majority of arrests it described showed up in the police court's ledgers. Portland newspapers seldom reported arrests for assaults. The few it did describe were sometimes absent from its police court records. The arrest records not only include just a small fraction of actual assaults, but the ones it does describe are difficult to interpret. The fact that one person was listed as being charged with an assault and another as the complainant did not of course necessarily mean simply that the former hit the latter, even if that is what the courts decided. Indeed, police court magistrates occasionally found both parties guilty of an assault. In any event, the Portland records, in particular, not infrequently listed as the complainant an arresting officer or some other official acting on the purported victim's behalf. The identities of principals were also obscured by recorders' use of initials rather than first names, a practice that usually, though not always, indicated that the person referred to was a male. Vancouver's arrest records seldom noted race or ethnicity, although people of Asian descent can usually be identified by their names. Portland's records identified the birthplace of those charged and noted if that person was "colored" but provided no such information for the complainants. Discerning how the court disposed of cases is also tricky. A fraction of those allowed out on bail failed to return. The term "discharged" appeared often in the Portland records and could indicate that the arrestee had been sent to another court or that he or she had been released from the custody of the legal system altogether. In neither set of records can one consistently tell whether "dismissed" indicated a decision from the complainant to drop

the charges, the prosecuting attorney not to prosecute, or the court's judgement that the defendant was not guilty. Since Portland was much larger than Vancouver during this time period, I have used the arrest records from March 1905 to December 1910 for Portland and records from January 1900 to December 1910 for Vancouver.

100. Some of these averages have to be interpreted gingerly because of low numbers. Some 389 native-born white men and 179 non-Asian immigrant men were fined, but only 24 African American men, 17 women, and 8 Chinese or Japanese men. On judicial bias against African Americans accused of violent crimes see: Roger Lane, *Murder in America: A History*, 197–199; Clare V. McKanna Jr., *Homicide, Race, and Justice in the American West, 1880–1920*, 61–63; Jess Spirer, "Negro Crime," *Comparative Psychology Monographs* 16 (June 1940): 1–64.

101. Only 24 percent of the seventy-one women sentenced were fined; 42 percent of all men.

102. The Vancouver magistrates did not impose fines or jail time in roughly four cases out of ten, not quite as frequently as their Portland counterparts. Portland fines almost always appeared in monetary values rather than in days to be served in jail. Vancouver sentences appeared to be more consistent in the number of days in prison that they charged a defendant with than in the amount of their fines, hence I have used the former measure. Vancouver magistrates charged roughly $2.00 in fines for each one day in jail. Both localities were apt to fine people more heavily for assaulting women than for assaulting men. Portlanders convicted of hitting non-Asian men paid average fines of $25.75 compared to $41.98 for hitting women. The average jail time for Vancouver residents was 16.8 days for hitting a non-Asian male, 25.5 days for hitting a woman. Other types of sentences also expressed the relative seriousness of hitting a woman. Portlanders who hit a woman were about twice as likely to be sent to a higher court than those who hit men. None of the seventy-four people accused of hitting an Asian man were sent to the grand jury. Portland and Vancouver residents convicted of hitting women were much more likely to receive suspended sentences and to be asked to deposit money to guarantee that they would keep the peace than were those who hit men, a sentence that freed the accused of punishment, but warned him or her that subsequent violations would be dealt with much more severely. This was a particularly popular sentence to impose on a man who had beaten his wife, in part because fine or imprisonment in such cases often imposed financial difficulties on the woman he had hit.

103. If we were to consider only adults, immigrants would have constituted a substantially larger proportion of these two cities' populations.

104. Jess Spirer found that African Americans convicted in Pennsylvania of murder or assault from 1906 to 1935 were nearly thirty times more likely to be committed to the penitentiary than were their native-born, white counterparts. Spirer, "Negro Crime."

105. *VDP*, 31 July 1909, p. 6.

106. *VDP*, 24 September 1904, p. 8.

107. Letter from the Vancouver Moral Reform Association to the Mayor and Board of Police Commissioners, 5 May 1906, file 5, series 181, 75–A-5, City of Vancouver Archives.

108. *VDP*, 28 December 1903, p. 1. Mary E. Hallett, "A Governor-General's Views on Oriental Immigration to British Columbia, 1904–1911," *BCST*, 14 (summer 1972): 51–52; Vancouver Police Scrapbook, 1908–1909, p. 91, series 204, 42–B-33, City of Vancouver Archives; *VDP*, 5 December 1900, p. 1; 2 September 1905, p. 24; 21 February 1903, p. 1; 25 February 1905, p. 1; 2 August 1905, p. 1.

109. *Vancouver Daily World*, 3 August 1909, p. 1. *VDP*, 3 April 1905, p. 3.

110. *PO*, 6 January 1909, p. 11.

111. *PO*, 29 October 1900, p. 5. *VDP*, 25 February 1905, p. 1; *SPI*, 23 September 1910, p. 5; *SDT*, 13 March 1900, p. 8; *PODJ*, 28 October 1907, pp. 1–2.

112. *SDT*, 31 March 1900, p. 3; 10 March 1900, p. 8; *SPI*, 29 March 1910, p. 2; *SDT*, 5 August 1905, p. 1; 20 July 1905, p. 1.

113. *VDP*, 24 April 1905, p. 1; *PODJ*, 27 November 1904, p. 11; 2 October 1910, p. 1; *PO*, 23 July 1907, p. 1.

114. *VDP*, 4 April 1902, p. 1.

115. *PODJ*, 26 January 1910, p. 1. *VDP*, 27 September 1904, p. 1.

116. *SR*, 1 June 1906, p. 1. *SR*, 4 January 1901, p. 1.

117. *SR*, 20 July 1900, p. 1.

5 / TO DO JUST AS HE PLEASED

1. Robert Ormond Case, *Riders of the Grande Ronde* (Garden City, New York: Doubleday, Doran, and Company, 1928), 68.

2. John Fahey, *The Inland Empire: Unfolding Years, 1879–1929* (Seattle: University of Washington Press, 1986), 157–171; Carlos Arnaldo Schwantes, *The Pacific Northwest: An Interpretive History*, rev. ed., 363–374; Jean Barman, *The West Beyond the West: A History of British Columbia*, rev. ed., 225–230, 236–247; Dorothy E. Chunn, "'Just Plain Everyday Housekeeping on a Grand Scale': Feminists, Family Courts, and the Welfare

State in British Columbia, 1928–1945," in *Law, Society, and the State: Essays in Modern Legal History,* ed. Louis A. Knafla and Susan W. S. Binnie (Toronto: University of Toronto Press, 1995), 379–404; Norah L. Lewis, "Creating the Little Machine: Child Rearing in British Columbia, 1919–1939," *BCST* 56 (winter 1982–1983): 44–60; Lewis, "Reducing Maternal Mortality in British Columbia: An Educational Process," in *Not Just Pin Money: Selected Essays on the History of Women's Work in British Columbia,* ed. Barbara K. Latham and Roberta J. Pazdro, 337–349; Megan J. Davies, "'Services Rendered, Rearing Children for the State': Mothers' Pensions in British Columbia, 1919–1931," in *Not Just Pin Money,* 249–263; Carolyn Strange and Tina Loo, *Making Good: Law and Moral Regulation in Canada, 1867–1939* (Toronto: University of Toronto Press, 1997).

    3. Warren I. Susman, *Culture as History: The Transformation of American Society in the Twentieth Century* (New York: Pantheon, 1984), 105–149; Kevin White, *The First Sexual Revolution: The Emergence of Male Heterosexuality in Modern America* (New York: New York University Press, 1993); Gail Bederman, *Manliness and Civilization: A Cultural History of Gender and Race in the United States, 1880–1917* (Chicago: University of Chicago Press, 1995); D. Owen Carrigan, *Crime and Punishment in Canada: A History* (Toronto: McClelland and Stewart, 1991), 74–81; Harrow Van Brummelen, "Shifting Perspectives: Early British Columbia Textbooks from 1872 to 1925," in *Schools in the West: Essays in Canadian Educational History,* ed. Nancy M. Sheehan, J. Donald Wilson, and David C. Jones (Calgary: Detselig Enterprises, 1986), 18–22; Arnoldo Testi, "The Gender of Reform Politics. Theodore Roosevelt and the Culture of Masculinity," JAH 81 (March 1995): 1515–1518; Cleve Dheensaw, *Lacrosse 100: One Hundred Years of Lacrosse in B.C.* (Victoria: Orca, 1990), 10–12.

    4. Arthur Mayse, *My Father, My Friend,* ed. Susan Mayse (Madeira Park, British Columbia: Harbour, 1993), 9–12, 74–75.

    5. Garry Andrews, *Metis Outpost: Memoirs of the First Schoolmaster of the Metis Settlement of Kelly Lake, B.C., 1923–1925* (Victoria, British Columbia: G. Smedley Andrews, 1985), 135. In both this example and the preceding one, parents objected to their sons boxing.

    6. Robert Ballou, *Early Klickitat Valley Days* (Goldendale, Washington: Goldendale Sentinel, 1938), 482, 484. Play was also rough on and around the lacrosse fields of Vancouver and New Westminster early in the twentieth century, as players and fans alike sometimes brawled. One of Vancouver's most noteworthy sports riots occurred in 1908, when fans poured onto the field and attacked the visiting players, apparently because their manager had the temerity to walk intentionally the home team's lead-

ing hitter. Robin John Anderson, "'On the Edge of the Baseball Map' with the 1908 Vancouver Beavers," *CHR* 77 (December 1996): 570–571; *VDP*, 26 July 1901, p. 4; 14 August 1901, p. 9; 10 June 1909, p. 8; *Vancouver Daily World*, 12 August 1909, p. 8; *(Vancouver) Western Call*, 8 July 1910, p. 1; Colin D. Howell, *Northern Sandlots: A Social History of Maritime Baseball* (Toronto: University of Toronto Press, 1995), 97–119. Early-twentieth-century baseball games in mining and logging communities often included fights as well. Diane Olson and Cary Olson, eds., *Black Diamond: Mining the Memories: An Oral History of Life in a Company Town* (Seattle: Frontier, 1988), 173; Sam Churchill, *Don't Call Me Ma* (Garden City, New York: Doubleday, 1977), 63; Merritt Des Voigne, *Being Small Wasn't Bad at All* (Seattle: Littleman Press, 1982), 6.

7. Egbert S. Oliver, *The Shaping of a Family: A Memoir* (Portland, Oregon: Ha Pi Press, 1979), 193. Jean Barman, *Growing Up British in British Columbia: Boys in Private School* (Vancouver: University of British Columbia Press, 1984), 63–77; Edmund Arthur Hunt, "A History of Physical Education in the Public Schools of British Columbia from 1918 to 1967" (M.A. thesis, University of Washington, 1967), 6–21; Elliott J. Gorn, *The Manly Art: Bare-Knuckle Prize Fighting in America* (Ithaca, New York: Cornell University Press, 1986), 179–206; Norbert Elias and Eric Dunning, "The Quest for Excitement in Unexciting Societies," in *The Cross-Cultural Analysis of Sport and Games*, ed. Gunther Lüschen (Champaign, Illinois: Stipes, 1970), 31–51; Joan Adams and Becky Thomas, *Floating Schools and Frozen Inkwells: The One-Room Schools of British Columbia* (Madeira Park, British Columbia: Harbour, 1985), 144; Wallace Ohrt, *The Rogue I Remember* (Seattle: Mountaineers, 1979), 23; Bob Barry, *From Shamrocks to Sagebrush* (Lakeview, Oregon: Examiner, 1969), 187–193; Henry Penner, *Chiefly Indian: The Warm and Witty Story of a British Columbia Half Breed Logger*, ed. Herbert L. McDonald (West Vancouver: Graydonald Graphics, 1972), 44–46.

8. Alex Philip, *The Painted Cliff* (Ottawa: Graphic Publishers, 1927), 171; Bertrand W. Sinclair, *Poor Man's Rock* (New York: A. L. Burt, 1920); Sinclair, *The Inverted Pyramid* (Toronto: Frederick D. Goodchild, 1924); Robert Watson, *The Spoilers of the Valley* (Toronto: McClelland and Stewart, 1921); Watson, *Gordon of the Lost Lagoon: A Romance of the Pacific Coast* (New York: Minton, Balch, and Company, 1924).

9. Charles Alexander, *The Splendid Summits* (New York: Dodd, Mead, and Company, 1925), 278; Ernest Haycox, *Free Grass* (Garden City, New York: Doubleday, Doran, and Company, 1929). Stephen L. Tanner, *Ernest Haycox* (New York: Twayne; London: Prentice Hall International, 1996); Richard Wayne Etulain, "The Literary Career of a Western Writer: Ernest Haycox, 1899–1950" (Ph.D. diss., University of Oregon, 1966); Etulain, *Ernest Haycox* (Boise, Idaho: Boise State University, 1988);

Howard McKinley Corning, "Charles Alexander: Youth of the Oregon Mood," *OHQ* 74 (March 1973): 34–70.

10. Edison Marshall, *The Isle of Retribution* ([New York: A. L. Burt, 1923]); Ernest Haycox, *Chaffee of Roaring Horse* (New York: Popular Library, 1930); Case, *Riders of the Grande Ronde*. An earlier novel by Marshall, *The Strength of the Pines* (Boston: Little, Brown, and Company, 1921), features a masculine protagonist who is more wary of physical combat. Jane Tompkins, *West of Everything: The Inner Life of Westerns* (New York: Oxford University Press, 1992), is a provocative study of westerns and gender.

11. Corning, "Charles Alexander," 44–45.

12. Warren L. Clare, "Big Jim Stevens: A Study in Pacific Northwest Literature" (Ph.D. diss., Washington State University, 1967), 5, 7, 87–88, 129; James Stevens, *Brawny-Man* (New York: Alfred A. Knopf, 1926); Stevens, *Homer in the Sagebrush* (New York: Alfred A. Knopf, 1928).

13. Churchill, *Don't Call Me Ma*, 63.

14. Virgil Davis Jackson, "Social Conflict in Rural Communities of Oregon" (M.S. thesis, Oregon State Agricultural College, 1932), 112. Joe Garner, *Never Chop Your Rope: A Story of British Columbia Logging and the People Who Logged* (Nanaimo, British Columbia: Cinnibar Press, 1988), 198.

15. Bill Riley and Laura Leake, *History and Events of the Early 1920s: A Mounted Policeman's Bird's-eye View of the Old Cariboo Country, British Columbia, Canada* (New York: Vantage, 1980), 31, 14–16, 22. Files KIT 75–37sa, Jack Ness interview, KIT 76–64sa, Neil McGovern interview, KIT 76–70sa, Steve Labusky interview, Kittitas County Oral History Project, Washington State Archives, Olympia; PGC, 14 April 1922, p. 1; Ralph R. Sawdy, "Woolgathering: 1924, or 1924: The Year I Grew Up," *Pacific Northwest Forum* 9 (winter 1984): 44–46; Ray Nelson, *Memories of an Oregon Moonshiner* (Caldwell, Idaho: Caxton, 1980), 76.

16. W. L. Morton, ed., assisted by Vera K. Fast, *God's Galloping Girl: The Peace River Diaries of Monica Storrs, 1929–1931* (Vancouver: University of British Columbia Press, 1979), 11, 23.

17. Roger Lane, *Murder in America: A History*, 241, 239–240. Lane notes that the decline may well have flattened out during the 1920s. Mortality Statistics [1920–1929] (Washington, D.C.: Government Printing Office, [1922–1932]); Registers and Indexes to Coroners' Inquiries and Inquests, GR 432/B7894, British Columbia Archives and Records Service, Victoria. It was necessary to check some of these cases further, in Coroners' Inquiries and Inquests, GR 1327/B2404–26, British Columbia Archives and Records Service.

18. Judy M. Torrance, *Public Violence in Canada, 1867–1982* (Kingston, Ontario: McGill-Queen's University Press, 1986), 124; Angus McLaren, "Males, Migrants, and Murder in British Columbia, 1900–1923," in *On the Case: Explorations in Social History,* ed. Franca Iacovetta and Wendy Mitchinson (Toronto: University of Toronto Press, 1998), 159–180.

19. Priscilla Tiller, *The Wooden Bench: Inkwells, Slates, and Coping Saws* (Adna, Washington: Fernwood Press, 1991), 369. Michel Foucault, *Discipline and Punish: The Birth of the Prison,* trans. Alan Sheridan (New York: Vintage, 1995, orig. 1977); Herbert Arnold Falk, *Corporal Punishment: A Social Interpretation of Its Theory and Practice in the Schools of the United States* (New York: Columbia University, 1941), 124, 137; Veronica Strong-Boag, "Intruders in the Nursery: Childcare Professionals Reshape the Years One to Five, 1920–1940," in *Childhood and Family in Canadian History,* ed. Joy Parr (Toronto: McClelland and Stewart, 1982), 160–178; F. Henry Johnson, "Changing Conceptions of Discipline and Pupil-Teacher Relations in Canadian Schools," 54–56; Norah Lillian Lewis, "Advising the Parents: Child Rearing in British Columbia During the Inter-War Years" (Ph.D. diss., University of British Columbia, 1980), 107–109.

20. *(Coupeville) Island County Times,* 21 October 1921, p. 2. *PGC,* 13 February 1923, p. 1.

21. Frank Pierce, *Pierce's Code: State of Washington* (Seattle: National Law Book Company, 1921), vol. 2: 2551.

22. *Revised Statutes of Canada,* 1927 (Ottawa: Frederick Albert Acland, 1927), vol. 1: 681.

23. Thomas Fleming and Carolyn Smyly, "The Diary of Mary Williams: A Cameo of Rural Schooling in British Columbia, 1922–1924," in *Children, Teachers, and Schools in the History of British Columbia,* ed. Jean Barman and Neil Sutherland (Calgary: Detselig Enterprises, 1995), 275. Mel Rothenburger, *Friend o' Mine: The Story of Flyin' Phil Gaglardi* (Victoria: Orca, 1991), 7; *(Raymond) Advertiser,* 21 October 1926, p. 1; Tiller, *Wooden Bench,* 323; Keith Franklin James, *Corporal Punishment in the Public Schools* (Los Angeles: University of Southern California, 1963), 52; Ralph William Macy, *Wooden Sidewalks: Growing Up in Western Washington,* 2nd ed. (Portland, Oregon: Hapi Press, 1983), 171–172; Elda Copley Mason, *Lasqueti Island: History and Memory* (n.p.: AdMan Printing, 1976), 39; Jackson, "Social Conflict in Rural Communities of Oregon," 73–74; Fred C. Bohm and Craig E. Holstine, *The People's History of Stevens County* (Colville, Washington: Stevens County Historical Society, 1983), 66; Ohrt, *Rogue I Remember,* 21; Jessie Bond Sugden, *In the Shadow of the Cutbanks* (n.p.: n.p., 1985), 3.

24. Grace Brandt Martin, *An Oregon Schoolma'am* (Brownsville, Oregon: Calapooia Publishers, 1981), vol. 2: 11. Andrews, *Metis Outpost*, 135; File KIT 75–19sa, Fern Haberman interview, Kittitas County Oral History Project; E. R. Huckleberry, *The New Adventures of Dr. Huckleberry: Tillamook County, Oregon* (Portland: Oregon Historical Society, 1970), 101–102.

25. Johnson, "Changing Conceptions of Discipline," 49–50; Tiller, *Wooden Bench*, 213, 214–215. Falk, *Corporal Punishment*, 124, 126–127, 137; James, *Corporal Punishment in the Public Schools*, 26–27.

26. Olson and Olson, *Black Diamond*, 145.

27. Richard Hugo, *The Real West Marginal Way: A Poet's Autobiography*, ed. Ripley S. Hugo, Lois M. Welch, and James Welch (New York: W. W. Norton, 1986), 5. Brent Walth, *Fire at Eden's Gate: Tom McCall and the Oregon Story* (Portland: Oregon Historical Society Press, 1994), 44.

28. Rothenburger, *Friend o' Mine*, 6, 9. Phil reported that his father stopped this sort of extreme punishment when he converted from Catholicism to Pentecostalism. Beverly Cleary, *A Girl from Yamhill: A Memoir* (New York: William Morrow, 1988), 46–47; Des Voigne, *Being Small Wasn't Bad At All*, 74–76. Mary E. Steele, *I'll Make a Face: The Story of My Life* (Stanwood, Washington: n.p., [1985]), 55; Dorothy Gallagher, *Hannah's Daughters: Six Generations of an American Family, 1876–1976* (New York: Thomas Y. Crowell, 1976), 159, 163; Tiller, *Wooden Bench*, 326; Johnie (Cactus) Smyth, *Footloose and Ahorseback: Memories of a Buckaroo on Steens Mountain, Oregon*, ed. Marilyn Carter (Bend, Oregon: Maverick Publications, 1984), 123; Monty R. Eaton, *Out Behind the Barn* (Spokane: Kroma International Graphics Center, 1982), 67; Cyril Shelford, *From Snowshoes to Politics* (Victoria: Orca, 1987), 23; Dennie D. McCart, *Memories of Edenbrook Farm* (Portland, Oregon: Binford and Mort, 1984), 48–49, 59; Ed Gould, *Ralph Edwards of Lonesome Lake* (North Vancouver, British Columbia: Hancock House, 1981), 137; Huckleberry, *The Adventures of Dr. Huckleberry*, 101–102; Lila Fuhriman, *In Our Day* (Fairfield, Washington: Ye Galleon Press, 1989), 11; Joe Garner, *Never Fly over an Eagle's Nest* (Nanaimo, British Columbia: Cinnabar Press, 1982), 165–166; Garner, *Never Chop Your Rope*, 165. As in the nineteenth century, newspapers and divorce-seekers complained only of extreme acts of parental cruelty. Neil Sutherland, *Growing Up: Childhood in English Canada from the Great War to the Age of Television* (Toronto: University of Toronto Press, 1997), 84–89; David I. Macleod, *The Age of the Child: Children in America, 1890–1920* (New York: Twayne; London: Prentice Hall International, 1998), 54–60, 92–94; Robert L. Griswold, *Fatherhood in America: A History* (New York: Basic Books, 1993), 49–51, 104; *PRDN*, 8 April 1926,

p. 1; *Powell River News,* 19 April 1928, p. 2; *Greenwood Ledger,* 13 September 1923, p. 1; cases 1772, 2077, 2652, 3027, Deschutes County Circuit Court, Deschutes County Courthouse, Bend; case JR 1306–4481, Grant County Circuit Court, Grant County Courthouse, Canyon City; case 8/1928, British Columbia court, further information withheld to protect privacy, British Columbia Archives and Records Service; case 17592, Whatcom County Superior Court, civil case files, Washington State Archives, Northwest Region, Bellingham; cases 2308, 2508, 3151, 6856, 7071, 7249, 7306, 7350, Coos County Circuit Court, Coos County Courthouse, Coquille; case 931, Wheeler County Circuit Court, Wheeler County Courthouse, Fossil; case 6/1928, British Columbia court, further information withheld to protect privacy; cases 7071, 7897, Benton County Circuit Court, Oregon State Archives, Salem.

29. Multnomah County Coroner's investigation books, Multnomah County Medical Examiner's Office, Portland; U.S. Bureau of the Census, *Mortality Statistics* [1908–1910, 1920–1929] (Washington, D.C.: Government Printing Office, [1910–1913, 1922–1932]).

30. Case 3151, Deschutes County Circuit Court.

31. Walth, *Fire at Eden's Gate,* 44.

32. Case 18473, Whatcom County Superior Court, civil case files. Jill Beth Schlessinger, "'Such Inhuman Treatment': Family Violence in the Chicago Middle Class, 1871–1920" (Ph.D. diss., University of California, Berkeley, 1998), 72–105.

33. *Reports of Cases Decided in the State of Oregon* (San Francisco: Bancroft-Whitney, 1922), vol. 100: 398. Case 7455, Coos County Circuit Court; cases 1909, 1979, 2176, Deschutes County Circuit Court.

34. Case 2652, Deschutes County Circuit Court. Case 931, Wheeler County Circuit Court.

35. Case 3/1929, court location withheld to protect privacy, British Columbia Archives and Records Service.

36. Case 1927, British Columbia court, location withheld to protect privacy. Case 86/1926, BCAGC.

37. Case 78/1922, BCAGC. The daughter had never told anyone because "he said that he had me between his thumb and fingers," that he "would put me where the dogs would not bark at me whenever he wanted to." This father also asserted this prerogative to his wife: "Whatever he said she had to abide by it . . . whatever he did she had nothing to say."

38. Case 120/1922, BCAGC.

39. Case 78/1922, BCAGC. Linda Gordon and Paul O'Keefe, "Incest as a Form of

Family Violence: Evidence from Historical Case Records," in *Family in Transition: Rethinking Marriage, Sexuality, Child Rearing, and Family Organization,* 5th ed., ed. Arlene S. Skolnick and Jerome H. Skolnick (Boston: Little, Brown, 1986), 456–467; Gordon, *Heroes of Their Own Lives: The Politics and History of Family Violence, Boston, 1880–1960,* 204–249.

40. Case 121/1928, BCAGC.

41. Case 92/1922, BCAGC.

42. Cases 36/1929, 28/1928, BCAGC.

43. Case 36/1929, BCAGC.

44. Newspapers, further information withheld to protect privacy, pp. 1, 6, pp. 1, 4, 6. The complainant did not claim that the defendants had penetrated her. She said that they held her down and bruised her before fleeing.

45. Newspaper, further information withheld to protect privacy, p. 4. Case 105/1928, BCAGC; newspapers, further information withheld to protect privacy, p. 5, pp. 1, 5.

46. Case 8445, Benton County Circuit Court. *PRDN,* 23 March 1920, p. 2; cases 2000, 2038, 2176, 2186, 2714, 2849, Deschutes County Circuit Court; case 8428, Benton County Circuit Court; cases 6555, 7260, Coos County Circuit Court; cases 3714, 3756, Crook County Circuit Court, Crook County Courthouse, Prineville.

47. David Peterson del Mar, *What Trouble I Have Seen: A History of Violence Against Wives,* 120–126.

48. Case 3480, Deschutes County Circuit Court. Case 11/1928, British Columbia court, further information withheld to protect privacy; case 994, Wheeler County Circuit Court; case 1936, Deschutes County Circuit Court; *(Colfax) Statesman Index Patriot,* 6 May 1927, p. 6. Peterson del Mar, *What Trouble I Have Seen,* 113–118; White, *First Sexual Revolution;* Schlessinger, "'Such Inhuman Treatment,'" 106–163; Terry L. Chapman, "'Til Death Do Us Part': Wife Beating in Alberta, 1905–1920," *Alberta History* 36 (autumn 1988): 13–22. The number of Oregon women who were victims of homicide had decreased by the 1920s. Some 22 percent of Oregon's murder victims in 1895 were women, 24 percent for five years in the 1920s. Yet women were a much larger proportion of the population by the latter dates. The proportion of homicide victims in British Columbia who were female grew dramatically from the 1890s to the 1920s, rising from 18 percent to 23 percent. But women's proportion of the province's population had also increased markedly, from 36 percent to 44 percent.

49. Case 2731, Deschutes County Circuit Court.

50. *Reports of Cases Decided in the Supreme Court of the State of Oregon* (San Francisco: Bancroft-Whitney, 1922), vol. 100: 174.

51. Case 11/1928, British Columbia court, further information withheld to protect privacy.

52. *Reports of Cases Decided in the Supreme Court of the State of Oregon* (San Francisco: Bancroft-Whitney, 1922), vol. 100: 403. *Reports of Cases Decided in the Supreme Court of the State of Oregon* (San Francisco: Bancroft-Whitney, 1925), vol. 111: 640.

53. *Cases Determined in the Supreme Court of Washington* (Seattle: Bancroft-Whitney, 1921), vol. 113: 251.

54. *Reports of Cases Decided in the Supreme Court of the State of Oregon* (San Francisco: Bancroft-Whitney, 1920), vol. 95: 578–579.

55. Case 7616, Benton County Circuit Court. James Snell, "Marital Cruelty: Women and the Nova Scotia Divorce Court, 1900–1939," *Acadiensis* 18 (autumn 1988): 20–21.

56. Case 2728, Deschutes County Circuit Court. Case 2844, Deschutes County Circuit Court.

57. Case 3322, Deschutes County Circuit Court. This woman's testimony suggested that her purported submission was tinctured by a lack of respect. She remarked that she had "humored him in every way I could, —made a baby out of him."

58. Case 2236, Deschutes County Circuit Court. Case 2982, Deschutes County Circuit Court.

59. Cases 2982, 3195, 3318, Deschutes County Circuit Court.

60. Case 3219, Deschutes County Circuit Court.

61. Case 3294, Deschutes County Circuit Court.

62. Case 2840, Deschutes County Circuit Court. Cases 1678, 1819, 2859, 3411, Deschutes County Circuit Court.

63. Case 28/1920, British Columbia court, further information withheld to protect privacy. Cases 6555, 6561, 6580, 6667, 7292, Coos County Circuit Court; cases 7624, 8469, Benton County Circuit Court; cases 2683, 3480, Deschutes County Circuit Court.

64. Case 6539, Coos County Circuit Court.

65. Peterson del Mar, *What Trouble I Have Seen*, 132.

66. Case JR 1557/4688, Grant County Circuit Court.

67. Case 728A/CC220, volume 1529, Capital Cases, RG 13, National Archives of Canada, Ottawa. Cases 1856, 2508, Deschutes County Circuit Court; cases 6593, 7172, Coos County Circuit Court.

68. Case 972, Wheeler County Circuit Court.

69. *Kamloops Sentinel*, 14 October 1924, p. 1; 24 October 1924, p. 1; 31 October 1924, p. 4.

70. Gallagher, *Hannah's Daughters,* 159–160.

71. Case 1925, British Columbia court, further information withheld to protect privacy. Case 2176, Deschutes County Circuit Court; cases 7455, 7071, 6667, 7427, Coos County Circuit Court; cases 1909, 2077, Deschutes County Circuit Court.

72. Case 1924, British Columbia court, further information withheld to protect privacy; case 7310, Coos County Circuit Court; case 3677, Crook County Circuit Court; cases 3027, 3219, Deschutes County Circuit Court.

73. *PRDN,* 15 September 1922, p. 1. Case 2373, Deschutes County Circuit Court; case 6946, Coos County Circuit Court; cases 1626, 2130, 2186, 2772, Deschutes County Circuit Court.

74. Case 3480, Deschutes County Circuit Court. Some husbands became violent when their wives refused to go out or stay out with them. Case 8515, Benton County Circuit Court; cases 1819, 3294, Deschutes County Circuit Court.

75. Case 3411, Deschutes County Circuit Court.

76. Case 3347, Deschutes County Circuit Court.

77. Case 3448, Deschutes County Circuit Court.

78. Case 2849, Deschutes County Circuit Court. Cases 2087, 2096, 2114, 2330, Deschutes County Circuit Court. One wife complained that her husband threatened to beat her when she refused to pack up and leave their home. Case 7249, Coos County Circuit Court.

79. Case C-83, box 1, Thurston County Prosecuting Attorney, criminal cases, Washington State Archives Southwest Region, Olympia.

80. Case 1626, Deschutes County Circuit Court. Case 6736, Coos County Circuit Court; cases 2079, 2287, Deschutes County Circuit Court.

81. Case 1979, Deschutes County Circuit Court. Cases 1926, 1678, Deschutes County Circuit Court; cases 6903, 6593, Coos County Circuit Court.

82. Case 3490, Deschutes County Circuit Court.

83. Case 10/1928, British Columbia court, further information withheld to protect privacy.

84. Case 227/1921, British Columbia court, further information withheld to protect privacy.

85. Nelson, *Memoirs of an Oregon Moonshiner,* 19–20. Estelle Freedman, "Separatism as Strategy: Female Institution Building and American Feminism, 1870–1930," *Feminist Studies* 5 (fall 1979): 512–529; Alice Echols, *The Demise of Female Intimacy in the Twentieth Century* (Ann Arbor: Women's Studies Program, University of Michigan, 1978); Alice Kessler-Harris, *Out to Work: A History of Wage-Earning Women in the*

United States (Oxford: Oxford University Press, 1982), 217–249; Veronica Strong-Boag, *The New Day Recalled: Lives of Girls and Women in English Canada, 1919–1939,* rev. ed. (Toronto: Copp Clark Pitman, 1993), 42, 51–53, 85–86, 97–99; Mary Vipond, "The Image of Women in Mass Circulation Magazines in the 1920s," in *The Neglected Majority: Essays in Canadian Women's History,* ed. Susan Mann Trofimenkoff and Alison Prentice (Toronto: McClelland and Stewart, 1977), 116–124; Pamela S. Haag, "In Search of 'The Real Thing': Ideologies of Love, Modern Romance, and Women's Sexual Subjectivity in the United States, 1920–40," *Journal of the History of Sexuality* 2 (April 1992): 547–577; Paula Fass, *The Damned and the Beautiful: American Youth in the 1920s* (Oxford: Oxford University Press, 1977), 260–290; Joseph F. Kett, *Rites of Passage: Adolescence in America, 1790 to the Present* (New York: Basic Books, 1977), 258–264; Suzanne Morton, *Ideal Surroundings: Domestic Life in a Working-Class Suburb in the 1920s* (Toronto: University of Toronto Press, 1995), 83–85; Beth L. Bailey, *From Front Porch to Back Seat: Courtship in Twentieth-Century America* (Baltimore: Johns Hopkins University Press, 1988), 13–24. Ellen Kay Trimberger, "Feminism, Men, and Modern Love: Greenwich Village, 1900–1925," in *Powers of Desire: The Politics of Sexuality,* ed. Ann Snitow, Christine Stansell, and Sharon Thompson (New York: Monthly Review Press, 1983), 131–152.

86. Robert Pike, "Legal Access and the Incidence of Divorce in Canada: A Sociohistorical Analysis," *CRSA* 12 (May 1975): 128, 125. James G. Snell, *In the Shadow of the Law: Divorce in Canada, 1900–1939* (Toronto: University of Toronto Press, 1991), 75–266.

87. Case 19/1929, British Columbia court, further information withheld to protect privacy.

88. Case 13792, Whitman County Superior Court, Whitman County Courthouse, Colfax.

89. Case 19768, Whatcom County Superior Court, civil case files, emphasis in the original.

90. Case 18/1925, British Columbia court, further information withheld to protect privacy.

91. Case 3309, Deschutes County Circuit Court. Peterson del Mar, *What Trouble I Have Seen,* 110–113. Nancy Maclean, *Behind the Mask of Chivalry: The Making of the Second Ku Klux Klan* (New York: Oxford University Press, 1994), 113–124, argues that the Ku Klux Klan opposed women's autonomy and sought to shore up the traditional, male-dominated, paternalistic family.

92. *Kamloops Standard-Sentinel,* 1 June 1923, pp. 1, 6.

93. Case 46/1928, BCAGC. The names used in this case and the next are pseudonyms.

94. Cases 36/1920, 37/1920, British Columbia court, further information withheld to protect privacy.

95. Case 36/1920, British Columbia court, further information withheld to protect privacy.

96. Newspaper, further information withheld to protect privacy, p. 1.

97. Peterson del Mar, *What Trouble I Have Seen*, 127–128.

98. Ibid., pp. 144–146; Gordon, *Heroes of Their Own Lives*, 180, 185; *VDP*, 8 February 1967, p. 2; *VS*, 9 January 1973, p. 2; *PO*, 2 May 1996, p. B1; U.S. Bureau of the Census, *Mortality Statistics* [1920–1929] (Washington, D.C.: Government Printing Office, 1922–1932); *Vital Statistics of the United States* [1950–1969] (Washington, D.C.: Government Printing Office); Rosemary Gartner, "Homicide in Canada," in *Violence in Canada: Sociopolitical Perspectives*, ed. Jeffrey Ian Ross (Don Mills, Ontario: Oxford University Press, 1995), 196; James Q. Wilson and Richard J. Herrnstein, *Crime and Human Nature* (New York: Touchstone, 1986), 430–437; Carrigan, *Crime and Punishment in Canada*, 97–100; John Demos, *Past, Present, and Personal: The Family and Life Course in American History* (New York: Oxford University Press, 1986), 68–91; *PO*, 11 February 1996, p. G4. A provincial official noted in 1967 that British Columbians beat to death about six children per year. Six years later that estimate had doubled, to twelve. Washington criminal statistics registered 133 children who had died from abuse between 1987 to 1996, 5.2 percent of the state's total homicides for those years.

6 / BIG AS GOD ALMIGHTY AND UNDEMANDING AS DEW

1. Box 1, file B1, 75–2em, Sandy Moses interview, Black Oral History Project, Washington State Archives, Olympia.

2. Monica Sone, *Nisei Daughter* (Seattle: University of Washington Press, 1979, orig. 1953), 114.

3. John Dollard, *Caste and Class in a Southern Town* (New Haven, Connecticut: Yale University Press, 1937), 339–340; Eugene D. Genovese, *Roll, Jordan, Roll: The World the Slaves Made* (New York: Pantheon, 1974); Stewart E. Tolnay and E. M. Beck, *A Festival of Violence: An Analysis of Southern Lynchings, 1882–1930* (Urbana: University of Illinois Press, 1995), 1–16; Stewart E. Tolnay and E. M. Beck, "Black Flight: Lethal Violence and the Great Migration, 1900–1930," *Social Science History* 14 (fall 1990): 347–370; J. William Harris, "Etiquette, Lynching, and Racial Boundaries in Southern

History: A Mississippi Example," *American Historical Review* 100 (April 1995): 387–410; Leon F. Litwack, *Trouble in Mind: Black Southerners in the Age of Jim Crow* (New York: Alfred A. Knopf, 1998), 150–163.

4. Lawrence W. Levine, *Black Culture and Black Consciousness: Afro-American Folk Thought from Slavery to Freedom* (New York: Oxford University Press, 1977), 419–420 (quote), 407–420. Dollard, *Caste and Class in a Southern Town*, 358–361, 274–275. Litwack, *Trouble in Mind*, 422–428, 433–447; Jeffrey T. Sammons, *Beyond the Ring: The Role of Boxing in American Society* (Urbana: University of Illinois Press, 1988), 39–40; Richard Wright, *Black Boy: A Record of Childhood and Youth* (New York: Harper and Row, 1937).

5. Roger Lane, *Violent Death in the City: Suicide, Accident, and Murder in Nineteenth-Century Philadelphia*, 112 (quote), 104–113. H. C. Brearley, *Homicide in the United States* (New Jersey: Patterson Smith, 1969, orig. 1932), 97–116; Lane, *Roots of Violence in Black Philadelphia, 1860–1900* (Cambridge, Massachusetts: Harvard University Press, 1986); Clare V. McKanna Jr., *Homicide, Race, and Justice in the American West, 1880–1920*, 45–77.

6. *VDBC*, 30 April 1863, p. 3. Kinahan Cornwallis, *The New El Dorado; or, British Columbia* (New York: Arno Press, 1973, orig. 1858), 283; *VDBC*, 26 September 1861, p. 3; 25 February 1862, p. 3; 2 April 1862, p. 3; 12 December 1863, p. 3; *PO*, 26 July 1865, p. 3.

7. *CC*, 8 August 1890, p. 1; *(Colfax) Weekly Commoner*, 6 March 1894, p. 1; *EC*, 7 August 1890, p. 3.

8. *Sixteenth Census of the United States: 1940, Population, Volume 2, Characteristics of the Population* (Washington, D.C.: Government Printing Office, 1943), part 7: 421, part 5: 1048; Dorothy O. Johansen and Charles M. Gates, *Empire of the Columbia: A History of the Pacific Northwest*, 2nd ed., 608; Calvin F. Schmid, assisted by Laura Hildreth Hoffland and Bradford H. Smith, *Social Trends in Seattle* (Seattle: University of Washington Press, 1944), 130.

9. Robert W. O'Brien, "Profiles: Seattle," *Journal of Educational Sociology* 19 (October 1945): 148; Daniel G. Hill, "The Negro in Oregon: A Survey" (M.A. thesis, University of Oregon, 1932), 48–49.

10. Virgil Davis Jackson, "Social Conflicts in Rural Communities of Oregon" (M.S. thesis, Oregon State Agricultural College, 1932), 112–113.

11. Case 3162, Deschutes County Circuit Court, Deschutes County Courthouse, Bend.

12. Races and Crimes Research Paper, Sociology 156, mid-1930s, file 8–26, Norman S.

Hayner Papers, University of Washington Manuscripts and University Archives, Seattle.

13. Henry Broderick, *The Commandment Breakers of Walla Walla* (Seattle: Frank McCaffrey, 1934), 66.

14. "Kathryn Hall Bogle's 'An American Negro Speaks of Color,'" *OHQ* 89 (spring 1988): 78. Marilyn P. Watkins, *Rural Democracy: Family Farmers and Politics in Western Washington, 1890–1925* (Ithaca, New York: Cornell University Press, 1995), 40–44.

15. "Kathryn Hall Bogle's 'An American Negro Speaks of Color,'" 79.

16. Hill, "Negro in Oregon," 119, 54–58. Elizabeth McLagan, *A Peculiar Paradise: A History of Blacks in Oregon, 1788–1940*, 114–117.

17. Quintard Taylor, *The Forging of a Black Community: Seattle's Central District from 1870 through the Civil Rights Era*, 62, 75, 49–78.

18. Box 1, file B1, 75–3em, Ernest White interview, and box 4, file B1, 76–55em, Elva Nicholas interview, Black Oral History Project.

19. Edwin C. Berry, "Profiles: Portland," *Journal of Educational Sociology* 19 (October 1945): 158–159. Taylor, *Forging of a Black Community*, 81–98, 137–142; McLagan, *Peculiar Paradise*, 142–144, 129–133, 118–127; Hill, "Negro in Oregon," 59–61, 112–113, 52–54; Diane L. Pancoast, "Blacks in Oregon (1940–50)," in *Blacks in Oregon: A Statistical and Historical Report*, ed. William A. Little and James E. Weiss (Portland, Oregon: Portland State University, 1978), 39–40; box 1, file B1, 75–8em, Gertrude Simons interview, and box 5, file B, 76–60em, Albert Smith interview, Black Oral History Project; *PO*, 16 February 1939, p. 4.

20. Taylor, *Forging of a Black Community*, 155. Schmid, *Social Trends in Seattle*, 140.

21. Horace R. Cayton, *Long Old Road* (New York: Trident Press, 1965), 5, 42–48. McLagan, *Peculiar Paradise*, 110–111; Hill, "Negro in Oregon," 122; Lane, *Roots of Violence in Black Philadelphia*, 95–133, 144–161; Clifford Frederick Johnson, "An Analysis of Negro News and Non-News Matter Appearing in Four Oregon Daily Newspapers During the Years, 1931, 1936, 1941, 1945, and 1948" (M.A. thesis, University of Oregon, 1949), 79–80; Tolbert Hall Kennedy, "Racial Survey of the Intermountain Northwest," *Research Studies of the State College of Washington* 14 (September 1946): 223.

22. Box 3, file B1, 76–42em, Elva Nicholas interview, Black Oral History Project, emphasis in the original.

23. Box 4, file B1, 76–55em, Elva Nicholas interview, Black Oral History Project. Box 2, file B1, 75–27em, Joseph Staton interview, Black Oral History Project; "Kathryn Hall Bogle's 'An American Negro Speaks of Color,'" 73.

24. Box 1, file B1, 75–18em, Fern Proctor interview, box 2, file B1, 75–22em, Arlie Chappel interview, box 3, file B1, 76–45em, Louise Gayton Adams interview, Black Oral History Project.

25. Cayton, *Long Old Road*, 80–92.

26. Cayton, *Long Old Road*, 29, 10–11.

27. McLagan, *Peculiar Paradise*, 141.

28. Box 3, file B1, 76–42em, Nicholas interview.

29. Esther Hall Mumford, ed., *Seven Stars and Orion: Reflections of the Past* (Seattle: Ananse Press, 1986), 34.

30. Box 3, file B1, 76–42em, Nicholas interview.

31. Box 4, file B1, 76–57em, Juanita Proctor interview, Black Oral History Project.

32. Mumford, *Seven Stars and Orion*, 34–35. Box 5, file B1, 76–66em, George Scott interview, Black Oral History Project.

33. Box 1, file B1, 75–14em, Letcher Yarbrough interview, Black Oral History Project. Moses interview; McLagan, *Peculiar Paradise*, 135–139; Staton interview; Cayton, *Long Old Road*, 80.

34. Staton interview.

35. Box 5, file B1, 76–69em, Genevieve Roberts interview, Black Oral History Project. Box 5, file B1, 76–68 em, Ernest White interview, Black Oral History Project. Robin D. G. Kelley, "'We Are Not What We Seem': Rethinking Black Working-Class Opposition in the Jim Crow South, *JAH* 80 (June 1993): 75–112.

36. Sylvia Junko Yanagisako, *Transforming the Past: Tradition and Kinship Among Japanese Americans*, 17, 143–144, 28; Yasuo Wakatsuki, "Japanese Emigration to the United States, 1866–1924: A Monograph," *Perspectives in American History* 12 (1979): 387–516; Calvin F. Schmid, Charles E. Nobbe, and Arlene E. Mitchell, *Nonwhite Races, State of Washington* (Olympia: Washington State Planning and Community Affairs Agency, 1968), 85; Yugi Ichioka, *The Issei: The World of the First Generation Japanese Immigrants, 1885–1924*, 52–90; Ken Adachi, *The Enemy That Never Was: A History of the Japanese Canadians*, 13–18; Daniel P. Johnson, "Anti-Japanese Legislation in Oregon, 1917–1923," *OHQ* 97 (summer 1996): 176–210; Eiichiro Azuma, "A History of Oregon's Issei, 1880–1952," *OHQ* 94 (winter 1993–1994): 315–367.

37. Schmid, Nobbe, and Mitchell, *Nonwhite Races, State of Washington,* 99; S. Frank Miyamoto, *Social Solidarity among the Japanese in Seattle* (Seattle: University of Washington Press, 1984, orig. 1939), 16; Miyamoto, "An Immigrant Community in America," in *East Across the Pacific: Historical and Sociological Studies of Japanese Immigration and Assimilation*, ed. Hilary Conroy and T. Scott Miyakawa (Santa

Barbara, California: ABC-Clio Press, 1972), 223; Miyamoto, "The Japanese Minority in the Pacific Northwest," *PNQ* 54 (October 1963): 143–149; Ichioka, *Issei*, 146–153, 164–169; Azuma, "History of Oregon's Issei," 315–367; Adachi, *Enemy That Never Was*, 133–156; Yanagisako, *Transforming the Past*, 3–4; William Toll, "Permanent Settlement: Japanese Families in Portland in 1920," *Western Historical Quarterly* 28 (spring 1997): 18–43; Ann Gomer Sunahara, *The Politics of Racism: The Uprooting of Japanese Canadians During the Second World War* (Toronto: James Lorimer, 1981), 171.

38. Schmid, Nobbe, and Mitchell, *Nonwhite Races, State of Washington*, 10; Quintard Taylor, "Blacks and Asians in a White City: Japanese Americans and African Americans in Seattle, 1890–1940," *Western Historical Quarterly* 22 (November 1991): 422–424; Jean Barman, *The West Beyond the West: A History of British Columbia*, rev. ed., 233; Forrest E. La Violette, *The Canadian Japanese and World War II: A Sociological and Psychological Account*, 77; Laurel Kimbley, interviewer and compiler, *Hastings and Main: Stories from an Inner City Neighbourhood*, ed. Jo-Anne Canning-Dew (Vancouver, British Columbia: New Star Books, 1987), 97; Ichioka, *Issei*, 244–254.

39. Linda Tamura, *The Hood River Issei: An Oral History of Japanese Settlers in Oregon's Hood River Valley*, 274. Katharine Jane Lentz, "Japanese-American Relations in Seattle" (M.A. thesis, University of Washington, 1924), 11–12; Miyamoto, *Social Solidarity among the Japanese in Seattle*, 17–18, 21, 70–71; Miyamoto, "Japanese Minority in the Pacific Northwest," 143–149; Forrest E. La Violette, *Americans of Japanese Ancestry: A Study of Assimilation in the American Community* (Toronto: Canadian Institute of International Affairs, 1945), 121–122; Adachi, *Enemy That Never Was*, 110, 157–178; Charles H. Young, Helen R. Y. Reid, and W. A. Carrothers, *The Japanese Canadians*, ed. H. A. Innis, 2nd ed. (Toronto: University of Toronto Press, 1939), 96–98, 122–131; K. Victor Ujimoto, "Contrasts in the Prewar and Postwar Japanese Community in British Columbia: Conflict and Change," *CRSA* 13 (February 1976): 81–82; Barry Broadfoot, *Years of Sorrow, Years of Shame: The Story of the Japanese Canadians in World War II* (Don Mills, Ontario: Paper Jacks, 1979, orig. 1977); La Violette, *Canadian Japanese and World War II*, 77–79; Yasuko I. Takezawa, *Breaking the Silence: Redress and Japanese American Ethnicity* (Ithaca, New York: Cornell University Press, 1995), 71.

40. Adachi, *Enemy That Never Was*, 32.

41. Daphne Marlatt, ed., *Steveston Recollected: A Japanese-Canadian History* (Victoria: Provincial Archives of British Columbia, 1975), 11.

42. Cases 151/1925, 37/1926, BCAGC. Chris Friday, *Organizing Asian American Labor: The Pacific Coast Canned-Salmon Industry, 1870–1942* (Philadelphia: Temple University Press, 1994), 106–107.

43. *SNE*, 3 April 1942, p. 1. Adachi, *Enemy That Never Was*, 388, 121–122; Kennedy, "Racial Survey of the Intermountain Northwest," 223; Norman S. Hayner, "Delinquency Areas in the Puget Sound Region," *American Journal of Sociology* 39 (November 1933): 319–321. See also: Young, Reid, and Carrothers, *Japanese Canadians*, 90–94; Lentz, "Japanese-American Relations in Seattle," 30; Daphne Marlatt and Carole Itter, eds., "Opening Doors: Vancouver's East End," *SH* 8 (1979): 84; Kazuo Ito, *Issei: A History of Japanese Immigrants in North America*, trans. Shinichiro Nakamura and Jean S. Gerard (Seattle: Executive Committee for Publication of *Issei*, 1973), 515–516, 746–749, 754–756, 758; Rolf Knight and Maya Koizumi, *A Man of Our Times: The Life-History of a Japanese-Canadian Fisherman* (Vancouver: New Star Books, 1976), 59–60; Gordon G. Nakayama, *Issei: Stories of Japanese Canadian Pioneers* (Toronto: NC Press, 1984), 82; Ichioka, *Issei*, 176–179.

44. David Suzuki, *Metamorphosis: Stages in a Life* (Toronto: Stoddart, 1987), 48–49.

45. Broadfoot, *Years of Sorrow, Years of Shame*, 21. Harami Befu, *Japan: An Anthropological Introduction* (San Francisco: Chandler, 1971), 50–55; Yanagisako, *Transforming the Past*, 18, 57–61, 105–109; La Violette, *Americans of Japanese Ancestry*, 16–19, 49–51, 112–113; Adachi, *Enemy That Never Was*, 89–91; Miyamoto, *Social Solidarity among the Japanese in Seattle*, 40–41; Tamura, *Hood River Issei*, 39, 97–100; Toll, "Permanent Settlement," 40; Evelyn Nakano Glenn, "The Dialectics of Wage Work: Japanese-American Women and Domestic Service, 1905–1940," *Feminist Studies* 6 (fall 1980): 443, 460–464; Amerika Nadeshiko, "Japanese Immigrant Women in the United States, 1900–1924," *Pacific Historical Review* 49 (May 1980): 339–357; Ito, *Issei*, 282.

46. Midge Ayukawa, "Good Wives and Wise Mothers: Japanese Picture Brides in Early Twentieth-Century British Columbia," *BCST* 105–106 (spring/summer 1995): 117–118. Karen Van Dieren, "The Response of the WMS to the Immigration of Asian Women, 1888–1942," in *Not Just Pin Money: Selected Essays on the History of Women's Work in British Columbia*, ed. Barbara K. Latham and Roberta J. Pazdro, 90–91; Tomoko Makabe, *Picture Brides: Japanese Women in Canada*, trans. Kathleen Chisato Merken (n.p.: Multicultural History Society of Ontario, 1995, orig. 1983), 78–79.

47. Ito, *Issei*, 281; case 95/1924, BCAGC.

48. Miyamoto, *Social Solidarity among the Japanese in Seattle*, 41–42. Lauren Kessler, *Stubborn Twig: Three Generations in the Life of a Japanese American Family*, 84, 148–149; Yanagisako, *Transforming the Past*, 67–70, 146–148, 170–172.

49. Sone, *Nisei Daughter*, 25.

50. Tamura, *Hood River Issei*, 16–17; Suzuki, *Metamorphosis*, 30. Sone, *Nisei Daugh-*

ter, 28, 43; La Violette, *Americans of Japanese Ancestry*, 19–29; Takezawa, *Breaking the Silence*, 64–66; Kessler, *Stubborn Twig*, 134–136.

51. Alfred W. Moltke, *Memoirs of a Logger* (College Place, Washington: College Press, 1965), 9. Miyamoto, "Japanese Minority in the Pacific Northwest," 149. Those who profited by working for or dealing with such farmers were of course not so critical of them. Jackson, "Social Conflict in Rural Communities of Oregon," 84–85.

52. Broadfoot, *Years of Sorrow, Years of Shame*, 54.

53. Adachi, *Enemy That Never Was*, 173. Hilda Glynn-Ward, *The Writing on the Wall* (Toronto: University of Toronto Press, 1974, orig. 1921); Lentz, "Japanese-American Relations in Seattle," 44–45; Carol Popp, *The Gumboot Navy* (Lantzville, British Columbia: Oolichan Books, 1988), 65; Johnson, "Anti-Japanese Legislation in Oregon," 176–210; Robert W. O'Brien, "Evacuation of Japanese from the Pacific Coast: Canadian and American Contrasts," *Research Studies of the State College of Washington* 14 (June 1946): 113–120; Roger Daniels, "The Japanese Experience in North America: An Essay in Comparative Racism," *Canadian Ethnic Studies* 9 (1977): 91–100; Daniels, "Chinese and Japanese in North America: The Canadian and American Experiences Compared," *Canadian Review of American Studies* 17 (summer 1986): 173–187; Broadfoot, *Years of Sorrow, Years of Shame*, 2–3; Rolf Knight and Maya Koizumi, *A Man of Our Times: The Life-History of a Japanese-Canadian Fisherman* (Vancouver, British Columbia: New Star Books, 1976), 72.

54. Kessler, *Stubborn Twig*, 70, 158–159.

55. Ito, *Issei*, 261, 133, 186–188. Adachi, *Enemy That Never Was*, 59–60; Stefan Tanaka, "The Toledo Incident: The Deportation of the Nikkei from an Oregon Mill Town," *PNQ* 69 (July 1978): 116–126; Lentz, "Japanese-American Relations in Seattle," 84; Tamura, *Hood River Issei*, 136–137.

56. Gordon Hirabayashi, "Growing Up American in Washington," in *Washington Comes of Age: The State in the National Experience*, ed. David H. Stratton (Pullman: Washington State University Press, 1992), 32.

57. Katsuyoshi Morita, *Powell Street Monogatari*, trans. Eric A. Sokugawa (Burnaby, British Columbia: Live Canada Publishing, 1989), v.

58. Broadfoot, *Years of Sorrow, Years of Shame*, 17. Taylor, *Forging of a Black Community*, 119–120; Ichioka, *Issei*, 180–196. Taylor, "Blacks and Asians in a White City," 403, 416–420, attributes the relative political quiescence of Seattle's Japanese Canadians to their leaders' fears that confrontation would drive white customers away from their merchants.

59. Ito, *Issei*, 185, 133.

60. Ito, *Issei*, 129. Takezawa, *Breaking the Silence*, 72; Broadfoot, *Years of Sorrow, Years of Shame*, 21; Sone, *Nisei Daughter*, 93–94, 98–99.

61. Ito, *Issei*, 263.

62. Ito, *Issei*, 131.

63. Broadfoot, *Years of Sorrow, Years of Shame*, 29.

64. Umeo Uyeda, "My Migration from British Columbia to Quebec," box 20, file 1, Japanese Canadian Research Collection, University of British Columbia Special Collections, Vancouver. Muriel Kitagawa, *This Is My Own: Letters to Wes and Other Writings on Japanese Canadians, 1941–1948*, ed. Roy Miki (Vancouver, British Columbia: Talonbooks, 1985), 91, 116–117, 191; La Violette, *Canadian Japanese and World War II*, 53; Keibo Oiwa, ed., *Stone Voices: Wartime Writings of Japanese Canadian Issei* (Montreal: Vehicule Press, 1991), 120; *(Seattle) Japanese American Courier*, 27 February 1942, p. 1; *VS*, 17 April 1943, p. 3; G. Thomas Edwards, "The Oregon Coast and Three of Its Guerrilla Organizations, 1942," *Journal of the West* 25 (July 1986): 20–34; Adachi, *Enemy That Never Was*, 200–201; Kennedy, "Racial Survey of the Intermountain Northwest," 186; Tamura, *Hood River Issei*, 169–174; Suzuki, *Metamorphosis*, 40.

65. Kathy Hogan, *Cohasset Beach Chronicles: World War II in the Pacific Northwest*, ed. Klancy Clark de Nevers and Lucy Hart (Corvallis: Oregon State University Press, 1995), 152. Deena K. Nakata, *The Gift: The Oregon Nikkei Story Retold* (n.p.: n.p., 1995), 92–93.

66. Emilie L. Montgomery, "'The war was a very vivid part of my life': The Second World War and the Lives of British Columbian Children," in *Children, Teachers, and Schools in the History of British Columbia*, ed. Jean Barman, Neil Sutherland, and J. Donald Wilson (Calgary: Detselig, 1995), 165. Craig M. Cameron, *American Samurai: Myth, Imagination, and the Conduct of Battle in the First Marine Division, 1941–1951* (Cambridge: Cambridge University Press, 1994), 124–126. Some Caucasians and particularly African Americans expressed support and sympathy for the Issei and Nisei during the war. Kitagawa, *This Is My Own*, 91; *SNE*, 3 April 1942, p. 1.

67. *VS*, 1 October 1942, p. 17; *Victoria Daily Times*, 2 April 1943, p. 2.

68. *VDP*, 17 January 1942, p. 2. *VS*, 17 January 1942, p. 17; 19 January 1942, p. 13; 17 April 1942, pp. 17, 10; *VDP*, 17 April 1942, p. 13.

69. *VS*, 18 April 1942, pp. 1, 9. Jim Fairley, *The Way We Were: The Story of the Old Vancouver Courthouse* (Burnaby, British Columbia: Hemlock Printers, 1986), 85–86.

70. *VDP*, 17 April 1942, p. 15; 18 April 1942, p. 3; 20 April 1942, p. 4. *VDP*, 27 April 1942, p. 4.

71. VS, 6 May 1943, p. 4. VS, 21 April 1942, p. 4; 23 April 1942, p. 4.

72. VDP, 27 April 1942, p. 4.

73. VDP, 21 April 1942, p. 4.

74. VS, 22 April 1942, p. 4. VS, 25 April 1942, p. 4; VDP, 24 April 1942, p. 4.

75. VS, 19 April 1943, p. 8. VDP, 1 May 1942, p. 4; 2 May 1942, p. 4. Three of the defendants were sentenced to ten years, the fourth to nine years. VS, 5 May 1943, p. 1.

76. Marlatt and Itter, "Opening Doors," 23, 122; Kitagawa, This Is My Own, 245.

77. Adachi, Enemy That Never Was, 252; O'Brien, "Evacuation of Japanese from the Pacific Coast," 113–120; Tolbert H. Kennedy, "Racial Tensions Among Japanese in the Intermountain Northwest," Research Studies of the State College of Washington 14 (June 1946): 145–150; Patricia E. Roy, "A Tale of Two Cities: The Reception of Japanese Evacuees in Kelowna and Kaslo, B.C.," BCST 87 (autumn 1990): 23–47; Marlatt and Itter, "Opening Doors," 22, 124; VS, 16 April 1943, p. 9; Broadfoot, Years of Sorrow, Years of Shame, 227; Personal Justice Denied: Report of the Commission on Wartime Relocation and Internment of Civilians (Washington, D.C.: Civil Liberties Public Education Fund; Seattle: University of Washington Press, 1997), 137–140.

78. Broadfoot, Years of Sorrow, Years of Shame, 144. Roger Daniels, "The Exile and Return of Seattle's Japanese," PNQ 88 (fall 1997): 166–171; Nakata, The Gift, 102–112.

79. Sunahara, Politics of Racism, 59. Kitagawa, This Is My Own, 116.

80. Kitagawa, This Is My Own, iv. Sunahara, Politics of Racism, 65–71; Adachi, Enemy That Never Was, 243.

81. Oiwa, Stone Voices, 121.

82. Adachi, Enemy That Never Was, 225. Takezawa, Breaking the Silence, 83; La Violette, Canadian Japanese and World War II, 154; Broadfoot, Years of Sorrow, Years of Shame, 55.

83. Broadfoot, Years of Sorrow, Years of Shame, 198–199.

84. Yon Shimizu, The Exiles: An Archival History of the World War II Japanese Road Camps in British Columbia and Ontario (Wallaceburg, Ontario: Shimizu Consulting and Publishing, 1993), 95, 96, 253, 410; Broadfoot, Years of Sorrow, Years of Shame, 147; Adachi, Enemy That Never Was, 270, 406. The crime rate of Japanese Americans during the course of the war was very low among those who moved to Spokane, in eastern Washington. Kennedy, "Racial Survey of the Intermountain Northwest," 220–221, 223–224.

85. Suzuki, Metamorphosis, 76. La Violette, Canadian Japanese and World War II;

Adachi, *Enemy That Never Was,* 269–270, 245; Sunahara, *Politics of Racism,* 60–65; [Shizuye Takashima], *A Child in Prison Camp* (New York: Tundra Books, 1971), chapter 2, p. 6.

86. Adachi, *Enemy That Never Was,* 270–271; Broadfoot, *Years of Sorrow, Years of Shame,* 199, 220–221; Oiwa, *Stone Voices,* 130–131, 138; L. J. Evenden and I. D. Anderson, "The Presence of a Past Community: Tashme, British Columbia," in *Peoples of the Living Land: Geography of Cultural Diversity in British Columbia,* ed. Julian V. Minghi (Vancouver: Tantalus Research, 1972), 54; Shimizu, *Exiles,* 413; Takezawa, *Breaking the Silence,* 94–95; Yanagisako, *Transforming the Past,* 73–75; Takashima, *Child in Prison Camp,* chapter 9, p. 1; Takeo Ujo Nakano, with Leatrice Nakano, *Within the Barbed Wire Fence: A Japanese Man's Account of His Internment in Canada* (Seattle: University of Washington Press, 1980), 14, 99; Knight and Koizumi, *A Man of Our Times,* 81–82; Valerie Matsumoto, "Japanese American Women During World War II," *Frontiers* 8 (1984): 6–14; Tamura, *Hood River Issei,* 206–207; La Violette, *Canadian Japanese and World War II,* 93, 100–101.

87. O'Brien, "Profiles: Seattle," 147–148; Charles U. Smith, "Social Change in Certain Aspects of Adjustment of the Negro in Seattle, Washington" (Ph.D. diss., State College of Washington, 1950), 79; Rudy N. Pearson, "African Americans in Portland, Oregon, 1940–1950: Work and Living Conditions—A Social History" (Ph.D. diss., Washington State University, 1996), 2, 51; Manly Maben, *Vanport* (Portland, Oregon: Oregon Historical Society, 1987), 87–88; Berry, "Profiles: Portland," 159; James T. Wiley Jr., "Race Conflict as Exemplified in a Washington Town" (M.A. thesis, State College of Washington, 1949), 9–17; Lillian Kessler, "The Social Structure of a War Housing Community: East Vanport City" (B.A. thesis, Reed College, 1945), 21–24; Quintard Taylor, "The Great Migration: The Afro-American Communities of Seattle and Portland During the 1940s," *Arizona and the West* 23 (summer 1981): 109–126; Taylor, *Forging of a Black Community,* 160–163.

88. Pearson, "African Americans in Portland, Oregon," 29.

89. June Herzog, "A Study of the Negro Defense Worker in the Portland-Vancouver Area" (B.A. thesis, Reed College, 1944), 62. Pearson, "African Americans in Portland, Oregon," 52–53, passim.

90. *SNE,* 20 January 1943, p. 1. *SNE,* 31 November 1945, p. 4

91. *SNE,* 13 January 1943, p. 2.

92. Mumford, *Seven Stars and Orion,* 64.

93. Mumford, *Seven Stars and Orion,* 15. Taylor, *Forging of a Black Community,* 172–173; Taylor, "The Great Migration," 123–124; Howard A. Droker, "Seattle Race

Relations During the Second World War," *PNQ* 67 (October 1976): 167–168; Pearson, "African Americans in Portland, Oregon," 68–69, 112–113; Berry, "Profiles: Portland," 159; Smith, "Social Change in Certain Aspects of Adjustment of the Negro," 92–94; box 2, file B1, 75–26em, Sara Oliver Jackson interview, Black Oral History Project; Smith interview; box 5 file B1, 76–61em, Ina Toney interview, Black Oral History Project; box 3, file B1, 76–38em, Ruby Bell interview, Black Oral History Project.

94. Taylor, *Forging of a Black Community*, 159–189; Taylor, "Great Migration," 113; Droker, "Seattle Race Relations During the Second World War," 164–167; Pearson, "African Americans in Portland, Oregon," 97–108, 158–159; Robert W. O'Brien and Lee M. Brooks, "Race Relations in the Pacific Northwest," *Phylon* 7 (1946): 25, 28–29; O'Brien, "Profiles: Seattle," 150, 152–154; Berry, "Profiles: Portland," 160; Kennedy, "Racial Survey of the Intermountain Northwest," 237–242; Herzog, "Study of the Negro Defense Worker in the Portland-Vancouver Area," 64–81; Pancoast, "Blacks in Oregon," 42–45; Stuart McElderry, "Vanport Conspiracy Rumors and Social Relations in Portland, 1940–1950," *OHQ* 99 (summer 1998): 158–159; *PO*, 2 October 1942, p. 10; 21 March 1943, p. 15; 24 June 1945, sec. 4, p. 2.

95. Box 4, file B1, 76–55em, Elva Nicholas interview. Taylor, "Great Migration," 115–116.

96. Pearson, "African Americans in Portland, Oregon," 74–75.

97. Staton interview, emphasis in the original.

98. Smith interview.

99. Elva Nicholas interview. *PPO*, 31 July 1944, p. 7.

100. *SNE*, 29 March 1944, p. 1.

101. *SNE*, 1 July 1943, p. 1. Pearson, "African Americans in Portland, Oregon," 160–161; Droker, "Seattle Race Relations During the Second World War," 171–172; Herzog, "Study of the Negro Defense Worker," 79; *SNE*, 29 March 1944, p. 1; Kelley, "'We Are Not What We Seem,'" 102–110.

102. Herzog, "Study of the Negro Defense Worker," 75, 77; Pearson, "African Americans in Portland, Oregon," 110; Maben, *Vanport*, 89; *SNH*, 13 March 1945, p. 1; *SNE*, 8 September 1943, p. 1; Harvard Sitkoff, "Racial Militancy and Interracial Violence in the Second World War," *JAH* 58 (December 1971): 661–681; Neil A. Wynn, *The Afro-American and the Second World War* (London: Paul Elek, 1976), 100–106.

103. *PO*, 24 June 1945, sec. 4, p. 7.

104. *SNE*, 19 July 1944, p. 1. *PPO*, 15 April 1944, p. 6.

105. *SNE*, 23 August 1944, pp. 4, 1.

106. *SNE*, November 1941 to November 1945. One of the victims was sitting with

a Black man who was also killed, another was a police officer killed in a shootout, and two were store owners shot by African Americans who were apparently intending to rob them.

107. *SNE*, 31 July 1942, p. 1. *SNE*, 8 May 1942, p. 2.

108. *SNH*, 23 January 1945, p. 8.

109. See chapter two. Thirteen of the sixteen killings by African Americans in Seattle during World War II involved the use of a gun.

110. *SNE*, 30 December 1942, p. 1; 7 November 1941, p. 1; 19 January 1944, p. 1; 16 May 1945, p. 1. Two husbands killed their wives. *SNE*, 23 June 1943, p. 4; 21 March 1945, p. 3. Roger Lane, *Murder in America: A History*, 233–234, reports that 124 of 161 women committed to prison for homicides in 1926 in the United States were African American. The Seattle killings may or may not indicate that violence against wives was relatively common in the African American community; there is insufficient documentary evidence to address that question. One woman said that she killed her husband when he hit her for the first time in their ten-year marriage.

111. *SNE*, 13 January 1943, p. 1. *SNE*, 29 March 1944, p. 1.

112. *SNE*, 11 August 1943, p. 1.

113. *SNE*, 19 July 1944, p. 1. *SNE*, 5 May 1943, p. 4; *SNH*, 30 October 1945, p. 1; *PPO*, 15 April 1944, p. 6.

114. *SNE*, 29 March 1944, p. 2. *PPO*, 18 January 1945, pp. 2, 6; 31 August 1945, p. 4; *SNE*, 26 September 1941, p. 3; 24 October 1941, p. 3; 16 June 1943, p. 1; 5 April 1944, p. 1; 12 April 1944, p. 1; 21 November 1945, p. 1.

115. *SNE*, 23 August 1944, p. 1.

116. *SNE*, 27 December 1944, pp. 1, 3. *SNE*, 23 August 1944, pp. 1, 4; 13 September 1944, p. 1; 8 November 1944, pp. 1, 4; 22 November 1944, pp. 1, 4; 29 November 1944, pp. 1, 4; 6 December 1944, pp. 1, 4; 13 December 1944, pp. 1, 4; 20 December 1944, pp. 1, 5.

117. *SNE*, 28 November 1945, pp. 1, 4. *SNE*, 21 November 1945, pp. 1, 3.

118. *SNE*, 28 November 1945, pp. 1, 4.

119. *SNE*, 21 November 1945, p. 1.

120. Richard Wright, *Native Son* (New York: Harper and Row, 1966, orig. 1940), 101.

121. Ibid., 224–225, 328.

122. Ibid., xi.

123. Chester Himes, *If He Hollers Let Him Go* (New York: Thunder's Mouth Press, 1986, orig. 1947), 35.

124. Ibid., 38.

125. Ibid., 74.

126. Wright, *Native Son,* 366, emphasis in the original.

127. Willliam Attaway, *Blood on the Forge* (New York: Monthly Review Press, 1987, orig. 1941), 286, passim.

128. Ann Petry, *The Street* (London: Michael Joseph, 1947), 308, 311.

129. Arthur P. Davis, *From the Dark Tower: Afro-American Writers, 1900 to 1960* (Washington, D.C.: Howard University Press, 1974), 193–194, 162–163.

130. *PPO,* 17 August 1945, p. 4. *PO,* 16 August 1945, p. 10. *PODJ,* 16 August 1945, p. 8; Pearson, "African Americans in Portland, Oregon" 173–174.

131. Kelley, "'We Are Not What We Seem,'" 88, emphasis in the original. A number of scholars have argued that violence among poor African Americans and Natives is not as purposeless or irrational as it appears to be. Some suggest that the relatively high number of unpremeditated, alcohol-related homicides between impoverished family members or friends has expressed, albeit unconsciously, rage over marginalization. This violence, to be sure, arises from many factors, including stubborn poverty, family disintegration, and the proliferation of crack cocaine and handguns. But it is also, as several scholars have observed, "a form of achievement when everything else has failed," reflecting "a personal and subconscious struggle . . . against the threat of complete despair"—this notwithstanding the self-destructive spiral that such violence and the drug dealing that commonly accompanies it perpetuate. Richard Majors and Janet Mancini Billson, *Cool Pose: The Dilemmas of Black Manhood in America* (New York: Lexington, 1992), 33; Carl Husemoller Nightingale, *On the Edge: A History of Poor Black Children and Their American Dreams* (New York: Basic Books, 1993), 49, 130–133. Guy Lanoue, *Brothers: The Politics of Violence Among the Sekani of Northern British Columbia* (New York: Berg, 1992); Lee Maracle, *Bobbi Lee: Indian Rebel* (Toronto: Women's Press, 1990); John Edward Michael Kew, "Coast Salish Ceremonial Life: Status and Identity in a Modern Village" (Ph.D. diss., University of Washington, 1970), 56; David T. Courtwright, *Violent Land: Single Men and Social Disorder from the Frontier to the Inner City,* 225–268; James M. Messerschmidt, *Masculinities and Crime: Critique and Reconceptualization of Theory* (Lanham, Maryland: Rowman and Littlefield, 1993), 119–153; Philippe Bourgois, *In Search of Respect: Selling Crack in El Barrio* (Cambridge: Cambridge University Press, 1995); Cornel West, *Race Matters* (New York: Vintage, 1994), 128–129; Ellis Cose, *The Rage of a Privileged Class* (New York: Harper Collins, 1993), 93–110.

132. Joy Kogawa, *Obasan* (Markham, Ontario: Penguin, 1983, orig. 1981), 112.

133. Joy Kogawa, *Itsuka,* rev. ed. (Toronto: Penguin, 1993), 124.

EPILOGUE

1. *PO*, 19 September 1993, p. A1; *PWW*, 7 October 1993, p. 20; 16 December 1993, p. 23. Carl Husemoller Nightingale, *On the Edge: A History of Poor Black Children and Their American Dreams* (New York: Basic Books, 1993), 121–130; Hugh Brody, *Indians on Skid Row* (Ottawa: Northern Science Research Group, 1970), 46–48.

2. *ST*, 2 March 1991, p. A13; *VS*, 9 September 1976, p. 13; *SW*, 25 May 1994, p. 15. *PGC*, 8 October 1994, p. 5; *PO*, 2 April 1995, p. A14; 7 May 1995, p. L1; *Vancouver Times*, 3 December 1964, p. 6. Thomas Gabor, *'Everybody Does It!' Crime By the Public* (Toronto: University of Toronto Press, 1994), 23–50, points out that criminal behavior is both widely distributed in the population and identified as somebody else's problem. This fear has been fanned by popular media and politicians. The *Willamette Week*, Portland's leading alternative newspaper, in 1993 published a story entitled "The *Oregonian*'s Crime Wave," which argued that the state's large daily had been placing increased emphasis on violent crime despite statistics indicating that the violent crime rate had been steady or even declining. Likewise, the *Seattle Post-Intelligencer*, one of the city's two major newspapers, noted that it had published 648 substantial stories on crime in 1994, nearly twice as many as it had published in 1987, when the crime rate was higher. Newspapers were of course not operating in a vacuum. Crime stories had become a mainstay of television news by the 1990s and apparently translated into increased popularity and advertising revenue. Expressing concern about crime had also become a reliable way for politicians to elicit attention and support. People had become very worried about crime, especially violent crime. *PWW*, 7 October 1993, pp. 18–24; *SPI*, 27 October 1995, p. A13. Elliott Leyton, *Men of Blood: Murder in Everyday Life* (Toronto: McClelland and Stewart, 1997), ix–xvi; Leyton, "Homicide," in *Violence in Contemporary Canadian Society*, ed. James M. MacLatchie (Ottawa: John Howard Society of Canada, 1987), 238–240; *SW*, 25 May 1994, pp. 15–16; *SPI*, 14 June 1995, p. A13; *VC*, 20 August 1997, p. 1; *ST*, 9 January 1994, p. A13; *VS*, 9 September 1976, p. 13; *PRDN*, 24 August 1994, p. 4.

3. *PGC*, 2 December 1995, p. 5. People had become very sensitive to nonviolent crimes, as well. In 1996 the owner of a Vancouver security service asserted that "the psychological effect of being raped and having one's house burgled is essentially the same." *VBCR*, 7 October 1996, p. 35. *VDP*, 3 March 1985, p. 5; *ST*, 28 March 1986, p. A9. Some scholars have pointed out that crime had become, as Elliott Leyton put it, "the symbol of everything that was wrong with our society." Leyton, "Homicide," 239. Stuart Scheingold, a University of Washington professor, argued that this concern offered

"a way to channel public anger and anxiety away from amorphous social and economic threats and toward criminals, who in their own much more concrete ways threaten our well-being." SPI, 27 October 1995, p. A13. Stuart A. Scheingold, *The Politics of Street Crime: Criminal Process and Cultural Obsession* (Philadelphia: Temple University Press, 1991), 172–178; Erich Goode and Nachman Ben-Yehuda, *Moral Panics: The Social Construction of Deviance* (Oxford: Blackwell, 1994), 31–41, 129–130; Philip Jenkins, *Moral Panic: Changing Concepts of the Child Molester in Modern America* (New Haven: Yale University Press, 1998), 10, 119–134, 191–193, 237–238; Henry Brownstein, "The Media and the Construction of Random Drug Violence," *Social Justice* 18 (winter 1991): 85–103; Joel Best, *Random Violence: How We Talk about New Crimes and New Victims* (Berkeley: University of California Press, 1999), 1–27.

4. *PO*, 10 July 1993, p. B8. *PO*, 14 December 1991, p. D6; 15 January 1992, p. B2; 25 August 1992, p. C2; 30 August 1992, p. O2; 17 October 1992, p. A1; 12 March 1993, p. C3; 7 January 1994, p. C8; 22 October 1994, p. C9; Katherine Dunn, "Fibbers," *New Republic*, 21 June 1993, pp. 18–19.

5. *PO*, 21 October 1992, p. F1.

6. *PO*, 13 April 1994, p. B2. *PO*, 24 December 1991, p. B3; 28 January 1992, p. B6; 21 October 1992, p. F1; 27 October 1992, p. B4; 25 December 1993, p. D9; 2 May 1993, p. D9.

7. *VS*, 22 February 1997, p. A1. *VDP*, 5 July 1965, p. 1; 6 July 1965, p. 1; 21 November 1986, p. 48; 13 March 1998, p. A30; 25 July 1975, p. 30; 8 March 1985, p. 24; 12 June 1986, p. A12; *Revised Statutes of Canada, 1985* (Ottawa: Queen's Printer for Canada, 1985), vol. 3: 24–27.

8. *PO*, 22 November 1993, p. B8. *VS*, 10 July 1965, p. 6; 26 April 1975, p. 5; *ST*, 1 August 1993, p. B7; 17 April 1998, p. B5.

9. *PGFP*, 25 May 1995, p. A8. *PWW*, 2 April 1987, p. 14; James William Gibson, *Warrior Dreams: Paramilitary Culture in Post-Vietnam America* (New York: Hill and Wang, 1994), 75.

10. *VS*, 11 April 1996, p. A19.

11. *PWW*, 11 February 1993, pp. 22, 28. Suspicion of firearms certainly varied by region. A 1969 *Oregonian* editorial wondered if urbanites in the eastern United States felt that "westerners are a little psycho on the subject of gun restrictions," but a few years later it published a poll revealing considerable variation within the state. *PO*, 15 September 1969, p. 22. Residents of eastern and central Oregon were nearly twice as likely to oppose handgun restriction as those who lived in metropolitan Portland, where only 25 percent declared themselves opposed to handgun registration. A quarter cen-

tury later, in 1993, the dichotomy persisted. An Oregon political analyst, commenting on the sharp debates over a bill that would make carrying guns into schools a felony, observed that rural Oregonians associated guns "with the freedom to go out in the fields hunting, to be free of restraints which they associated with cities." For urban legislators, on the other hand, "guns are a symbol of crime and violence." *PO*, 11 May 1993, p. B4; 16 November 1975, p. A1. British Columbia residents, rural and urban alike, shared a nationalistic orientation that prompted many to associate firearms with the United States. *VS*, 2 June 1995, p. A23; 23 December 1996, p. A1; *VDP*, 9 August 1972, p. 4; *VTC*, 30 December 1990, p. A4.

12. *VS*, 3 March 1976, p. 4. *PODJ*, 11 June 1968, p. 7; PO, 1 February 1972, sec. 2, p. 1; Peter and Judith DeCourcy, *A Silent Tragedy: Child Abuse in the Community* (n.p.: Alfred Publishing, 1973); *PO*, 16 May 1973, sec. 2, p. 1; *PODJ*, 16 May 1973, p. 2; 10 June 1968, p. 7; *VT*, 14 November 1964, mag. p. 2; Elizabeth Pleck, *Domestic Tyranny: The Making of American Social Policy against Family Violence from Colonial Times to the Present*, 167–181; LeRoy Ashby, *Endangered Children: Dependency, Neglect, and Abuse in American History* (New York: Twayne, 1997), 134–137, 151; Stephen J. Pfahl, "The 'Discovery' of Child Abuse," *Social Problems* 24 (February 1977): 310–323; John M. Johnson, "Symbolic Salvation: The Changing Meanings of the Child Maltreatment Movement," *Studies in Symbolic Interaction* 6 (1985): 289–305. For 1966 British Columbia recorded 47 deliberate instances of child injury, apparently a significant increase from earlier in the decade. In 1971 there were 180. Oregon recorded 347 cases of child abuse in 1971, 8,991 in 1995. *PO*, 2 December 1996, p. A8; *VS*, 18 May 1967, p. 37; 9 January 1973, p. 2.

13. *VS*, 4 September 1974, p. 49; *ST*, 22 November 1992, p. K1; 16 October 1986, p. D1. Joel Best, *Threatened Children: Rhetoric and Concern about Child-Victims* (Chicago: University of Chicago Press, 1990), 171–175.

14. *VS*, 15 February 1973, p. 2.

15. *VC*, 27 February 1995, p. 1.

16. *PO*, 19 April 1992, p. L8. *VDP*, 17 October 1974, p. 1; 21 February 1974, p. 4; *VS*, 22 May 1976, p. 5; *ST*, 4 February 1989, p. A11; *(Tacoma) News Tribune*, 16 August 1997, p. B1.

17. *VS*, 21 January 1998, p. A15.

18. *VTC*, 17 September 1988, p. A4.

19. *PO*, 30 December 1997, p. B2. *Victoria Daily Times*, 7 February 1961, p. 5; *VDP*, 23 November 1967, p. 10; *VS*, 14 March 1972, p. 4; *ST*, 11 October 1985, p. D1; 15 December 1985, p. A18; 4 March 1988, p. A7; Phillip W. Davis, "The Changing Meanings of

Spanking," in *Troubling Children: Studies of Children and Social Problems*, ed. Joel Best (New York: Aldine de Gruyter, 1994), 142–144. See Lawrence Wright, *Remembering Satan* (New York: Alfred A. Knopf, 1994) and Kathryn Lyon, *Witch Hunt: A True Story of Social Hysteria and Abused Justice* (New York: Avon, 1998) for purported examples of overzealous child protection in Washington.

20. *(Tacoma) News Tribune*, 16 August 1997, p. B1. *VBCR*, 26 February 1996, p. 30. Ashby, *Endangered Children*, 147–149, 152–155; Davis, "Changing Meanings of Spanking," 137–138.

21. *VS*, 15 February 1973, p. 2.

22. *ST*, 2 September 1985, p. A9. Violence has come unhinged from any sort of objective definition, has become a sort of shorthand term to connote a broad range of objectionable attitudes and actions. It "is seen in every unjust act or instance of wrong behavior," as Sergio Cotta puts it. Sergio Cotta, *Why Violence? A Philosophical Interpretation*, trans. Giovanni Gullace (Gainesville: University of Florida Press, 1985), 12.

23. Ken Kesey, *Sometimes a Great Notion* (New York: Bantam Books, 1965, orig. 1964), 144, 150. Kesey, *One Flew Over the Cuckoo's Nest* (New York: Signet, 1962). Robert P. Waxler, "The Mixed Heritage of the Chief: Revisiting the Problem of Manhood in *One Flew Over the Cuckoo's Nest*," *Journal of Popular Culture* 29 (winter 1995): 225–235.

24. Paul Kooistra, *Criminals as Heroes: Structure, Power and Identity* (Bowling Green, Ohio: Bowling Green State University Popular Press, 1989), 163–173; Stephen Powers, David J. Rothman, and Stanley Rothman, *Hollywood's America: Social and Political Themes in Motion Pictures* (Boulder, Colorado: Westview Press, 1996), 104–106; Gibson, *Warrior Dreams;* James P. Leary, "Fists and Foul Mouths: Fights and Fight Stories in Contemporary Rural American Bars," *Journal of American Folklore* 89 (January-March 1976): 27–39; Vicki Goldberg, "Death Takes a Holiday, Sort of," in *Why We Watch: The Attractions of Violent Entertainment*, ed. Jeffrey Goldstein (New York: Oxford University Press, 1998), 49–50.

25. David Guterson, *Snow Falling on Cedars* (New York: Harcourt Brace, 1994); Guterson, *East of the Mountains* (New York: Harcourt Brace, 1999); Guterson, *The Country Ahead of Us, the Country Behind* (New York: Harper and Row, 1989).

26. *Summary Statistics: Police, Crime* (n.p.: Police Services Division, Ministry of Attorney General, Province of British Columbia, 1995), 30; annual homicide data from 1989 to 1993, the Law Enforcement Data System, Salem; *Crime in Washington State* annual reports of 1980 to 1996, published in Olympia by the Washington Association

of Sheriffs and Police Chiefs, especially *Crime in Washington State Annual Report, 1996* (Olympia: Washington Association of Sheriffs and Police Chiefs, n.d.), 16; Statistics Canada Web Site, Homicide Offences, Number and Rate; Federal Bureau of Investigation, *Uniform Crime Reports* (issued annually); Richard Maxwell Brown, *No Duty to Retreat: Violence and Values in American History and Society*, 139–153; Roger Lane, *Murder in America: A History*, 295–303, 324–330.

27. Chris Hables Gray, *Postmodern War: The New Politics of Conflict* (New York: Guilford Press, 1997).

28. Leyton, *Men of Blood*, 221. Jack Katz, *Seductions of Crime: Moral and Sensual Attractions in Doing Evil* (New York: Basic Books, 1988), 44–47; Edward Green and Russell P. Wakefield, "Patterns of Middle and Upper Class Homicide," *Journal of Criminal Law and Criminology* 70 (summer 1979): 172–181.

29. Richard J. Gelles and Murray A. Straus, *Intimate Violence* (New York: Touchstone, 1989, orig. 1988), 85–86; David Peterson del Mar, *What Trouble I Have Seen: A History of Violence against Wives*, 151–152; Gunnar Almgren, Avery Guest, George Immerwahr, and Michael Spittell, "Joblessness, Family Disruption, and Violent Death in Chicago, 1970–90," *Social Forces* 76 (June 1998): 1465–1493.

30. Robert Leo Heilman, *Overstory Zero: Real Life in Timber Country* (Seattle: Sasquatch Books, 1995), 24.

31. Pierre Bourdieu, *Distinction: A Social Critique of the Judgement of Taste,* trans. Richard Nice (Cambridge: Harvard University Press, 1984), 384.

32. *VC*, 15 August 1997, p. 1.

33. Indeed, the protagonist in Aldous Huxley's futuristic novel *Brave New World* concludes that whipping himself is the only way to break out of the modern cocoon of anesthetized and tedious pleasure.

34. Peterson del Mar, *What Trouble I Have Seen*, 161–162.

35. *PGFP*, 16 May 1996, p. A9. *VBCR*, 23 March 1998, p. 41; *PO*, 7 October 1991, p. B1; Donald Dutton, "Patriarchy and Wife Assault: The Ecological Fallacy," *Violence and Victims* 9 (summer 1994): 167–182; Michael P. Johnson, "Patriarchal Terrorism and Common Couple Violence: Two Forms of Violence Against Women," *JMF* 57 (May 1995): 283–294; William A. Stacey, Lonnie R. Hazlewood, and Anson Shupe, *The Violent Couple* (Westport, Connecticut: Praeger, 1994).

36. *VGS*, 7 May 1998, p. 19. *VBCR*, 3 November 1997, p. 36; *PO*, 12 June 1996, p. A1; *VS*, 28 June 1988, p. B2; *VC*, 8 May 1998, p. 1.

37. Aafke Komter, " Hidden Power in Marriage," *Gender and Society* 3 (June 1989): 187–217. Barbara J. Morse, "Beyond the Conflict Tactics Scale: Assessing Gender

Differences in Partner Violence," *Violence and Victims* 10 (winter 1995): 251–272; Dair L. Gillespie, "Who Has the Power? The Marital Struggle," *JMF* 33 (August 1971): 445–458. See James C. Scott, *Domination and the Arts of Resistance: Hidden Transcripts* (New Haven, Connecticut: Yale University Press, 1990), especially 86–87 on subordinates' interest in concealing their discontent.

38. Alexis J. Walker, "Couples Watching Television: Gender, Power, and the Remote Control," *JMF* 58 (November 1996): 813–823; William T. Bielby and Denise D. Bielby, "I Will Follow Him: Family Ties, Gender-Role Beliefs, and Reluctance to Relocate for a Better Job," *American Journal of Sociology* 97 (March 1992): 1241–1267; Karen D. Pyke, "Class-Based Masculinities: The Interdependence of Gender, Class, and Interpersonal Power," *Gender and Society* 10 (October 1996): 527–549; Cecilia L. Ridgeway, "Gender, Status, and the Social Psychology of Expectations," in *Theory on Gender/Feminism on Theory*, ed. Paula England (New York: Aldine de Gruyter, 1993), 175–197.

39. Court case, BCAGC, further information withheld to protect privacy.

40. Sibylle Artz, *Sex, Power, and the Violent School Girl* (Toronto: Trifolium Books, 1998), 53–55, 166–172, 176–179, 195–196, 199–201. Much rhetoric around youth violence also obscures children's vulnerability to violence. Many adults worry over children's apparent attraction to violence, that "it's considered 'not cool' to find peaceful resolutions to arguments," as the *Seattle Times* put it in 1993. *ST*, 17 October 1993, p. A1. *SW*, 22 September 1993, p. 17; *PO*, 23 February 1993, p. D2. Adults have become particularly worried about juvenile crimes. In British Columbia, for example, growing numbers have been demanding changes to Canada's Young Offender's Act, which shields children from long prison terms. Such concerns have fueled greater attention to youth violence, artificially inflating juvenile arrest statistics. British Columbia charged 915 youths with crimes against the person in 1985; 3,063 in 1994. But the number of youths charged with homicide remained stable over that decade. *Summary Statistics: Police, Crime*, 96–97; *ST*, 24 May 1993, p. A1; 17 December 1993, p. A1; *SPI*, 21 December 1980, p. A1; *PO*, 4 May 1992, p. B1; 9 January 1994, p. E1; Lane, *Murder in America*, 322–323; John Devine, *Maximum Security: The Culture of Violence in Inner-City Schools* (Chicago: University of Chicago Press, 1996); Arnold P. Goldstein, Steven J. Apter, and Berj Harootunian, *School Violence* (Englewood Cliffs, New Jersey: Prentice-Hall, 1984); D. Owen Carrigan, *Crime and Punishment in Canada: A History* (Toronto: McClelland and Stewart, 1991). 229–241. Washington homicide statistics indicate a rise in extreme violence by youth there, however. The state identified only nine children under age fifteen as perpetrators of homicides from 1981 to 1985, twenty-seven from

1992 to 1996. *Crime in Washington State Annual Reports. VS,* 26 September 1994, p. A1; T. C. Caputo, "The Young Offenders Act: Children's Rights, Children's Wrongs," in *Youth Injustice: Canadian Perspectives,* ed. Thomas O'Reilly-Fleming and Barry Clark (Toronto: Canadian Scholar's Press, 1993), 1–30; *(Victoria) Colonist,* 22 January 1960, p. 1; *Dawson Creek Star,* 3 June 1960, p. 2; *VBCR,* 22 June 1992, pp. 29–30; 2 June 1997, pp. 12–13; 2 March 1998, p. 19; *VS,* 12 June 1986, p. A12; *PGC,* 2 December 1995, p. 5; *Prince George This Week,* 25 September 1994, p. 9; *PRDN,* 1 November 1994, p. 4. Fear of violent young people has been far outpacing their actual violent acts. Indeed, the quintessential juvenile delinquents, street children and child prostitutes, have been extremely vulnerable to violence themselves. Most cite physical or sexual abuse as their reason for leaving their families. "Is it worse on the streets or worse at home?" asked an operator of a Portland youth shelter in 1991. "If it was worse on the streets, they would go back home." *PO,* 25 August 1991, p. D1. "It was better to sleep in a park or under a bridge or with men who I didn't know than to be at home in a place that's supposed to be safe and have a relative crawl into bed with you each night," explained a woman who had left her suburban home for Portland's streets at the age of fourteen. *PO,* 1 October 1995, p. D1. *PO,* 3 August 1980, p. B1; *PODJ,* 18 August 1982, p. 6; *SW,* 13 December 1995, pp. 32–33; *ST,* 14 June 1985, p. D1; *SPI,* 1 November 1982, p. A7; *VS,* 5 July 1979, p. A2; 17 August 1988, p. A10; *Vancouver Courier,* 6 July 1979, p. 7; Sheila Baxter, *A Child Is Not a Toy: Voices of Children in Poverty* (Vancouver, British Columbia: New Star, 1993); Evelyn Lau, *Runaway: Diary of a Street Kid* (Toronto: Harper Collins, 1989), 1–5. But prostitution was a dangerous way to make a living. Boys and particularly girls were at risk of being beaten by customers. Physical violence became an intrinsic part of prostitution for Evelyn Lau, who ran away from her Vancouver home in 1986, in her mid-teens. After less than two years at it she wrote that her "breasts were amputated long ago—the men touch them so much, move them around, squeeze them. . . . The next thing that will go will be my vagina, because of their probing fingers." Lau, *Runaway,* 319. A British Columbia man was overheard in 1980 telling a prostitute who was objecting to a sex act that he had proposed that "you are in a tough business baby and you have got to learn to take it." *British Columbia Law Reports, Second Series* (Toronto: Carsell, 1987), vol. 14: 199. Prostitutes also experienced a great deal of violence at the hands of their pimps, men who took the majority of their often substantial earnings and threatened to disfigure or kill them if they tried to leave. The homicide rate was especially high among Vancouver prostitutes. At least thirty-five reportedly died between 1989 and 1995. *VS,* 6 September 1995, p. B1. *VS,* 16 September 1995, p. A3; 8 July 1976, p. 2; 23 April 1981, p. A3; *VDP,* 22 July 1968, p. 2; 21 May 1969,

p. 1; 9 October 1988, p. 14; *Vancouver Express*, 16 April 1970, p. 28; *ST*, 25 January 1970, p. C8; 5 December 1982, pp. A1, C2; 24 March 1986, p. C1; 17 January 1993, p. B5; *Seattle Sun*, 20 December 1978, p. 10. Low status and vulnerability to violence are positively correlated.

41. Court case, BCAGC, further information withheld to protect privacy.

42. Clifford Geertz, *The Interpretation of Cultures: Selected Essays* (New York: Basic Books, 1973), 452.

43. Lawrence M. Friedman, *Crime and Punishment in American History*.

44. Emanuel Marx, *The Social Context of Violent Behaviour: A Social Anthropological Study of an Israeli Immigrant Town* (London: Routledge and Kegan Paul, 1976), 87.

45. Mikal Gilmore, *Shot in the Heart* (New York: Anchor, 1994), 360–361.

46. Ibid., xii.

47. Ibid., 398, emphasis in the original.

48. Ibid., 386–387.

SELECTED BIBLIOGRAPHY
OF SECONDARY SOURCES

Adachi, Ken. *The Enemy That Never Was: A History of the Japanese Canadians.* Toronto: McClelland and Stewart, 1991, orig. 1976.

Asher, Brad. "Coming Under the Law: Indian/White Relations and Legal Change in Washington Territory, 1853–1889." Ph.D. diss., University of Chicago, 1996.

Barman, Jean. *The West Beyond the West: A History of British Columbia,* rev. ed. Toronto: University of Toronto Press, 1996.

Brown, Richard Maxwell. *No Duty to Retreat: Violence and Values in American History and Society.* New York: Oxford University Press, 1991.

Bunting, Robert. *The Pacific Raincoast: Environment and Culture in an American Eden, 1778–1900.* Lawrence: University Press of Kansas, 1997.

Burley, David V., J. Scott Hamilton, and Knut R. Fladmark. *Prophecy of the Swan: The Upper Peace River Fur Trade of 1794–1823.* Vancouver: University of British Columbia Press, 1996.

Courtwright, David T. *Violent Land: Single Men and Social Disorder from the Frontier to the Inner City.* Cambridge: Harvard University Press, 1996.

Dodds, Gordon B. *The American Northwest: A History of Oregon and Washington.* Arlington Heights, Illinois: Forum Press, 1986.

Ferguson, Brian. "Warfare and Redistributive Exchange on the Northwest Coast." In *The Development of Political Organization in Native North America,* ed. Elisabeth Tooker, 133–147. Washington, D.C.: American Ethnological Society, 1983.

Ferguson, R. Brian. "A Reexamination of the Causes of Northwest Coast Warfare." In *Warfare, Culture, and Environment,* ed. R. Brian Ferguson, 267–328. Orlando: Academic Press, 1984.

Fisher, Robin. *Contact and Conflict: Indian-European Relations in British Columbia, 1774–1890,* 2nd ed. Vancouver: University of British Columbia Press, 1992.

Friedman, Lawrence M. *Crime and Punishment in American History.* New York: Basic Books, 1993.

Gordon, Linda. *Heroes of Their Own Lives: The Politics and History of Family Violence, Boston, 1880–1960.* New York: Viking, 1988.

Gough, Barry M. *Gunboat Frontier: British Maritime Authority and Northwest Coast Indians, 1846–90.* Vancouver: University of British Columbia Press, 1984.

Greenburg, Kenneth S. *Honor and Slavery: Lies, Duels, Noses, Masks, Dressing as a Woman, Gifts, Strangers, Humanitarianism, Death, Slave Rebellions, the Pro-Slavery Argument, Baseball, Hunting, and Gambling in the Old South.* Princeton: Princeton University Press, 1996.

Harris, Cole. *The Resettlement of British Columbia: Essays on Colonialism and Geographical Change.* Vancouver: University of British Columbia Press, 1997.

Ichioka, Yugi. *The Issei: The World of the First Generation Japanese Immigrants, 1885–1924.* New York: Free Press, 1988.

Johansen, Dorothy O., and Charles M. Gates. *Empire of the Columbia: A History of the Pacific Northwest,* 2nd ed. New York: Harper and Row, 1967.

Johnson, F. Henry. "Changing Conceptions of Discipline and Pupil-Teacher Relations in Canadian Schools." Ph.D. diss., University of Toronto, 1952.

Johnston, Hugh J. M., ed. *The Pacific Province: A History of British Columbia.* Vancouver: Douglas and McIntyre, 1996.

Kessler, Lauren. *Stubborn Twig: Three Generations in the Life of a Japanese American Family.* New York: Penguin, 1994, orig. 1993.

Lane, Roger. *Murder in America: A History.* Columbus: Ohio State University Press, 1997.

Lane, Roger. *Violent Death in the City: Suicide, Accident, and Murder in Nineteenth-Century Philadelphia.* Cambridge: Harvard University Press, 1979.

Latham, Barbara K., and Roberta J. Pazdro, eds. *Not Just Pin Money: Selected Essays on the History of Women's Work in British Columbia.* Victoria: Camosun College, 1984.

La Violette, Forrest E. *The Canadian Japanese and World War II: A Sociological and Psychological Account.* Toronto: University of Toronto Press, 1948.

McDonald, Robert A. J. *Making Vancouver: Class, Status, and Social Boundaries, 1863–1913.* Vancouver: University of British Columbia Press, 1996.

McKanna, Clare V., Jr. *Homicide, Race, and Justice in the American West, 1880–1920.* Tucson: University of Arizona Press, 1997.

McLagan, Elizabeth. *A Peculiar Paradise: A History of Blacks in Oregon, 1788–1940.* Portland: Georgian Press, 1980.

McLaren, John, Hamar Foster, and Chet Orloff, eds. *Law for the Elephant, Law for the*

Beaver: Essays in the Legal History of the North American West. Regina: Canadian Plains Research Center; Pasadena: Ninth Judicial Circuit Historical Society, 1992.

Peterson del Mar, David. *What Trouble I Have Seen: A History of Violence against Wives*. Cambridge: Harvard University Press, 1996.

Pleck, Elizabeth. *Domestic Tyranny: The Making of American Social Policy Against Family Violence from Colonial Times to the Present*. New York: Oxford University Press, 1987.

Rotundo, E. Anthony. *American Manhood: Transformations in Masculinity from the Revolution to the Modern Era*. New York: Basic Books, 1993.

Sandwell, R. W., ed. *Beyond the City Limits: Rural History in British Columbia*. Vancouver: University of British Columbia Press, 1999.

Schwantes, Carlos Arnaldo. *The Pacific Northwest: An Interpretive History*, rev. ed. Lincoln: University of Nebraska Press, 1996.

Suttles, Wayne, ed. *Northwest Coast*. Washington, D.C.: Smithsonian Institution, 1990.

Swadesh, Morris. "Motivations in Nootka Warfare." *Southwestern Journal of Anthropology* 4 (spring 1948): 76–93.

Tamura, Linda. *The Hood River Issei: An Oral History of Japanese Settlers in Oregon's Hood River Valley*. Urbana: University of Illinois Press, 1993.

Taylor, Quintard. *The Forging of a Black Community: Seattle's Central District from 1870 through the Civil Rights Era*. Seattle: University of Washington Press, 1994.

Walker, Deward E., Jr. *Plateau*. Washington, D.C.: Smithsonian Institution, 1998.

Ward, W. Peter. *White Canada Forever: Popular Attitudes and Public Policy Toward Orientals in British Columbia*. Montreal: McGill-Queen's University Press, 1978.

Yanagisako, Sylvia Junko. *Transforming the Past: Tradition and Kinship among Japanese Americans*. Stanford: Stanford University Press, 1985.

INDEX

Printed in the United States
36452LVS00005B/49-69